CAMBRIDGE HISTORY PROJECT

PEOPLE, POWER AND POLITICS

Was there a mid-seventeenth-century English Revolution?

A Study in Depth
Modules 3 & 4

Angela Anderson

Stanley Thornes (Publishers) Ltd

First published in 1994 by:
Stanley Thornes (Publishers) Ltd
Ellenborough House
Wellington Street
CHELTENHAM GL50 1YD
England

Reprinted 1995

ISBN 0–7487–1497–9

A catalogue record for this book is available from the British Library.

Cover illustration:
By permission of the
British Library

Typeset by Tech-Set, Gateshead, Tyne & Wear
Printed and bound in Great Britain at The Bath Press, Avon

Contents

Introduction

This volume is one of four written for the Cambridge A-Level History Project syllabus, *People, Power and Politics,* and the second relating to the Depth Study, *Was there a mid-seventeenth-century English Revolution?;* the other two relate to the Development Study, *Political change through time.* One of the principal aims of the Project is to develop understanding of what history is, and of the methodologies involved in the study of history. To this end, all four volumes contain sections explaining historical concepts and techniques. However, *People, Power and Politics* is a syllabus about history, not the philosophy of history, and the sections of this volume dealing with concepts and techniques should be regarded as providing advice about how to explain aspects of the English Revolution rather than as having a life of their own.

Depth Book 1 contains an introductory unit, *Boudicca and Roman Britain,* which provides a methodological introduction and seeks to establish certain basic concepts about sources, evidence and hypotheses. This is followed by Module 1 which establishes certain characteristics of seventeenth-century government and society in England, and provides a contextual outline of developments which enables some preliminary conclusions to be drawn about the nature and significance of the 'English Revolution' of 1640-60. Module 2 examines five important stages in the 'Revolution', allows its outbreak, development and conclusion to be considered and explained, and enables more sophisticated assessments to be made as to how far England experienced a constitutional revolution.

The present volume re-examines this question from a variety of different perspectives. It is not an exhaustive study of the English Revolution; its purpose is to allow students to explore specific issues and draw their own conclusions as to the nature and significance of what occurred in England (and to a lesser extent Britain) between 1640 and 1660. Module 3 looks at the emergence and development of radical religious and political groups, whose contribution to the ferment of ideas that characterised the period far outweighed their numbers. If there was a revolution, then the radicals did much to create it. Students are asked, therefore, to explain why such individuals and groups developed at this particular time, their importance in influencing the events of their own time, and to assess their significance in the longer-term development of popular protest and mass politics in Britain. This enables a consideration of the issue of whether or not England experienced a revolution in the mid-seventeenth century from a different perspective, by considering changes in the ideas, attitudes and beliefs that shape the practice of politics.

Module 4 continues this approach by examining the English Revolution within different temporal and spatial contexts. It begins with a local dimension, exploring the variety and complexity of attitudes and responses to the war and its aftermath, as revealed in a series of local studies. In indicating the importance of local, rather than national, considerations in the choice of 'sides' and the reluctance with which many participants took up arms, this raises questions as to how far such actions and events can be considered revolutionary. These issues are further explored in a local case study. The perspective is then widened, to allow the English Revolution to be viewed as part of a general European crisis, and to be compared with other revolutions (in France and Russia particularly) in order to assess its nature and significance. Finally, these explorations are used to establish a number of criteria against which the events studied throughout the course are measured, in order to produce a final response to the question, *Was there a mid-seventeenth-century English revolution?*

Acknowledgements

Like Book 1, this volume owes much to the extensive trialling of teaching materials in over 80 schools and colleges between 1988 and 1992, and to the efforts and enthusiasm of the many teachers and students who participated in the process. In some areas I have drawn directly on trial materials for sections of this book, but even where my material is new, it has been shaped and influenced by the experience, the responses and the ingenuity of colleagues, and by their generosity in sharing their ideas.

Special thanks are due to Denis Shemilt and Peter Lee for conceiving the Project and for guiding it through its early stages; to the University of Cambridge Local Examinations Syndicate for funding and support of both the original trials and the rewrite of materials; to Alan Kelly and Robert Ellis for their work as Executive Directors of the Project; and to the following for their major contributions to the trial materials which provided the inspiration for the present volume:

Rosalyn Ashby   Jeff Lord
Graham Berry   Robert Ellis
Susan Carpenter   Martin Palmen
Ian Coulson   David Parker
Andy Harmsworth   Roy Parkin
Ben Jones   Russell Sherman
Alan Kelly   Rob Wilkinson
Peter Lee

While I have utilised the trial material as a whole, I have made particular use of the work on the Levellers carried out by Russell Sherman, and drawn extensively on the Ranter material produced by Peter Lee; I would like to express my gratitude to them both. My thanks are also due to Barry Page of Stanley Thornes (Publishers) Ltd. for his advice, and expert help in providing illustrations, and to Graham Berry for reading and commenting upon the manuscript. I am grateful to my family for their forbearance during the writing of this volume, and to my sons, Stephen and Stuart, for occasional employment of their typing skills. Above all, I am indebted to Bob Ellis, author of the other books in this series, for placing his experience at my disposal, for his constructive criticism, and his unfailing support. He contributed much to what is good about this book – the errors and shortcomings are all my own.

Angela Anderson
Hornsea, October 1993

The author and publishers are grateful to the following for their permission to reproduce copyright material in this book:

Illustrations (numbers refer to sources, except in cases where a page number is given)

Module 3
Bodleian Library, Oxford 124, 127; The British Library 4, 6, 8, p. 28 (right), p. 51, 77, 80, 81, 82, 85, 86, 87, 99, 100, 141; British Museum 158, 167, 168; Hulton Deutsch Collection 2, p. 27, p. 40, p. 41, 116; Mansell Collection 1, p. 3, p. 24 (Lilburne portrait), p. 28 (left), 117

Module 4
Hulton Deutsch Collection 64, p. 172; Popperfoto p. 179

Text material
Philip Allan Publishers Ltd. for material from W. Doyle, 'The Legacy of the French Revolution', *Modern History Review*, February 1992; B. T. Batsford Ltd. for material from A. G. Dickens, *The English Reformation*, 1989; Blackwell Publishers for material from F. D. Dow, *Radicalism in the English Revolution 1640–60*; 1989; Cambridge University Press for material from J. C. Davis, *Fear, Myth and History*, 1986, and W. C. Braithwaite, *The Beginnings of Quakerism*, 1955; A. M. Heath & Company on behalf of the author for material from Christopher Hill, *The World Turned Upside Down*, 1975; Historical Association for material from A. Everitt, *The Local Community and the Great Rebellion*, 1969, and F. C. Mather, *Chartism*, 1965; History Today Ltd. for material from M. Mullett, 'George Fox and the Origins of Quakerism', *History Today*, 41, May 1991, and G. Watson, 'How Radical is Revolution?', *History Today*, November 1988; Kingston upon Hull City Council for material from the Hull Corporation Bench Books, and P. McNichol, *Horrible News from Hull*, 1987; Lawrence & Wishart Ltd. for material from A. L. Morton, *Freedom in Arms*, 1974; Longman Group UK for material from H. Shaw, *The Levellers*, 1973; R. J. Acheson, *Radical Puritans in England 1550–1660*, 1990; J. Morrill, *The Revolt of the Provinces*, 1980; E. Royle, *Chartism*, 1986; and cartoons by Margaret Hunt in D. Richards, *Modern Europe*, 1945; Macmillan Publishers Ltd. for material from R. B. Dobson, *The Peasants' Revolt of 1381*, 1986; Mr Pye Books for B. N. Reckitt, *Charles the First and Hull*, 1988; Oxford University Press for material from Kenneth O. Morgan, ed., *The Oxford Illustrated History of Britain*, 1984; J. F. McGregor and B. Reay,

Module 3: A popular revolution?

UNIT 3.1

POLITICAL AND RELIGIOUS RADICALISM

Introduction

In Modules 1 and 2 the English Revolution has been studied from the viewpoint of those most closely involved – the governing class or 'those who ruled'. The 'revolution' centred on changes in the distribution of power within and between the existing institutions of monarchy, Lords and Commons. If the involvement and attitudes of the common people are considered at all, it is assumed that they simply reacted as best they could to the decisions made by their superiors. They are seen as supporting the political and religious claims initiated by their betters or clinging to familiar loyalties for safety. Hence the people of London can be manipulated by Pym in 1641 to pressurise Charles into signing Strafford's death warrant, and by Holles and others in 1647 to support a conservative settlement and the rapid return of the king. In both cases the common people are portrayed as essentially passive, no more than a weapon to be utilised by different factions within the governing élite. Where they do take independent action for themselves, they are seen as taking refuge in resentful neutrality as a means of survival in a period of high taxation, bad harvests and dislocated trade. The natural reaction of 'those who did not rule' is typified by the Clubmen, who took up arms in the south and west of England in 1645 to drive from their locality both Royalist and Parliamentarian armies, and reappeared in the Severn valley in 1649 to seize corn for local distribution in a time of shortage. In short, the Civil Wars and their aftermath are viewed as a power struggle within the governing élite, into which the common people were reluctantly drawn by the political and military needs of their betters.

This account needs to be qualified at a number of levels. The role of the 'middling-sort' in the boroughs which supported Parliament, in the Puritan Churches and in the New Model Army has been widely accepted. A more comprehensive reappraisal has been put forward by historians who have studied the various radical groups which emerged in this period, most notably in the work of Christopher Hill. He has argued that there was a genuinely popular revolution which sought to bring about fundamental changes in the nature of society as well as in its political and religious institutions. In his view the quarrel within the governing élite created the opportunity for radical, popular alternatives to emerge, particularly in the crisis years of 1647–53, whose limited numbers and poor organisation disguised the extent to which they reflected widespread popular aspirations. Their impact and the threat that they represented led the governing class to close ranks, and ultimately restore the monarchy as the guarantee of social and political stability. Thus the radicals failed in their ambitions at this time, but the attempt had led them to formulate and develop ideas about individual liberty and the nature of power which could not be eradicated and which have influenced and informed political developments ever since.

The purpose of Module 3 is to examine a number of these issues, and to facilitate some conclusions about the nature, extent and significance of radical activities in the English Revolution. Thus unit 3.1 seeks to establish what we mean by the radicals, what radicalism consisted of, and why such groups emerged at this time. Units 3.2, 3.3 and 3.4 examine particular groups and investigate their ideas in more depth. They also allow us to consider why

1

some groups were short-lived, while others resisted all attempts to destroy them. Unit 3.5 considers the radical movements in a wider context in order to assess both their significance and the extent to which they represented something new. Finally, it should be possible at the end of this module to revise and reformulate ideas about the English Revolution as a whole – what it was, what took place, and what, if anything, was revolutionary about it.

The rise and decline of radicalism

In 1641–2 the parliamentary attack on the bishops and their authority, combined with the abolition of the Prerogative Courts, effectively destroyed the normal controls exercised over the pulpit, press and religious meetings. The speed with which an array of separatist Churches, tub-thumping preachers and dangerously radical ideas emerged in this new freedom is evidence that political and religious radicalism did not begin in 1641, although, since it was illegal, its earlier history is fragmentary and difficult to trace. What is revealed in the attempt is that radical ideas sprang from the same roots as those sanctioned by the government and by the established Church, being a logical, if unorthodox, outcome of the Protestant Reformation.

Roots and origins

The Reformation

Religion and politics had always been closely linked. The authority of government, of monarchy and of the social order was justified by its claim to be ordained by God, with the king as God's representative on earth. The English Reformation, establishing the king as Head of the Church had enormously strengthened these links, giving the monarch power over doctrine and belief as well as the administration and form of government used in the Church. While this greatly enhanced his power, it raised the problem that disputes about doctrine and matters of belief would also imply an attack on royal authority and might involve some form of resistance, if not rebellion. By uniting secular and spiritual authority in one person, the Reformation extended the integration of religion and politics to the point where governments saw religious uniformity as a political necessity. Hence unorthodox beliefs would be seen as a political threat, even if they did not involve any direct attack on the government; simply to hold and defend them was an act of subversion, and would be punished as such.

Source 1

William Tyndale, whose English translation of the New Testament in 1526 did much to encourage Protestantism in England. He was later executed for heresy.

This might have been less significant if the Reformation in England and elsewhere in Europe had not also shattered religious unity, and introduced a Protestant creed which emphasised the private and highly personal nature of religious belief. In 1521 Martin Luther publicly rejected the authority of Rome in favour of individual faith based on the authority of God's Word as written in the Bible. The ensuing decades saw his ideas taken up and developed by other scholars, each producing and defending his own variations. Theological debate in itself was nothing new, having always been a part of Christian scholarship. What was new was that it now extended beyond the ministry to include ordinary lay men and women, and that there was no longer a universally accepted authority able to adjudicate between the different views. In England that responsibility had devolved to the monarchy, but the orthodoxy of Henry VIII had been followed by the Protestant reforms of Edward VI's reign and the reversal attempted by Mary. This was a bewildering sequence of change for many of their subjects. Thus, in 1558–9 the new queen, Elizabeth, and her advisers saw a need for religious unity and uniformity in a society which had learned to question. The Elizabethan settlement with its attempt to encompass a broad range of opinions was politically motivated and politically successful, but it left a dissatisfied minority who believed that the new Church contained traces of popery which would corrupt and destroy it, if they were not removed.

Puritans and separatists

Puritans, as this minority were called, wished to reform and purify the Anglican Church after the settlement of 1559–60. Their ideas were not, in themselves, revolutionary or radical. The objectives of the Puritan ministers and their allies in parliament were threefold: to remove all trace and taint of popery, to reform the government and practice of the Church and to bring about a 'reformation of manners' which would create a more decent society. Their chosen model was the Church established by John Calvin in Geneva. In their own eyes they were the queen's most loyal and devoted subjects, seeking only to establish religion according to God's Word for the benefit and protection of queen, Church and nation. However, their beliefs and attitudes had potentially radical implications. Some of these, the emphasis on individual faith and conscience, the authority accorded to the Bible as God's Word and the encouragement to ministers and people to study the Bible and discuss its message, were common to most forms of Protestantism, but among those of Puritan tendencies they were heightened and intensified. What gave Puritanism its particular force and character was the Calvinist theology of Predestination: the belief that God had selected certain souls to be saved, to become his chosen 'saints' and gain eternal salvation. The evidence that an individual was one of these chosen few lay in the willingness and desire to follow God's laws as laid out in Scripture. The Bible provided rules for both Church organisation and individual belief. It was therefore essential that all, rich and poor alike, should have access to God's Word through Bible reading (if they could) and through the words and advice of good preachers. The main guide and interpreter of God's Word was the Minister, whose most important function and duty was to preach the word, but Bible classes, discussions and prayer meetings also played a role in both establishing and strengthening the faith of the Saints. The result was a faith which was vigorous, active and confident, and in which the laity were required to participate, to take a measure of responsibility, and to exercise what gifts and skills they possessed.

If English Puritans had been able to establish a fully Calvinist system, the radical potential of these beliefs would probably have been held in check, as

JOHN CALVIN (1509–64)

John Calvin was a French reformer who established a Protestant Church in the Swiss city of Geneva. He became the most influential reformer after Luther. Calvin argued that men were too sinful to save themselves by their own efforts but that God had chosen some to receive the gift of his saving grace, who were thus predestined to be saved. The mark of these 'Saints' was that they chose to join Calvin's Church and obey its rules, which were drawn from God's own Word (the Bible) and therefore had divine authority. The Minister's role was to preach and teach the Word of God so that the Saints could obey it, and to uphold strict discipline in the congregation with the help of lay Elders. Calvin's ideas demanded great dedication from his followers, but offered the certainty of salvation to those who were able to stay the course.

in Presbyterian Scotland. During the reigns of Elizabeth and James, however, Puritan ministers were able to preach, to enthuse their hearers, and to organise congregational activities at a local or parish level, but never to reform the Church as a whole. The concept of a national Church meant that they could not limit membership to 'saints' but were expected to welcome everyone who lived in the parish – saints and sinners alike. This meant that they could not maintain discipline and morality within the congregation at the level that they regarded as necessary. More seriously, they were forced to conform, at least occasionally, to ceremonies and forms of worship that they regarded as popish, sinful and idolatrous. The vast majority of Puritan ministers accepted this, albeit reluctantly; they tried to spread their message through preaching to any who would listen, and to persuade and influence those in authority towards further reform. It was not surprising, however, that some ministers and their followers should come to regard this as unacceptable and seek to form separate 'true' Churches of their own.

It is in this establishment of independent, voluntary congregations that the roots of radicalism are to be found. In the first place, separatism was in itself illegal, since it involved a rejection of authority and a threat to the established order. Secondly, once separated and able to draw on their own interpretations of the Bible for their rules and practices, congregations tended to become more unorthodox and less willing to conform to conventional rules and assumptions. One immediate consequence of separation was that the minister became reliant on his congregation for support, and therefore more dependent on their views and opinions. Alternatively, he had to find some way of earning a living. Not only did this blur the distinction between clergy and laity to a degree which was considered dangerous, but the tendency for congregations to participate in discussions led to growing confidence among gifted laymen of their own ability to analyse the scriptures, to develop and express their own views, and ultimately, to preach. In the end this would produce men like Lilburne, who was able and willing to argue his case against lawyers, bishops, Lords and Commons. It is hardly surprising that the authorities, both religious and secular, should regard these developments as a threat to the social order, and the range and extent of ideas which were to emerge from the separatist groups between 1640 and 1660 illustrates how well-grounded were their fears.

Separatist development to 1640

It is difficult to trace the development of separatist groups with any precision before 1640, because their position was often hesitant and confused, as well as illegal and therefore secretive. Such evidence as there is suggests that the early separatists, or sects, fall into one (or sometimes more than one) of three categories:

1. A few examples can be found of genuinely radical groups, pursuing unorthodox ideas, often imported from the more eccentric continental congregations. Examples such as the Anabaptists discovered in Guildford, Surrey in 1561, and the stronger group of Familists (or Family of Love) detected in Ely in the 1580s fall into this category. However, there were very few such groups, and where they did exist they were apparently short-lived.

2. Much more frequent are examples in the second category, of *enforced* separatism, where congregations gathered around a minister who was deprived of his living, or attended private conventicles [religious meetings] because they lacked effective ministry in their own parish. Groups of this kind met for some years in the Church of Holy Trinity in the Minories in London and around some of the 'stranger' Churches of foreign residents which were permitted to use their own forms and rituals. Separatism of this kind often overlapped with a form of partial or semi-separatism in which members occasionally attended their parish church in order to show Christian goodwill and conform to the necessities of the law. One such example was the Church gathered in London by Henry Jacob in 1616 after he had been deprived of his living by Archbishop Bancroft. Jacob spent a period of exile in Holland, where he associated with other radicals, but he then returned to London and gathered a congregation which included members with separatist views alongside others who also attended their parish church. Jacob's flexible approach was continued by his successor as pastor, John Lathrop, and by 1641 some eight different separatist congregations had developed from Jacob's work.

3. The third, and most genuinely separatist, category consisted of those who adopted separatism as a matter of principle and who regarded the Anglican Church as ungodly and 'untrue'. The earliest statement of the separatist argument came in 1580 from Robert Browne, who argued that only a voluntary covenant by believers could create a 'true' Church and that earthly governments should have no authority over their rules, practices and forms of worship. Not surprisingly, by 1582 Browne had been forced into exile to escape persecution, but the name 'Brownist' was to remain a common term for separatists. When Henry Barrow and John Greenwood were deprived of their livings during Archbishop Whitgift's attack on Puritan

practices in the 1580s, they joined up with a group of separatists in London, who appear to have maintained a murky existence since the 1560s. By 1593 the group had been crushed and both Barrow and Greenwood had been executed for sedition. Little more is heard of separatism (although this does not mean that no congregations existed) until after 1604. In that year a group of Puritan ministers presented the Millenary Petition (advocating reform of the Church) to the new king, James I; his rejection of the petition and Archbishop Bancroft's ensuing issue of strict new canons [church rules] made it clear that change would not come in the foreseeable future, and drove into separatism many waverers who had hoped for reform.

Separatist development in the early seventeenth century can be illustrated most effectively by examining two distinct, but related, congregations gathered in Lincolnshire by John Robinson and John Smyth. Their history reveals the shifts and complexities involved in the development of separatism, as well as the way in which radical ideas continued to develop in a variety of directions after separation. Smyth and Robinson were both Lincolnshire men, educated and ordained at Cambridge, preaching in Lincoln and Norwich respectively in 1602. In that year Smyth lost his post, presumably because of his Puritan leanings, since he reappeared in 1606 as pastor to a separatist congregation in Gainsborough. Shortly after this, Robinson left Norwich to lead a similar group in Scrooby, near Gainsborough, and by 1608 both groups had been forced into exile in Holland. There, Robinson settled his congregation in Leyden, where they apparently became prosperous and successful. After being joined by other dissatisfied Puritans from Sandwich, where a group had been gathered by a woolcomber named Richard Masterson, the congregation seems to have tired of living in a foreign land, and set out to find a new home in America, where their Congregationalist model was to flourish and grow. Smyth, however, had gone further than this. Once separated from the national establishment, and possibly influenced by Dutch Anabaptists, he had re-baptised his members, as a sign of their full and conscious choice in joining the Church. This action reflected the belief that infant baptism, as practised in the Anglican Church, was a superstitious relic of popery, for only an adult could make a conscious and genuine choice to take on the responsibilities of church membership. Smyth also came to the conclusion that a God who offered such a gift of salvation would not offer it to only a few, and hence he rejected the Calvinist orthodoxy of Predestination. His members appear to have

accepted these views, but there were disagreements, and as Smyth seemed to be moving yet further towards full Anabaptism the majority left him. One member, Thomas Helwys, returned to England to establish the first General Baptist Church in Spitalfields in London, and by 1626 there were Baptist Churches gathered in London, Canterbury, Salisbury, and Tiverton, Devon. Baptist Churches fell into two categories, for while the Particular Baptists retained the Calvinist belief in Predestination, the General Baptists followed Smyth in arguing that salvation was open to all men who would follow God's way. This argument would, in time, influence early Leveller ideas about natural rights.

As yet, fully separatist Churches were few, especially outside the peculiar conditions of London, but already they were beginning to develop new and significant ideas and practices. In the decade before 1640 their numbers would increase, partly because of the policies of Laud in redefining Anglicanism and rigidly enforcing its laws. Ministers who had previously conformed to the extent of occasionally wearing a surplice or employing the Prayer Book at monthly intervals now found themselves forced to change or lose their livings. Parishioners who had accepted a few ceremonies in order to hear good preaching found their communion tables turned into High Altars, railed off from the laity, and their preachers silenced. Meetings and Bible classes held in private houses were rigorously suppressed, whether or not their members also attended their parish church. In these circumstances, enforced separatism increased, but as the gathered churches developed their own ideas and beliefs they also refined and strengthened the arguments for separatism as a principle. By 1640 a small, but significant, minority had rejected the whole idea of a national Church in favour of a voluntary gathering of individuals, members by their own choice and responsible for their own destiny. As yet their claims and ideas were not overtly political, but their congregational practice encouraged the independence and confidence of the laity, and their very existence was a challenge to authority. Until 1640, authority was able to respond with repression, but by 1642, with the collapse of traditional restraints and the system of censorship, radical voices were free to make themselves heard.

The emergence of the radicals

In 1641–2 the attack on the bishops and the abolition of the Prerogative Courts removed the restraints which controlled the pulpit and press, creating a hitherto unknown freedom of expression.

THE DEVELOPMENT OF SEPARATISM 1530–1640: A SUMMARY

Period	Events in England	Events in Europe
1530–47	Henry VIII became Head of the Church but doctrine and ceremonies remained largely untouched. Protestants still persecuted.	Lutheranism gained support in Germany and Scandinavia. In 1534 a brutal Anabaptist rising in Munster shocked Europe.
1547–53	Reign of Edward VI. Protestant reforms (e.g. New Prayer Book in 1549 set Protestant services).	Calvin's Geneva became a centre of Protestant faith. Catholic reform and counter-reformation began with the Council of Trent and the founding of the Jesuits. A Catholic counter-attack began across Europe.
1553–8	Mary became queen, restored the Pope's authority, and married Philip of Spain. Protestants persecuted. Many in exile, e.g. in Geneva.	
1558–1603	Reign of Elizabeth. Moderate religious settlement with state Church based on Protestant doctrines, retaining bishops and some traditional ceremonies. Demand for further reform, especially from returning exiles. This is rejected by the queen, but Puritan ministers allowed to preach and spread ideas. Early separatists, Browne and Barrow. Also a few Anabaptist or Familist groups.	Catholic powers of France and Spain threatened England, but Elizabeth able to exploit their rivalry. England the main Protestant power, with Scotland Calvinist after 1560. Civil war in France caused by religion; Protestants in the Netherlands rebelled against Spain, with English help. War and Spanish Armada. The Netherlands became Protestant state.
1603–25	Accession of James raised hopes of Puritan reformers, but the king rejected Millenary Petition and appointed Bancroft as Archbishop. Church rules enforced: ministers like Smyth, Robinson and Jacob forced out; encouraged early Independent and Baptist groups; but the more tolerant Archbishop Abbot after 1611 allowed most Puritans to stay in the Church. Some separatist Churches, e.g. Jacob, General Baptists by 1616, but only a few.	James made peace with Spain in 1604, but religious wars in Europe spread. Catholics won in France, but Protestant Huguenots tolerated. Rivalry in Germany erupted in 1618 – the Thirty Years War. Armies of the Holy Roman Emperor and Spain attacked the Protestant princes of northern Germany and Scandinavia. The war fed English fears of a Catholic conspiracy, and affected the relationship of both James and Charles with their subjects. The effect on trade created problems, and Charles I's refusal to intervene in the cause of Protestantism was regarded with suspicion. These events were particularly unfortunate for Charles, with his French Catholic wife; in this context, the reforms of Laud and Charles' high church views, as well as his high-handed methods, were all too easily interpreted as part of a Catholic conspiracy, and fed radical perceptions that the final struggle with the Antichrist was about to begin.
1625–40	Charles I held Arminian views. Laud at Canterbury from 1633: reforms drove out Puritans. Many emigrated to New England, others to The Netherlands. Fears of Catholics at Court. In 1636, Burton, Bastwick and Prynne published pamphlets attacking the queen and Bishops: mutilated and imprisoned in 1637. In 1638, Lilburne imprisoned and flogged for importing pamphlets. Separatists increased, but conventicles harshly persecuted. In 1637, imposition of Prayer Book in Scotland led to the Bishops' Wars (1638–40) and calling of the Long Parliament. Laud's impeachment, attack on Bishops and abolition of Prerogative Courts. Emergence of radicals.	

According to Clarendon 'the license of preaching and printing increased to that degree that all pulpits were freely delivered to the schismatical and silenced preachers [separatists who had been forbidden to preach by Laud] who till then had lurked in corners or lived in New England: and the presses [were] at liberty for the publishing the most invective, seditious and scurrilous pamphlets that their wit and malice could invent'. The majority in Parliament shared his concerns, and in 1643 censorship was reimposed but could not be effective in wartime conditions. In the same year their need for allies led to the Covenant with the Scots, whose stern Presbyterianism stiffened the resolve of their English allies to establish a new discipline in the Church. By the end of the year an Assembly of Divines [ministers] had been summoned to Westminster, meeting amid high hopes of a new settlement which would accommodate the separatists alongside a reformed national Church. In January 1644, however, five leading Independent ministers issued an *Apologetical Narration*, in which they defended separatism and demanded a measure of religious toleration. When the Presbyterian majority refused to concede this, the Independents resorted to delaying tactics and long debates in order to prevent the re-imposition of controls. By the time that the Directory of Worship [which established a Presbyterian discipline] was published in 1645, the situation had slipped out of the control of its authors and supporters and separatism had become an open, if uncomfortable, reality.

Source 2

Richard Baxter, a leading Presbyterian minister

Already, in 1644, the argument for religious toleration had been put forward by William Walwyn and Richard Overton (later to lead the Leveller movement in co-operation with John Lilburne) and a powerful plea for freedom of thought, speech and worship had been published in John Milton's tract *Areopagitica*. In the same year radicals gained a solid base in the formation of the New Model Army. In 1645 when Richard Baxter visited the army at its camp near Naseby, he was horrified at the scope and variety of religious practice that he saw: at ordinary troopers preaching in the place of ordained ministers and at the open debating of 'State democracy and sometimes Church democracy' around the camp fires. By 1646 there were separatist groups of one kind or another

in most English counties, and complaints at the spread and behaviour of sectaries had multiplied. At the moment of its triumph over bishop and king, Puritanism had fragmented, and the variety of thought and practice that had been disguised by the struggle against a common enemy was now laid bare for all to see. Worse still for those concerned with order and discipline in society, radical thought and activity had now acquired a political shape and identity in the form of the Leveller movement.

The movement was centred around three leading figures – John Lilburne, William Walwyn and Richard Overton. Both Walwyn and Overton had been active in the press campaign for religious toleration, but both had already moved beyond the ideas and aspirations of the majority of Puritan separatists. In 1643 Walwyn's *Power of Love* had linked religious freedom with a wider range of social concerns and in 1644 Overton's *Man's Mortality* had shocked more orthodox sympathisers by denying the existence of Heaven, Hell and man's immortal soul. To argue that man was a rational being whose spirit died with his body was a serious matter in a society which relied on the threat of Hell and damnation as a means of defending the social and moral order. In the following year Overton published his *Martin Marpriest* tracts – a series of bitterly anti-clerical attacks on the Presbyterians and their new church order. By this time John Lilburne, a product of the General Baptists and the parliamentarian armies, had joined the political discussions which Overton and others held at the Windmill Tavern in London. In 1645–6 his personal struggles against high-handed imprisonment by both Houses of Parliament led Lilburne to formulate and develop claims to individual rights under the law. His arguments were based on the same 'ancient and fundamental constitution' that the parliamentary apologists had used to justify their opposition and resistance to the king. Thus, by the summer of 1646, when Walwyn, Overton and Lilburne's wife began a public campaign on his behalf, the ingredients of Leveller philosophy were already present, and were given public expression in their campaign pamphlet *A Remonstrance of many thousand citizens*. Drawing on parliament's own arguments in favour of law and popular sovereignty, and on the egalitarian experience and practice of the Baptist Churches, the Levellers formulated demands for individual liberty, social justice and political reform. More importantly, these were justified, not as limited rights belonging to a religious élite of 'saints', but as natural rights applicable to all men as rational human beings. The historian Howard Shaw describes its significance in Source 3.

Source 3

From H. Shaw, *The Levellers* (Longman, 1973) pp. 46–7.

A Remonstrance is important for two main reasons. First, it shows Leveller recognition that a watershed in the revolution had been reached. If the conservatives in parliament had their way, the king, his powers suitably curtailed, would slip back onto his throne and there would be no more changes. In *A Remonstrance* the Levellers developed their own constitutional theory and proclaimed their challenge from the left. Secondly ... [it] foreshadows the breadth of the future Leveller platform. Religious toleration remained one of their foremost demands, but it had been joined by social and economic grievances. The pamphlet was at once the statement of a radical philosophy with far-reaching constitutional implications, and the beginning of a popular programme designed to obtain maximum support.

The political crisis, 1646–9

Whatever significance Leveller ideas would have acquired, it is doubtful if they would have achieved much as a political movement without the opportunity created by a growing rift between parliament and army. By the end of 1646 the Presbyterian majority in the Commons was seriously concerned by the religious radicalism of the troops and, desirous also of reducing the burden of taxation, determined to disband them. With the king safely in their hands at Holdenby House in Northamptonshire, the conservative majority wanted a speedy settlement and a return to normality. Ignoring army complaints over religious oppression and arrears of pay, they ordered that the regiments disband except for those willing to volunteer for service in Ireland, offering only six weeks' arrears to men who had not been paid for months. There was also no guarantee of indemnity for actions taken in parliament's name during the Civil War, leaving the soldiers vulnerable to prosecution or civil lawsuits. Those who volunteered for Ireland would be placed under the command of new officers, and the removal of those with radical or separatist tendencies left no doubt as to what the planned religious settlement would be. Army reaction was swift. In March 1647 the cavalry regiments organised a petition laying out their religious and financial grievances, which parliament ignored, and by April they had proceeded to the election of 'agents' or 'agitators' who presented an open letter to General Fairfax. By May 1647 it was clear that some concession was necessary, and the Commons issued a slightly improved offer, to be conveyed by a group of sympathetic officers led by Fairfax, Cromwell, Fleetwood and Philip Skippon.

It is difficult to be certain what part the Levellers had played in these events. To some extent the Army's reaction was spontaneous, and shared by men who were far more concerned with arrears of pay than political or religious reform. On the other hand, there were clear Leveller contacts with some agitators and junior officers. A leading spirit behind the cavalry petition was Colonel Robert Lilburne, the elder brother of John, while the agitators, Edward Sexby and William Allen had attended Leveller debates and demonstrations in London. Whatever their original role, there is no doubt that the Leveller leaders sought to exploit the crisis, and for several months they were able to exert considerable influence. In April 1647 Overton appealed to the army to take control of the proposed settlement, rid them of the parliament and establish a radically reformed system in both Church and State. On 25th May, when Parliament ordered the disbanding to go ahead, the leading officers, or Grandees, supported their men. This was probably because they feared that the troops would otherwise act without them. A General Council of the Army was established, consisting of the Grandees and representatives of the junior officers and men, and on June 3rd, Cornet Joyce seized the king at Holdenby, transferring him to army headquarters at Newmarket. On June 5th a general rendezvous of troops was held at which the Army and its officers bound themselves by a Solemn Engagement to hold together until their demands were met. Expressed in a written *Representation of the Army*, penned by Henry Ireton, these demands emphasised that they were 'not a mere mercenary army, hired to serve any arbitrary power of a state, but called forth and conjured by the several declarations of Parliament to the defence of our own and the people's just rights and liberties'. In pursuit of these liberties they demanded the dissolution of parliament, new elections based on a reformed franchise and a redistribution of seats, and a guarantee of liberty of conscience. The same conditions were included in the *Heads of the Proposals* presented to the king in July. Mainly the work of Cromwell and Ireton, they represented a genuine attempt at compromise, allowing for the restoration of bishops alongside liberty of conscience for Protestants, a reformed franchise and a range of social and legal reforms. Unfortunately, Charles did not have the political sense to accept them.

In the meantime the political divisions between parliament and army had increased. In June the army's *Representation* had accused 11 leading conservatives in the Commons of treason, and they had, not surprisingly, found it wise to absent themselves. In July, encouraged by their Presbyterian allies in the City of London, mobs attacked the House and demanded their return, forcing the Speaker and a number of Independent MPs to flee to the army for safety. Refusing Leveller demands that parliament be dispersed and new elections held, Cromwell and Fairfax restored their Independent allies and settled the army in quarters at Putney while continuing their negotiations with the king. Frustrated, but still influential, the Levellers and their allies attacked the Grandees for half-measures in the *Case of the Army Truly Stated*, which was presented to the General Council in October. This clearly laid down the principles of popular sovereignty, manhood suffrage, and complete religious toleration. Challenged by Ireton, they agreed to produce a simplified version for consideration by the Council, and at the end of October a meeting in Putney church was presented with the first *Agreement of the People* as the basis of a Leveller constitution.

The ensuing Putney Debates produced a clear enunciation of Leveller principles. They also revealed the political gulf which separated the Levellers and their allies from the Grandees. While religious toleration of some kind was a common cause, there were significant differences of definition and extent, and while social and legal reforms were acceptable to the Grandees, the threat to property embodied in both franchise reform and the abolition of tithes remained a sticking point. Whether or not the Levellers and agitators could have won the day remains a matter of debate. In the event it proved academic when the escape of Charles to the Isle of Wight on 11 November brought the discussions to a premature end. With the threat of renewed fighting, the army had to be returned to military discipline and regiments were ordered to assemble at three separate rendezvous, thereby dividing and weakening the radical element. An attempt by the regiments of Robert Lilburne and Thomas Harrison to join the rendezvous at Corkbush Field near Ware was easily defeated by Cromwell, with only three troopers arrested and one shot. Although not entirely apparent at the time, these events represented a serious defeat for the Levellers. They had lost their most important forum, and failed to capture the army as a power base. In January 1648 the Army Council met for the last time; two months later the expected fighting began and when the Scottish invaders were finally defeated at Preston in August, the situation had changed.

Source 4

Title page of The Agreement of the People

Although the army now demanded the removal of the king it was Ireton and the Grandees who led the call and dictated the process. In November, Cromwell renewed contact with the Leveller leaders, and discussions were held to formulate a new *Agreement of the People*, but when Parliament voted on 5th December to proceed with negotiations with the king, the army made no attempt to consult with the Levellers before Pride's Purge, and when the Council of Officers found that Leveller ideas on religious toleration were far more sweeping and radical than their own, they had no hesitation in rejecting the *Agreement* and terminating the discussions. When Charles was tried and executed in January 1649, it was at the behest of the army and the Rump of Independent MPs, and on their terms. Despite the continued publication of pamphlets, the vitriolic attacks on the Grandees, the failed Leveller rising at Burford in 1649 and the abortive plots of the 1650s, it was clear that political opportunity had passed them by.

While Leveller ideas might survive to inspire later generations of political reformers, their influence on the new regime was minimal.

For the majority of Puritan separatists who dominated the army and the Council of State in 1649, the revolution had now achieved most of its aims. The abolition of the monarchy and House of Lords had forestalled any conservative backlash and secured their political and religious rights. Further reform, for example changes in the franchise or simplification of the law, could proceed at a safe and reasonable pace while the new regime secured and consolidated its gains. Republican writers like John Milton justified the regime in the name of the people, while reserving to the men of property the right to actually govern. With toleration for Puritan dissenters secured in the new religious settlement, Baptist Elders like William Kiffin (once an apprentice with Lilburne but now a successful merchant) could dissociate themselves and their Churches from political radicalism. This would prove to be a major factor in the defeat of Leveller aspirations. If they believed, however, that they could stop the 'revolution' in its tracks, they were soon to learn otherwise. In April 1649 the Council of State received disturbing reports of a group of 'True Levellers', or Diggers, who had established a Commune on waste land at St George's Hill, Walton, in Surrey, and whose manifesto claimed that the king's execution had destroyed any legal basis of private property. Within months there were reports of strange new sects, of Seekers who denied that any earthly Church was valid in God's eyes, of millenarians who argued that all earthly law had been wiped away in preparation for the coming of King Jesus, and of Ranters who claimed that acts of immorality were no sin for those who had received the gift of God's grace. Exaggerated though these reports were, they demonstrated the impossibility of limiting the visions of 'a new heaven and a new earth' which were sparked off by the collapse of the earthly kingdom of Charles I.

POLITICAL AND RELIGIOUS RADICALISM: 1640–60

Year	Main events	The development of radicalism
1640		
November	Long Parliament summoned.	Lilburne's release called for by Cromwell. He was released shortly afterwards, with Burton, Bastwick and Prynne.
December	Root and Branch Petition.	Puritan attack on authority of Bishops began.
	Laud imprisoned.	Milton wrote in defence of Presbyterian tracts.
1641		
July	Prerogative courts abolished.	Meeting of London General Baptists revealed three Churches in existence at this time. Collapse of censorship permitted expression of radical views. Conservatives complained about activities of radical preachers such as Thomas Lambe and Samuel Oates, who were preaching in London.
1642		
February	Bishops deprived of secular power by the Clerical Disabilities Act.	1642–4: tracts published by Henry Parker justified rebellion on the basis of a claim to popular sovereignty.
August	Civil War began.	
1643–4	Alliance with the Scots (Covenant). Westminster Assembly convened to set up new (Presbyterian) Church.	London Particular Baptists (seven Churches) issued joint Confession of Faith – differentiated them from the Independents, with whom they were often linked. Five Independents in Assembly issued *Apologetical Narration* claiming right to toleration; refusal led to disruption and delayed work of Assembly. Dagger Lane church (the first Congregational church in England) founded in Hull, followed by Canterbury in 1645. By 1646 there were six in Yorkshire alone.
1645		
January	Laud executed.	John Lilburne left the army rather than take the Covenant. Returning to London, he joined a group campaigning for religious toleration.
	Directory of Worship issued.	
April	Parliament condemned lay preaching.	Walwyn and Overton were already active, and had already published arguments in favour.
	Formation of the New Model Army.	Richard Baxter visited the army at Naseby, and was shocked by lay preachers, radical sects and their ideas.

1646		
May	King surrendered to the Scots.	Lilburne brought before House of Lords, claimed rights under Magna Carta and refused to plead. Imprisoned. Public campaign for his release began, and widened into demand for political and social reform. (*A Remonstrance* etc.). The campaign marked the true beginning of the Leveller movement.
October	Episcopacy formally abolished.	
1647		
January –March	Scots handed King to Parliament. The army ordered by parliament to disband, with no indemnity or pay arrears secured.	George Fox began preaching doctrine of Inner Light. Parliament concerned at radicalism of army and growing demand for religious toleration. In March, Leveller *Large* Petition presented to Parliament, and increased conservative fears.
April	Army petition rejected.	The army elected agitators to meet Fairfax and officers, who were clearly sympathetic. Levellers saw opportunity to influence the army; new agitators elected, including Leveller sympathisers (Sexby, Everard). On 5 June the army held a general rendezvous; *Solemn Engagement* signed; Army Council established. Ireton produced second *Declaration of the Army*. *Heads of the Proposals* showed signs of Leveller influence.
May	Disbandment to go ahead.	
June	Joyce seized the King.	
July	Demonstrations in London for settlement with the king.	
October	King rejected army *Proposals*.	Independent MPs fled to join the army. Cromwell and Ireton seeking to maintain army unity in the face of Leveller demands. Leveller demonstrations in London continued, calling for the army to take control and draw up a new constitution. Ideas outlined in *Case of the Army Truly Stated* and in *Agreement of the People*. Putney Debates represented high point of Leveller influence. King's escape enabled Cromwell to end debates and restore military discipline; Leveller mutiny at Ware easily suppressed. Lilburne and Wildman arrested and imprisoned in the Tower of London by parliament. Charged with treason.
November	King escaped to Isle of Wight.	
December	King negotiating secretly with the Scots.	
1648		
March– August	Second Civil War: Royalist rising in Wales; joined by Colchester, and Scots; army defeated Scots at Preston.	Levellers refrained from further agitation during Second Civil War. Gerrard Winstanley published *Saints' Paradise* in which he argued that God existed within, and denied the existence of an external heaven or hell. With victory in war, Leveller activity renewed; petitioned Parliament (September) demanding reforms. Suspicious of army intentions, but attacks on Grandees cost support among separatist Churches; Cromwell renewed contact, and second *Agreement* was discussed in Whitehall debates; talks failed over religious toleration, and officers presented amended version to parliament, which laid it aside. Levellers outflanked, and very bitter.
November	Army issued *Remonstrance* demanding trial of king.	
December	Parliament voted to resume addresses to the king, resulting in Pride's Purge.	
1649		
January	Trial and execution of King Charles I.	Renewed Leveller agitation in the army based on demands for political and social reform and claims that Rump's proceedings were illegal. Attempts to elect new agitators were quickly stopped by Grandees. *England's New Chains Discovered* presented to Rump by Lilburne. Virulent attack on Grandees. Attempted mutiny; five troopers cashiered. Overton's *Hunting of the Foxes* and arrest of Leveller leaders. Third *Agreement* published, led to army mutiny at Burford, crushed by Cromwell – effective end of Leveller threat. Disowned by separatist Churches. However, other radical groups were appearing: a Digger colony founded in Surrey, and complaints about Seekers and Ranters already multiplying.
February	Charles II proclaimed king in Edinburgh.	
March	Monarchy and House of Lords abolished.	
May	England declared a Commonwealth; Council of State established. Cromwell in Ireland.	

The era of the Enthusiasts, 1649–54

The groups that now emerged to terrify and shock society have been characterised by J.F. McGregor under the title of 'Enthusiasts'. For the most part they originated in the congregations of Puritan separatists, whose elevation of individual faith and conscience over church rules and authority had justified their own separation. Within the separate congregations the individual was expected to accept the guidance of Elders and the words of the Bible as restraints on speculation and interpretation, but in the conditions of the 1640s, this was to prove impossible, as J.F. McGregor explains in Source 5.

Source 5

From J.F. McGregor and B. Reay, *Radical Religion in the English Revolution* (OUP, 1986) pp. 57–8

In the climate of revolution, with unprecedented liberty of expression, the Puritan principle of the supremacy of individual conscience, instructed by Scripture and guided by grace, inevitably developed into less restrained claims to enthusiasm: direct inspiration by the divine spirit. No congregational system could possibly have accommodated the resulting confusion of enthusiastic speculation. Enthusiasm was intrinsically anarchic: the authority of the divine light within was supreme, autonomous and self-sufficient. … The enthusiast is subject to no external religious authority. The Scripture … is an inferior source of revelation to the inner light.

Source 6

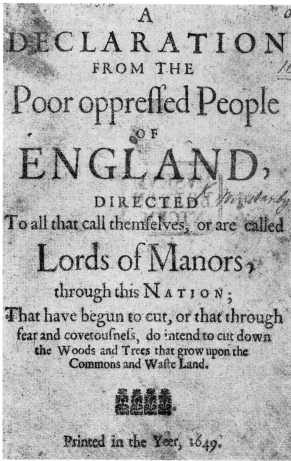

The title page of the Digger Manifesto, *1649*

The enthusiastic groups varied considerably in both longevity and significance, although this was not always perceived by contemporaries. The Digger experiment in Surrey lasted a little over a year. Fairfax, who was ordered to investigate them by the Council of State, concluded that they were harmless, but the local gentry disagreed with his interpretation and began a campaign of harassment which eventually brought the commune to collapse. Other Digger groups appeared briefly in neighbouring Cobham, in Wellingborough, Northants, and in Buckinghamshire, but amounted to very little. By 1650 attention had shifted to the Seeker and Ranter groups. The Seekers, identified as a threat to the Church by Thomas Edwards as

early as 1646, probably did not exist as a sect at all. The process of 'seeking the Lord' in different Churches was not uncommon in this period of experimentation, and many of those associated with the 'group', like John Milton and William Dell were rational intellectuals who did not really deny the validity of existing Churches, but argued that church organisation and practice were matters of indifference, not central to salvation. Evidence of the groups of northern 'Seekers', who have been claimed as the fore-runners of Quakerism, is remarkably scanty, apart from those led by Thomas Taylor in Westmorland. When converted by Fox in 1652, they had already established some meetings to arrange poor relief, suggesting a definite membership. In many other places it is likely that meetings of this kind, attached to no formal church organisation, were simply a reflection of the widespread uncertainty and dissatisfaction with existing Churches that enabled the Quaker evangelists to gain converts with such startling success when they began their first mission in 1652.

The Quaker movement was, in fact, one of two enthusiastic groups which seem to have had real significance and influence on people and events in this period, the other being the millenarian, or 'Fifth Monarchist' movement. The titles are not synonymous, for while the Fifth Monarchy Men constituted a distinct and organised sect, millenarianism represents something far more widespread.

Source 7

From B. Capp, 'The Fifth Monarchists and Popular Millenarianism', in McGregor and Reay (ed.), *Radical Religion in the English Revolution* (OUP, 1986) pp. 165–7.

Millenarianism may be defined broadly as belief in an imminent kingdom of heaven on earth to be established with supernatural help; its inspiration sprang from the biblical prophecies, especially in Revelation. … Professor William Lamont demonstrated some years ago how apocalyptic hopes [of the end of the world and the second coming of Christ] … formed part of the mainstream of English thought in the Elizabethan and early Stuart period. By the sword of the monarch and the zeal of the preacher Rome would be thrown down and a godly commonwealth would arise in England. From 1640 many moderate parliamentarians believed passionately that the Long Parliament would take over the duty long ignored by the Stuarts and at last erect the New Jerusalem through a godly, ordered reformation of church, state and society. … This sense of living in the shadow of the Apocalypse produced strong and confused emotions which help to explain the extravagant language and behaviour of the time. … In the turbulent years of civil war and revolution it was easy to be swept along by the fiery rhetoric of prophecy, and in varying ways the creed also influenced the Baptists, Congregationalists, Ranters, Diggers and Quakers. … Fifth Monarchism was, in fact, only one of many forms which such hopes could take.

It was this widespread millenarianism which explains the influence that the Fifth Monarchy movement exercised, especially within the army, in the early 1650s. For Cromwell and his supporters the king's refusal to settle, his fomenting of a second Civil War and his consequent trial and execution were acts of Providence, foreshadowing the fulfilment of God's purpose. With growing frustration they watched the Rump Parliament quibble, delay the work of reformation and pass a new Blasphemy Act in 1650 to suppress the over-enthusiastic rather than fulfil their hopes of a new society. In 1651 the 'crowning mercy' of Cromwell's victory over Charles II at Worcester seemed to confirm that they were doing God's work and the Fifth Monarchy Men emerged as a pressure group, dedicated to the establishment of his kingdom on earth. At this stage they called for the army to take power and establish a government of Saints, based

on the Jewish Sanhedrin, to prepare the way. The high point of their influence came in 1653, when Cromwell's patience finally snapped and he drove the Rump from Westminster. Encouraged by millenarian friends like Colonel Thomas Harrison, he agreed to replace them with an assembly nominated by the Puritan Churches and their allies. There is no doubt that the Barebones Parliament, as it came to be known, represented widely-held millenarian hopes. In a welcoming speech peppered with references to the prophecies of Daniel and Revelations, Cromwell charged its members with the task of constructing a godly settlement. Their failure, brought about mainly by the speed with which the radical element addressed the need for reform, and specifically by the scheme to abolish tithes, was a massive blow to radical hopes, and does represent a significant turning point in the history of radical movements. It was increasingly clear thereafter that while Cromwell would defend and maintain a significant measure of religious toleration, the remaking of society would take second place to the need for 'healing and settling'.

Source 8

Woodcut from the title page of The Quaker's Dream, *an anti-Quaker pamphlet*

Conservative fears had already been further exacerbated by the emergence of a new threat to order from the North. In 1652 George Fox and a small group of Friends began their journeys through the north of England, preaching their message to existing groups of separatists and linking them together in the beginnings of a Quaker movement. The Quaker message – that God existed within all men and women, that sin could be conquered and salvation assured to all who would seek the inner light – was not entirely new. Elements of it had been put forward by the General Baptists, the Levellers, and Winstanley the Digger, and had already created fears among conservatives. If sin could be overcome, if Hell did not exist, how could they be used as a threat to enforce social order and discipline? The Quakers not only developed these ideas further, but by denying marks of outward respect to human superiors, by attacking the role of the Church and the Ministry, by eccentric mannerisms, ecstatic 'quaking', the interruption of church services and public haranguing of ministers, they set up a coherent and public challenge to the basic foundations of conventional society. Worse still, they were highly successful. Other radical groups had, deliberately or otherwise, challenged the existing social and political structure, but few, if any, had threatened to become anything approaching a mass movement. By comparison, the rate of Quaker conversions was astonishing. In 1654–5 the movement had extended to the south. Centres of support grew up in London and Bristol, but more significantly, the movement spread rapidly through rural towns and villages. By the early 1660s, there were at least 35–40,000 Quakers in England and possibly as many as 60,000. In Ireland and Scotland the movement had developed among and around the English army, forcing Monck and Henry Cromwell to carry out extensive purges of both officers and rank and file. Although the Quaker leaders had no political programme, and would support whatever government seemed to be willing to further the work of reformation, their attitude towards authority, willingness to lecture those who did not meet their requirements and refusal to be intimidated carried an unmistakable political message. It is not surprising, therefore, that they suffered extensive persecution, despite the official policy of toleration. Their eccentricities laid them open to the use of the Blasphemy Act of 1650, but it is probably more significant that the majority of prosecutions were brought under the Vagrancy Acts, or for non-payment of tithes. Whatever the impact of their religious message, for the rest of society they were, first and foremost, a threat to property and to social order; and this fear of social upheaval that they engendered among men of property, which reached new heights in the Quaker scare of 1659, is the main reason for the failure of radical ambitions.

Failure, suffering and survival, 1653–89

The failure of radical hopes and schemes can be traced through a series of events and disappointments from 1649 onwards, marked by gradual disillusionment and growing bitterness. In 1649 the Leveller rising was crushed at Burford, and although John Lilburne was acquitted of the charge of treason, he was to spend most of his life in exile or in prison until his death in 1657. In 1650 a new Blasphemy Act marked the beginning of an onslaught on the more outrageous of the radical groups. Although the Puritan separatists were able to worship freely, and within the Cromwellian Church many ministers were able to enjoy parish livings alongside their work with independent congregations, hopes of political and social reform gradually faded. Disillusioned and not infrequently the target of persecution, radical leaders differed as to how to react. Some continued a propaganda war, others plotted. An increasing number found personal fulfilment in the growing ranks of the Quakers. From 1649 the Levellers John Lilburne and John Wildman were in touch with the Royalists and Edward Sexby had become a royalist agent. After the failure of the Barebones Parliament, some army millenarians like Colonel Nathaniel Rich remained loyal to Cromwell and refused to contemplate action without a clear sign that this was God's Will, but the more fanatical members of the Fifth Monarchy sect plotted to seize power in the name of King Jesus. In 1657 the Sindercombe Plot involved the attempted assassination of Cromwell, and later in the year the *Humble Petition And Advice* , offering the crown to Oliver Cromwell, sparked off a Fifth Monarchy rising led by Thomas Venner. Such outbreaks achieved nothing, except to fuel conservative fears and increase persecution. Never more than a tiny minority of the population, the radicals failed to touch the majority, and as the years progressed it became increasingly clear that, in political terms at least, they had nothing new to offer.

Nothing illustrates this more clearly than the events leading to the Restoration in 1659–60. When the Republicans and junior officers of the army combined to bring about the resignation of Richard Cromwell in April 1659, their desire was to bring about a restoration of the 'good old Cause': instead they demonstrated its complete bankruptcy. While Rump and officers squabbled about the balance of power between them, complaints of radical excesses, especially the activities of the Quakers, multiplied. Yet when Lambert attempted to raise an army to prevent Monck from reaching London, his troops simply melted away. Not only were radicals and their ideas unpopular in the country, but more important, they had apparently lost belief in themselves. A decade of persecution had deprived them of their most effective leaders. More important, a decade of failure had deprived them of their most powerful belief – that they were the instruments of God, executing his Will, and therefore assured of ultimate success. A few, like John Milton in his pamphlet *The Readie and Easie Way*, published in 1659, argued that the

establishment of the godly commonwealth was still possible, but for the majority their continued failure was evidence that God had turned from them, that the English nation was not yet ready to leave the wilderness. 'We have waited for liberty, but it must be God's work, not man's,' wrote Moses Wall to John Milton in May 1659. It is this disillusionment, more than any other factor, which explains the rapid disappearance of political radicalism after 1660. It is no coincidence that the one group which continued to expand, the Quaker movement, was characterised by its lack of interest in political power and its message that the victory of the saints, 'the people of God' was a personal victory, to be found within.

POLITICAL AND RELIGIOUS RADICALISM: 1649–60

Year	Main events	The development of radicalism
1650		
June	Cromwell made commanding general. Led army into Scotland.	Complaints against Ranters led to Blasphemy Act and attack on radicals and unorthodoxy. Puritan radicals (Baptists, Independents etc.) generally tolerated. Regional Associations of General Baptists established. Lilburne tried for treason and acquitted. Diggers forced to move to Cobham by local opposition; agents sent out; by April, ten Digger groups formed when Surrey group crushed; others quickly disappeared.
August	Blasphemy Act passed.	
September	Cromwell's army win victory at Dunbar.	
1651		
January	Charles II was crowned in Scotland.	Activities of radical Enthusiasts continued despite Blasphemy Acts, but increasing persecution had the effect of driving them underground. John Robins and Thomas Tany were active Ranters at this time, also Lodowick Muggleton and John Reeve who soon set up their own millenarian group – the Muggletonians.
August	Charles led army into England.	
September	Defeated at Worcester.	
1652	Anglo-Dutch War (1652–3)	Winstanley published *Law of Freedom in a Platform*, an appeal to Cromwell; communes appeared briefly in Buckinghamshire, but no real momentum. Lilburne in personal feud with Sir Arthur Haselrig; summoned by Rump and banished into exile – apparently had some contacts with Royalist agents while abroad. Ranter activities declining but Quaker missions began in north, and quickly became very successful.
1653		
April	Dissolution of the Rump.	Lilburne returned, promising to live quietly, but put on trial by Rump. Although acquitted, returned to prison. Growing army anger at lack of reform shows some radical ideas persisted. Fifth Monarchist hopes raised, but very different vision from Levellers; dissolution of Barebones Parliament infuriated them. Some influence remained in the army, but radicals increasingly isolated. Most sectarian Churches able to compromise with new regime.
July–December	Barebones Parliament.	
December	Instrument of Government. Cromwell as Lord Protector.	
1654–8	Cromwell established a broad state Church with basic orthodoxy and ministers tested on quality and fitness.	Period of decline and disillusionment for most radical groups, but of development for separatist Churches and for Quakers. In 1654 the General Baptists held their first national Conference, and many Congregationalist ministers found benefices within Cromwell's Church, while maintaining their separate groups alongside their parish. The Quakers extended their missions to the south with remarkable and rapid success. They were persecuted harshly, particularly after James Nayler re-enacted at Bristol Christ's entry into Jerusalem. Nayler was flogged and mutilated and even Fox expressed disapproval of his actions. Despite this, Quaker groups increased. Fifth Monarchists were purged from the army, especially after Venner's Rising in 1657; Walwyn abandoned political activity, Overton and some other Levellers became royalist agents. Lilburne died in 1657, a Quaker. In 1659, the Rump again proved politically bankrupt, but no radical alternative emerged.
1655	Penruddocks's royalist rising.	
1656	Rule of the Major-Generals.	
1657	*Humble Petition and Advice.*	
1658	Death of Oliver Cromwell.	
1659	Resignation of Richard Cromwell. Army/Rump rivalry.	
1660	Restoration.	

The history of religious dissent after 1660 is one of persecution, endurance and ultimate survival, but it is important to distinguish between the religious groups whose radicalism was confined mainly to a refusal to conform to the Anglican Church, and the political radicals whose visions of a new earth as well as a new heaven had dominated the period of revolution. The two are not entirely separable; in the eyes of contemporaries they were synonymous, and religious dissenters certainly suffered in the wake of political plots. Nevertheless there are important differences, if only in the survival and significance of the one and the rapid disappearance of the other. By 1663, radical politics had been effectively eradicated. An abortive Fifth Monarchy rising led by Thomas Venner in 1661 led to the arrest and imprisonment of many radical leaders, and the so-called Yorkshire Plot of 1663 enabled most others of significance to be eliminated. The Yorkshire Plot was a projected rising in Yorkshire, Durham and Westmorland by religious dissidents and former members of Cromwell's army intent on achieving religious liberty and reduced taxation.It is highly likely that the plot was, if not manufactured by government agents, at least encouraged and fomented by them in order to entrap as many potential dissidents as possible. With the exception of a few old soldiers who reappeared in the Rye House Plot of 1683 and the Monmouth Rebellion of 1685, political radicals vanished into prison, exile or their graves, or found refuge in purely religious activity.

For religious dissenters the years 1660–89 produced varied results. For the Quakers, persecution began immediately, with the passing of a draconian Quaker Act in 1662 which prescribed imprisonment, transportation and even death for persistent offenders. Fortunately, the Act was rarely applied in full, and many Quakers continued to be prosecuted for non-payment of tithes or refusal to attend their parish churches rather than specifically Quaker activities. In addition, they were prevented by their beliefs from taking an oath; many were arrested on patently false charges, but kept in prison because they refused to take the Oath of Allegiance to King Charles. In most of these cases they offered to make a declaration of their loyalty, but this was rejected. Both they and the itinerant Baptist preachers were arrested in the aftermath of radical plots and spent many years in prison as a result. More widespread persecution began after 1662, when the Act of Uniformity drove Puritan ministers from the Church. Despite the king's attempt to secure a measure of toleration through a royal Declaration of Indulgence in 1662, a series of Acts followed which were directed at those who

refused to conform to the new regime. In 1661 the Corporation Act drove Dissenters from local government positions in the boroughs, although sympathisers who were prepared to conform occasionally by taking communion in their parish church, were often able to retain their places. In 1664 the first Conventicle Act laid down a system of fines for private religious meetings, in 1665 the Five Mile Act forbade ministers to live within five miles of their previous livings, or of a chartered borough (an attempt to separate them from their congregations), and in 1670 a harsher Conventicle Act renewed the onslaught. These Acts were known collectively as the Clarendon Code.

The effects of this persecution varied from group to group and place to place. In many places the dissenters were helped and protected by sympathisers, especially among the wealthier classes who employed ejected ministers as private chaplains or refused to prosecute peaceful conventiclers. In 1672 the King's Declaration of Indulgence, rejected by many dissenters as a cloak for tolerating Catholics, nevertheless provided a measure of relief until parliament forced him to withdraw it in 1673. Many congregations established at that time were never eradicated again. In Hull, noted for its Puritan sympathies, the two Puritan congregations were virtually undisturbed until 1682, when a visit from the Earl of Plymouth as newly appointed Governor forced the reluctant Corporation to act. Even then one Alderman, Mr Humphrey Duncalf, resigned from his position, declaring to the Earl that he had no intention of hounding 'peaceable neighbours' for their religious beliefs. Hull was, however, something of an exception and even there the Quakers had suffered fines and imprisonment. It is difficult to make general statements about the impact of persecution, but it is clear that the range of congregational activities, the personal and social influence held by members and sympathisers, and the extent to which enemies associated a group with 'political' radicalism directly affected the extent to which they were persecuted. Hence there were individual cases of great suffering. Some died in prison, others lost their health and fortunes. The Presbyterians suffered least, the Quakers worst. The effect of persecution and isolation also varied. Those groups who required the services of a trained ministry, like the Presbyterians and Congregationalists, found survival difficult, and by 1689 there were few such congregations outside urban centres. Even the Quakers found it necessary to organise a much clearer structure and establish a network of meetings to support and encourage members, as well as to uphold discipline and protect the name and reputation of the movement. Survival required a new maturity, a compromise with harsh reality. For the Presbyterians, the new reality was ultimately disastrous. Believing in a single, disciplined State Church, they were unable to come to terms with separatism even when legally permitted. When the Toleration Act of 1689 eventually made their separation permanent, the English Presbyterian movement crumbled, and its Churches gradually drifted towards Congregationalism or adopted new Unitarian beliefs. For other dissenters, however, the Act of 1689 represented their final victory in the long struggle for existence.

The Toleration Act illustrates both the fact of toleration and the price that had been paid for it. Religious liberty was granted to Protestants, but positions in local and central government as well as some professions required at least occasional attendance at the parish church and the taking of the Anglican communion. What the Act granted was the right to worship freely in return for the abandonment of political ideals and aims. In 1660 the radicals were feared and hated because they threatened the existing social and political structure. In the years that followed they gradually abandoned whatever ambitions they had entertained in this area, their energies becoming almost entirely absorbed in the struggle to maintain their religious identity. In the struggle to survive, the radicals were forced to return to the original core and inspiration of radicalism – the belief of individuals in their right to seek God and find salvation according to their consciences. In their initial pursuit of this cause, they had developed ideas about heaven, earth and society which would never totally disappear. The idea of religious uniformity, of a single Church with a single creed to which all citizens should belong, had been destroyed. The achievement of the radicals was a major extension of individual freedom – but only when this had ceased to be a threat to the social and political structure were they permitted to enjoy it in peace.

Political and religious radicalism: 1640–60

What was radicalism?: Interpretation of sources

The sources below are all written by members of different radical groups and sects which were active between the calling of the Long Parliament in 1640 and the Restoration in 1660. As a first step in

understanding and defining radicalism, you should read the sources and try to summarise the ideas, attitudes and aspirations that are contained there. It is important to realise that there were many different kinds of radicals, and that while some ideas were common to them all, each group had its own, unique combination of beliefs. At this stage, however, we are not seeking to identify particular groups, but to gain an initial understanding of the ideas and beliefs which challenged conventional assumptions about God and Man, Church and State, society and the individual. The introductory narrative, and your own knowledge of the period, will help you to interpret the sources, and within that context you should concentrate on collecting and cross-referencing the information contained in the set of sources that you have.

Question

1. What conclusions can you draw about the ideas and beliefs put forward by political and religious radicals from the evidence provided in Sources 9–25?

Source 9

From the Covenant of the Canterbury Congregational Church, 1645. This is an example of the kind of agreement, or Covenant, made by congregations when they chose to set themselves up as separate, independent, or 'gathered' Churches.

We poor Creatures, [being sinful by nature and having no hope without God] believe that God, out of rich mercy, has provided salvation in Christ by making a Covenant of Free Grace, in which he offers everlasting life … fully and freely, to all those that shall take hold of the same. … We acknowledge ourselves unworthy, yet … our desire is to take hold on the Covenant of Free Grace, and we do solemnly avow and sincerely profess … that we do accept and acknowledge God for our God and will endeavour (by the power of the Spirit of Christ) to live as his People … And we do also profess, that the sincere desire of our souls is with full purpose of heart to cleave to, and walk with one with another … in a way of Christian and brotherly love, admonishing, exhorting, reproving, counselling, comforting; and helping one another forward in the way to heaven.

Source 10

From *The Apologetical Narration* issued by five Congregationalist members of the Assembly of Divines in 1644. This was the first public appeal

for some religious toleration for the separatist groups; the ministers hoped that the Presbyterian majority in the Assembly would allow it to be written into the new settlement of the Church.

We could not ... but judge it a safe and an allowed way to retain the government of our several congregations in matters of discipline within themselves, to be exercised by their own elders, whereof we had ... three at least in each congregation, whom we were subject to; yet not claiming to ourselves ... [a total independence] ... to be subject to none others; but only a full and entire power complete within ourselves, [unless] we should be challenged to err grossly, such as corporations enjoy, who have the power and privilege to [control their membership] within themselves, and yet are accountable to the state they live in.

Source 11

From *The Ancient Bounds*, an anonymous pamphlet published in 1645.

There are two things contended for in this liberty of conscience: first to instate every Christian in his right of free, yet modest, judging and accepting what he holds; secondly, to [encourage a search for] the truth, and this is the main end and respect of this liberty. I contend not for variety of opinions; I know there is but one truth. But this truth cannot be so easily brought forth without this liberty; and a general restraint, though intended but for errors, yet through the unskilfulness of men, may fall upon the truth. And better many errors of some kind suffered than one useful truth be obstructed or destroyed ....

Nor yet may all principles that derive themselves from conscience have the benefit of this plea of liberty ... if they shall be found of a disabling [dangerous] nature, or wanting in their due proportion of benevolence to public peace, liberties, societies.

Source 12

From Roger Williams, *The bloody tenent of Persecution*, 1644. Williams had emigrated to the American colonies to escape persecution, but found the Puritans of Massachusetts as hostile to toleration as Laud. With help from sympathisers like Lord Brooke, he founded the colony of Rhode Island, which permitted complete religious liberty.

It is the will and command of God that ... a permission of ... consciences and worships be granted to all men in all nations and countries; ... God requireth not an uniformity of religion to be enacted and enforced in any civil state; which enforced uniformity, sooner or later, is the greatest occasion of civil war, ravishing of conscience, persecution of Christ Jesus in his servants, and of the hypocrisy and destruction of millions of souls.

Source 13

From William Walwyn, *A Word More*, 1646. A leader of the Leveller movement, Walwyn had campaigned publicly for religious toleration since 1643.

I find by myself that Christians cannot live, though they enjoy all natural freedom and content, where they are not free to worship God in a way of religion, and I find also by myself that Christians cannot worship God in any way but that which agreeth with their understandings and consciences.

Source 14

From John Milton, *Areopagitica*, 1644; an outstanding plea for freedom of expression. Milton was writing to protest at plans to reintroduce the censorship which had collapsed with the power of the Bishops. The plans involved setting up a licensing committee of twenty.

I cannot set so light by all the invention, the art, the wit, the grave and solid judgement which is in England, as [to believe] that it can be comprehended in any twenty capacities [minds] however good, much less that it should not pass except their superintendence be over it, except it be sifted and strained with their strainers. ...Truth and understanding are not such wares as to be monopolised and traded in by tickets and statutes and standards ...

While Bishops were to be baited down [those who now want censorship argued] that all Presses might be open; it was the people's birthright and privilege in time of Parliament, it was the breaking forth of light. But now the Bishops [are driven] out of the Church, ...liberty of printing must be enthralled again under a Prelatical commission of twenty, the privilege of the people nullified, and which is worse, the freedom of learning must groan again, and [go back] to her old fetters.

Source 15

Extracts from the works of John Smyth and other General Baptists, quoted in W. Haller, *The Rise of Puritanism* (Harper Torchbooks, 1938)

Original sin is an idle term ... man is yet free to adhere to good or evil as he will.

God is no respecter of persons, he calleth all effectually [equally] and in good earnest, and whosoever holdeth otherwise, he hath an evil conceit [idea] of God.

Christ lives in every man ... and is as much in the [sinners] as in the [saints]: But, I say, here is all the difference, to the one Christ is manifested, to the other he is not; God lives in all, but all know it not.

Source 16

From Laurence Clarkson, *The Lost Sheep Found*, 1660. The extract below refers to Clarkson's activities in 1644–5, when he was associated with the Baptists, several years before he became a Ranter. It refers to the Baptist insistence on adult baptism, as a sign of the conscious choice made in joining their Church.

Now dipping being a command of Christ, I judged them rebels that did profess the name of Christ, and not submit their bodies to the ordinance of Christ, and that Christ requires obedience from none but such as was capable of being taught, and therefore no children, but men and women, ought to receive the ordinance of baptism.

Source 17

From William Walwyn, *The Compassionate Samaritan*, 1644.

They would not have us to think that a minister comes to be so, as another man comes to be a merchant, bookseller, tailor etc. ... by his own making choice to be of such a trade: no, there must be something spiritual in the business, a *Iure Divino* [Divine Right] must be brought in, and a succession from the Apostles ... as some would have us think kings to be anointed of God, because the Israelite kings were by his command.

... If the people did not believe so, they would examine all that was said, and not take things upon trust from the ministers. ... They would then handle their ministers familiarly, as they do one another, shaking off that timorousness and awe which they have of the Divines, with which they are ignorantly brought up. ...

They have ... made it a difficult thing to be a minister, and so have engrossed the trade to themselves ... so that hereby they become masters of all discourses, and can presently stop the people's mouths that put them too hard to it, by telling them that it is not for laymen to be too confident, being no scholars ... and thus they keep all in a mystery, that they may be the only oracles.

Source 18

From William Hartley, *The Prerogative Priest's Passing Bell*, 1651. It was written in response to Thomas Hall's, *The Pulpit Guarded*, which argued that preaching should be restricted to the ordained ministry.

Your animosity is against laymen's preachings. Sure you are from Rome for your speech betrays you. In the commonwealth of Saints there is no such distinction of laity and clergy, but all are one, or alike in Jesus Christ ... One main argument wherewith you deceive the people is drawn, as you say, from God's eternal decree who, as you argue, hath appointed every man a calling, viz. some carpenters, fishermen, tent makers, etc., others to be set apart for the ministry. ...

We answer that persons are qualified by God (the wise disposer of all things) with abilities in the management of the arts, mysteries and sciences for the benefit of the creation, but that persons, so qualified, are prohibited the ministerial function, viz. preaching of the Gospel, that I utterly deny. ...

Peter was a catcher of fish by nets, and men by preaching, and both allowable by Jesus Christ. Therefore trading and preaching is legitimate in the self-same person.

Be it granted that human learning, rightly sanctified, may help the sight, yet in itself it gives no more light than spectacles to a blind man.

Source 19

From Hanserd Knollys, *A Glimpse of Sion's Glory*, a millenarian tract published in 1641.

At the pouring forth of the first vial, there was a voice saying: *Babylon is fallen, it is fallen.* ... Babylon's falling is Sion's raising. Babylon's destruction is Jerusalem's salvation. ... This is the work that is in hand. As soon as ever this is done, that Antichrist is down, Babylon fallen, then comes in Jesus Christ reigning gloriously. ... It is the work of the day to cry down Babylon, that it may fall more and more; and it is the work of the day to give God no rest till he sets up Jerusalem as the praise of the whole world. Blessed is he that dasheth the brats of Babylon against the stones. ...

The voice of Jesus Christ reigning in his Church comes first from the multitude, the common people. The voice is heard from them first, before it is heard from any others. God uses the common people and the multitude to proclaim that the Lord God Omnipotent reigneth. As when Christ came at first the poor received the Gospel – not many wise, not many noble, not many rich, but the poor – so in the reformation of religion, after Antichrist began to be discovered, it was the common people that first came to look after Christ. ...You that are of the meaner rank, common people, be not discouraged; for God intends to make use of the common people in the great work of proclaiming the kingdom of his Son. ...

But though it be dark for a while, certainly he shall reign. ... It is true, this is ... interpreted in a mystical sense; but there is no reason why we may not take it literally ... it is said, *The Saints shall reign with him a thousand years*, which cannot be meant reigning with him in heaven. For after these thousand years there shall be many enemies raised against the Church. ...If it were meant of heaven that could not be and therefore it must be meant of Jesus Christ coming and reigning here gloriously for a thousand years. ...

But when shall these things be? Truly brethren, we hope it is not long before they shall be; and the nearer the time comes, the more clearly these things shall be revealed.

Source 20

From Richard Overton, *A Remonstrance of Many Thousand Citizens*, 1646. The *Remonstrance* was a petition presented to Parliament in 1646. Sparked off by the problems of John Lilburne, it was the first clear expression of Leveller philosophy and the political programme that had begun to develop from it. Overton's use of 'we' reflects his claim to be speaking on behalf of the petitioners, and by implication, the nation as a whole.

We are well assured, yet cannot forget that the cause of our choosing you to be Parliament-men, was to deliver us from all kind of bondage, and to preserve the commonwealth in peace and happiness. For effecting whereof, we possessed you with the same power that was in ourselves, to have done the same; for we might justly have done it ourselves without you, if we had thought it convenient, choosing you as persons whom we thought fitly qualified and faithful, for avoiding some inconveniences.

But ye are to remember, this was only of us but a power of trust, which is ever revocable and cannot be otherwise, and to be employed to no other end than our own well-being …

It is high time we be plain with you: we are not, nor shall not be so contented; we do expect, according to reason that ye should, in the first place, declare and set forth King Charles his wickedness openly before the world, and withal, to show the intolerable inconveniences of having a kingly government, from the constant evil practices of those of this nation; and so to declare King Charles an enemy, and to publish your resolution never to have any more, but to acquit us of so great a charge and trouble for ever, and to convert the great revenue of the crown to the public treasure, to make good the injuries and injustices done heretofore, and of late, by those that have possessed the same; and this we expected long since at your hand, and until this be done, we shall not think ourselves well dealt withal in this original of all oppressions, to wit, kings.

… Whereas truly we are well assured, neither you, nor none else, can have any … power at all to conclude [decide for] the people in matters that concern the worship of God, for therein every one of us ought to be fully assured in our own minds, and to be sure to worship him according to our consciences …

Ye know the laws of this nation are unworthy [of] a free people, and deserve from first to last to be considered and seriously debated, and reduced to an agreement with common equity [fairness] and right reason, which ought to be the form and life of every government. …

Source 21

From *The case of the Army Truly Stated*, a Leveller manifesto published in 1647. It claimed to speak for the army, but was probably written by the civilian Leveller, John Wildman.

Whereas all power is originally and essentially in the whole body of the people of this Nation, and whereas their free choice or consent by their Representors is the only original or foundation of all just government; and the reason and end of the choice of all just Governors whatsoever is their apprehension of safety and good by them. … That the supreme power of the peoples representors or Commons assembled in Parliament be forthwith clearly declared, as their power to make laws or repeal laws … as also their power to call to an account all officers in this nation whatsoever …

Source 22

From John Lilburne, *England's New Chains Discovered*, 1648. Lilburne was a prominent Leveller leader.

When we consider what rackings and tortures the people in general have suffered through decay of trade and dearness of food, and very many families in particular, through Free-quarter, Violence, and other miseries incident to war, having nothing to support them therein, but hopes of Freedom and a well-settled Commonwealth in the end. …

[We are] resolved to take away all known and burdensome grievances, as Tithes, that great oppression of the Country's industry and hindrance of tillage: Excise and Customs, those secret thieves and Robbers, Drainers of the poor and middle sort of people, and the greatest Obstructers of trade … also to take away all Monopolising Companies of Merchants, the hinderers and decayers of Clothing and Cloth-working, Dying and the like useful professions; … [We] also have in mind to take away all imprisonment of disabled men for debt; and to provide some effectual course to enforce all that are able to a speedy payment, and not suffer them to be sheltered in Prisons, where they live in plenty, whilst their creditors are undone … and to establish some more speedy, less troublesome and chargeable way for deciding of Controversies in Law, whole families having been ruined by seeking right in the ways yet in being. … For which end we most earnestly desire and propose. …

5. That you will open the Press . … which is a liberty of greatest concernment to the Commonwealth, and which such only as intend a tyranny are engaged to prohibit. …

6. That you will (whilst you have opportunity) abate the charge of the Law, and reduce the stipends of Judges and all other Magistrates and Officers in the Commonwealth, to a less, but competent, allowance, converting the overplus to the public Treasury, whereby the taxes of the people may be much eased. …

10. That the so many times complained of Ordinance for Tithes … may be forthwith taken away;

Source 23

From Gerrard Winstanley, *The True Levellers' Standard Advanced*, 1649. Winstanley was the leader of a group of 'Diggers' who set up a commune on waste land in Surrey. The pamphlet sets out the purpose and justification of the commune, which was quickly suppressed by the local authorities. Equally important, Winstanley identifies God with Reason, and by claiming that God/Reason exists within all human beings, is moving towards modern ideas of natural, or human, rights.

In the beginning of time, the great Creator, Reason, made the earth to be a common treasury, to preserve beasts, birds, fishes, and man, the lord that was to govern this creation. For man had domination given to him over the beasts, birds and fishes. But not one word was spoken in the beginning, that one branch of mankind should rule over another.

And the reason is this. Every single man, male and female, is a perfect creature of himself. And the same Spirit that made the globe dwells in man to govern the globe; so that the flesh of man, being subject to Reason, his Maker, hath him to be his teacher and ruler within himself, therefore need not run abroad after any teacher and ruler without him. ...

But since human flesh. ... began to delight himself in the objects of the creation more than in the Spirit ... then he fell into blindness of mind and weakness of heart, and ... set up one man to teach and rule over another. And thereby the Spirit was killed, and man was brought into bondage and became a greater slave to such of his own kind than the beasts of the field were to him.

And hereupon the earth, which was made to be a common treasury of relief for all, both beasts and men, was hedged into enclosures by the teachers and rulers, and the others were made servants and slaves. And that earth that is within this creation made a common storehouse for all, is bought and sold and kept in the hands of a few; whereby the great Creator is mightily dishonoured: as if he were a respecter of persons, delighting in the comfortable livelihood of some, and rejoicing in the miserable poverty and straits of others. From the beginning it was not so. ...

Wherefore is it that there is such wars and rumours of wars in the nations of the earth? And wherefore are men so mad to destroy one another? But only to uphold civil propriety of honour, dominion and riches one over another, which is the curse the creation groans under, waiting for deliverance. But when once the earth becomes a common treasury again ... then this enmity in all lands will cease. ... The work we are going about is this: to dig up George's Hill and the waste ground thereabouts, and to sow corn and to eat our bread together by the sweat of our brows. ... That which encourages us to go on in this work is this. We would have none live in beggary, poverty or sorrow, but that everyone might enjoy the benefit of his creation. ...

For by this work we are assured, and reason makes it appear to others, that bondage shall be removed, tears wiped away, and all poor people by their righteous labours shall be relieved and freed from poverty and straits.

Source 24

From Abiezer Coppe, *A Fiery Flying Roll*, 1650.

Thus saith the Lord: Be wise now therefore, O ye rulers etc. Be instructed etc. Kiss the sun [son?] etc. Yea, kiss Beggars, Prisoners, warm them, feed them, clothe them, money them, relieve them, take them into your houses, don't serve them as dogs, without door, etc. Own them, they are flesh of your flesh, your own brethren, your own Sisters, every whit as good (and if I should stand in competition with you) in some degrees better then yourselves. Once more I say own them; they are yourself, make them one with you, or else go howling into hell: howl for the miseries that are coming upon you, howl.

The very shadow of levelling, sword-levelling, man-levelling frighted you, (and who, like yourselves, can blame you, because it shook your Kingdom?), but now the substantiality of levelling is coming.

The Eternal God, the mighty Leveller is coming, yea come, even at the doore; and what will you do that day.

Source 25

From James Nayler, *The Power and Glory of the Lord Shining out of the North*, 1656. Nayler was one of the early Quaker leaders, whose famous entry into Bristol on Palm Sunday 1656 brought notoriety to his movement and great suffering to Nayler himself. The extract below concentrates on the Quaker rejection of tithes; they were not alone in this, but their ideas were reinforced by their rejection of any priesthood in favour of the spirit of Christ found within the individual.

All your hirelings [paid priests] are strangers to Christ, and he knows them not: for though they may prophesy in his name, and in his name cast out devils, yet if they be workers of iniquity, Christ knows them not and such know not Christ. ... Now all people, cease from your strange guides and outside lights and return to the Light of Christ in you, that which shows you sin and evil and the deeds of darkness.

For your tithes, augmentations and set benefits, when did ever God require any such thing from any magistrates under the Gospel? And doth it serve for any other end but to hold up an idle, loitering ministry, one pulling another out of places and setting themselves in their stead that they may heap up riches and live in their lusts? ... Those who are sent by Christ take little care for such earthly things, having a better reward in durable riches. And can you ever keep the ministers of Antichrist out of places (who will conform to anything for gain) so long as they can have you to feed them with money? … when you leave all that say they are Christ's ministers to Christ's maintenance, set down in the Gospel, then it will appear who have run unsent and have not profited the people.

What was radicalism?: Interpretation of sources in context

The set of sources 9–25 that you have read provides a basic understanding of some of the main radical ideas that were held and expressed in the mid-seventeenth century; but if you are to form opinions about their meaning and significance, it is necessary to know a great deal more about who wrote them, in what circumstances, and for what purposes. If you are to make judgements about the nature of radicalism, you need to know how far these sources are representative of radical thinking, how widely these views were held, by what groups and individuals, and whether some ideas can be seen as more important than others. In short, the sources need to be read and interpreted in the context of what is known about the situation in which they were produced.

The sources below provide information of this kind, taken from historians who have studied the full range of radical writings and the lives of those who were called radicals. Sources 26 and 27 describe the Baptists, who were among the earliest of the separatists and whose ideas paved the way for many later developments. They are followed by a brief summary of the early life of John Lilburne, whose experience in the Baptist meetings shaped and prepared the future Leveller leader. Source 28 then discusses the emergence of the Levellers, and shows how their religious inspiration stimulated and encouraged the demands for political reform that were the hallmark of the mature Leveller movement. In Source 29, F.D. Dow analyses a range of radical groups and their ideas, revealing the variety of beliefs that developed as well as the common and overlapping elements that were shared by all or most radicals. To illustrate this there are brief biographies of John Milton and Gerrard Winstanley. Born within a year of one another, both were to challenge accepted conventions on the basis of their religious beliefs, but with different characters and experiences, their concerns and their challenge would take very different forms. Milton remained, above all else, an individual

campaigning for individual freedom, while Winstanley's thought led him to attempt, on God's authority, a major change in the social and economic organisation of society. What is perhaps equally significant is the extent to which their very different visions had a common root and purpose. Finally, in Source 30, Dow addresses the important question of how numerous and how powerful the radical groups came to be. His survey considers the geographical distribution of radicalism and the social groups from which the radicals drew support.

As a whole, Sources 26–30 and the accompanying biographies should provide you with a context in which you can interpret the radical ideas that you have studied in Sources 9–25, and enable you to make some judgements as to what radicalism was.

Question

2. Read Sources 26–30 and the mini-biographies of Lilburne, Milton and Winstanley. Compile a list of radical groups or sects mentioned.

   (a) Using information from the historians' analyses and the introductory narrative to help you interpret Sources 9–25, briefly summarise the characteristics of each group under the following headings:

   period of activity, size/numbers, individuals/ leaders, main aims and ideas.

   (b) Place each group in what you consider to be their correct position on the matrix provided on p. 30.

   (c) What difficulties are there in defining and arranging radical groups in this way? Why do these difficulties arise?

   (d) What conclusions can you draw at this point about radicals in the 'English Revolution'?

Source 26

From J.F. McGregor, 'The Baptists – Fount of all Heresy', in McGregor and Reay (ed.), *Radical Religion in the English Revolution* **(OUP, 1986) pp. 23–63.**

While continental Anabaptism did have some influence on the English Baptists, the movement which emerged in the early 1640s was essentially a product of native English Puritanism. The Baptists were part of a separatist tradition which saw little prospect of Christian reformation in a national Church tainted with relics of popery and too lax in its admission of the ungodly to communion. The saints, those confident of their election to salvation, must withdraw to form their own Churches ... Between 1640 and 1642 both Particular and General Baptists further demonstrated their exclusive separatism by adopting the dramatic ritual of baptism by total immersion. Henceforth they were known by their opponents as Dippers as well as Anabaptists. ... Most contemporaries failed to grasp the distinction between General and Particular Baptists ... [but]the Particular Baptists condemned [the doctrine of] general redemption as heresy: the General Baptists tended to regard this doctrine, rather than believers' baptism as the foundation of their faith. Strictly, they were distinct Churches with many common sectarian attitudes. ... In the first years of the civil war, the London Baptists refined their evangelical techniques: revivalist meetings, public debates, and printed propaganda. ... Baptist publications were not particularly well designed as propaganda. They were more concerned to counter the attacks of their opponents than to develop an effective polemical style. Nevertheless they were the first radical, popular movement able to take advantage of the freedom and relative cheapness of the printing press in the unique conditions of revolution to appeal to an increasingly literate population. ... Presbyterian opposition to the Independents' doctrine of the Church as autonomous congregations of saints ... pushed the Independents into alliance with the separatists and obliged them reluctantly to defend liberty of worship for all Puritan saints, including Baptists. The growing influence of the Independents, in both Parliament and its armies, protected religious radicals from the punitive actions of hostile magistrates and clergy. The dynamic energy of separatism, which had previously been absorbed in surviving the rigours of persecution, was increasingly channelled into evangelism. ... The victories of the parliamentary armies in 1644 and 1645 allowed them to expand their missionary activities into most of England. In the vanguard were the many saints who had volunteered for military service. The Anabaptist principle of pacifism found little sympathy with either wing of the Baptists, both of which were prepared to fight for a just cause and serve in the armies of a godly regime. They shared the Puritan conviction that Parliament's forces, and particularly the New Model Army, were God's instrument for the destruction of popery and tyranny. ...

The Baptist church was a gathering of those whom the Lord had sanctified by his grace, called out of the ungodly world into the fellowship of saints. As a voluntary association of God's chosen, the Church was necessarily an egalitarian, democratic and consensus society. The sect allowed for no distinction between clergy and laity. In the vast majority of Baptist congregations, the ruling ministry consisted of lay Elders who exercised the functions of both pastor and teacher as well as the disciplinary duty 'to oversee the lives and manners of men'. Elders were chosen by the congregation from those brethren gifted in preaching and teaching the gospel ... [and] acquired no special status. ... Elections and congregational business were decided by consensus. ... [but] the principle of consensus in practice required uniformity. ... There was no provision for principled dissent from the will of the congregation except for defection or expulsion. ...

The Baptist saints had come out of the world into Christ's spiritual kingdom but they were neither willing nor able to divorce themselves from the revolutionary events of their time. They ... held to the Puritan ideal that reformation of society and its institutions was possible through the action of godly men. Radical zeal, however, was frequently constrained by sectarian interest. To the Baptists the foundation of Puritan reformation was the guarantee of liberty of worship for the saints and in defence of this liberty they made a substantial contribution to the cause of toleration. They argued that the true Church was the creation of divine grace, not of man. Since it was not of this world, it must necessarily be completely separate from the state. The magistrate, therefore, had no power in religious matters: the state must allow total liberty of religious opinion and worship. ... In support of their principle of the separation of Church and state, much of the Baptists' propaganda was directed against the foundations of the traditional ecclesiastical system: a professional clergy financed by a compulsory tithe. ... Clergy, like lawyers, used their professional monopoly to line their own pockets. ... Baptists shared the general radical criticism of the university as 'a factory of divines'. But the corrupt foundation of the state Church was 'that Jewish and Antichristian yoke of tithes ... an intolerable burden, inconsistent with the liberty of conscience unto all'.

In their contributions to the religious controversies of the 1640s, the Baptists developed from their fundamental doctrine of the separation of Church and state the elements of a radical reform programme. The general expectation of the movement, however, was that change would come about through the chosen instruments of the Lord, whether Parliament, Army or Protector, rather than direct action of the saints themselves. ... [Thus] the London leaders were content with the Independents' strategy of discreetly lobbying their sympathisers in government as they feared that any attempt at popular agitation would only provoke cries of Munster and John of Leiden [leader of a violent Anabaptist rebellion in Germany in 1534]. Their timidity allowed the Levellers to mobilise from 1646 the discontent of the rank and file separatists, turning the principle of religious liberty into a secular theory of natural rights. The Leveller party built its ideology and organisation on the foundations of London separatism. It is likely that Leveller egalitarianism owed much to General Baptist theology, with its greater emphasis on human accountability and the innate goodness and equality of all mankind. ... If all mankind were even potentially of the elect, then there could be no practical distinction between the civil rights of saints and citizens. To guarantee the liberty of the saints, it was necessary to seek freedom for all. Furthermore, the General Baptists' fluid membership, mass meetings, evangelical campaign tactics, and wide social appeal provided the Levellers with the basis of a popular political organisation.

Source 27

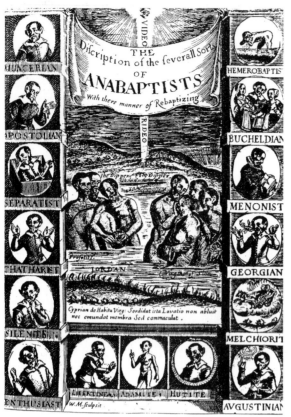

An anti-Baptist tract, enumerating the different heresies of which they were accused

JOHN LILBURNE: THE MAKING OF A LEVELLER

John Lilburne was born in 1614, the son of Richard Lilburne, a member of the minor gentry in the county of Durham. About 1630 his father apprenticed him to one Thomas Hewson, a London cloth merchant, with whom he apparently remained until 1636–7. In this period London was the centre of a religious and intellectual ferment, stimulated by the words and visions of radical preachers whose sermons the young Lilburne would undoubtedly have heard. According to his friend and fellow-apprentice, William Kiffin, they were members of a group who regularly met on a Sunday morning 'in order to pray, communicate their experiences, repeat a sermon and read scripture'. Such young men were powerfully affected in 1637 by the mutilation and imprisonment of Burton, Prynne, and Bastwick whose acquaintance Lilburne had apparently made in 1636. He had been introduced to Bastwick by Kiffin and one Edmund Rozer, whom Lilburne describes as teacher to the (Baptist) congregation of which he was a member. In 1637, therefore, Lilburne was already associated with the London Baptists, and with the underground opposition to Laud's religious policies and the Anglican uniformity that the Archbishop sought to maintain. At this point he seems to have left his master, who was looking to retire, and was seeking to raise some capital to establish himself. Both conviction and the hope of a profit, therefore, led him into the scheme whereby he arranged the printing of Bastwick's *Letany* (an attack on the Bishops) in Holland, and its illegal importation. As a result he found himself before the Star Chamber. On this first of many occasions, Lilburne defied his persecutors, standing on his rights as a freeborn Englishman to follow his conscience – a defiance which earned him a £500 fine, a public whipping and the pillory, and imprisonment in the Fleet. According to his own account, Lilburne's sufferings marked the moment of his spiritual conversion. Certainly they marked the beginning of his career as an agitator. Standing in the pillory he harangued the crowd as to their right to freely seek and serve God, the right to freedom of conscience and expression, and the illegality of persecuting him thus, contrary to the law, the Petition of Right, and the law of nature. If Lilburne's legal knowledge was less than accurate, his political instincts were immaculate – his frustrated judges had him gagged 'so that blood issued from his mouth' in an attempt to silence him, but their success was temporary. Even before the sentence was executed in April 1638, Lilburne had written an account of his wrongs, and between 1638 and 1640 he succeeded in publishing at least four petitions and pamphlets, detailing the injustices that had been perpetrated upon him, and by implication upon the rights of all Englishmen. Although his ideas had yet to fully form, the future Leveller had already begun to take shape.

Source 28

From B. Manning, 'The Levellers and Religion', in McGregor and Reay, *Radical Religion in the English Revolution* (OUP, 1986) pp. 65–90.

The Levellers were the left wing of the parliamentarian party which won the English civil war. They became increasingly disillusioned with the outcome of victory. They sought to explain the cause for which they thought they had been fighting and why they felt it was being betrayed. At the same time the Levellers sprang from the radical religious groups of the period and the major problem for historians has been to identify and analyse the relationship between their religious beliefs and their political thinking. The question has been whether the movement remained religious in its primary inspiration and ultimate aims or became wholly secular in ideas and objectives. The Levellers did not all hold exactly the same views on religion, but ... [they] believed that the essential points of religion were simple and within the grasp of all men. The people did not have to depend on the teachings of clergymen or the judgements of learned men but could discover for themselves all they needed to know. In tracts published in 1643 and 1644 William Walwyn put forward the view that everything necessary 'either for the enlightening of our understandings, or the peace of our minds' had been set forth so plainly in the Bible 'that the meanest capacity is fully capable of a right understanding thereof'. ...

The implications of Walwyn's argument extended beyond religion. The Levellers saw a parallel between the capacity of all men to discover for themselves true principles of religion and the demand that the laws of the land should be accessible to all citizens. Although the Bible had been translated into English ... the laws of England were 'locked up from common capacities in the Latin or French tongues'. ... The Levellers claimed that just as the clergy made religion difficult and uncertain in order to monopolise it and to dominate and exploit the people, so the lawyers made the law complex and confusing in order to keep the exclusive control of it by which they grew rich and powerful. ... The Levellers wanted to reduce the laws to 'express and plain rules' which would 'be comprised in one volume in the English tongue', 'to be kept in every church throughout the land; and to be read over at several appointed Times and Seasons, in open Congregation' so that 'every free Commoner might understand his own proceedings'. ... The simple rules and basic principles which lay behind, or ought to lie behind, the laws, were the same as those which were the essence of Christianity as the Levellers understood it, and were similarly within the capacity of all men to understand. The rules and principles which they had in mind are revealed, therefore, in their notion of true religion.

The foundation of true religion in the view of the Levellers was 'doing good'. ... This doctrine of 'practical Christianity' shifted the emphasis in religion away from devotion and virtue towards concern for mankind – not that ... the Levellers would have seen this in any other light than that of obeying God's commands and worshipping him by doing good ... The individualism of the Levellers ... was 'balanced by a ... sense of community'. 'As I am an individual, I am part of the whole Nation', wrote Lilburne, and so bound up with the fate of the whole nation. 'For what is done to any one may be done to every one: besides, being all members of one body, that is, of the English Commonwealth, one man should not suffer wrongfully, but all should be sensible, and endeavour his preservation'. It was the sense of personal responsibility for the good of their fellow men and of the society to which they belonged – the English nation – that provided the Levellers with the religious and philosophical justification for defying the tradition that private individuals did not pronounce on public affairs and for campaigning for the political rights and liberties of all Englishmen ... The principle which linked [their] religious beliefs ... to political action was the 'golden rule' – 'to do unto others as you would have them do unto you' ... This was not just a scriptural law binding only upon Christians, it was also a natural law binding upon all mankind and upon all secular authorities ... Overton saw it as the basic principle which made civil society possible ... [It] led them to fight against political [and religious] oppression and poverty ... but it did not provide them with an ideology of social change. It operated within the traditional notions of good neighbourliness held by the people they represented – the small producers (craftsmen and peasants) ...

The Levellers escaped from exclusive dependence on religion for their critique of society by adopting and developing a secular theory – the myth of the Norman Yoke: the people had been free in Anglo-Saxon England but they had ben deprived of their liberty by the Norman Conquest, from which came the ruling class and all the oppressions and injustices of which the Levellers complained. This enabled them to express and explain the divergences between, on the one side, the people, and on the other side, Kings, lords, gentry, clergy, lawyers, merchants. It facilitated their insight that what they called 'false religion' was a cloak for class interests and disguised from the people their true interests or 'true religion'. This led the Levellers to see the ending of compulsion in religion and the leaving of each individual free to follow his own judgement, together with the reduction of the power and influence of the clergy, as the way both to promote true Christianity and to diminish the opportunities for the ruling class to exploit religion in its own interests against those of the people. Their aim in both religion and politics was the same and that was to reduce the power of the ruling class.

Source 29

From F.D. Dow, *Radicalism in the English Revolution, 1640–60*, Historical Association Studies (Blackwell, 1989) pp. 57–8.

The challenge to the established order in mid-seventeenth-century England was not confined to those who devised new theories of the origins of government, or to those who advanced plans for the reshaping of the political order. The 1640s and 1650s also witnessed a proliferation of radical religious groups whose immediate concern was to attack the notion of a disciplined, established, national Church. These radicals included Particular and General Baptists, Quakers, Ranters, Seekers, Muggletonians and Fifth Monarchists, as well as members of separatist Churches with no specific name. Some contemporaries would also have included the Independents with the sects because they adhered to the idea of the 'gathered Church', but with the exception of a radical wing the Independents insisted that, church membership apart, they believed and worshipped very much as the Presbyterians did.

In a negative sense the religious radicals had much in common: they were opposed to the notion of enforced religious uniformity within one national Church, territorially organised and universal in membership; they wished to extend liberty of conscience and worship; and they wanted to end the system of compulsory tithes. As such, they were united in condemning the theory and practice of the Anglican Church before 1642, and also the system of Presbyterian church government which parliament erected in its place. However, beyond this desire for greater religious toleration and freedom of worship there was room for considerable diversity among the radicals. They differed, for example, on how complete the separation between Church and state should be, and on what role (if any) was to be left to the civil magistrate in spiritual matters; they reached no exact consensus on whether to tolerate certain blasphemous or heretical opinions and certain politically suspect groups such as Catholics; and there were differences of opinion on what form of maintenance ministers should be afforded once tithes were abolished. In the 1650s, most religious radicals stood to gain from the looser, more tolerant and more liberal framework which Oliver Cromwell set up, but the retention of tithes and the setting up of boards of 'triers' and 'ejectors' to judge the fitness of candidates for, and incumbents in, parochial livings still aroused great hostility. Some radicals collaborated with the arrangements for a loose 'national Church', but most continued to press for greater freedom and the end to all forms of state maintenance for the clergy.

Across the radical spectrum there was also great diversity in theological opinion, in the degree of formal organisation and internal unity which different groups demanded of their members, and in the political, social, economic and moral conclusions which the radicals drew from their religious beliefs. Some radicals, for example, such as Baptists and radical Independents, came together in recognisable 'Churches' which had a formal structure; others, like Ranters and Muggletonians [millenarians who believed that Christ had given a special commission to two prophets, John Reeve and Lodowick Muggleton, to prepare for his second coming] were so loose and informal in their organisation that one instinctively calls them 'groups' rather than 'Churches'. Flexibility and fluidity were among the essential characteristics of many religious groupings, and the boundaries between them are hard to define: the gathered Churches were not like present-day denominations which strive to maintain their distinctiveness in doctrine and organisation. The dividing lines between different groups were often so confused that individuals could, and did, step over them easily and, indeed, numerous outstanding radical figures of this period made many transitions from one sect to another. This was in part a measure of the great variety of religious experiences on offer and the great spiritual excitement of those times, which encouraged men and women to abandon traditional restraints and seek out new forms of worship and belief. One such figure was Laurence Clarkson … brought up in the pre-war Anglican Church [who] then progressed through Presbyterianism to become successively an Independent, a Baptist, a Seeker, a Ranter, and finally, a Muggletonian. Abiezer Coppe, a fellow-Ranter, had also been both a Presbyterian and a Baptist. John Milton, likewise, moved away from orthodox Calvinism to develop a highly personal and individual set of near-heretical beliefs, while John Lilburne, the separatist and Leveller, ended his life as a Quaker. …

What many radicals did, in effect if not in intention, was to exploit the ambiguities and contradictions of Calvinist theology and Puritan belief, and develop and extend them in different directions. Predestinarian beliefs – that is, the notion that some men (the elect) are saved and preordained by God to receive everlasting life while others (the reprobate) have been damned and condemned to everlasting death – were retained by Particular Baptists, Fifth Monarchists, Muggletonians and by very many radical Independents. But both the Muggletonians and the Fifth Monarchists gave this basic doctrine a distinctive twist. The Fifth Monarchists interpreted the doctrine in a highly élitist way, believing that only members of their own sect were the elect, or the 'saints' who had the right to destroy the kingdoms of this world and rule in readiness for the (imminent) Second Coming of Christ. Other radicals repudiated altogether the predestinarian distinction between the elect and the reprobate, and believed that anyone who opened his heart to God could receive God's saving grace. The notion of salvation through God's free grace was what distinguished the General Baptists from their predestinarian, and hence 'Particular' brethren. Quakers believed that 'God would have all men be saved'. … The more extreme radicals like the Ranters espoused antinomianism, the belief that Christ's atonement on behalf of mankind was sufficient to save all, so that men and women lived on earth in a state of grace and were not subject to external laws or the dictates of a moral code. Not all antinomians, however, took this doctrine to the extreme that the Ranters did in using it to justify strongly libertarian social and moral behaviour.

Attitudes to the question of salvation were closely linked to beliefs about the Spirit of God and its working within men … The mainstream position was to believe that the Spirit spoke to man in, by or through the Word (or Scriptures). This was designed to uphold Scriptural authority and restrain purely individualistic interpretations, or spiritual fancies. Radicals however, upset this equilibrium by putting their emphasis on the Spirit, stressing as the Quakers did that it dwelt within man, or even more extremely, that it dwelt in all creation.[Pantheism] … The elevation of the authority of the Spirit against that of the Scriptures led to a variety of approaches to biblical interpretation. Some radicals remained directly inspired by what they regarded as the Bible's divine revelations but stressed the role of the Spirit in guiding their interpretations … others … were interested in what we would regard as rigorous textual criticism; while the most extreme group began to highlight the mythical or allegorical nature of Bible stories, and use them merely to illustrate arguments arrived at by other means. [Few] … would have accepted William Walwyn's argument that 'the Scriptures is so plainly and directly contradictory to itself' that he did not believe it to be the Word of God. …

Most radicals responded in some way to the millenarian impulse which was also a part of Puritanism. Many historians now accept William Lamont's argument that in the early seventeenth century, some brand of millenarianism … was integral to the character of Puritanism and indeed to the whole of English Protestantism … Encouraged by [the words and visions of the Puritan preachers and] the evident victories of the people of God in the Civil War … many religious radicals … began to feel that the millennium was almost upon them. Only the Fifth Monarchists, however, who drew much of their strength from the more millenarian-minded Baptists and Independents, translated their beliefs into an organised political movement, and perhaps only a minority of these were prepared to undertake revolutionary activity, in order to destroy the institutions of the old world in preparation for the Second Coming of Christ.

JOHN MILTON: POET PROPHET

Born in 1608, John Milton was the son of a London scrivener, prosperous enough to have bought property at Horton in Cambridgeshire, and to educate his sons for the Ministry and the Law. In 1625, John entered Christ's College, Cambridge already a talented scholar and poet, but intending to make his career in the Church. Over the next seven years he saw the influence of Laud and the Arminians grow, to the point where such a career was impossible, and in 1632 he left the University, intending to use his talents as a poet and scholar to further the cause of reformation. In 1638 his poem *Lycidas* constituted a thinly veiled attack on the Bishops, but it was in 1641 that he became fully involved in controversy, publishing a series of tracts in defence of Presbyterian reform. At this point Milton clearly identified with the Puritan mainstream, but he was too much an individualist to accept the bonds of Presbyterian discipline for long. In the first place his claim that a godly layman like himself, a poet-prophet, had a role to play in guiding and informing the English people constituted a threat to the clerical monopoly; secondly, he claimed freedom for individual judgement in matters of belief or morality. In 1642,

his royalist wife having returned to her family home, he published a tract in favour of divorce, and was immediately labelled immoral by his erstwhile friends. Infuriated by their censure, Milton published the tract *Areopagitica*, a powerful plea for intellectual freedom. Religion, he argued, was a personal search for truth and no man could predict where truth and the knowledge of God might be found. Therefore all should be allowed to express themselves freely, and to hear the views of others. It was possible that this would allow error, but God had given man the gift of Reason, with which to distinguish good from bad. The English were chosen to bring about God's kingdom on earth through a godly reformation which would make them an example to the world. How could this work go forward if God's people were not free to search for truth and reveal what they found? This plea for rational freedom was Milton's central contribution to radical thought, although he was active in several capacities. In 1649 as Cromwell's secretary he published a telling justification of the regicide based on the argument that the people were the source of power; in 1659 he argued fiercely for the preservation of the Republic. His schemes for educational reform combined godly purpose with rational learning, foreshadowing the best developments of the Restoration era. Yet through it all, what moved Milton was a belief in individual freedom: his theology remained largely Calvinist, he never joined a gathered Church, and his lack of concern with forms and organisation led him to be labelled a Seeker. He showed little interest in social reform. What Milton struggled for was the personal and intellectual freedom for every individual to search for truth in his own way, and the political structure to guarantee this freedom.

WINSTANLEY: THE DIGGER

Gerrard Winstanley was born in 1609, near Wigan in Lancashire, where his father seems to have been a fairly prosperous mercer. Since Winstanley could write and use some Latin, it seems likely that he was educated at a grammar school, before being apprenticed to a member of the London Merchant Taylors Company in 1630. In 1637 he was himself admitted to the Company, and apparently went into business. By 1643, however he was living in Surrey, where his wife's family had property, and seems at one stage to have been employed as a herdsman. Unlike Milton, he had firsthand experience of the economic disruption caused by the war, and of the difficulties faced by the labouring classes in these years. Like Milton, however, Winstanley had moved beyond his orthodox Puritan background to develop religious views based on a concept of human reason. Reason, the voice of God within, was the mainspring of much radical thinking in this period, but the resulting conclusions took different forms. For Milton, reason was the means by which God revealed his truth, for the Levellers it was the basis of natural rights to which all men were entitled. For Winstanley, it was the spirit of God himself, existing within the human heart and mind. In his first published works in 1648, he argued that God lives in man, and that the struggle between good and evil in the world takes place within the human soul. Thus the kingdom of God will be established on earth when it is established in the hearts and minds of men. Similar ideas were to be put forward by the Ranter and Quaker movements, but at this point Winstanley's beliefs took a new turn. In 1649 he published *The New Law of Freedom*, as a manifesto for the establishment of the first Digger commune on St. George's Hill in Walton, Surrey. Freedom, he argued, will be established when men are able to live by Reason, free from greed and oppression.

God created the earth as a 'common treasury' from which all creatures could draw life, with man given the power to rule the earth by the force of Reason, which is God living within them. Man's fall had come when some men gained power over others, claiming the earth for their own. True regeneration, therefore, requires that the earth is restored as a common source of life for all, releasing men from greed, wars and competition. Winstanley did not intend a direct attack on property; he claimed that two thirds of England existed as waste and common land and the aim of the communes in Surrey and elsewhere was to turn this to cultivation. This they regarded as God's work, an act of worship and an example for the regeneration of society. Not surprisingly, the gentry and JPs of Surrey took a different view, and after a year of harassment they succeeded in breaking up the commune. In 1652 Winstanley appealed to Cromwell to take up the cause, but thereafter he seems to have lived quietly, eventually joining the Quakers whose belief in God as the 'Light within' accorded closely with his own.

THE **8**

Law of Freedom

I N A

PLATFORM:

Or, True

Magiſtracy Reſtored.

Humbly preſented to *Oliver Cromwel*, General of the Common-wealths Army in England, Scotland, and Ireland. And to all Engliſh-men my brethren whether in Church-fellowſhip, or not in Church-fellowſhip, both ſorts walking as they conceive according to the Order of the Goſpel: and from them to all the Nations in the World.

Wherein is Declared, What is Kingly Government, and what is Commonwealths Government.

By *Ferrard Winſtanley*.

In thee, O England, is the Law ariſing up to ſhine,
If thou receive and practiſe it, the crown it wil be thine.
If thou reject, and ſtil remain a froward Son to be,
Another Land wil it receive, and take the crown from thee.
Revel. 11. 15. ———— Dan. 7. 27.

LONDON,
Printed for the Author, and are to be ſold by *Giles Calvert* at the black Spred-Eagle at the Weſt end of *Pauls.* 1651.

An early seventeenth-century woodcut of haymaking and the title page of Winstanley's Law of Freedom in a Platform, *1652*

Source 30
From F.D. Dow, *Radicalism in the English Revolution 1640–1660* (Blackwell, 1989) pp. 65–8.

The radicals' threat to the established political and social order was much exaggerated by conservatives. But their norms and values did prove attractive to elements within the middling and lower orders, who preferred to exchange their experience of traditional patterns of ecclesiastical and social discipline for the mixture of excitement and security offered by the sects. The appeal of some brands of radicalism to the lower orders was especially worrying to contemporaries, who were almost certainly led into overestimating their numbers by the public demonstrations of the more volatile radicals. A recent estimate by the historian John Morrill suggests that probably 'at no point in the critical period 1643–54 did more than five per cent attend religious assemblies other than those associated with their parish churches', although this figure probably rose after the emergence of the Quakers in the mid-1650s. ... Even the most sympathetic historians would not accept contemporary claims for the strength of the radicals. Quakers may have numbered at most tens of thousands, Baptists several thousands, grouped in about two hundred Particular and General congregations by the time of the Restoration, but Muggletonians and Ranters were perhaps never more than a few hundred in number, despite a contemporary claim that three thousand people were converted to Ranterism on a single occasion. Even the charge that sectaries and separatists were drawn from the lower classes has to be examined with care, for although the radicals undoubtedly lacked the degree of upper-class patronage which pre-war Puritanism had enjoyed, their attraction for other social groups was not always out of proportion to the latter's distribution in the population as a whole.

In geographical terms, the influence of some form of religious radicalism was felt in most parts of the country, but areas where new patterns of social organisation flourished, or where the traditional hierarchical chains of deference were weak, may have been especially conducive to the growth of Dissent. Thus some radical groups flourished in the so-called 'dark corners of the land' especially the north and west, and in other fen, moor and woodland areas where ... manorial control was weak and where orthodox Puritanism had not taken hold. Many groups also found ready support in towns, above all in London, where by 1646 there were already about three dozen separate Churches in existence, with several thousand adherents.

Fifth Monarchists ... were not a discrete denomination or group in themselves but ... the political expression of a certain kind of millenarianism which drew heavily on extant Baptist and Independent congregations ... 'an essentially urban movement' ... [which] never numbered more than 10,000. ... The movement was to be found largely in the southern half of England [and] ... in North Wales [where] the charismatic appeal of Vavasor Powell and Morgan Llywd attracted a wide following ... There were three distinct elements in the movement: a number of army officers (some gentlemen, some not) a number of clergy (some with army connections) and thirdly, more typical of the rank and file than the leadership, persons in mechanic occupations. Cloth workers were dominant, comprising perhaps one third of the membership, whereas agricultural workers (the largest group in the population as a whole) provided only about one-seventh of Fifth Monarchists. In general, many supporters were drawn from occupations with a high level of social and economic insecurity.

In contrast to the urban base of the Fifth Monarchists and other radical groups, the Quakers were extremely successful in building up a rural following. In part this was because they were in the vanguard of popular agitation against tithes [and] ... were able to harness existing feeling against tithes to their cause. ... In 1659 they were able to collect 15,000 signatures for a petition against tithes solely from the counties of Westmorland, Cumberland, Lancashire and Cheshire. Especially in the north, Quakerism may also have advanced in some communities because of the precedent set by older radical traditions, such as the Familist or Grindletonian, so that in its early days there may have been many kinds of Quakerism rather than one coherent movement. From its base in Westmorland and among the yeomanry of the West Riding of Yorkshire, Quakerism nonetheless launched a nationwide campaign which drew support away from other radical groups as it spread south. The social composition of the early Quakers shows that the movement appealed to fairly prosperous yeomen and traders as well as to humbler husbandmen and artisans, with the upper ranks of the middling sort being in some areas very prominent. Some gentlemen and some professional men were also among the first converts. Perhaps only the very top (aristocracy) and the very bottom (paupers and landless labourers) of the social scale were under-represented in the early movement.

Muggletonians tended to be slightly more wealthy than the average citizen ... but ... principally drawn from shopkeepers and artisans ... Literacy standards were relatively high in the group, which also indicates that its following came from among the middling orders. London was an important centre of Muggletonian activity, but groups were also formed in various parts of the Midlands, the south of England and in Ireland.

Ranters ... are hard to identify, but their historian, A.L. Morton, claimed that, despite the paucity of numbers, their influence was felt throughout England. Individual groups of Ranters may only have numbered about a dozen, but they had some strength in the poorer areas of London, among depressed artisans and labourers. ... In general terms, Ranterism seems to have attracted the support of wage-earners and small traders in towns rather than agricultural workers in the country.

Finally, General Baptists were particularly noticeable in the east Midlands and Kent, while Particular Baptists – a much larger and altogether more structured and formal group than some of the extremists – had centres of strong affiliation in London, Berkshire, the Midlands and the western counties, as well as Wales and Ireland. The Particular Baptists, in fact, built up successful regional associations to support and lend succour to weaker churches, each of which had close relations with a group of London advisers.

The radical groups

The matrix below uses two sets of criteria for defining the nature of the radical groups that the sources have revealed. The vertical axis represents the range and extent of individual freedom favoured by different groups, from Discipline at one extreme to Libertarianism at the other. Personal freedom might refer to freedom of worship, but also to personal behaviour, the extent to which any moral code was enforced by a Church, and to the right to make personal decisions including the right to accept or reject salvation. Thus the Presbyterians would be placed at the Discipline end of the axis, partly because they claimed power for the Church to control moral behaviour, but also because their belief in Predestination meant that individuals did not choose to be saved – they were predestined. The horizontal axis refers to the aims and interests of the group, and the relative importance given to political or religious issues. Thus Presbyterians are placed at the centre because their concern with a single, national Church makes politics and religion impossible to separate.

The Presbyterians have been placed as an example for you – although they cannot be considered a radical group. Consider how and where you would place the groups that you have identified as radicals.

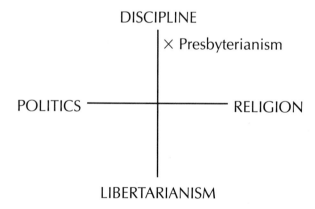

The significance of radicalism

Having established the nature and characteristics of the various radical groups, it is now possible to consider their significance in the events and developments of the revolutionary years from 1640 to 1660. This is not a matter of historical significance, which requires a much longer temporal perspective, but of their significance to contemporaries – how the radicals affected the events of their own time and the ensuing decades. Significance may be judged by various criteria – what, if anything, they achieved, what they represented in terms of contemporary attitudes and beliefs – but significance within their own period may also be influenced less by what they were than by what others perceived them to be. As Dr Dow has indicated above, conservatives reacted strongly to the existence of radical groups and seriously overestimated both their numbers and the threat that they represented to society. This complicates the historian's task in two ways. In the first place, evidence from conservative opponents of the radicals is often the main source of information about them. Secondly, in assessing the significance of radical movements, we must consider both their direct contribution to events, and their indirect contribution i.e. the extent to which they influenced and affected the decisions and actions of others.

Source evaluation

Before any historical source can be used it needs to be evaluated to assess its accuracy and reliability, to consider in fact what weight of interpretation the evidence will bear. Conservative descriptions of the radicals pose a particular problem. Clearly, the evidence is likely to be biased, but for several reasons it cannot simply be dismissed or used only as evidence of conservative attitudes. The paucity of radical sources, particularly coherent statements of belief from some of the less formal groups, means that conservative descriptions may well be the only evidence available to historians on some issues. Nor can historians assume a consistent degree of hostility – conservatives varied in attitude and temperament, and evidence may also be influenced by the kind of source from which it is drawn. An entry in a diary or autobiography may well differ in tone and accuracy from a public speech or a pamphlet written as part of an ongoing debate. Moreover, while hostility might lead one observer to exaggerate the threat posed by radicalism, another, equally hostile, might react by dismissing or minimising its importance. It is therefore necessary to evaluate each source carefully, for example by considering the following:

- what you already know of the radicals;
- how the source in question relates to other sources;
- the time and situation in which the source was written;
- the purpose for which the source was written.

Below are three sources taken from conservatives who opposed and disapproved of the radicals and their ideas. The first, Thomas Edwards' *Gangraena*, was written in 1646. Edwards was a bitter opponent of radical ideas, and his purpose, as the title of his work indicates, was to warn the parliament and its conservative supporters about the poisonous radical minority who were threatening to undermine the godly reformation from within. His account of radical views and activities is notable for its extremism rather than its accuracy. Thomas Hall, the author of the second source, was of a more moderate temperament, but like Edwards, he was writing as part of a public debate. As a member of a Presbyterian group in Warwickshire in the 1650s, he was concerned with establishing Presbyterian discipline and control over ministers and laymen, although his entry into the realms of public debate had been sparked off by radical attacks on the ministry and tithes. As well as the extract printed below, he published several attacks on lay preachers, defending the claims of the ministry to the exclusive right to preach. Richard Baxter, author of the third source, was one of the leading Presbyterian ministers of his age. For most of his career he was the Vicar of Kidderminster, and succeeded in establishing a Presbyterian organisation in that area. In 1660 he was offered a bishopric, but was unable to conform to the Anglican Church of 1662 and after. Moderate in both views and temperament, Baxter's letters and diaries, as well as his published works, reveal a man who tried to be fair to all, although his personal opinions were clearly conservative. He disliked persecution, and was widely respected by contemporaries. It is also important to note that the work from which Source 33 is taken, *Reliquae Baxterianae*, was published in edited form in 1696, after Baxter's death.

Question

3. (a) Read sources 31–3, and use the questions which follow them to analyse and evaluate the evidence that they provide.

   (b) Compile a list of valid statements that can be made on the basis of these sources, interpreted in context, concerning:

   ● the radicals;

   ● their opponents;

   ● their impact.

Source 31

From Thomas Edwards, *Gangraena*, 1646.

The Army that is so much spoken of upon all occasions in the newsbooks, pulpits, conferences, to be Independent (though I conceive upon good information, that upon a true muster of the whole, commanders and common soldiers, there would not be found above one in six of that way); yet of that Army, called by the sectaries, Independent, and of that part of it which truly is so, I do not think there are 50 pure Independents, but higher flown, … made up and compounded of Anabaptism, Antinomianism, Enthusiasm, Arminianism, Familism; all these errors and more too sometimes meeting in the same persons, strange monsters, having their heads of Enthusiasm, their bodies of Antinomianism, their thighs of Familism, their legs and feet of Anabaptism, their hands of Arminianism, and Libertinism as the great vein going through the whole; in one word, the great religion of that sort of men in the Army, is liberty of conscience, and liberty of preaching. …

(i) What was Edwards' view of the army?

(ii) How far was his description of 'strange monsters' intended to be taken literally?

(iii) Using your knowledge of the period, consider:

   (a) what complaints he was trying to make;

   (b) how far his complaints were valid.

Source 32

From Thomas Hall, *A Looking Glass for Anabaptists*, 1651.

Their first tenet is, that infant-baptism is a childish, needless thing; and that none must be baptised till he come to a perfect age, and can make a confession of his faith; that infant-baptism came from the Pope and the Devil.

2 That all gifted persons may preach without ordination.

3 That God reveals his will, not only by the written word, but also by dreams and visions; which they believe more than the word.

4 That the Saints in this life are pure, without spot, and need not use that petition 'Forgive us our sins'.

5 No man can with good conscience exercise the office of Magistrate under the New Testament.

6 They are rigid separatists; they separate themselves from all Reformed Churches.

7 They are tumultuous; they raised tumults in Germany and filled it with the fire of sedition.

8 They deny original sin to be in infants, that so they might overthrow baptism.

9 They hold free-will by nature in all spiritual things.

10 That a man may have more wives than one.

11 That clothes discover sin; therefore they being as perfect and pure as Adam in his innocency, they ought to go naked.

12 That Christ died intentionally for all.

13 No Christian ought with a safe conscience take an oath, nor by oath promise fidelity to a Magistrate.

14 That a Christian cannot with a safe conscience possess anything proper to himself; but he must let all be common. ...

20 That the Magistrate must compel none in matters of religion; but must tolerate all. ...

26 After rebaptisation we cannot sin.

27 We may dissemble our Religion, deny Christ before men, so we keep the truth within our hearts. God delights not in our blood, nor requires that we die for the truth.

28 The Scripture is to be turned into allegories.

29 Heaven and Hell are nowhere but within a man.

30 They give a supreme and independent power, in all ecclesiastical causes and censures, to their single congregations.

(i) Using your knowledge of the attitudes and beliefs of radical groups, consider which of the above statements were:

(a) true of Baptists;

(b) untrue of Baptists but true of other groups;

(c) distortions of genuine radical beliefs;

(d) completely untrue.

(ii) Why do you think Thomas Hall made errors of this kind?

Source 33

From Richard Baxter, *Reliquae Baxterianae*, 1696.

The Quakers who were but the Ranters turned from horrid prophaneness and blasphemy to a life of extreme austerity on the other side. Their doctrines were mostly the same with the Ranters': they make the light which every man hath within him to be his sufficient rule, and consequently the scripture and ministry are set light by. They speak much for the dwelling and working of the spirit in us, but little of justification and the pardon of sin, and our reconciliation with God through Jesus Christ ... They will not have the scripture called the word of God; their principal zeal lieth in railing at the ministers as hirelings, deceivers, false prophets etc., and in refusing to swear before a magistrate, or to put off their hat to any, or to say 'You' instead of 'Thou' or 'Thee' which are their words to all. At first they did use to fall into tremblings and sometimes vomitings in their meetings, and pretended to be violently acted by the spirit, but now that is ceased; they only meet and he that pretendeth to be moved by the spirit speaketh, and sometime they say nothing, but sit an hour or more in silence and then depart. One while divers of them went naked through divers chief towns and cities of the land, as a prophetical act; some of them have famished and drowned themselves in melancholy, and others undertaken by the power of the spirit to raise them ... Many Franciscan friars and other papists have been proved to be disguised speakers in their assemblies and to be among them, and it's like are the very soul of all these horrible delusions.

(i) Using your knowledge of the period, decide:

(a) which of Baxter's statements about the Quakers and their religion are likely to be true.

(b) which of his statements are likely to be untrue.

(c) what sort of facts about the Quakers he could have seen at first hand or verified.

(d) what he could only know by report or hearsay.

Question

4. On the basis of Sources 9–33 and your own knowledge of the period, what significance would you attribute to radical groups and ideas in the years between 1640 and 1660?

Judgements about the contemporary significance of radicalism also raise another, related issue – the question of why this radical upsurge occurred at this particular time. As Professor Aylmer explained in his address to the Royal Historical Society in 1987, the matter of why radicalism developed has implications for our understanding of the period and the place of radicalism within it. In his words, 'Did their open emergence on the public scene from 1641 on ... represent the re-appearance under more favourable conditions of ideas long latent among sections of the population, now freed from censorship and other constraints, indeed positively encouraged to seek articulate expression? Or were they to a greater extent the short-term product of a conflict within the traditional ruling class, which split apart the upper and middle levels of society, thereby stimulating those below them in the social hierarchy to put forward their own contributions to solving the country's problems?' The answer to this question carries implications for both the historical significance of radicalism (which will be considered in Unit 3.5) and its contemporary meaning, particularly in relation to its apparently rapid disappearance. If radicalism was merely the product of war and upheaval, its ultimate failure was both predictable and easily explained. If it represented something more deep-seated in English life, then its failure must have arisen from contemporary, and avoidable, errors. It is necessary, therefore, to consider why radicalism emerged, and in particular whether it was the natural result of long-term developments and conditions, or whether it owed its existence to the peculiar situation and events pertaining in the period after 1640.

Historical explanations of mid-seventeenth-century radicalism

Radicalism has been the subject of much debate and disagreement. Many contemporary observers offered explanations which were heavily influenced by their own commitment or hostility to radical ideas; many historians have since addressed the issue with similar variation in interests and approach. Their collective efforts have revealed a range of factors which, it is widely agreed, contributed to the emergence of radicalism and which are summarised in the sources below; but an explanation requires more than a list of contributory factors. It is necessary also to consider the *interaction* between and *relative importance* of different factors, to weigh up the part that they played in creating and bringing about the emergence of mid-seventeenth-century radicalism.

The interaction between different factors is revealed by considering the patterns of ideas, actions and events which help to bring about a particular outcome. Thus the spread of radical ideas in 1641–2 could be explained by linking the breakdown of censorship, which allowed radical ideas to be expressed publicly, with the millenarian mood created by the upheavals, which made many people more receptive to ideas of that kind. The result arises from a combination of the two. However, it is not enough to simply state that such a combination existed. If the explanation is to be taken further, we need to explore how the factors combined, what part each played in the eventual outcome, and what was their relative importance.

One way of doing this is to consider the role and function of *conditional* factors which make an outcome possible or probable, and *contingent* factors which actually make it happen. For example, it could be said that the influence of Puritanism and the weakening of traditional patterns of employment created the possibility or probability of radical development, while the collapse of censorship provided the opportunity and the upheaval of war the inspiration to trigger the explosion. This approach involves analysing the *function* of different factors in order to explain the interaction between them and to show which seem to have played the most important part in producing a particular result.

Another way of approaching the process is through analysing and defining the occurrence that we are trying to explain. For example, if we are considering the emergence of radicalism, we may define this as an *event*, in which case we will employ a causal mode of explanation. This will involve considering the pattern of events and factors that brought about the emergence of radical movements, such as the spread of Puritanism, Laud's persecution and the political crisis of 1640–2. If, however, we consider that the emergence of radicalism involves the development of a set of ideas, then we will employ an empathetic mode of explanation which requires us to focus on the attitudes and beliefs in which the ideas had their roots, and on the reasons why such ideas were held at this time. By defining the occurrence in these terms and employing the appropriate mode of explanation, we are thereby selecting certain factors as having particular importance in explaining the emergence of radicalism.

However, a simple causal or empathetic explanation is insufficient to explain any historical occurrence – while it answers some questions, it inevitably raises others. For example, an explanation of how radical ideas developed will inevitably raise the question of why they should have become more widespread at this time. This will invoke a causal explanation of the emergence of radicalism and/or an intentional explanation of the actions of radical leaders who contributed to the development. By defining what is to be explained (in this case radical ideas) and using the appropriate mode of explanation, we are defining the core of the occurrence and the factors which directly influence it. Other factors (the events and actions which led to radicalism becoming more widespread) will also need to be examined, but as indirect or secondary influences which arise in the course of the initial explanation. What finally emerges from this process is an explanation which reveals the interaction of ideas, actions and events, shows how they combined to bring about a particular result, and attributes relative importance to different factors by the place that they are given in the explanation.

It is also possible to further clarify the relative importance of different factors by considering which of them are *necessary* (that the occurrence would not have been possible without that particular factor) or by considering what combination of factors would have been *sufficient* to bring it about. For example, we may argue that radical ideas had existed for some time before 1640, but had never been widely disseminated until the collapse of censorship in 1641–2. Therefore both the ideas and the opportunity to publish them were necessary factors in the emergence of radicalism. However, the opportunity to express ideas and opinions does not guarantee that they will be heard and accepted. Therefore we do not have a sufficient explanation of the emergence of radicalism until we consider the mood and expectations which were generated by the crisis of 1640–2 and the upheaval of war. Thus these three factors can all be considered to be of major importance in our explanation, while others (the cheapness and ease of establishing a printing press, for example) may well have contributed to the occurrence in a less important way.

Whatever method we use, historical explanation requires that we:

- define what is to be explained;
- establish what factors brought it about;
- explain how those factors combined to bring it about, and their relative importance in the process;
- repeat the procedure for any new questions that this raises, and summarise the whole in a coherent conclusion.

In the light of these considerations, you should now read Sources 34–44 and the introductory narrative on pages 2–17; then answer Question 5.

Question

5. Why did so much political and religious radicalism develop in England in the years following the calling of the Long Parliament?

Source 34

From W. Haller, *Rise of Puritanism* (Harper Torchbooks, 1938) pp. 172–9 and 271.

The object of the Puritan reformers was the reorganisation of English society in the form of a Church governed according to Presbyterian principles. Until they were summoned by Parliament to the Westminster Assembly [see pages 6–7], they were granted no opportunity to put their ideas into effect, but they were allowed within limits to preach to the people and to publish books. ... The immediate result was that, in the hope of establishing ultimately their cherished scheme of uniformity, they spent two generations preaching a doctrine and a way of life which promoted active, individual religious experience and expression, promoted it much faster than means could be found to control or direct it. ... Belief in the eventual coming of the new Jerusalem ... too confidently proclaimed from the pulpit, led some men to grow impatient with the slow processes of reform and to attempt the erection of the true Church for themselves in

their own time. The doctrine, too convincingly set forth, of God's immediate concern in the individual soul and of the individual's aptitude for understanding what the Holy Spirit revealed through the spoken and the printed word, encouraged some to the idea that they need trust nothing so much as their own, untutored notions. ... Having made them a reading people, an articulate people and a confident people, the preachers told the people that they must obey conscience, thinking that they could hold the conscience of the saints in their own keeping. But when they said one thing to the saints, and conscience said another, the reformers were destined to find their authority as fragile as that of pope and prelate had been ... By 1640 the more extreme separatists were persuaded not only that the saints knew all they needed for salvation in the next world, but also that they were, by the authority of the spirit destined in the not distant future to assume sovereignty in this one.

Source 35

From B. Capp, 'The Fifth Monarchists and Popular Millenarianism', in McGregor and Reay, *Radical Religion in the English Revolution*, pp. 165–7.

Though millenarianism was certainly popular it cannot be seen as part of a distinct, self-contained 'popular culture'. Millenial hopes were by no means confined to the lower classes or the radical sects and influenced many prominent politicians, intellectuals and clergymen. From the Reformation onwards, many contemporaries had interpreted current events in the light of biblical prophecies of the latter days. ... Early in Elizabeth's reign John Foxe the martyrologist had set out a version of Church history in which ... the small band of true Christians struggled against the might of antichristian Catholicism. ... The obvious fact that England was the major Protestant state ... led patriots to believe that their nation had a special role to play in God's providential scheme. ... In the excitable mood of [1640 and after] the apocalyptic dream [that Christ would return to earth in judgement] made a greater impact on the lower classes than ever before and, more important, began to take new forms which used the language of the common people and reflected their particular hopes and fears. ... In the turbulent years of civil war and revolution it was easy to be swept along by the fiery rhetoric of prophecy. ... As the landmarks of the old order were thrown down one by one – bishops, the House of Lords, monarchy, Parliament itself – many people were led to believe that these must be the upheavals foretold in Scripture to herald the world's end or its transformation.

Source 36

From H. Shaw, *The Levellers*, pp. 12–16.

The smaller copyholder was frequently ejected from land his family had farmed for centuries. His resentment was increased and his economic position further endangered by the enclosure that often took place on the land that he, and others like him had left. ... The extent of enclosure varied from place to place and should not be exaggerated, but it was clearly a constant irritant. ... The pressure that forced copyholders downwards had its parallel in the industrial sphere. ... By the seventeenth century the woollen industry, the oldest and most important of English industries, had for some time been completely dominated by the capitalist clothier. Other industries followed suit. ... The decline of the small operator was taking place all over the country; it was mirrored and magnified in London.

It is impossible to understand the Civil War or the Leveller movement if one does not grasp the importance of London. Its recent growth in population had been remarkable. ... From a figure of about 60,000 early in the sixteenth century, it had risen to something in the region of 350,000 by 1650 ... it sprawled five miles along the northern bank of the Thames and three along the south. A wide belt of country was dedicated to providing its food; it handled the bulk of English trade; its capital reached out to control provincial economic development. Seat of court and government, centre of trade and law, London exercised a dominance that was, as Christopher Hill has said, 'unique in Europe'.

The prosperity of the city was not shared by all its inhabitants: the master-craftsman was a victim of the new capitalist age. ... Increasingly he now exercised his skills for an entrepreneur. He sold his labour; he was a wage-earner. It was possible, of course to go up rather than down ... but in general, the craftsman was being depressed. Many apprentices would never become 'masters' at all ... [and] these men often came from a prosperous background – apprentice weavers had to be sons of freeholders. ... They were bitterly mortified to find themselves descending the social scale, a slide often [symbolised] by a move from the streets of the City to the suburbs of Southwark and Bermondsey across the Thames.

The stresses within society brought about by the declining fortunes of copyholders and craftsmen were the result of basic structural changes within agriculture and industry. Between 1646 and 1649, however, these tensions were brought into high relief by the more normal uncertainties of war and nature. In 1646 there began a series of poor harvests that had a catastrophic effect on food prices. The price of bread more than doubled in a short time; oats, rye, peas, and beans rose in proportion. The plight of thousands who always lived on or near subsistence level was doleful. ... Wages failed to rise and unemployment was widespread. ... There was genuine hardship in these years ...

These privations were ... countrywide, but it was in London that they merged with virulent Puritanism. London had long been the centre of opposition to the Anglican Church ... based primarily on a few parishes that had the right to appoint their own clergy. ... Sermons and lectures by popular preachers were attended by large crowds; the punishment of Prynne, Bastwick and Burton in 1637 for their attacks on the bishops took place before an audience that was plainly sympathetic to the sufferers. Already industrial suburbs like Southwark, Wapping, Blackfriars and Whitefriars had gained something of a reputation for extremism. When episcopal censorship was abolished in 1641, these areas soon showed themselves susceptible to the more radical preachers.

Source 37

From F.D. Dow, *Radicalism in the English Revolution*, pp. 58–60.

Without the conflicts and controversies of mid-seventeenth-century England and the breakdown of the old order in Church and state, it is impossible to imagine such a flowering of radical religious beliefs. Yet it had its precursors in pre-Civil War England. At least as far back as Elizabethan times, radical dissent had had a shadowy, underground existence in areas such as the Weald of Kent, parts of Essex and Cambridgeshire, the Chiltern Hills and parts of the West Riding of Yorkshire. Familist and Grindletonian groups had made their appearance, and their heterodox ideas were similar to some of those aired in the 1650s. The Elizabethan Barrowists and Brownists had enunciated the principle of separation of Church and state, and separatist Churches had been formed. ... After the Elizabethan persecution, the existence of separate Churches is hard to prove, but before the Civil War they had certainly been formed in London and Bristol, and probably in Cambridgeshire and Wales. In the 1620s there were at least five General Baptist congregations in England, but their membership numbered perhaps only 150 in total. By far the most important centre of radical activity was London, where from at least 1616 the Church of Henry Jacob spawned separatist offspring; yet on the eve of Civil War only about 1,000 people attended the small group of separatist Churches there. But as the political crisis between king and parliament deepened, so radical opinions began to surface. Lay preaching in London caught the public's attention, and separatists were crucially involved in popular demonstrations in the capital in 1641–2. Throughout the country, hostility to the payment of tithes found expression in riots and disturbances, and the question of lay – even popular – participation in the Church at national and local level began to be discussed.

After 1642, the breakdown of the old order in Church and state and the expression of radical opinion became mutually reinforcing. The inability of the parliamentarians to agree on what should replace the Laudian Anglican Church opened the way for a proliferation of ideas on doctrine and Church government. The relaxation of censorship allowed the radicals an outlet for their ideas, while social and economic dislocation provided a further stimulus to men to rethink their world. In this period it is impossible to separate political from religious thinking: the circumstances which promoted the rise of the Leveller movement also encouraged the emergence of religious radicalism. Moreover, just as hostility to an established Church and the desire for religious toleration drove many men to espouse radical politics, so too the failure of direct political activity or disillusionment with overtly political solutions may have driven them back to a reliance on specifically religious change. It must also be remembered that some radical demands, especially that for religious toleration, were the product of expediency as well as of principle. Once the proliferation of opinions and the splintering of groups had taken place, toleration was the only way for minorities to ensure their own survival; but once a measure of toleration had been conceded, then this in turn ensured the perpetuation of dissent. Thus in the 1650s the increase in the number of radical groups was not merely the cause, it was also the consequence of the regime's initial concession to radical demands.

Puritan beliefs played an important part in the parliamentarian cause after 1642 ... [but] it would be wrong to see religious radicalism in the 1640s and 1650s as simply the logical 'left-wing' extension of the type of Puritanism that had attracted a large following before the war. Other streams flowed into it too; some radical beliefs looked back to pre-Reformation heresy; and radical dissent often flourished in areas which had been relatively untouched by conventional Puritan piety ... Yet the background to much radical religious thinking is undeniably formed by the loose cluster of beliefs, attitudes and assumptions which we call Puritanism.

Source 38

From H. Tomlinson and D. Gregg, *Politics, Religion and Society in Revolutionary England, 1640–60* (Macmillan, 1989) pp. 85 and 88.

Much of the import of recent historical work on the Civil War stresses the underlying conservatism of the king's parliamentary opponents between 1640 and 1642. ... We are assured that opposition to the crown in the early 1640s was naturally defensive and that future parliamentarians desired no political or social revolution. However, in the course of the Civil War, an unexpected but not unnatural expansion of political consciousness occurred, leading to active popular consideration of various issues which were purely latent in 1642. Moreover, the breakdown in effective censorship of press and pulpit ... enabled 'the lower sort' to participate more fully in political processes, and the focus of political debate gradually extended beyond Westminster to include Churches, taverns and places of work. ...

Those participants in the conflict who hoped for more radical change in English society tended to present their arguments in terms of freedom: liberty to express opinions verbally or in print; liberty to attend whatever form of religious service one desired; freedom of trade from monopolies, and liberty to play an active role in political affairs through the franchise. The quest for liberty was first and foremost an attack on religious uniformity ... [but] rapidly extended beyond the issue of conscience in the 1640s. ... The desire for toleration in religion naturally led to a campaign for secular liberties. Milton's tract *Areopagitica* represented an early statement of the case against censorship of publications. A pamphlet produced by urban apprentices, *The Mournful Cries of Many Thousand Poor Tradesmen*, requested the end of restrictions upon commerce. Parliament treated popular petitions with contempt, causing the radicals finally to

advocate political remedies for their grievances. Disenchantment with the effectiveness of parliamentary government inspired a series of Leveller pamphlets ... [whose main] argument was the claim that parliament had consciously denied the liberties of the subject. The only conceivable remedy lay in fundamental political reform – giving the common people a significant political voice by extending the franchise.

Source 39

From J. Morrill, *The Impact of the English Civil War* (Collins and Brown, 1991) p. 69 and 78.

In England during the 1640s parliament's rebellion against the king was often defended with reference to resistance theories of a sort first developed in sixteenth-century Scotland and France. ... Because the theory had generally been used to defend the resistance of Calvinist minorities against their rulers, it has come to be called the Calvinist theory of resistance. In fact, much of its theoretical basis was first developed by late-medieval Catholic writers ... [but] the English writers did not simply copy the ideas of their sixteenth-century predecessors. They used them creatively, often combining them with native English ideas such as those attached to the common law.

The Calvinist theory of resistance had two characteristic components. First, it was a populist theory which argued that the entire community (acting as a collective unit) had chosen its own rulers and had given them authority, and retained the right to take action should the ruler use such authority in a tyrannical fashion. For many the community had a duty to take action against a king who broke the laws of God by favouring false religion. The second distinctive feature of the theory, especially in its French forms, was that it was a theory of lesser magistrates. For though the people had a collective right to resist a tyrant, it was generally thought that this right could not be exercised by any individual but only on the initiative of lesser magistrates. These people were those who held public office beneath the king. In England during the 1640s some, like the Levellers, began to play around with the idea that individuals too had rights of resistance that they could exercise on their own initiative ... [Thus] one of the features of the language and rhetoric of the radical writers was that it reworked themes first put forward in the propaganda of the Parliamentarians.

Source 40

From F.D. Dow, *Radicalism in the English Revolution* (Blackwell, 1989) p. 69.

An additional factor in the rise of many radical groupings was the influence of charismatic preachers and leaders. Just as the intellectual abilities and personal qualities of William Walwyn, Richard Overton and, above all, John Lilburne, were crucial to the success of the Leveller movement, so too the inspiration and appeal of individual religious leaders was central to the advance of the separatist or sectarian cause. ... All movements, of course, have their leaders, but the stamp of some radical ideologues – and demagogues – on their followers was particularly strong. The Muggletonians, for example, relied heavily on the inspiration of John Reave and Lodowick Muggleton, under whom each local area had its special leaders ... The Quakers' evangelical drive owed much to several outstanding figures including George Fox, Edward Burroughs and James Nayler. Abiezer Coppe, Laurence Clarkson, Joseph Salmon and Joseph Bauthumley played a crucial role in articulating the tenets of the Ranters. Fifth Monarchism owed much to the talents of Thomas Harrison, John Rogers and Vavasor Powell, as well as to ministers like Christopher Feake and John Simpson. Indeed, the history of religious radicalism is littered with a host of exciting and adventurous characters whose personal eccentricities often rivalled their intellectual power, but whose contribution to the radical ferment was immense. William Erbery, William Sedgewick, John Saltmarsh, William Dell, Arise Evans, Richard Coppin, Samuel Fisher, John Warr and, towering above them all, Gerrard Winstanley, are crucial figures in the story of those who in their contemporaries' eyes tried to turn the world upside down.

Source 41

From Christopher Hill, *The World Turned Upside Down* (Penguin, 1975) pp. 85–6.

Historians of Science distinguish between 'internal' and 'external' causes of advance in scientific knowledge; between the logical development of structures of ideas on the one hand, and response to social pressures and technical needs on the other. ... I attempt in this book to look at the external and internal causes of the florescence [flowering] of radical ideas of all kinds in the decade after the end of the English Civil War.

... I have stressed the social background – the isolation and freedom which permitted radical ideas to develop among some communities in woodland and pasture areas; the mobile society of early capitalism, serviced by itinerant merchants, craftsmen, pedlars; the crowds of masterless men, vagabonds and urban poor, who no longer fitted into the categories of a hierarchical agrarian society. The great shake-up of the Civil War suddenly and remarkably increased social and physical mobility. The New Model Army itself can be regarded as a body of masterless men on the move. Just as – given religious freedom – itinerant craftsmen and merchants could become itinerant ministers, so the New Model Army – the main protagonist in the fight for religious liberty – contained mechanic preachers and gathered Churches. It linked up the hitherto obscure radical groups scattered up and down the kingdom, and gave them new confidence, especially in the lonely North and West. It was also itself an outstanding example of social mobility. ... The New Model was the match which fired the gunpowder. But once the conflagration started there was plenty of combustible material lying around. To appreciate this we must look at the development of radical and heretical ideas in England, some religious, others secular; some inherited from the Lollards, some imported from the continent, all modified in the rapidly changing society of sixteenth and early-seventeenth-century England.

Source 42

From Richard Baxter, *Reliquiae Baxterianae,* 1696.

When the court news-book told the world of the swarms of Anabaptists in our armies, we thought it had been a mere lie, because it was not so with us, nor in any of the garrison or county forces about us. But when I came to the army among Cromwell's soldiers ... I heard the plotting heads very hot upon that which intimated their intention to subvert both Church and State. Independency and Anabaptistry were most prevalent; Antinomianism and Arminianism were equally distributed; and Thomas Moor's followers had made some shift to join these two extremes together.

Abundance of the common troopers, and many of the officers, I found to be honest, sober, orthodox men ... but a few proud, self-conceited, hot-headed sectaries had got into the highest places, and were Cromwell's chief favourites, and by their heat and activity bore down the rest ...

Source 43

From J.F. McGregor, 'The Baptists – Fount of all Heresy', in McGregor and Reay, *Radical Religion in the English Revolution* (OUP, 1986) pp. 31–2.

Military service in a regiment with sympathetic senior officers gave considerable scope for lay evangelism. Many Baptists became unofficial preachers in companies dominated by zealous Puritans. In June 1645 ... Paul Hobson, a prominent London Particular Baptist [was] arrested by Sir Samuel Luke ... for unlicensed preaching. Having despatched [him] to London for examination by Parliament, Luke was furious to find [him] returned several weeks later to resume ... preaching with a safe conduct from ... colonel Charles Fleetwood, a radical Independent. It ... brought home to local authorities the futility of attempting to suppress military preachers when they had the support of sympathetic Independents such as Fleetwood and General Oliver Cromwell. Objecting a year before to a fellow general's cashiering of one of his officers for Anabaptist principles, Cromwell claimed that 'the State, in choosing men to serve it, takes no notice of their opinion; if they be willing to serve it, that satisfies'.

Civilian preachers also relied on military support to protect them from local hostility. For Baptist evangelists, complained a beleaguered clergyman, 'it is ordinary to come with a gang of soldiers, and prate on a tombstone while the Minister preacheth in a pulpit'. Despite the hostility which they aroused among the political nation, there were relatively few cases of Baptist preachers being apprehended by local authorities. ... Local magistrates were generally uncertain of the law, and lacked confidence in their power to deal with lay preachers.

Source 44

From H. Shaw, *The Levellers* (Longman, 1973) pp. 44, 49 and 53.

Lilburne's punishment [imprisonment by order of the House of Lords] raised fundamental issues that had been foreshadowed by his earlier imprisonment by the Commons – issues which were secular, not religious. And there were wider implications, as Lilburne showed in a speech he made to the Lords shortly before his sentence: 'All you intended when you set us a-fighting was merely to unhorse and to dismount our old riders and tyrants, that so you might get up and ride us in their stead … '

The disillusionment expressed here mirrored the feelings of many who, as the Civil War lay in its death throes, wondered just what they had been fighting to achieve. …

Early in 1647 parliament decided to dispense with the services of the New Model Army. The last royalist garrisons had surrendered some time ago, the Scots had retired across the border, and the king was safely in residence at Holdenby, where he would no doubt soon come to see the advantages of a compromise. Only the army, victorious, confident and – at least in the view of its enemies – riddled with sectarian heresies, stood between the Presbyterians and a swift return to peacetime stability. Anxious to gain popularity by cutting taxation and to ensure that any constitutional settlement would remain wholly in its own hands, parliament voted the army's disbandment. Had parliament shown any real understanding of the men who had fought for it, the demobilisation might well have been carried through with little overt criticism. As it was, the terms of disbandment suggested at best black ingratitude, at worst outright hostility. Six weeks arrears of pay were offered to men who … were owed several times this amount; no security was offered for the remainder. No provision was made for those maimed in battle, or for the widows and orphans of those killed. Nor was any indemnity given to cover their actions during the war, though a number of soldiers had recently been arrested for horse stealing and rumour had it that some had actually been hanged. … Added to all this was a parliamentary proposal for a new army to subdue Ireland. This, it was true, was to consist of volunteers, but the scheme to remove Independent officers and entrust the new force to reliable conservatives did not commend itself to soldiers shrewd enough to see the motives behind it. It would be difficult to imagine a programme more likely to unite officers and men in outspoken opposition.

Having constructed an explanation of why Radicalism emerged and developed at this time, it is important to evaluate it, in order to test whether the factors which apparently had greatest significance were indeed the most influential. One way of doing this is to use a comparative explanation – comparing the situation with other similar events in order to pick out common factors which brought about a similar outcome, or to establish that the absence of certain factors creates a different result. In either case, the comparison can be used to establish the particular importance of certain factors in encouraging radical ideas to develop, or radical groups to emerge, in England in the years of Civil War and Interregnum.

Comparisons may relate to seventeenth-century England or to other times and places. For example, it is possible to compare the situation of the 1640s in England with that of the 1630s, when Laud's reforms placed Puritan reformers within the Church in great difficulties and forced many into a more radical, separatist position; yet there was no major development of radical movements such as emerged in 1641–2. Alternatively, the 1640s can be compared with the situation in 1659 when the collapse of the Protectorate created the opportunity to initiate new schemes and plans for reform. Again, there was little response from the radicals. In both of these cases it is necessary to consider what factors that were present in 1640–53 were not present in the other situations, to explain the difference in outcome. These factors may well be considered therefore, to have a particular importance in the events of 1640–53, or to have contributed to a combination which was necessary to bring about radical development. In either case, the comparison serves to enhance and refine the explanation that we can offer.

Whatever comparisons are used, the process must follow three important steps:

1. the similarities in the situations which make the comparison valid must be explained;

2. the similarities and differences which explain the eventual outcomes must be analysed;

3. the resulting lessons must be applied to the events of 1640–60 in order to evaluate the significance of factors contributing to the emergence and development of Radicalism in this period.

The result will serve to evaluate and develop the original explanation that you constructed in response to Question 5, by highlighting or placing special emphasis on certain factors or combinations of factors within it.

Question

6. Changes in religion, and in the economic base of English society, had been creating upheaval since the early sixteenth century.

   (a) At what other times, before 1640, might radical movements have developed and emerged?

   (b) Why did they not do so on any significant scale?

   (c) What does this indicate about the reasons why radicalism developed in the years after 1640, rather than earlier?

UNIT 3.2

THE LEVELLERS

Introduction

The Leveller movement began as part of the campaign for religious toleration which drew together radicals of many different kinds in the mid-1640s; it went on, however, to become something new in English politics. By adopting plans for social, economic and legal reform, and most importantly for political changes in the system of government, the Levellers created a movement whose principles, aims and methods have become an accepted part of modern political activity. Popular protest was not, in itself, new. From the Peasants' Revolt of 1381 to the Tudor rebellions the common people had demonstrated their ability to defend their interests and draw attention to their grievances. Their methods, however, were based on armed insurrection, often led (if not exploited) by factions within the governing class, and their objectives were based on putting right the faults of an existing political system, often resisting rather than demanding change. What made the Levellers new and different was that they developed methods of peaceful protest aimed at radically changing the system of government, and reforming it on the basis of democratic principles and natural, human rights.

The purpose of this unit is to examine what the Levellers stood for, what they were attempting to achieve, and why, ultimately, they failed. The flood of Leveller pamphlets published between 1646 and their collapse in 1649 offers abundant evidence of their ideas and activities; yet the extent to which the Levellers can be considered democrats, and therefore how far they were advocating new political principles, has been the subject of some debate among historians. On the one hand they have been hailed as the founding fathers of modern democracy: on the other, dismissed as representing little more than the interests of their own 'middling-sort', the tradesmen, master-craftsmen and smaller merchants of London. Much of the debate has centred around their plans for the new parliamentary franchise – to whom would they have accorded the right to vote? The principle of popular sovereignty had been advanced by parliamentarian writers like Henry Parker in

1642–4; what was crucial was the question of who would express that sovereignty by electing the representatives who were to exercise it. Leveller writings were often imprecise on this subject. At Putney in 1647, Col. Rainsborough clearly set out a principle of universal manhood suffrage, but this was not explicitly stated in their various plans and schemes for reform. Professor C.B. McPherson has argued that their willingness to exclude 'servants and paupers' because they were economically dependent on others meant that they had abandoned any universal, democratic principle, and that in practice they would have increased the electorate by relatively little. If the term 'servant' is interpreted in its old sense, as meaning *employees* as well as those who were part of their master's household, then his assessment of its effects is probably accurate. It must be remembered, however, that the Levellers were creating both a blueprint for society and a practical scheme of reform to be adopted by sceptical army leaders in the immediate future. Their writings are part philosophy, part practical plans, part propaganda. To expect these to produce a coherent and unambiguous programme would be unrealistic, but what can be defined are the basic principles upon which they stood, and the broad outline of what they sought to achieve. At no point did they retreat from the claim that the changes they advocated were based upon ideas of natural law and individual rights arising from it. Some might be temporarily unable to exercise these rights because their economic dependence laid them open to influence by others, but the principles and the rights remained. They consistently campaigned for individual rights, social justice and freedom from oppression – and they claimed these, not for a social class or a band of saints, but for all, as their natural entitlement.

The Leveller movement

The Leveller movement emerged in recognisable form in the year 1646, when the imminent defeat of the king raised urgent questions about what settlement would follow, how power would be distributed, and liberty guaranteed within it. Its origins, however, lie in the earlier activities of its three main leaders – John Lilburne, William Walwyn and Richard Overton – and in the ideas and beliefs that they had developed. Although other individuals would later be of significance in the movement, it was these three who consistently inspired and shaped its development. Their coming together in the year of 1645–6 created a particular blend of character and talent which was to prove exceptional, if not unique.

WILLIAM WALWYN (1600–80)

William Walwyn was born in 1600, the second son of a prosperous landowner in Worcestershire and the grandson of a Bishop of Hereford. Like Lilburne and Winstanley, he was apprenticed in London, but in his case this led to membership of the Merchant Adventurers Company, and considerable prosperity. A man of good education, his pamphlets show wide classical knowledge and the humanist influence of Renaissance scholarship. He also benefited from a happy family life – a successful marriage producing 19 children!

Walwyn's radicalism seems to have developed from the application of this classical background, with its respect for human reason, to the questions about God and salvation that troubled his Puritan soul. Like most orthodox Calvinists, he accepted the doctrine of Predestination, but was unable to come to terms with the idea of a God who condemned millions of souls to everlasting damnation. Some time prior to 1640, through study of the Bible and debate with friends, he came to the conclusion that, while humans were indeed sinful, God's love offered hope and forgiveness to all. As a result he rejected both Presbyterian beliefs and the ministers' claims of an exclusive right to teach and interpret the word of God; he became an advocate of free speech, the right of laymen to preach, and complete religious toleration. Others, such as the General Baptists, followed a similar path to belief in free will and salvation, but Walwyn took his ideas further by advocating that God's love for mankind should be reflected in human love and brotherhood, including the care of the poor and the unemployed. In this practical expression of religious belief lay the origin of the Leveller 'golden rule' and the basis of their social and economic programme. By 1643, when he published *The Power of Love*, Walwyn had moved to the view that society was responsible for the removal of poverty and economic inequality.

This theme, combined with his constant advocacy of religious liberty, led to bitter attacks by parliamentary conservatives, and also by the more cautious and conventional members of the sectarian Churches. In 1649 a virulent attack upon him was published under the title of *Walwyn's Wiles*, by William Kiffin and others of the Particular Baptist and Congregational Churches. In the same year the failure of Leveller hopes and the rising at Burford led to his arrest and brief imprisonment. Thereafter he seems to have retired into private life and the needs of his large family, becoming a medical practitioner and surviving to see the Restoration and beyond. Always the most private of the Leveller leaders, lacking the personality of Lilburne or the bitter invective of Overton, he contributed greatly to the development of Leveller ideas. With wide interests and contacts (including the Digger, Winstanley) he provided breadth of vision and philosophical justification for the new society that the Levellers sought to achieve.

RICHARD OVERTON (dates uncertain)

Very little is known of the early life of Richard Overton; his personality, as revealed in his pamphlets, suggests a man of lower social status and more abrasive temperament than Walwyn, but a man of some education, capable of clear and disciplined argument. First appearing in Amsterdam, as a member of an English Baptist group, but undoubtedly of English birth, it seems likely that he had been forced into exile by his religious beliefs. By 1641 he had returned to England and was publishing pamphlets attacking Laud and prelacy. From this time, unlicensed printing seems to have been his main source of income. In 1644, he published *Man's Mortality*, a tract in which he denied the immortality of the soul, and came dangerously close to atheism. This shocked many Independents and Baptists as well as Presbyterians. In 1645 he followed it by a series of satirical attacks on the clergy under the name of Martin Marpriest, which were remarkable for their vitriolic language as well as making the case against tithes and in favour of complete religious liberty. By now he was clearly in contact with Walwyn, and probably with Lilburne. The latter had returned to London, and in joining the campaign for religious toleration, seems to have used the same secret press as Overton, run by one William Larner. Indeed, Lilburne was suspected by some in parliament of being the real author of Overton's tracts.

By 1645 the Leveller leaders were emerging as a coherent group, and were treated as such by opponents like Thomas Edwards, the author of *Gangraena*. When Lilburne was imprisoned by the House of Lords it was Walwyn and Overton who orchestrated the campaign for his release, and produced in the process the first clear statement of Leveller principles and objectives. Taking the form of a petition to the House of Commons, *A Remonstrance of Many Thousand Citizens* demanded the abolition of the monarchy and a range of constitutional reforms to secure a new and representative parliament, elected on a wide franchise. Individual rights were to be protected, and a variety of legal and social reforms were to be introduced.

From this point, the Leveller movement began to develop, with Overton playing an active role. His main function seems to have been as a propagandist, often in co-operation with Lilburne. In 1649, with the Levellers facing defeat, he published a bitter attack on the army Grandees in *The Hunting of the Foxes*, a slanderous attack on Cromwell and Ireton, and also an incitement to mutiny. Overton was arrested with the other Leveller leaders and imprisoned in the Tower of London. In May 1649 the Leveller rising was crushed at Burford. When Overton was released in 1650 he returned to a shadowy world of illicit publishing and plotting; still pursuing some kind of cause, he was in touch with royalist agents in the 1650s and survived the Restoration. However, in 1663 he attacked government handling of the Yorkshire Plot (see page 16) and was imprisoned again, after which his fate is unknown.

JOHN LILBURNE (1615–57)

Of all the Leveller leaders, it was John Lilburne who dominated the movement, shaping it in his own image and imposing on it both his ideas and his character. Warm-hearted, generous and passionately opposed to injustice of any kind, he was also stubborn, argumentative and quick to take offence. With an unerring gift for publicity he was able to use his own personal wrongs to create a dramatic focus for the general political issues that lay at the heart of Leveller ideas. He had already shown his natural talent as a popular leader in his opposition to Laud and the Bishops in 1638, which led to his imprisonment in the Fleet (see Unit 3:1, p.24). Ironically, his release in 1640 was obtained from the House of Commons by Oliver Cromwell, who was to become, first, a political ally, and later the target of Lilburne's bitter attacks. Upon his release, Lilburne was able to set up as a brewer and to marry. In 1641 he was active in the London elections and the disturbances that drove the bishops from the Lords in December. In 1642 he enlisted in a regiment raised by Lord Brooke, a prominent champion of religious toleration. Captured by the Royalists after Edgehill, and put on trial for treason, he refused to accept the power of the court and defied them in terms which raised doubts about his sanity – which may have saved his life! He was included in an exchange of prisoners, and re-enlisted in a regiment of the Eastern Association, where he provided valuable support for Cromwell in his quarrel with the Earl of Manchester. When the New Model Army was formed, however, he returned to civilian life rather than take an oath to the Solemn League and Covenant, as it would have bound him to accept a Presbyterian settlement in the Church.

In London, Lilburne quickly became involved with the campaign for religious toleration by Walwyn, Overton and others, who often met at the Windmill and Whalebone taverns. However, it was to be Lilburne's own troubles that shifted the focus of activity from religion to politics. In 1645 he was accused by a group of Presbyterians of slandering William Lenthall, the Speaker of the Commons. Summoned before a parliamentary committee, he refused to answer their questions and read extracts from Magna Carta to prove that they had no right to act as a court. Committed to Newgate gaol for three months, he published a pamphlet, *England's Birthright Justified*, in which he attacked the Commons for infringing individual rights. In 1646, after his release, he claimed a right to compensation for his various imprisonments, and in making his case, he made a slighting reference to the Earl of Manchester, now Speaker of the Lords. This time he was summoned before the Upper House, where his arrogant defence of his rights as a 'free-born commoner' infuriated the Lords into fining him and committing him to the Tower. Impossible as Lilburne was, his case raised a genuine issue about an individual's right to a fair trial, and the abuse of parliament's power in order to punish individuals. The resultant campaign waged by Walwyn, Overton and Lilburne's wife led to the first publication of a coherent Leveller programme, based on popular sovereignty, individual rights including religious liberty, and the free exercise of trade. The campaign of marches, petitions and popular demonstrations marks the emergence of the Levellers as an organised movement, the establishment of its means and methods and the position of Lilburne as its leader.

He was to fulfil that function largely from the inside of a prison cell. He remained in the Tower throughout the crisis of 1647, directing the efforts to capture the army through a flood of letters, pamphlets and instructions to visitors. These included the Agitator, Edward Sexby, and 'Major' John Wildman, who wrote *The Case of the Army* in October 1647. Released on bail in November, he was too late to influence the Putney Debates, and was unable to reach the rendezvous at Ware in time to support the mutineers. Cromwell's comfortable restoration of discipline was a serious blow to the Levellers, but their efforts to counter-attack by campaigning for the *Agreement of the People* led to the withdrawal of Lilburne's bail and return to prison in January. Released once more in August 1648, he refrained from further attacks on the Grandees during the second Civil War, a policy that seemed to have paid off in November when Cromwell renewed negotiations on a second *Agreement*. Compromise proved impossible, and after Pride's Purge, the Levellers were powerless to prevent the *Agreement* being laid aside. For Lilburne, the execution of the king was no more than a military coup, and the Rump an unrepresentative tyranny; but his vitriolic attacks and attempts to stir the old spirit in the army led only to the tragedy at Burford, and his own trial for treason. After his *England's New Chains Discovered* called for mutiny and rebellion, both Cromwell and the Council of State were determined to deal with the Levellers once and for all. The four leaders – Lilburne, Overton, Walwyn and Thomas Prince – were arrested in March, and could do little but watch helplessly as the risings were crushed. Although able to mount a spectacular funeral for Robert Lockyer, shot after an abortive mutiny in April, they could do nothing to prevent the failure at Burford Church in May. As a movement, the Levellers were finished.

Yet if the Levellers were defeated, Lilburne himself lived to fight another day. After his triumphant acquittal by a London jury in October 1649, he retired into private life as a soap-boiler. It was impossible, however, for him to stay quiet for long, and the trials and tribulations of his final years reveal both the strength and weaknesses of his character. In 1650 he emerged from obscurity to campaign on behalf of a group of commoners at Epworth, Lincolnshire, whose rights were threatened by enclosures. His final sufferings, however, were brought upon himself by a long-standing feud with the MP Sir Arthur Haselrig, who was a neighbour of the Lilburne family in Durham. In 1652 he launched a series of personal attacks on Haselrig, giving his enemies the opportunity to crush him. He was sentenced (without trial) to a fine of £7,000 and banishment for life; if he returned to England, he could be executed as a felon. Few things could have demonstrated more effectively how little the Leveller campaigns had achieved.

In exile in Holland, Lilburne came to know and like a number of Royalists, but unlike Overton and Wildman, he does not appear to have been involved in any plots. In 1653, saddened by separation from friends and family, he took the opportunity afforded by the dissolution of the Rump to return, promising to live quietly. He was immediately arrested and put on trial for his life. Once more there were petitions on his behalf, and a typical performance from the defendant himself. Although the jury found him 'not guilty of any crime worthy of death' he was remanded in prison, where he remained until 1657 when he died as a result of his many imprisonments. In his last years he appears to have found new comfort, and a new humility, in the Quaker religion.

Lilburne was a man of two personalities, both of which influenced the Leveller movement. His character is summed up by the historian Howard Shaw in Source 45.

Source 45

From Howard Shaw, *The Levellers* (Longman, 1973) pp. 27–8.

Obstinate, extrovert, arrogantly refusing to bow to any form of authority, he was a supreme egotist with an exaggerated sense of his own grievances. Lacking in humour and quick to take offence on his own and other people's behalf, he looks like a barrackroom lawyer of the worst type. One contemporary critic described him as 'never well but when fishing in troubled waters' ... the royalist weekly *Mercurius Pragmaticus*, designated him the 'lunatic Lieutenant Colonel'. Yet this is less than half the picture. Certainly he was a born rebel, but his was not the narrow prejudiced revolt of the man with a chip on his shoulder. He had a passionate hatred of injustice of any sort and his whole life was dedicated to the ideal of freedom in its widest sense. Willing to suffer any hardship if the cause was right, he constantly lashed out at the strong to protect the weak. ... His genius for putting his own wrongs at the centre of a conflict of principle was something more than mere exhibitionism. As champion of the oppressed, he felt it his duty to resist illegality at every turn, for 'what is done to anyone may be done to everyone'. For fulfilling his duty to his fellow men he was flogged, gaoled over and over again, and tried three times for his life. His turbulent career, in which comedy and tragedy are never far apart, was at all times worthy of respect.

In 1646, therefore, the Leveller leaders observed a political world which was at a crossroads. The Civil War was effectively won, but the peace had yet to take shape. The king was determined to retain his power in its essentials, the Presbyterian majority in parliament sought a reform of the Church, an adjustment of the constitution and a return to normality. The Independents and sectaries were waging a campaign for religious liberty, at least for themselves. Of the mass of the population, and even the ordinary soldier, we know little, but it is clear that there were many discontents – and it was these that the Levellers sought to represent and to mould in their own image.

What did the Levellers stand for?

Sources 46–53 provide extracts from the many Leveller writings to illustrate the range of arguments and ideas put forward by the Levellers. They do not, and cannot, constitute an exhaustive survey – it is possible only to provide an outline of their main aspirations and demands. However, the brief biographies on the preceding pages and the introductory narrative provided in Unit 3:1 will enable you to refer to the historical context in which the sources must be interpreted, and to establish a broader understanding of what these ideas implied at the time. You may also find it useful to re-read Unit 3.1, Sources 14, 18, 21–3, and 29.

Questions

1. Read Sources 46–53, and interpreting them in context, explain:

   (a) what popular grievances the Levellers claimed to express;

   (b) what the Levellers were trying to achieve;

   (c) what ideas and arguments about politics, religion and society they put forward in support of their demands.

2. Using these sources and the information contained in Unit 3.1, explain why the Leveller movement emerged and attracted support at this time.

Source 46

From John Lilburne, *England's Birthright Justified*, 1645.

For my part, I look upon the House of Commons as the supreme power of England, who have residing in them that power that is inherent in the people, who yet are not to act according to their own wills and pleasure, but according to the fundamental constitutions and customs of the land, which I conceive provides for the safety of the people.

Source 47

From a speech by Lilburne to the House of Lords, 11 July 1646.

All you intended when you set us a-fighting was merely to unhorse and dismount our old riders and tyrants, that so you might get up and ride us in their stead. And therefore my Lords … if you shall be so unworthy as to persevere … in the destruction of the fundamental laws and liberties of England … I will venture my life and heart's blood against you, with as much zeal and courage as ever I did against any of the king's party.

Source 48

From *A Remonstrance of Many Thousand Citizens*, 7 July 1646, largely written by William Walwyn and Richard Overton.

The history of our forefathers since they were conquered by the Normans, doth manifest that this nation hath been held in bondage all along ever since by the policies and force of the officers of trust in the commonwealth, amongst whom we always esteemed kings the chiefest. … Ye have experience that none but a king could do so great, intolerable mischiefs; the very name of king providing a sufficient charm to delude many of our brethren … so far as to fight against their own liberties, which you know no man under heaven could ever have done. And yet … you cannot fight for our liberties but it must be in the name of King and Parliament; he that speaks of his cruelties must be thrust out of your House and society; your preachers must pray for him as if he had not deserved to be excommunicated by all Christian society; or as if ye or they thought God were a respecter of the persons of kings in judgement.

By this and other your like dealings, your frequent treating and tampering to maintain his honour, we that have trusted you to deliver us from his oppressions and to preserve us from his cruelties, are wasted and consumed in multitudes to manifold miseries, whilst you lie ready with open arms to receive him, and to make him a great and glorious king.

We must deal plainly with you, ye have long time acted more like the House of Peers than the House of Commons; we can scarcely approach your door with a request or motion, though by way of petition, but ye hold long debates, whether we break not your privileges. … Your members in all impositions [taxes] must not be taxed in the places where they live, like other men … ye now frequently commit men's persons to prison without showing cause; ye examine men upon … questions against themselves, and imprison them for refusing to answer; … [you] vex and molest honest men for matters of religion … and thereby have divided honest people amongst themselves, by countenancing only those of the Presbytery and discountenancing all the separation, Anabaptists and Independents.

What a multitude of precious lives have been lost? What a mass of moneys have been raised? … Truly, it is a sad thing, but too true, a plain, quiet-minded man in any place in England is just like a harmless sheep in a thicket; [he] can hardly move or stir but he shall be stretched and lose his wool; such committees have ye made in all cities and counties, and none are so ill-used as honest, Godly men.

Source 49

From *An Arrow against all Tyrants*, 1646, written by Richard Overton.

For by natural birth all men are equal … born to like propriety [property] liberty and freedom, and as we are delivered of God by the hand of nature into this world, every one with a natural innate freedom and propriety … even so we are to live, every one equally … to enjoy his birthright and privilege, even all whereof God by nature hath made him free.

Source 50

From the *Large Petition*, March 1647, probably written by William Walwyn.

And although all new illegal Patents are … abolished, yet the oppressive Monopoly of Merchant Adventurers and others, do still remain to the great abridgement of the liberties of the people, and to the extreme prejudice of all such industrious people as depend on clothing, or other woollen manufacture. … Also the old tedious and chargeable way of deciding controversies, or suits in law is continued to this day. … Likewise, that old, but most unequal punishment of malefactors, … whereby men's lives and liberties are as liable to the law, and corporal pains [punishment] as much inflicted for small as for great offences, and that most unjustly upon the testimony of one witness, contrary both to the law of God and common equity, a grievance very great, but little regarded. Also tithes and other enforced maintenance are still continued, though there be no ground for either under the Gospel; … [and] multitudes of poor distressed prisoners for debt lie still unregarded, in a most miserable and woeful condition. … Likewise Prison-keepers, or gaolers, are as presumptuous as ever they were, both in receiving and detaining of prisoners illegally committed … [and] as oppressive and extorting in their fees. … Also thousands of men and women are still … permitted to live in beggary and wickedness all their life long, and to breed their children to the same idle and vicious course of life, and no effectual means used to reclaim either, or to reduce them to any virtue or industry.

Source 51

From *An Appeal* written by Richard Overton in July 1647, calling on the Army to take power and dissolve parliament.

And as for matters of conscience or opinion about Religion or Worship, with which human society, cohabitation and safety may freely subsist and stand together, that doth not fall under the power of the Magisterial sword, either for introduction and settlement, or for extirpation and subversion; for the limits of magistracy extend no further than humanity, or human subsistence, not to spirituality or spiritual being; and no further than its own nature extends, no further may its compulsive power be stretched: And this is the true distinction … betwixt God and Caesar, and what is God's we must in the first place give unto God, and what is Caesar's, in the second place, freely and readily, we must give unto Caesar; the inward man is God's prerogative, the outward man is man's prerogative.

Source 52

From *The Agreement of the People*, drafted 29 October 1647 and debated at Putney. This is the first of three versions, the others being devised in December 1648 and May 1649. Although the later versions contained some alterations, these were occasioned by circumstance rather than principle – the essence of Leveller constitutional thinking is contained in the Putney version. The Agreement sets out the powers and arrangements for a sovereign parliament, and the guarantees of individual liberty which were to be withheld from government control. It does not specify the franchise qualifications, but both Wildman (in the *Case of the Army*) and Col. Rainsborough in the Putney Debates (see below) spoke in terms of universal manhood suffrage. However, after the debates, the Levellers seem to have accepted some of Ireton's concerns, and were willing to exclude 'servants and alms-takers'.

An Agreement of the People for a firm and present peace upon grounds of common right.

… Since, therefore, our former oppressions and scarce-yet-ended troubles have been occasioned, either by want of frequent national meetings in Council [parliament] or by rendering those meetings ineffectual, we are fully agreed and resolved to provide that hereafter our representatives be neither left to an uncertainty for the time nor made useless to the ends for which they are intended. In order thereunto we declare:

That the people of England being at this day very unequally distributed by Counties, Cities and Boroughs for the election of their deputies in Parliament, ought to be more indifferently proportioned according to the number of the inhabitants; the circumstances whereof for number, place and manner are to be set down before the end of this present Parliament.

That to prevent the many inconveniences apparently arising from the long continuance of the same persons in authority, this present Parliament be dissolved upon the last day of September … 1648.

That the people do, [as a matter] of course, choose themselves a Parliament once in two years … after the manner as shall be prescribed before the end of this Parliament, to begin to sit upon the first Thursday in April … and to continue till the last day of September then next ensuing, and no longer.

That the power of this, and all future representatives of this Nation, is inferior only to theirs who choose them, and doth extend, without the consent or concurrence of any other person or persons, to the enacting, altering and repealing of laws, to the erecting and abolishing of offices and courts, to the appointing, removing and calling to account magistrates and officers of all degrees, to the making war and peace, to treating with foreign states, and, generally, to whatsoever is not expressly or impliedly by the represented to themselves:

Which are as followeth.

1 That matters of religion and the ways of God's worship are not at all entrusted by us to any human power … nevertheless the public way of instructing the nation (so [long as] it be not compulsive) is referred to their discretion.
2 That the matter of impressing and constraining any of us to serve in wars is against our freedom; and therefore we do not allow it … ; the rather because money … being always at their disposal, they can never want numbers of men apt enough to engage in any just cause.
3 That after the dissolution of this present Parliament, no person be at any time questioned for anything said or done in reference to the late public differences …
4 That in all laws made or to be made every person may be bound alike …
5 That as the laws ought to be equal, so they must be good, and not evidently destructive to the safety and well-being of the people.

Source 53

From the Putney Debates, October 1647.

Ireton: The exception that lies in it [*The Agreement of the People*] is this. It is said they [parliamentary seats] are to be distributed according to the number of the inhabitants. … And this doth make me think that the meaning is that every man that is an inhabitant is to be equally considered, and to have an equal voice in the election of those represeners. … And if that be the meaning, then I have something to say against it. …

Petty [an Agitator]: We judge that all inhabitants that have not lost their birthright should have an equal voice in elections.

Rainsborough: I desired that those engaged in it [might be included]. For really I think that the poorest he that is in England hath a life to live as the greatest he. And therefore truly, sir, I think it's clear that every man that is to live under a government ought first by his own consent to put himself under that government; and I do think that the poorest man in England is not at all bound in a strict sense to that government that he hath not had a voice to put himself under; and I am confident that, when I have heard the reasons against it, something will be said to answer those reasons insomuch that I should doubt whether he was an Englishman or no, that should doubt of these things.

While Ireton and the officers might resist such radical demands, there is no doubt that the Levellers touched a chord among the rank and file, particularly among the cavalry and among the sectarian Churches who were the allies of the army. The extent of Leveller influence in the spring and summer of 1647 has been a matter of debate, but they had certainly been able to seize the initiative in removing the king from the parliament's custody, in politicising the discontents of the army and in forcing the leading officers to consult the lower ranks through the medium of the Army Council. Added to their activities in London, these successes suggest a movement which had the capacity to influence the outcome of events. Yet within weeks of the Putney Debates, the initiative had slipped from their grasp, and they were never to regain it. Ultimately the Levellers failed in their objective of establishing a new political order in England based upon the rights, sovereignty and agreement of the English people.

Why did the Levellers fail?

For three years the Leveller movement appeared to be influential in shaping the settlement that would emerge from the upheavals of the Civil War, yet in 1649 the king was executed, the monarchy abolished and a new Commonwealth established without reference to them or their ideas; and the leaders' attempts to assert their power led only to a few failed mutinies and their own imprisonment. In their own eyes the reasons for this failure were clear. As Source 54 indicates, they blamed the ruthless ambition and deception of their erstwhile allies, the Grandees, and the determination of a Rump of Parliament to hold on to power. Historians, however, have taken a more complex view. While some have accepted the actions of Cromwell and Ireton as a significant factor in their failure, others have also pointed to errors and misjudgements on the part of the Levellers themselves. Others again have argued that failure was inevitable – that the situation and conditions of the period meant that a movement of this kind could not flourish for long enough to have a significant influence on events. G.E. Aylmer summarises this view:

Source 54

From G.E. Aylmer, *The Levellers in the English Revolution* (Thames and Hudson, 1975) pp. 9 and 12.

The leaders and others about whom enough is known are interesting in themselves … ; their ideas are remarkable; and so is the organisation they formed. Whether they wanted full manhood suffrage, or something like male household suffrage … it is no misnomer to call them the first democratic political movement in modern history. … Nowhere else before the 1760s, or even perhaps before 1789, do we find the combination of radical journalism and pamphleteering, ideological zeal, political activism, and mass organisation that prevailed in England from 1646 to 1649.

The circumstances of these years were, of course, exceptional. They alone made the Leveller movement possible as a major historical event. The essential elements were these: the personalities of the leading figures, of John Lilburne above all; the intellectual development of their ideas; and the juxtaposition of difficult economic conditions with the political and religious conflicts and dissatisfactions that followed the King's defeat in the First Civil War.

[By 1649] the movement [had] disintegrated. … Yet, if we consider the hierarchical nature of seventeenth-century society, the prevailing assumptions of the age, the deferential acceptance of upper-class rule, the cohesive nature of the local communities of rural and provincial England, the pervasiveness and force of preaching and writing against rebellion, popular tumult, anarchy and communism – then what is remarkable … is not the Levellers' failure, either to seize power or to see more of their demands implemented, but rather the amount of influence they did exercise … during these few years.

This explanation attributes the greatest relative importance to conditional, causal factors in bringing about the downfall of the movement – the political structure and the prevailing attitudes of the time. Even if this is accepted, and some historians have disagreed, it is still necessary to explore the contingent factors – the events and actions which shaped the failure and dictated its timing, extent and immediate effects – in order to show why the Levellers failed in the way that they did. Moreover, the explanation will inevitably raise further questions. What, for example, were the attitudes referred to above which so hindered Leveller efforts, why were they held at this time, and how did they work to counteract Leveller arguments? How did these attitudes shape the intentions, objectives and actions of those who opposed the Levellers? Why did the Levellers react in a particular way, and if they made mistakes, why did they make them?

A number of sources follow which will enable you to address these issues in order to offer your own explanation of why the Levellers failed. They include both primary sources which explain the views and attitudes of contemporaries, and historians' views about the situation and about the significance of particular events and actions. You may find that you agree with the weight and significance that some historians have attached to the conditional factors, or you may attribute more importance to the decisions and actions of various individuals. Either way, you will need to understand the nature and sequence of events from 1645 to 1649 when the Leveller movement was active. For that reason the material includes a summary of the events which have been explained above (in the introduction to Unit 3.1 and the biographies of Leveller leaders) and to which the sources refer.

THE LEVELLER MOVEMENT: SUMMARY OF EVENTS		
Year		**Events and Developments**
1645	July	Lilburne imprisoned by House of Commons for slandering Lenthall, raised awareness of the need to protect individual rights. Publication of *England's Birthright Justified* extended the argument to economic, social and legal rights and equality.
1646	July	Publication of Edwards' *Gangraena* attacks Levellers as a group. Lilburne imprisoned by House of Lords; replied by publishing *A Freeman's Freedom Vindicated*. Campaign begun for his release. Publication of *A Remonstrance* laid out the Leveller programme.
	August	Overton, arrested for a pamphlet attacking the Lords, won public sympathy.
1647	January	Lilburne published *Regal Tyranny Discovered*; argued that monarchy incompatible with government based on consent. Attacked Charles.
	February	Petition for release of Lilburne and Overton with 10,000 signatures. Party organisation being built up, probably by Walwyn; based on local wards throughout London.
	March	Leveller manifesto, *Large Petition*, presented to Parliament. First petitions against disbandment appeared in the army.
	April/May	The army elected Agitators; some (e.g. Sexby, William Allen, Captain White) had clear Leveller links. Appeal to Officers met with sympathy. Overton published *A Newfound Strategem*, appealing to the army to take up the cause of the people's liberties.
	25 May	Disbandment ordered to go ahead. The army in open revolt. Fairfax, Cromwell, etc. forced to lead, to preserve discipline.
	3/4 June	Cornet Joyce seized the king.
	5 June	General rendezvous held; Solemn Engagement adopted and Army Council set up.
	June/July	*Representation of the Army*, written by Ireton, called for the dissolution of parliament, redistribution of seats, franchise reform and religious liberty; shows Leveller influence. Similar terms retained in *Heads of the Proposals* (see Unit 2.2, p.118), presented to the king by Cromwell and Ireton. The Grandees refused forcible dissolution of Parliament which Levellers demanded. Attacks on Independent MPs led the army to enter London and set up quarters in Putney. King delaying response to *Heads of the Proposals*.
	August/ September	Levellers, fearing Grandees would settle with the king, attempted to maintain pressure. John Wildman drafted the *Case of the Army*.
	October	*Case of the Army* presented to Army Council for discussion. *An Agreement of the People* presented as Leveller constitution. Putney Debates revealed common aims of Levellers, Agitators and Grandees; also wide differences, especially over the franchise.
	November	King escaped to the Isle of Wight. Debates ended; call for a general rendezvous, but Fairfax ordered three, dividing radical strength. Attempt to mutiny at Ware easily defeated. Cromwell restored military discipline. Levellers furious but powerless.
1648 Second Civil War	January	Last meeting of General Army Council held at Windsor. Parliament voted No Further Addresses to the king, but no reform guaranteed. Levellers reverted to campaign in London; *Earnest Petition* taken to Parliament. Lilburne returned to prison. Attempting to widen support, built up party organisation and set up groups in Bucks, Herts, and Kent.
	July	The Levellers acquired the newspaper *The Moderate*.
	August	Petition of 10,000; Lilburne released but refused to attack the Grandees during the war. Hoped for further co-operation.
	November	Army determined to call the king to account. Levellers agreed but wanted constitutional change first. Army *Remonstrance* issued. Meetings of Levellers and officers held at Windsor to construct new *Agreement*; wide differences of view.
	December	Parliament voted to resume negotiations with the king, leading to Pride's Purge. New *Agreement* failed over religious toleration.

1649	January	Officers' version of *Agreement* laid aside by Rump. King executed. Levellers furious. They had been totally outmanoeuvred and had failed to effect any constitutional changes before the removal of the king. Now had no means of applying pressure to the Grandees, other than popular demonstrations or subversion of the army. Began both in February.
	February	Attacked trial of Charles as illegal and circulated petitions among the troops. Army petition requested restoration of the General Council. Grandees forbade meetings and complained of civilian agents stirring up the army.
	26 February	Lilburne presented *England's New Chains Discovered* to Rump. Set out constitutional plans and appealed to parliament. He also launched a vitriolic personal attack on the Grandees. Followed by national campaign in *The Moderate* but with relatively little effect.
	March	Scattered mutinies in the army were easily suppressed. Leveller frustration found outlet in attacks on Cromwell and Ireton, particularly in Overton's *Hunting of the Foxes*, accusing them of betrayal and inciting the army to mutiny. Followed by *England's New Chains Part 2*, in which Lilburne appealed to the Rump to adopt Leveller plans and again incited the army to mutiny. Levellers had gone too far. Baptist Churches rejected them and government determined to act. Four main leaders arrested.
	April	*English Soldier's Standard* published from within the Tower. Led to brief mutiny in London, and the execution of Robert Lockyer. Large funeral organised as a demonstration.
	May	Third *Agreement* published by Leveller leaders sparked off an army rising at Oxford, led by William Thompson. Grandees acted decisively. Leaders more rigorously confined in the Tower and troops sent to deal with the mutiny. Rebels caught at Burford and defeated; 300 prisoners taken, 3 shot as an example.

Further Leveller activity of sorts was carried out, such as the publication of *An Impeachment for High Treason* against Cromwell and Ireton, and Lilburne was acquitted by a London jury after his trial in September. Effectively, however, the movement was broken.

Question

3. Why did the Leveller movement fail to achieve its political and religious objectives in the search for a settlement after the Civil War?

Source 55

From *The Hunting of the Foxes*, written by Richard Overton in 1649. The pamphlet was a vitriolic attack on Cromwell and the Grandees, accusing them of having tricked the army and the Levellers into supporting plans that were really only intended to gain power for themselves.

O Cromwell! whither art thou aspiring? The word is already given out amongst their officers, that this Nation must have one prime Magistrate or Ruler over them; and that the General hath power to make a law to bind all the Commons of England: This was most daringly and desperately avowed at Whitehall [the Whitehall meetings of Levellers and officers held to discuss the Second *Agreement* in December 1648]; and to this temper these Court-Officers are now a-moulding, he that runs may read and fore-see the intent, a New Regality [monarchy]! And thus by their Machiavellian pretences, and wicked practices they are become masters and usurpers of the name of the Army, and of the name of the Parliament; Under which visors they have levelled and destroyed all the authority of this nation: For the Parliament indeed and in truth is no Parliament, but a representative ... of the Council of War; and the Council of War but the representative of Cromwell, Ireton and Harrison [Thomas Harrison, the leader of the Fifth Monarchists]; and these are the all in all of this nation which ... play all the strange pranks that are played.

Source 56

From Thomas Edwards, *Gangraena*, (1646). Despite the personal abuse and extremism found in Edwards' work, he did represent the feelings of many conservatives.

There is one Richard Overton, a desperate sectary, one of Lilburne's breed and followers, who hath printed many scandalous things against the House of Peers and ... there was an order granted for the taking of him and seizing of his press (a press that had printed many wicked pamphlets that have come out of late, against the King, the Lords, the Presbyterial government, the City [of London] and for a toleration and liberty, destructive to all religion, laws and government, yea, overthrowing by the principles laid down in them the power of the House of Commons, whilst they seem to cry up and invest that House with the monopoly of all power of the kingdom). ...

There is one John Lilburne, an arch sectary, the great darling of the sectaries, highly extolled and magnified by them in many pamphlets ... [whose] insolent, ungodly practices and ... anarchical principles [are] destructive to all civil government whatsoever. ...

Many ... instances I could give of those who have by the laws of England and other kingdoms, power of government, and that most justly, without any immediate election of the people. ... We must look for some other foundations and grounds of giving one man, or more, power in government over all ... which binds them before God and men to obedience and subjection in all lawful things.

Source 57

From the Putney Debates of 1647. This source shows the argument put forward by Henry Ireton in opposition to Leveller arguments about the franchise. Not only does it challenge the idea of universal suffrage, but it puts forward a totally different conception of what Parliament should represent – the *interests*, not the people, of the kingdom. In Ireton's view the right to vote was a matter of constitutional, not natural, law, and the purpose of the constitution was to protect existing legal rights and property. Any attempt to change this basic concept was a threat to property, and to the law itself. His argument would have been convincing to the conventional majority in seventeenth-century England.

Ireton: I think that no person hath a right to an interest or share in the disposing of the affairs of the kingdom, and in determining or choosing those that shall determine what laws we shall be ruled by here, no person hath a right to this that hath not a permanent, fixed interest in this kingdom, and those persons together are properly the represented of this kingdom ... who taken together do comprehend whatsoever is of real or permanent interest in the kingdom. ... We talk of birthright. Truly [by] birthright there is thus much claim: men may justly have by birthright, by their very being born in England, that we should not seclude them out of England. That we should not refuse to give them air and place and ground and the freedom of the highways and other things. ... But that by a man's being born here he shall have a share in that power that shall dispose of the lands here, and of all things here, I do not think it a sufficient ground. ... I am sure if we look upon that which is the utmost, within man's view, of what was originally the constitution of this kingdom, upon that which is most radical and fundamental, and which if you take away there is no man hath any land, any goods, you take away any civil interest, and that is this: that those that choose the representers for the making of laws by which this state and kingdom are to be governed, are the persons who taken together, do comprehend the local interest of this kingdom; that is the persons in whom all land lies, and those in corporations in whom all trading lies. This is the most fundamental constitution of this kingdom ... which if you do not allow, you allow none at all. This constitution hath limited and determined it , that only those shall have voices in elections. [And as for what] the meanest man in England ought to have ... those that have the meanest local interest, that man that hath ... forty

shillings a year [the lowest freehold qualification for voting in the counties] he hath as great voice in the election of a knight for the shire as he that hath ten thousand a year or more.

Source 58

From *Walwyn's Wiles*, published by William Kiffin and others in 1649. The tract is significant for two reasons. First it reiterates the belief that the Levellers were a threat to property, which was one of the most serious criticisms of their plans, in a more scurrilous form than Ireton would ever have used. Secondly, it was published by those who had once been allies of the Levellers, at least in the campaign for religious liberty. Kiffin was an Elder of the Particular Baptists, and the 'others' represented some of the London Congregationalists. Although there had always been significant differences between these orthodox Calvinists and the more libertarian sects from which the Levellers drew inspiration, the fact that they should now dissociate themselves from the Levellers in this public way indicates the growing isolation of the movement in the early months of 1649.

This Mr Walwyn, to work upon the indigent and poorer sort of people, and to raise up their spirits in discontents and clamours, did one time profess [that] he could wish with all his heart that there was neither pale, hedge nor ditch in the whole nation, and that it was an unconscionable thing that one man should have ten thousand pounds, and another, more deserving and useful to the commonwealth, should not be worth two pence. ...

At another time, discoursing [talking] of the inequality and disproportion of the estates and conditions of men in the world, [he] had words to this purpose, that it was a sad and miserable thing that it should so continue, and that it would never be well until all things were common; and it being replied, will that be ever? – answered, we must endeavour it. It being said that this would destroy all government; answered that then there would be less need of government, for then there would be no thieves, no covetous [greedy] persons, no deceiving and abusing of one another. ...

Source 59

From G.E. Aylmer, *The Levellers in the English Revolution*, pp. 13–14, 22 and 24–25.

The inception of the Leveller movement is correctly traced to the particular events and circumstances of the years 1644–6. In order to defeat the King, the Long Parliament had had to introduce numerous radical measures, which were no part of its original, pre-Civil War reform programme. ... At the same time some of Parliament's own erstwhile supporters became increasingly suspicious of the self-interest of MPs and committee-members. The deepening rift between the Presbyterian clergy ... and the other Puritan or ex-Puritan sects was paralleled by a widening gap between the conservative parliamentarians in both Houses ... and their radical ex-allies in London, in the Army, and among the sects. Here the position of the Army leadership and of the radical minority in the House of Commons was crucial, precisely because it was equivocal in relation to this split. A unique position within this radical group was occupied by Oliver Cromwell: Lt-General of Horse ... radical parliamentary leader, and 'darling of the sectaries' because of his championing of toleration for all brands of Protestant dissenters. The Levellers' fluctuating relations with Cromwell provide a vital thread in any understanding of the movement, and one explanation of its varying fortunes. ...

1647 was both the *annus mirabilis* [wonderful year] of Leveller writings and the year of crisis for the Levellers as an organised movement. ... In March the first of a long series of collective petitions was presented to the House of Commons. ... After two months of toing and froing, the Presbyterian, or conservative majority condemned it and ordered it to be publicly burnt by the common hangman. The Levellers, it must have seemed, could ... expect no reasonable voluntary response to their proposals from the present parliament as it was then constituted. What was the answer: a purged parliament, a new parliament, or a radically different constitution? But by the time the Levellers' challenge to parliament had raised these issues, the Long Parliament's parallel collision with the Army had opened up new, and dramatic possibilities for the radical, popular cause. ...

From May to November 1647, the fortunes of the Leveller movement were largely bound up with those of the Agitators and their few supporters among the more senior officers. ... It looked at first (May–June) as if the wishes of the Agitators and their allies might even determine the policy of the Army as a whole. ... Despite these appearances, ... realities were different. Cromwell and his son-in-law, Commissary-General Henry Ireton, and probably other senior officers too, had their own ideas about reaching a settlement with the King, if necessary at the expense of Parliament – and perhaps of their radical allies as well.

Source 60

From H. Shaw, *The Levellers* pp. 54 and 57–66.

Whatever Charles might think, the army was the ultimate arbiter of the kingdom. And within the army tensions were growing. Strong though their own grievances were, the officers knew full well their hands had been forced by the ordinary soldiers. As the summer of 1647 drew on, the Grandees struggled to reassert their authority. Moreover, a clash between the Grandees and those who had fallen under Leveller influence was more or less certain on other than military grounds. Cromwell and his colleagues were in no sense social radicals. They belonged to the moderate

gentry class that had been best represented by Pym. They had fought against the king to consolidate the gains made in 1641, not to inaugurate a social revolution. Although tending to be of lower social status than the Presbyterians, they had the same interest in maintaining stability and the sanctity of property. Only in a religious sense was Cromwell a radical; as an Independent he always supported toleration, but even here some consciences were to be regarded as more tender than others. The Levellers were more extreme in all fields and were unlikely to share common ground with the Grandees for long.

The Levellers never really trusted the Grandees. Both Lilburne and Overton urged the men to beware of their officers. ... Their behaviour after the seizure of London confirmed these suspicions. Parliament was not purged; negotiations with the king dragged on inconclusively; and, most important from the Leveller point of view, Lilburne and Overton remained in prison. Cromwell paid Lilburne a friendly visit in the Tower, but made it plain that he would not be released unless he would promise not 'to make new hurley-burleys' in the army. Caught between the crossfire of Presbyterians on the right and Levellers on the left, the Grandees did not intend to add to their embarrassments by allowing Lilburne a free hand with the agitators. These disappointments led to a new burst of Leveller energy aimed at regaining the initiative lost when the men's representatives had been absorbed into the General Council. ... In a public letter to Henry Marten [a republican MP who was sympathetic to the Levellers] Lilburne announced that, since Cromwell had failed him and planned 'to keep the poor everlastingly ... in bondage and slavery', he would henceforth appeal to the ordinary soldiers. Probably at Lilburne's instigation, several regiments elected new and more extreme agitators. Finally, in October, the agitators of five regiments stationed in Surrey signed *The Case of the Army Truly Stated*, a manifesto drawn up by civilian and army Levellers ... [and] presented to Fairfax in the middle of October 1647. ... It was agreed that the Leveller proposals should be considered by the General Council of the Army. [In fact a shortened version was drawn up and presented as *The Agreement of the People*.]

The General Council met in the church at Putney in the closing days of October and it was not long before the discussions revealed the basic differences between the Grandees, the new conservatives and their fiery critics on the left. ... The main battle was joined over the question of suffrage. ... Ireton ... expressed the traditional view with logic and clarity. ... The Levellers ... while feeling their way tentatively towards the democracy implicit in their belief in the sovereignty of the people, were increasingly handicapped by insinuations that they were greater social revolutionaries than they really were. ... [By early November] these debates were nearing their end. Ever since the beginning of June, when he threw in his lot with the agitators, Cromwell had realised that the army was the only guarantee for peace in the kingdom and that it only remained such a guarantee while under its officers' control. As the discussions at Putney progressed, he saw this discipline endangered by the extremists in the

General Council. The Levellers outvoted the Grandees for the restoration of their full suffrage proposals ...; a Leveller motion was carried for another general rendezvous. ... The signs were ominous and Cromwell launched an immediate counter-attack. He had a resolution passed that officers and agitators should return to their regiments pending the rendezvous; having scattered the troublemakers, he ensured that they should not re-unite by arranging the rendezvous in three separate places; lastly, he 'packed' another committee, whose task was to draft a non-controversial document for presentation to the troops. On 11 November the king fled from Hampton Court to the Isle of Wight. Several contemporaries charged Cromwell with complicity in the escape, for with the resurrection of the royalist threat he now had ample excuse to enforce strict discipline. In fact he almost certainly had nothing to do with it ... [but his] hand was strengthened for the critical meetings shortly to take place.

Source 61

The General Council of the Army, presided over by Fairfax, 1647

Source 62

From H. Shaw, *The Levellers*, p. 65.

Leveller hopes of recreating the exhilaration of the early days at Newmarket were sadly disappointed by the new rendezvous. Of the three rendezvous appointed, only one, at Corkbush Field, Ware, produced trouble for the Grandees. There two regiments, Harrison's and Robert Lilburne's [John Lilburne's brother] turned up against orders and with copies of the *Agreement* stuck in their hats. Harrison's cavalry removed the offending

documents after an address from Fairfax, but Lilburne's foot refused and the officers had to go in amongst them to pull them out. ... Several ringleaders were arrested and three were condemned to death immediately by drumhead court martial. These diced for their lives, and the loser, one Arnold, was shot in front of his regiment.

The Ware rendezvous was a notable victory for the Grandees. The seven regiments officially summoned accepted the moderate policy statement without fuss; the two mutinous regiments had wavered in the face of determined action and discipline had been restored with a minimum of bloodshed. For the Levellers, it was a sharp setback. Although John Lilburne, recently released on bail, had hastened to Ware, Leveller plans had been uncoordinated. ... The agitators had circulated a critical account of the Grandees' handling of the Putney debates and Rainsborough tried to present a copy of the *Agreement* to Fairfax on his arrival at the rendezvous, but Sexby, who was present, seems to have taken no action at all.

Undoubtedly the flight of the king had much to do with [their] indecision; the possibility of renewed civil war must have made any attack on the officers seem inopportune. ... Nevertheless whatever excuses may be made, Corkbush Field was a major reverse. Having helped to dictate the pace and direction of events for the last six months, the Levellers found at this vital point that the New Model remained a disciplined body with a powerful loyalty to Fairfax and Cromwell.

Source 63

From G.E. Aylmer, *The Levellers in the English Revolution*, p. 34.

If it deserves to be called a mutiny at all, rather than an indisciplined demonstration, it was one that went off at half-cock. Lilburne – now at last out of the Tower on parole – was at Ware, lurking in the background. Despite the presence of Rainsborough (at least for part of the time – the accounts are not quite clear about this) the soldiers allowed themselves to be overawed by the prestige of Fairfax and the sheer personality and courage of Cromwell. The 'mutiny' was suppressed at the cost of one soldier executed ... and three officers arrested. ... But the cost to the Leveller cause was in fact much heavier than this. For they had played their trump card – direct action by the rank and file of the Army – and it had failed. As events turned out, they were to try it only once more, and then under even less favourable circumstances.

Source 64

From A.L. Morton, *Freedom in Arms* (Lawrence and Wishart, 1974) pp. 48–60.

Looking back with the advantage of hindsight we can see that the events at Ware constituted a defeat for the Levellers from which recovery was hardly possible. Their one real hope of even temporary success was to win the support of the Army: the attempt had failed, the Council of the Army was soon to be dispersed, and no such opportunity ever presented itself again. Outside the Army they had many supporters, especially in and around London, but ... their [appeal was not to] the classes in which political power traditionally rested: they could protest, they could not make their protests effective. Only in the Army was there a possible alternative power base through which fundamental change might have been effected. This is obvious now, it cannot have been so at the time. All that could be seen was that a set-back had been received which made new tactics necessary, both in the Army and outside it.

In the Army a compromise was soon reached. In spite of their victory, Cromwell and Ireton must have seen the danger of their position. Discipline had been restored, but the Army had not changed its political convictions overnight. ... The result was another meeting of the Army Council at Windsor on December 15, the last which the Agents [agitators] attended, at which a reconciliation was effected. ... On the political side the Grandees undertook that there should be no more attempts at agreement with the King – a Leveller demand which had been strongly resisted at Putney. This proved to be a genuine change of policy when Cromwell on January 3 moved and carried in the House of Commons that no more addresses should be made to Charles. The unity of the Army was restored, but at the price of an important step to the left by the Grandees.

Meanwhile [the Levellers] were developing their own new campaign. Now that they had failed to win the support of the Army they resumed their petitioning [of Parliament] ... [which] had been purged of its leading Presbyterians. ... Alongside this petitioning [they] were seriously engaged in building the world's first organised radical-democratic political party. They made their headquarters at the Whalebone Tavern, 'in Lothbury behind the Royal Exchange' where the leadership seem to have held almost nightly meetings at this period. A substantial membership was soon recruited, paying weekly subscriptions according to their means and organised, in London at least, on a parish and ward basis. Similar groups or branches began to be built in the towns around London. ... There is evidence too that in this winter of famine prices and widespread unemployment and misery, they were trying to broaden the basis of their appeal. This can be seen in ... the *Petition* of January 1648. Here, in addition to the familiar constitutional demands, are new clauses directly affecting the poor and the wage-earner. ... There seems no doubt that the campaign was making considerable headway if one may judge by the amount of hostility it provoked both from Presbyterians and Independents, when it was interrupted in May by the renewal of war. There was serious fighting in South Wales, and in Kent and Essex. ... In August Cromwell, having disposed of the South Wales rising, marched to meet the invading Scots, leaving behind him a London whose richer citizens were looking forward to his defeat. ...

The relative isolation of the Army at this time made the support of the Levellers indispensable, and the ending of the war brought a new stage in Leveller tactics. ... *The September Petition* ... contained a demand for the execution of 'Justice upon the Capital Authors and Promoters of the former or late Wars'. This brought the Levellers into line with the feeling of the Army, where Grandees and rank and file were united in pressing for the immediate trial of the King. Parliament, meanwhile ... persisted in negotiations ... which would have involved the abandonment of much that had been won. ... so that once more the Grandees were forced to bid for Leveller support. [Lilburne] and Wildman were told that the first steps must be to execute the King and purge Parliament of its Presbyterian members (now all back in their places). Lilburne objected that, 'The Army had couzened [tricked] us the last year, and fallen from all their Promises and Declarations and therefore ... I pressed very hard for an Agreement amongst the people first, utterly disclaiming the thoughts of the other till this was done'. [A series of meetings followed at Whitehall, during which Pride's Purge was precipitated by parliament's negotiations with the King. There are different claims as to why the negotiations broke down (over religion) but the result was that the officers ignored the Leveller version of a new Agreement and presented their own to parliament on January 20; they showed little concern when it was laid aside].

It is clear that once again the Levellers had been out-generalled. The trial of the King and the setting up of a Council of State, in which all real power was centred, was pushed ahead while they were confused and divided ... [Walwyn had apparently argued for uniting behind the officers' Agreement]. Lilburne was offered a seat on the Court at which Charles was tried, but refused it, not because he was opposed to the trial in principle, but because he objected to the timing and method. ... One may doubt how far the mass of Leveller supporters, especially in the Army, were able to appreciate [his] rather legalistic objections. At any rate, the party was left isolated and floundering in the wake of events. ... Their failure was the more complete because of an extraordinary ... tactical blunder. At this most critical moment in their history they simply ceased to function. Towards the end of December Lilburne left London for Durham to settle private affairs. Walwyn temporarily ceased to be active in the Party leadership. Wildman deserted the cause. From the appearance of the second [Leveller] *Agreement* on December 15, till the end of February, no Leveller pamphlet of importance was issued. ... When the Leveller campaign was resumed, the Council of State, dominated by the Grandees, was firmly in control and could only have been dislodged by a new revolution, the conditions for which did not exist.

Source 65

From H. Shaw, *The Levellers*, pp. 77–90.

The Levellers greeted the New Year in a spirit of despondency. ... For a while ... [Lilburne] considered giving up politics. ... With the *Agreement of the People* amended and shelved, its conservative opponents firmly established in the seat of government, and its leader contemplating a withdrawal from politics, the Leveller party appeared to be dead. Appearances were deceptive. The Levellers ... still had their party organisation [and by February 1649 they] again looked to the Army; here lay both the strength and weakness of the Grandees. In mid-February, a petition containing a number of inflammatory demands was circulated through the ranks. ... The response of the Grandees was sharp and immediate. ... On 22 February an order of the day was issued forbidding meetings for the discussion of petitions and stating that all complaints should in future be channelled through the officers of the regiment. ... It was this action on the part of the officers' council that provoked Lilburne to resume wholehearted political agitation. Four days after the obnoxious order, he reappeared at the bar of the House of Commons to present *England's New Chains Discovered*, a paper containing a summary of Leveller constitutional ideas and, more important, a fierce denunciation of the leaders of the army and the Council of State.

England's New Chains ... marked the beginning of a fresh campaign in the country at large. ... The soldiers responded first ... [with] a Leveller-inspired petition to Fairfax, demanding restoration of the right to petition freely. ... The new attack from the left was gaining momentum. But it was not as dangerous as it looked. To undermine the authority of the Council of State the Levellers had to destroy the discipline of the army, and this was no easy task after the Grandees' resolute stand at Ware. ... The Leveller leaders were more aware of their weakness than their enemies. Following the cashiering of five troopers [after the February petition] Overton produced his most bitter pamphlet. ... *The Hunting of the Foxes* was a distorted history of the last two years in which Cromwell and Ireton were the hypocritical villains and the ordinary soldiers the heroes. ... Every charge – truth, half-truth and blatant falsehood was pressed into service. ... The Levellers were burning their boats. *The Hunting of the Foxes* was at once a frenzied cry to the ordinary soldiers to bestir themselves before it was too late, and a challenge to the Grandees to do their worst; there could be no rapprochement [reuniting] with the new rulers after this. As if to show that Overton's work was not the outburst of an isolated individual but part of a planned campaign, Lilburne followed it up with the *Second part of England's New Chains Discovered*, an equally strident paper ... [in which] the threat of rebellion was scarcely veiled. ... Cromwell's patience was exhausted. He was indifferent to personal criticism, but was acutely aware of the problems facing the Commonwealth and could not allow the Levellers to divide the army against itself. ... [The four Leveller leaders were arrested]. The inclusion of Walwyn, who had played no part in Leveller activities since the breakdown of the negotiations at Whitehall, suggests a determination to crush the whole group once and for all.

Outwardly, in spite of its setbacks, the party exhibited remarkable virility; beneath the surface there were ominous hints of disintegration. The Fifth Monarchists, believing Christ's Second Coming to be imminent, were already active and tended to draw off Leveller support. Several Independent congregations in London, hitherto

constant allies, announced not merely withdrawal of sympathy but outright opposition. Shocked by what they took to be evidence of scepticism and agnosticism [doubts about the existence of God] in Leveller thought, they first dissociated themselves ... and then fiercely attacked the party in general and Walwyn in particular. [This was followed by] the Levellers last major attempt to destroy the discipline of the New Model. On 1 May Lilburne, Walwyn, Overton and Prince published the final version of *The Agreement of the People*. Shortly afterwards six regiments elected new agitators ... and in Oxfordshire William Thompson, an aggressive Leveller [called] for full-scale revolt [and collected] a number of disaffected troops at Banbury. News spread of unrest elsewhere, including a Leveller rally at Aylesbury.

The Grandees acted swiftly. The Leveller prisoners were more rigorously confined in the Tower ... [and] the Generals set off westwards to prevent a projected junction of the units in revolt. They overtook the main body of Levellers, some 1200 men, at midnight in the Cotswold town of Burford. There was a little desultory fighting, but the bulk of the mutineers, surprised in their beds by superior numbers, dispersed or surrendered. ... Three hundred and forty prisoners were taken and shut up in Burford Church. Three days later, after all had been condemned to death by court martial, three men were shot in the churchyard, the remainder watching from the leads in the church. ... The Cause had failed again.

Source 66

From F.D. Dow, *Radicalism in the English Revolution* (Blackwell, 1989) pp. 48–56.

In attempting to build up the strength of their movement and win support for their programme, the Levellers showed themselves to be shrewd publicists and propagandists. They were very soon able to whip up demonstrations of pro-Leveller feeling in the capital, establish links with aggrieved elements in the counties, and tap feelings of discontent in the army. The use of the press, the organisation of petitions and demonstrations, the development of a party structure and the skilful deployment of the charismatic appeal of its leaders quickly built up the impression of a mass political movement, especially in London. ...

However, it would be misleading to infer from this that England was full of committed party supporters. The superficial strength of the Leveller movement during its petitioning campaigns masked underlying weaknesses. Sympathy with the grievances to which the Levellers gave voice was greater than support for the solutions to those problems which the Levellers advocated. Not all those who shared the Levellers' hostility to the 'powers that be' were prepared to translate their antagonism into demands for radical change; and of those who were prepared to countenance a radical solution, not all agreed that it should be the Leveller one. This last point was crucial to the party's fortunes: the Leveller movement rose in part because it fed on, inspired, and became part of a radical coalition of interests in London, in the army and in the counties; when deserted by and isolated from the other elements in this radical coalition, its weaknesses were exposed. The weaknesses were both organisational and ideological. Organisationally the Levellers were too dependent on the gathered churches; they had not built up their own representative machinery among the rank and file of the army; and they had done little to mobilise the peasantry as opposed to the urban middling orders. Ideologically, their programme was too frightening to the rich, too neglectful of the poor, and too innovative in its assumptions to embrace all the godly 'middling sort'.

On the whole the individualistic liberal ideology of the Leveller movement encouraged their belief that political reform, not economic or social reform, would be the fount from which all other blessings for the common people would flow. Just as they believed that the source of the people's suffering was intrinsically political (in the long term the Norman Conquest, in the short term the corruption of parliament) so they believed that the remedies for these ills lay essentially in the political sphere. The economic issues which concerned them were principally those which affected the middling sort, the people to whom all Levellers would have given the franchise. In truth, their economic and political thinking was all of a piece. They were against the agglomeration of wealth in a few hands, just as they opposed the concentration of political power in a few hands; conversely, they came out against the complete equality of wealth just as they retreated from universal manhood suffrage. [This did not prevent their opponents from using such accusations against them.] As Brian Manning concludes, if the Levellers hated the exorbitantly rich, they also feared the very poor. Theirs was the characteristic doctrine of the 'industrious' people or the middling sort.

The Levellers' stand on religious toleration had been an important part of their appeal to other radical groups, but not all sectarians were prepared to go [as far] along the road towards accepting the secular state [without interest or control of religion]. They were not willing to make the full transition from Christian liberty and virtue to equal natural rights. The loss of support among leaders of the sectarian community was extremely serious for the Levellers. As early as the autumn of 1647, although the movement had already gained the allegiance of many individual sectarians and much organisational help from some of the gathered churches in London ... the enemies of the Levellers in the 'generality of congregations' publicly declared themselves. *A Declaration by Congregational societies in and about the City of London* argued against the Levellers alleged attempt to make all men 'equal in power'. It was supported by several pastors, like the Baptists' William Kiffin and Hanserd Knollys whom Lilburne had counted among his associates. ... Throughout 1648 Levellers and sectaries continued to make common cause [but] by 1649 a great rift had opened up between the Levellers and the Baptist pastors. The latter had decided to come to terms with the new regime in return for toleration, and formally dissociated themselves from the Levellers in March. Thereafter it was difficult for the Levellers ... to assume the role of political spokesmen for the godly. [In that matter the Grandees were always genuine rivals, both in London and, more importantly, in the army].

In their heyday, then, it is clear that the Levellers exhibited great flair in exciting the popular imagination and dramatising public events, but ideologically and organisationally their movement was severely flawed. The Levellers alienated key groups above them in the political and social structure (the ruling classes generally, the Grandees of the army, and the establishment radicals of the 'honest party'[the godly]). They failed to consolidate their appeal [in both religion and economic matters] to the middling orders whose interests they especially represented. They did not capitalise on the grievances of the middling peasants, remaining an essentially urban party. They also neglected those below them in the social scale. The Levellers both went too far and not far enough in their espousal of a new political and social order: in the end, their ideological and organisational base proved too narrow to achieve political success.

Source 67

From H. Shaw, *The Levellers*, pp. 95–8.

For two years the Leveller party was a major factor in politics and at one point – in May 1647 at Newmarket – it seemed about to seize control of the revolution altogether. But it failed. Outmanoeuvred on the debating floor and crushed in the field, it collapsed as dramatically as it had grown. At the time contemporaries thought that the Levellers had a good chance of success and hoped or feared accordingly. In retrospect, we can see that their importance was over-estimated. The reasons for their failure were numerous. ...

In the first place, the strength of the Levellers was something of an illusion. It is true that they exerted pressure on the Independents ... but there were other pressures forcing the Grandees to the left. The duplicity of the king, the interference of the Scots and the reactionary policies of the English Presbyterians acted just as potently. ... The Levellers never dictated events; their influence grew or diminished according to the prevailing political situation. [They] flourished in the chronic political instability and economic hardship of the years 1647–9. The negotiating quadrilateral of King, Presbyterians, Scots and Grandees and the series of disastrous harvests together formed ideal conditions for radical agitation. But these did not last. The rule of the Rump after the death of the king may have been arbitrary and corrupt, but it provided efficient government. ...

There were fundamental weaknesses in the Leveller programme. It demanded at once too much and too little. Too little in that it offered real advantages to only a small proportion of the population; too much in that it used such revolutionary language and was aimed in so many directions that all vested interests clung together for protection. ... In any case, the Levellers tended to be preoccupied with constitutional theories which were too subtle for popular consumption. ... Nor did [they] enjoy the unity they needed to achieve greater success. ... [Too many of their supporters had specific grievances to pursue rather than embracing the Leveller vision as a whole]. Such disparate aims were reflected in a lack of coordination at times of crisis.

The Levellers real failure was in the army. The measure of importance they achieved depended almost entirely on their influence in the New Model. ... But from an early stage Cromwell discovered that respect for traditional social leadership, backed by the spirit of loyalty created in war, was more potent than the revolutionary propaganda permeating the ranks. ... [But] in the last analysis, the Levellers' failure was due to their inability to stir the lower classes to action on their own behalf. This may be explained partly by the shortcomings in their programme and partly by the simple physical problems of communication in the seventeenth century. But even if these had been overcome, it is very doubtful whether the supporters needed would have been forthcoming. The vast bulk of the population was socially conservative and politically apathetic. ... The Levellers did their best to counteract this political illiteracy with their petitions, designed to inform and educate as well as to elicit immediate support. ... In London and the army, where unique conditions prevailed, they achieved temporary success; elsewhere the Leveller dream was shared by too few and feared by too many.

Evaluating your explanation

The sources above have enabled you to develop an explanation of Leveller failure, in which by considering the role of conditional and contingent factors, and by defining what you are explaining in order to establish primary and second order issues, you will have been able to attribute relative importance to the different factors that you have discovered. This process, however, can be further developed by evaluating your explanation in order to highlight certain factors as crucial. In Unit 3.1 you utilised a comparative explanation for this, but the issues surrounding the Levellers lend themselves more naturally to the use of counterfactual explanation or the consideration of possible alternative outcomes. This is often used in explaining actions and decisions – considering what other options were available in a given historical situation, and explaining why these were not chosen in order to emphasise the advantages of, or reasons for, a particular decision or a particular action which was actually taken. Counterfactual explanation can, however, be equally effective in evaluating explanations of events – what we need to ask is whether any other outcome to those events was possible.

The question of why the Levellers failed has already raised the issue of whether this failure was more or less inevitable, given the strength of the conditional factors working against them. We can therefore naturally raise the question: *Could the Levellers have succeeded?* In other words, was any other outcome historically possible (i.e. possible in the conditions that existed at the time). This will then lead us to consider how they could have succeeded, or what would have had to be different to enable them to succeed. To establish a new constitution they needed to persuade parliament to accept it, but given the nature and attitudes of MPs, this was not a realistic possibility. Therefore they had to establish a power base from which to force Parliament to act, or to replace it. The two possible power bases available in 1646–9 were:

(1) the people themselves,
       or
(2) the army.

This, then, allows three other historically possible outcomes to Leveller activities:

(1) they could have brought about a popular revolution;
(2) they could have taken control of the army; or
(3) they could have persuaded the army leaders to act for or with them.

If we consider these in turn, and use our knowledge of the situation to determine what factors prevented any of these outcomes from occurring, we will have some indication of which factors were of particular importance in denying the Levellers success. We can then apply this back to the actual historical issue, the failure of the Levellers, in order to highlight which of the factors in our explanation seem to have been of crucial importance in the eventual outcome.

Question

4. (a) Explain whether, and how, the Levellers could have succeeded in their political and religious objectives.

    (b) Explain why this did not occur.

    (c) How does this help to explain why they failed?

UNIT 3.3

THE RANTERS: MYTH OR REALITY?

Who were the Ranters?

The Ranters came to public attention in the summer of 1650, in connection with the passing of a new Blasphemy Act, and in a period of concern about the beliefs and behaviour of the 'enthusiastic' radical groups which seemed to have multiplied since the execution of the king in 1649. In the spring of 1649, as the Leveller movement began to disintegrate, came news of the Digger experiment in Surrey. This lasted approximately one year, being suppressed in April 1650. The millenarian mood of the 1640s had been intensified, and eccentric visions of a new earth as well as a new heaven had been openly expressed. Amid general concern that new measures of control were required, the House of Commons appointed a committee 'to consider of a Way for suppression of the obscene, licentious and impious Practices used by Persons under pretence of Liberty, Religion, or otherwise'. No specific groups or persons were named, but a week later, on 21 June 1650, the committee reported on 'the several abominable Practices of a Sect called Ranters' and was instructed to prepare a Bill for suppressing such activities. This was passed by the House as the Blasphemy Act on 9 August 1650, specifying as punishable the beliefs and practices associated with Ranterism as well as many others. In the following months the leaders and many other Ranters were arrested, imprisoned, and forced to repudiate their beliefs. By early 1651 the movement seems to have been broken, although scattered references to Ranters and more frequent references to Ranter behaviour continued for some years thereafter.

It is difficult to determine how long the Ranters had been in existence before this. One of their leading figures, Joseph Salmon, had published, as early as 1647, a pamphlet entitled, *Anti-Christ in Man*, in which he stated that the devil existed within humans rather than as a separate person and implied that Christ also did so. While the work cannot be described as a Ranter pamphlet, it may suggest that by 1650 Salmon's ideas had been moving in that direction for some time. In 1649 Abiezer Coppe, undeniably a Ranter leader, published *A Fiery Flying Roll*, while Salmon's *A Rout, A Rout*, published in the same year, talks of the death of God. Organised activities of a sect called Ranters do not appear until 1650, when, according to J.F. McGregor, 'Throughout 1650 the catchpenny news-books were filled with tales of Ranter orgies.' Most of the Ranter publications, particularly those expounding their doctrines, seem to have been published in that year, while the surviving anti-Ranter tracts which detail their scandalous behaviour belong mainly to the autumn and winter of 1650–1. In 1651 Coppe petitioned parliament from prison, on behalf of himself, his suffering wife and innocent children, before publishing a repudiation of Ranter beliefs. It therefore seems reasonable to conclude that the Ranter movement, in the sense of any organised group with regular meetings, lasted little more than a year and quite possibly less.

The problems involved in defining the Ranters illustrate a wider difficulty in dealing with any of the 'enthusiastic' radical sects. The core of enthusiasm was that God spoke directly to the individual in his head and heart. Professions of faith, church practice and organisation, concepts of membership, all took second place to individual experience and individual conviction. This is true of the so-called Seekers, even of the early Quakers, and certainly of the many individuals who followed their own spiritual path in and through a number of sects and groups. To add to the problem, while each recognised sect can be said to have adopted its own particular combination of beliefs and its own distinctive interpretations, many of these beliefs overlapped. The Ranters believed that God existed within man – as did Winstanley the Digger, as did the Quakers. The Ranters believed that God existed within Nature – as did the scientist Robert Boyle, although he would not have interpreted it in the same way nor drawn the same conclusions. Moreover, ideas took time to develop, and different men (and women) might well start off in a similar direction, appear to think alike at a certain point, yet end up in very different places. The period of Civil War and Interregnum was one of philosophical, theological and intellectual exploration, and a number of ideas developed or spread in forms that were held by different people in different versions and with different implications.

Your study of radicalism in Unit 3.1 has introduced you to the broad range of developments, but of these, three are of particular importance in a study of the Ranters. To understand the Ranters it is necessary to have some knowledge of these ideas, but also to be aware that not everyone who expressed them was a Ranter and that not every Ranter accepted them all with the same commitment or intensity.

1. Millenarianism

Some form of millenarian expectation was common to many Protestants. The Bible told of the struggle between Christ and Antichrist, who had been identified with the Pope, and hence the Protestant Reformation was seen to herald the final phase of the struggle. Many orthodox Puritans believed that England had been chosen to play a particular role in this struggle, and that the overthrow of Charles had been a necessary step to enable this. After the king's execution, millenarian intensity increased, and as with every belief, different interpretations appeared. Religious radicals tended to be influenced by the writings of an influential twelfth-century thinker, Joachim of Fiore. He divided history into three ages: the age of the Father was dominated by the Old Testament and its law, and ran from the Fall of Adam to the Death of Christ; the age of the Son was governed by Christ's message, as expounded in the New Testament, and offered man the possibility of salvation or perfection in heaven; the Third Age, the age of the Spirit, was the time when man could attain perfection, or freedom from sin, on earth. God had partly revealed himself in Scripture, but during the Third Age he would do so in a more direct way. For some, this Third Age could not begin until Christ returned to earth, but many of the radicals, influenced by the momentous events of the 1640s, believed that it had begun and that Christ would return in person at the end. Hence some believed that man could now escape sin and attain perfection. Existing Churches and religious practices belonged to the Second Age, and were therefore seen as dark formal constraints upon the enlightened. Scripture remained a useful guide, as interpreted by the enlightened, but had no authority over them.

A variation of this was accepted by followers of Lodowick Muggleton and John Reeve. They believed that Reeve and Muggleton were God's new prophets; God had given them power, or his Commission, in the Third Age, and they had the power to recognise the damned and pronounce damnation. Hence the group came to be known as Muggletonians.

2. Antinomianism

Antinomianism arose from the Calvinist idea of Predestination: that some, the elect, were destined to be saved. This could work on people's attitudes in two ways. It could lead to endless anxiety as to whether one was chosen, and hence to very moral behaviour as a means of reassurance. This was the conventional interpretation, encouraged by the Puritan Churches. On the other hand, it could lead to the conviction that, if God had chosen to save an individual, then that individual's behaviour made no difference. The individual had no choice, and could not influence the decision. This was, in a sense, a logical conclusion to draw from the common Calvinist assertion that people could not *earn* salvation by what they did – it came as a free gift from God. While most people would take for granted that 'saints' would behave in a conventionally moral way, a minority who were carried away by the heady excitement of the times and of their own notions, could logically reverse the argument – that 'saints' could not lose what God chose to give them. It was not a matter of any crude licence to sin. Rather, it was a conviction that through faith and God's freely-given grace, the elect were freed from ordinary moral laws. What would be sin in others was no sin in them.

There were a number of different forms that antinomianism could take. It could be a belief about doctrine, a confidence in salvation, without any effect on behaviour. Alternatively it could be 'practical antinomianism', in which case people behaved as if they need obey no moral law. Practical antinomians could be Calvinists, seeing themselves as an exclusive group and anxious to demonstrate their membership, or they could base their beliefs on a complete rejection of Calvinism, believing that Christ's sacrifice on the cross had atoned for *all* sins and created a state of 'universal grace'. What was important for those who sought to follow Christ was to recognise that this state existed, and to behave accordingly. Sin was something in the mind, and one way of freeing oneself from it was to carry out 'sinful' acts in the consciousness that, because the spirit was pure, they were no sin. This could even be seen as a duty – a demonstration that the individual had recognised and accepted Christ's gift.

3. Pantheism

Pantheism was the belief that God existed in everything, including plants, animals and the earth, and also in thoughts and actions. Pantheism had many respectable guises, since it came from the orthodox Christian belief that the universe was God's creation. Early scientists like Newton and

Boyle studied the natural world in the belief that knowledge of its laws and structures would help them to know and understand God's will and purpose in the same way as the Scriptures did. However, it could also lead to a form of antinomianism. If God created everything, then he created 'sin' as well as goodness, sinners as well as saints. If the universe is good because it was the work of God, then nothing in it can be 'bad', including things which people mistakenly call sin. If God is in everything, then he is in the sinner as well as the godly – indeed, some argued that to know God fully and to be fully a part of God, it was necessary to act out sin as well as good works.

The purpose of this unit is to find out what the phenomenon of Ranterism, which so shocked and outraged contemporaries, actually meant. Who were the Ranters? What sort of people were they? What did they believe? What were they seeking to achieve? How widespread were they? Historians have provided different, and sometimes contradictory, answers to these questions. In some cases this occurs because they are trying to answer different questions, but debates also arise because of the nature of the sources with which they have to work. This is the case in many historical issues, but the Ranters provide a particularly good example of the complexities that may arise in using historical sources and the ways in which they have to be addressed. Therefore a second purpose is to consider and demonstrate the interpretation of sources, the problems that arise, and the extent and weight of conclusions that different sources can be expected to bear.

The unit is divided into three parts. Part one provides a number of contemporary sources which you will be asked to study in order to establish some preliminary conclusions about the Ranters. As always, you should treat these sources as a set, cross-referencing between them, and interpret them in context. For part one this context will consist of your general awareness of radical ideas and behaviour, and your knowledge of the events of the period.

Historical sources are not, however, all of the same kind. In deciding how much reliance can be placed upon a particular source, how definite or tentative are the conclusions that we can draw from it, it is necessary to know the conditions in which it was written, the purposes for which it was to be used and concepts that lay behind it. Part two, therefore, gives you more information about the sources, their authors and the context in which they were created, in order that you can develop and refine your conclusions. Finally, part three provides examples

of what historians have made of the Ranters, and allows you to adjudicate between various explanations and develop your own.

The Ranters in contemporary sources

Questions

Use Sources 68–76 to answer Questions 1–4. The sources were all written by individuals who were considered by contemporaries and/or by historians to be Ranters.

1. Who were the Ranters?

2. What did they believe:

    (a) about God, sin and human morality?

    (b) about politics and government?

    (c) about social and economic life?

3. Did Ranterism amount to:

    (a) a number of isolated individuals?

    (b) a loose-knit group?

    (c) a sect?

    (d) a broad religious or social movement?

4. How certain of your conclusions can you be on the basis of these sources?

Source 68

From Jacob Bauthumley, *The Light and dark sides of God, Or a plain and brief Discourse of the Light side (God, Heaven and Earth) The Dark side (Devil, Sin and Hell)*, 1650.

O God, what shall I say thou art, when thou canst not be named? What shall I speak of thee … ? For if I say I see thee, it is nothing but thy seeing of thyself;. … If I say I know thee, that is no other but the knowledge of thyself. …

[For] I see that God is in all creatures, Man and Beast, Fish and Fowl, and every green thing, from the highest Cedar to the Ivy on the wall; and that God is the life and being of them all. …

And God loves the Being of all creatures, yea, all men are alike to him. … Some live in the light side of God and some in the dark side; but in respect of God, light and darkness are all one to him. …

Sin is properly the dark side of God, which is mere [de]privation of light. … Sin itself doth as well fall in compliance with the glory of God, as well as that which we call grace and goodness; for sin abounds that grace may abound much more. … [The] reason why we call some men wicked and some godly is not anything in men; [only that] the divine Being appears more gloriously in one than in the other.

Source 69

From Joseph Salmon, *Anti-Christ in Man*, 1647.

[The true Christian] is not he that believeth the history [Bible]; but he that by the power of the spirit believes all this history to be verified [proved true] in the mystery. ... the history is Christ for us, the mystery is Christ in us. ...

Thou needest not to go to Rome, Canterbury or Westminster, but thou mayst find that Anti-Christ in thee, denying Jesus Christ to be come in thy flesh. ... Thou art therefore to expect Jesus to come to judgement in thee, and the end of the world to be in thee. ... This last day, this spiritual appearance of Christ in men and women, is the very origin of all these commotions that are amongst us ... because the last day dawns and the star of glory is risen more in one than in another.

Source 70

From Laurence Clarkson, *A Single Eye*, 1650.

Sin hath its conception only in the imagination. ... Consider what act soever, yea, though it be the act of swearing, drunkenness, adultery and theft; yet these acts simply, yea nakedly, as acts are nothing distinct from the act of prayer and praises. Why dost thou wonder? Why art thou angry? They are all one in themselves; no more holiness, no more purity in the one than the other. ...

To that man that so esteemeth one act unclean, to him it is unclean; as saith the History [Bible] there is nothing unclean of itself but to him that esteemeth it unclean. ...

No matter what Scripture, Saints or Churches say, if that within thee doth not condemn thee, thou shalt not be condemned; for saith the History, Out of thine own mouth, not another's, will I judge thee ... [Luke 19:22].

Source 71

From Laurence Clarkson, *The Lost Sheep Found*, 1660. This is a spiritual autobiography published by Clarkson in 1660, after he had renounced his Ranter beliefs. In 1650 Clarkson was already a well-known preacher, who had previously been associated with a variety of separatist groups.

A former friend of mine asked me if I heard ... of a people called My One Flesh? I said no, what was their opinion and how should I speak with any of them? Then she directed me to Giles Calvert [a radical printer]. ... So coming to Calvert and making enquiry after such a people, he was afraid I came to betray them, but exchanging a few words in the height of my language, he was much affected and satisfied [that] I was a friend of theirs; so he wrote me a note to Mr Brush, and the effect thereof was, [that] the bearer hereof is a man of the greatest light I ever yet heard speak, ... so to Mr Brush I

went and presented this note; which he perused, so bid me come in, and told me if I had come a little sooner I might have seen Mr Coppe. ...

Now observe, at this time my judgement was this; that there was no man could be freed from sin till he had acted that so-called sin as no sin; this a certain time had been burning within me, yet [I] durst not reveal it to any, in that I thought none was able to receive it; and a great desire I had to make trial, whether I should be troubled or satisfied therein. ...

On the day appointed I found Mr Brush, Mr Rawlinson, Mr Goldsmith with Mary Lake and some four more: now Mary Lake was the chief speaker [and] her discourse was something agreeable, but not so high as was in me experienced, and what I then knew with boldness declared ... [Clarkson seems to be suggesting that he was moved by some inner spirit]; so with many more words I affirmed that there was no sin, but as man esteemed it sin, and therefore none can be free from sin till in purity it be acted as no sin; for I judged it pure to me which to a dark understanding was impure, for to the pure all things, yea all acts, were pure; thus making the Scripture a writing of wax [distorting it], I pleaded the words of Paul, That I know and am persuaded by the Lord Jesus, *that there was nothing unclean but as man esteemed it*, unfolding [explaining] that was intended [to apply to] all acts as well as meats and drinks, and therefore till you can lie with all women as one woman, and not judge it sin, you can do nothing but sin: ... at which Mr Rawlinson was much taken, and Sarah Kullin being then present, did invite me to make trial of what I had expressed, so as I take it; after we parted she invited me to Mr Wats in Rood Lane, where was one or two more like herself and ... lay with me that night: now against next Sunday it was noised abroad what a rare man of knowledge was to speak at Mr Brush's; at which day there was a great company of men and women, both young and old, and so from day to day increased. ...

I was moved to write to the world what my principle was, so brought to public view a book called *A Single Eye*, so that men and women came from many parts to see my face and hear my knowledge ... being restless till they were made free as we then called it. Now I being, as they said, Captain of the Rant, I had most of the principle women came to my lodging for knowledge, which was then called the Head-Quarters. Now in the height of this ranting I was made still careful for moneys for my wife, only my body was given to other women: so our company increased, wanted for nothing that heart could desire, but at last it ... began to be a public reproach, [so] I broke up my quarters and went into the country to my wife, where I had by the way disciples plenty. ...

There ... was no small pleasure and delight in praising ... what great and glorious things the Lord had done in bringing us out of bondage, to the perfect liberty of the sons of God. ... God had made all things good, so nothing evil but as man judged it; for I apprehended there was no such thing as theft, cheat, or a lie, but as man made it so: for if the creature had brought this world into [no] propriety [property], as Mine and Thine, there had been no such title as theft, cheat, or a lie. ...

This I conceived, as I knew not what I was before I came into being [was born], so for ever after I should know nothing after [I die]; but even as a stream from the ocean is distinct in itself while it is a stream, but when returned to the ocean is therein swallowed and becomes one with the ocean, so the spirit of man while in the body is distinct from God, but when death comes returns to God and becomes one with God, yea God itself; yet notwithstanding this, I had sometimes a relenting light in my soul, fearing this should not be so ... but ... then a cup of Wine would wash away this doubt.

Source 72

From Abiezer Coppe, *A Fiery Flying Roll*, 1649.

Contents:

Chap. 2. Several new, strange, yet seasonable and good advice and wholesome admonitions, and the last warning to the great one, as from the Lord.

Chap. 3. Several dismal, doleful cries and outcries ... and how the King of Kings, the King of heaven charges the great ones of the earth.

Chap. 4. How the Judge of heaven and earth, who judgeth righteous judgement, passeth sentence against all those great ones, who like sturdy oaks and tall cedars will not bow, and how he intends to break them and blow them up by the roots. ...

Chap. 6. A terrible word and fatal blow from the Lord upon the gathered churches, who pretend most for God, yet defy the Almighty more than the vilest.

Source 73

From Abiezer Coppe, *A Fiery Flying Roll*, and *A Second Fiery Flying Roll*, 1649.

Chap. VI ... Thus saith the Lord; Kings, princes, Lords, great ones must bow to the poorest peasants; rich men must stoop to poor rogues, else they'll rue for it. ...

It is but yet a very little while; and you shall not say that aught you possess is your own ... and the strongest, yea the seemingly purest, propriety [ownership] which may most plead privilege and Prerogative from Scripture and carnal reason, shall be confounded ... into community and universality. And there's a most glorious design in it; and equality, community and universal love shall be, in request to the utter confounding of abominable pride, murder, hypocrisy, tyranny and oppression. ...

Chap. VII ... Howl, howl ye nobles, howl honourable, howl ye rich men for the miseries that are coming upon you. For our parts, we that hear the Apostle preach, will also have all things common; neither will we call anything we have, our own.

Source 74

From Joseph Salmon, *A Rout, a Rout.*, 1649.

[The Army generals are] the rod of God ... In this day of the Lord's wrath you strike through King, gentry and nobility; they all fall before you. ... [Yet] the Lord will ere long cast his rod into the fire of burning and destruction. It will be a sweet destruction, wait for it. [Those who cling to the sword to defend their liberty] are shut up in a darkness; ... you fear the world and they are afraid of you. [But soon] the whole edifice of this swordly power shall be annihilated ...

Source 75

From *A Justification of the Mad Crew*, anonymous pamphlet, 1650.

A Justification of the Mad Crew in their ways and principles
or
The Madness and Weakness of God in Man proved Wisdom and Strength

The immutable God (whom the nations and kindreds of the Earth, Churches and societies, because they know him not have not worshipped) is clearly manifesting the earth to be his foot-stool, and the heavens his throne, that every creature that moves in the earth and under the earth, in the sea and in the firmament above, is the seat of God, contains him, hugs him, embraces him, nay is really and truly God, even the living God: that ... he loves all sweetly, pouring out himself in and upon all, making all at peace with him, bowing and serving him, that the devil and he are one, and that the devil is but a part of God's backsides, which terrifies because of the curtain, that he sports and feasts himself in swearing, drinking, whoring, as when he is holy, just and good; that the holiness of man and unholiness of man are both one to him; that he loves and delights in one as well as the other: that the sons of God when they eat, eat God, and when they drink, drink God ...

1. Justified first in their Name.
They are named the mad crew: ... mad, so was David accounted ... so was Lot in his time, so was Paul a madman ... so was Christ a devil. ... It is a common thing for God in the many and several appearances of himself to be called of men, mad, a fool, a drunkard, a vain person ...

2. Justified in their Principles.
That there is but one God. ...
That this one God is served and gloriously worshipped in all, both things and persons. ...
That Good and Evil are both joined hand in hand. ...
That God is no respecter of persons. ...
That the righteous shall never be saved, that the Godly shall go to Hell, the Wicked to Heaven. ...
That they have overcome death, and mortality is in them swallowed up into immortality. ...
That being in Heaven (the light, glory and perfection of God) these neither marry nor are given in marriage. ...

They hold all things common and truly enjoy all things in common. …
That their counsel shall stand and they will do all their pleasure.

The Postscript, directed to all Nations

… O ye hypocrites … I hear your inward blaspheming and cursing me, that am risen up a holy generation of men, that can sin no more. … Ye Churches, ye Seekers are the veriest devils and prophanest wretches in the world; you have sworn, committed adultery before me, in your hearts, time after time; yea thou Preacher and thou great Prophet, I have seen thee (though thy neighbours never did) lie with twenty women in one night, nay in one hour, nay in one moment, in thy thoughts and desires. I could tell you of your cheating … the people in your shops, and your thieving and lying, and this you can digest [live with] because no eye sees you , and because of the great gain accruing thereby … But I spare you until the day which is at the very doors, that shall burn as an oven, and all the proud and all that do wickedly shall be burnt up, and as fuel to the fire.

Source 76

From Abiezer Coppe, *Copp's Return to the Wayes of Truth,* 1651.

The contents

I. The Preface or Epistle Dedicatory, wherein is hinted what the Author has been and now is.
II. The Several Errors protested against:
1. That there is no sin.
2. That there is no God.
3. That Man, or the mere creature, is very God.
4. That God is in man, or in the creature and nowhere else.
5. That Cursing and Swearing is no sin.
6. That Adultery and Fornication is no sin.
7. That Community of wives is lawful.

All which you may find in the Pages where the contrary Truths are asserted. …

Now will I lay the Axe to the root of the tree, even to this grand Error, This:

I. **Error** That there is no sin.
Concerning this Error,
1. I disown, detest and protest against it.
2. I assert and prove the contrary.
I. **Assertion** I assert and prove, that there is sin:
For, there is not a just man upon Earth, that doth good, and sinned not, as it is written, (Ecclesiast: 7. 20) …
We, our Kings, our Rulers, our Priests, our Judges,
All have sinned, and gone astray,
Do sin, are sinners. …
Woe be to the inhabitants of the Earth –
That Earth is full of sin,
There is sin, sin with a witness. …

IV. Error That God is in man, or in the creature only, and nowhere else. Concerning this Error,
1. I utterly disown, detest and protest against it. …
3. I assert the very truth, which is contrary to this error
IV. Assertion That God is not confirmed in man, or in the creature only, but is omnipresent, or everywhere. …
The Darkness and the Light are both alike to thee,
He is in Heaven, Earth, Sea, Hell. …
He is near and afar off, … He filleth all things, all places.
Can you have any more than all?

Question

5. Your conclusions so far are based on the evidence provided by the Ranters themselves. Sources 77–88 below are taken from anti-Ranter tracts and Quarter Sessions records, and are largely hostile views. Read these sources, and review your answers to Questions 1–4 in the light of any new evidence that they provide.

Source 77

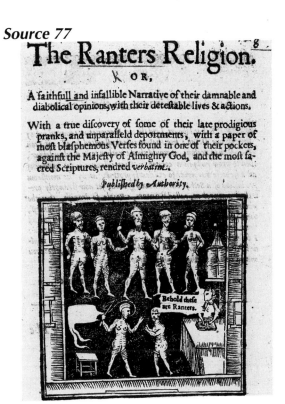

Title page from The Ranters Religion, *1650*

Source 78

From *The Ranters Religion,* 1650.

An Advertisement to the Reader

He that labours … is tempted but by one Devil; he that is idle is assaulted by all … That idleness is the mother of all mischief was never so evidently proved as by the monstrous production of a Sect, but of novel growth, yet now strangely prevalent amongst us, called Ranters, a people so dronish, that the whole course of their lives is but one continued Scene of Sottishness, their gestures filthy, their words obscene, and blasphemous, and all their deeds which they wretchedly glory in, impious and horrid; I beseech thee, good Reader, to peruse this pamphlet … with a will to know such filthiness, that if thou mayest be incited the more heartily to abominate it. …

These Ranters … affirm that God is so far from being offended at the crying sins of drunkenness, swearing, blaspheming, adultery, etc. that he is well pleased therewith, and that (O strange and horrid impiety!) it is the only way of serving him aright … these licentious Sciolists [people who have only a superficial knowledge] affirm that each whimsey … whether to swear, to whore, yea to commit incest or buggery, is of God, and proceeds from him; he being the author, Orderer, and origin of it; a doctrine which the very Devils sure would tremble to hear.

These monsters … make the Almighty not only the Countenancer, which but to imagine is damnable blasphemy, but the efficient cause of sin, and dare impiously to affirm, that that man who tipples deepest, swears the frequentest, commits Adultery, Incest or Buggery the oftenest, blasphemes the impudentest, and perpetrates the most notorious crimes with the highest hand, and rigidest resolution, is the dearest darling to Heaven.

The Heads of their damnable Errors and horrid Blasphemies.

1. They believe (and these are the wisest sort of them) that a Resurrection is possible, and that there may be a Restitution of our bodies, but then they say that stars and planets … are the only causes of it. …
2. They affirm that all women ought to be in common, and when they are assembled all together (this is a known truth) they first entertain one another, the men those of their own sex, and the women their fellow females, with horrid oaths and execrations; then they fall to boozing and drink deep healths (Oh cursed caitiffs! [despicable people]) to their brother God, and their brother Devil; then being well heated with liquor, each brother takes his she-otter upon his knee, and the word (spoken in derision of the sacred Writ) being given, viz. *Increase and Multiply*, they fall to their lascivious embraces with a joint motion, etc.
3. … Their opinion about resurrection of the body is so strange, and withal so absurd, that I must by no means omit to recite it.
4. They tell you there is a certain little bone in every man's back that shall never be subject to any putrefaction, and this bone, say they, at the last day shall be mollified and softened by a Dew from Heaven, and it shall swell having the nature of leaven, and it shall diffuse its virtue to the collecting of all the dust that belongs to its own body, and prepare it for resurrection.
5. They maintain, that to have their women in common

is their Christian liberty, and very prettily, indeed la, that the sister among them who can make the beast with two backs the most strenuously, viz. entertain most men the longest and the oftenest, has a sufficient canonization for a saint triumphant. This they frequently, and with much fervency affirm.

These Beasts of Ephesus do not tremble over a pint pot, or in the parenthesis of a whiff of tobacco, to vaunt blasphemously their dissatisfaction in matters of religion, and … send challenges to reason, to prove there is a God, and the scriptures are but a mere romance …

One of these Roysters sitting over his cups (with the rest of his companions) evacuating wind backwards, used this blasphemous expression, *let everything that has breath, praise the Lord.*

Another of them taking a piece of boiled beef betwixt his hands, and tearing it in pieces, gave part thereof to one of his companions using these words (in derision of the blessed sacrament) *the body and blood of our lord Jesus Christ.*

A she-Ranter said openly in the hearing of many (a friend of mine accidentally one of them) that she should think herself a happy woman, and should esteem herself a superlative servant of Gods, if any man would accompany with her carnally in the open market place.

Source 79

From *The Routing of Ranters*, 19 November 1650.

The Ranters Ranting

or

A true Relation of a sort of People called Ranters, with some of their abominable and wicked carriages, and behaviour at their private meetings.

I shall in the first place give you, my friends, a brief character of a sort of people … newly sprung up among us, called Ranters, alias Coppanites, or Claxtonions … seducing men and women to commit all manner of mad and desperate wickedness …

The chief ringleaders of this viperous generation, are one Copp and Claxton … [This] Copp being lately brought before a committee to be examined, feigned himself mad, used strange kind of uncouth behaviour, throwing nutshells and other things about the room, and talked to himself when questions were put to him, which some thought to be God's just judgement on him, and others were of the opinion that … he merely acted the part which at length will no way stand him in stead.

[Ranters met recently near] White Chappel: where after a time they were discovered by officers of the place, who with a guard repaired to the house where they were: and to the end that none might make an escape, the business was carried out with such secrecy, that it was not known to others till they came to the door … ; which the officers had no sooner entered, but they found some of these lascivious openly satisfying their lusts. Amongst this company was … Claxton, … who with undaunted boldness and audacious carriage spoke to the officers, that came with authority to apprehend them, to this effect.

Gentlemen, I perceive you have come to seize us, your fellow creatures, for what cause I know not, I pray use no violence or terrify ... those of our fellow creatures here, that are of a weak and tender constitution: if we have offended the law, we shall ... willingly submit to be tried by it. And taking up his cloak he said, Gentlemen, ... I am ready to go along with you. And forth he went ... ; and as the others were coming forth (about thirty in number), he framed an excuse to return back again to the house, pretending he had left something of great use behind him, and so escaped away at the back door; but is re-taken, and at this day in prison.

Copp (when he was fitter to have gone to bed and slept, than to have spoken in a public place) bestowed an hours time in belching forth imprecations, curses, and other such like stuff, as is not fit to be once named among Christians: and when he perceived that he should be called to answer for the wicked blasphemies that he had uttered at sundry times, took two of his she-disciples, and went to the city of Coventry, where it was soon dispersed abroad, that he commonly lay in bed with two women at a time: whereof he being soberly admonished by an officer of the army, he replied, that it was his liberty, and he might use it. With many other speeches to justify himself in his ungodly practices, for which he was apprehended and brought up to London, and by the magistrate committed to Newgate.

Source 80

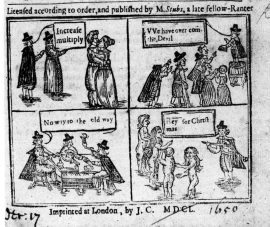

Title page from Gilbert Roulston, The Ranters Bible, 9 December 1650

Source 81

Title page from M. Stubbs, The Ranters Declaration, 16 December 1650

Source 82

Title page from Strange Newes from Newgate, 21 January 1651

Source 83

From Strange Newes from Newgate, 21 January 1651.

Strange Newes from the Old Bailey

The Proofs, Examinations, Declarations, Indictments and Conviction of the Ranters, at the sessions of Gaol-delivery, held in the Old Bailey, 18, 19 and 20 of this instant January. …

Two of the Ranters which were taken in More Lane, the first of November last, viz. Jo. Collins, and Tho. Reeve, were indicted upon the late act against blasphemy [under the Blasphemy Act, see Introduction]. …

[This] Collins, Reeves and others were sitting at a table, eating a piece of beef, one of them took it in his hand, tearing it asunder, said to the other, *this is the flesh of Christ, take it and eat.*

The other took a cup of ale and threw it into the chimney corner, saying, *There is the blood of Christ.* And … it was proved that one of these said, That he could go into the house of office, and make a God every morning, by easing of his body, and blowing through two pieces of tobacco pipes he said, *That was the breath of God.* …

There is one example of God's judgement upon an open and profane Ranter. … It is not more than three days since God's hand was stretched out in severe punishing of Kendall in Drury Lane. This Kendall was discoursing with a woman which he called his fellow-creature, and was persuading her to have his pleasure with her, and he said that there was no God or Devil, affirming that everything came by nature, &c. whereupon it is said that she gave her consent and appointed him a place where he should meet her.

When they had made this wicked compact and agreement together they parted with an intention to go two separate ways and meet again at the assigned place, but the man was no sooner gone from her, but he was suddenly struck dead in the place to the great amazement and astonishment of many beholders.

Source 84

From *The Ranters Monster*, 30 March 1652.

Strange and terrible news from Essex; being a true relation of the most impious life, and blasphemous action of one Mary Adams, who named herself the Virgin Mary and said she was conceived with child of the Holy Ghost: but being cast into prison, soon after she was delivered of the ugliest, ill-shapen monster that eyes ever beheld.

Source 85

Title page from The Ranters Monster, *30 March 1652*

Source 86

Title page from Samuel Tilsbury, Bloudy Newes from the North, *20 January 1651*

Source 87

THE DECLARATION OF JOHN ROBINS, the false Prophet, otherwise called the Shakers God, and Joshua Beck, and John King, the two false Disciples, with the rest of their Fellow-Creatures now prisoners in the New-prison at Clarkenwell : Delivered to divers of the Gentry and Citizens, who on Thursday, Friday, and Saturday last resorted thither to dispute with them : With their Citizens Proposals to the said John Robins, concerning his Opinion and Judgment, and his Answer thereunto : Together with his Prophesie of what is to come to pass this year, 1651 & the strange things revealed to him : his Religion, Principles, and Creed : as also his blasphemous Tenents, in attributing an inspiration from the Holy Ghost : with the manner of their Diet, and his Woe pronounced concerning all those that drink Ale. By G. H. an Eye-witness.

London, Printed by R. Wood, 1651.

Title page from G.H., The Declaration of John Robins, *2 June 1651*

Source 88

From Wiltshire Quarter Sessions, Great Roll, Easter 1656.

Indictment of William Bonds, Laycock, weaver: for saying at Laycock, 'that there was no God or power ruling above the planets, and that there was no Christ, but the scripture'; on 3rd March, 'that if the scriptures were made again that Tom Lampire [a husbandman of Melksham] would make as good a scripture as the bible: And there was neither Heaven nor Hell but in a man's own conscience for if he had a good fortune and lived well in the world that was Heaven and if he lived poor and miserable that was Hell and death itself, for then he would die like a cow or a horse'. Pleads not guilty; found guilty.

Indictment of Thomas Hibbard, Laycock, weaver: said on 1st January 1656:' that he … believed God was in all things, and if he was … drunk, God was drunk with him, and any sins he committed … God was the author of them all and committed those sins as well by his own power' …; on 3rd January 'would sell all religions for a jug of beer'. Pleads not guilty; found guilty.

Information of Harry Arnold, Cosham, gent.: W.B. said 'that there was no Hell and if there were any it was a grave … and as for God said he, that God was everywhere. … God was in the flagon, in this jug and everywhere, and that Christ saveth all, he would save him or else he would shit as good as Christ out of his arse … but he believed that God would save … every man'. Said this about twelve months ago.

The Ranters in context

The attention of historians was drawn to the Ranters by the publication of A.L. Morton's *The World of the Ranters*, in 1970. Studying the sources in the context of violent upheaval, radical enthusiasm and visions of a new earth as well as a new heaven, he found it quite possible to accept the truth of contemporary accounts ascribing eccentric behaviour and beliefs to the Ranters. Morton's interpretation was further supported by the work of other historians of radicalism such as Christopher Hill. In 1986, however, J.C. Davis published a study of Ranter sources entitled *Fear, Myth and History*, in which he challenged the accepted view. Based on a careful study of how and by whom the sources were produced, Davis's view was that many of them were unreliable and could not be accepted at face value, and that the Ranters were, in fact, a myth created by conservatives to justify a new policy of repression and restrictions on religious toleration. Referring to the general context of upheaval just as Morton did, Davis argued that this supported his view, in that it created the conservative fears that lay behind the policy; indeed, many conservatives may well have believed in the existence of Ranters – they were the creation of their own fears and concerns.

Davis's interpretation has, in turn, been challenged and a considerable debate has developed. While many historians do not accept the view that the Ranters were a myth, it is clear that the sources have to be carefully examined and that Ranter activities may well have been significantly exaggerated. What is also clear is that interpretation of the sources in context does not provide certainty in history, nor prevent disagreement and debate. Examining sources within their contemporary context informs and influences their interpretation – but the result nevertheless remains an interpretation. Reference to the context can be used to support and strengthen an argument and to demonstrate that the interpretation is justified – it cannot place the argument beyond challenge.

The sources which follow provide evidence of the context in which Ranterism – whatever it was – came into existence. They will enable you to review your own interpretation of the contemporary sources in order to strengthen, change or refine it. Sources 89–93 focus on the sources themselves and the conditions in which they were produced; sources 94–7 deal with radicalism and the nature of radical activity in this period, and sources 98–102 relate to conservative fears and reactions. You may also find it useful to refer back to the Introductory narrative and the summaries of radical activities provided in Unit 3.1.

Questions

6. Read Sources 89–102. In what ways might the evidence contained in these sources lead you to change your view of the meaning, significance or reliability of any or all of Sources 68–88?

7. Can any of sources 68–88 be interpreted in more than one way? If so, do sources 89–102 help to support or undermine one interpretation more than another?

8. On the basis of the sources interpreted in context, do you now regard the Ranters as

   (a) a myth?

   (b) isolated individuals?

   (c) a small group whose significance was exaggerated?

   (d) an important radical movement?

   (e) a symptom of social breakdown?

   (f) a combination of more than one of the above?

   Explain your choice.

Source 89

Seventeenth-century spiritual autobiography: Clarkson's *The Lost Sheep Found*. From J.C. Davis, *Fear, Myth and History* (Cambridge, 1986) pp. 64–5, 67–70 and 72.

In 1660 Clarkson published a work, *The Lost Sheep Found*, of which the first half is cast in an autobiographical frame. … To see any kind of autobiography, in this period or others, as essentially an accurate, factual narrative is to engage in a form of naivety. Far more is invariably going on than the simple recording of the facts of a life. Moreover, early modern biography and autobiography are loaded with rhetorical [there for effect], theatrical and polemical [debating] purposes and devices over which 'the facts' by no means necessarily predominate. Indeed, 'the facts' may be so subservient to the main purpose of the work as to permit fictional characters to emerge.

The Lost Sheep Found is a much more carefully crafted … work than has been generally allowed. Its immediate

context is a sequence of Muggletonian writings … which formed the basis of a bid for leadership of that sect by Laurence Clarkson. … The fundamental proposition is that the authority of the old Churches is spent, their time is over. But Clarkson no longer wants to accept the sectarian consequence that inner illumination or 'Reason' replaces the authority of institutional faith. The sects have also to be inadequate and all of this must lead towards the inevitability … of an authoritative Third Commission [see Introduction, Millenarianism]. … In fact, Clarkson had a polemical interest in emphasising the blackness of the principles of the Ranters … to show where the folly of reason might lead.

The object of the work is to follow a spiritual progress. … [Clarkson describes his progress from Anglicanism through Presbyterianism, Independency, antinomianism and Baptist beliefs, to a Seeker position. His journey through these stages is a consequence of his rejection of existing formal religious authority, and of reliance on individual reason.] We are wondering how far this process can go when Clarkson encounters the group 'My one flesh'. … The image of 'My one flesh' is by no means clear. In particular, we are not told what they believed before Clarkson joined them. Finally, nowhere in this section of the work is there any indication of the pre-existence of a Ranter group which Clarkson could be said to have joined.

Source 90

The nature of Ranter recantation. From N. Cohn, *The Pursuit of the Millennium* (Heinemann, 1962) pp. 333–4.

Faced with persecution many Ranters seem to have adopted a secret language and to have carried on … clandestine propaganda. After listening to the 'recantation sermon' preached by the Ranter Abiezer Coppe at Burford in September 1651, John Tickell, Minister of Abingdon, commented on these tactics. …

'They use to speak one thing and mean another. … Before the late Act against Ranters, they spake boldly, now they dare not. … It seems to me from what I have known of them, they will put themselves on all expressions, ways and windings, to keep themselves from being known, but to their own: you shall not know where to find them, so as to fasten on them, but their own shall know their meaning, and so may you when you have once got their Key. … They will first insinuate an interest in your affections, and then corrupt your judgements. They will smile upon you and cut your throat: use melting words, honeysweet, smooth as oil but full of poison.

Source 91

Contemporary authors and publishers of Ranter material. From J.C. Davis, *Fear, Myth and History*, pp. 108–9.

Most of these works were published anonymously, but almost wherever we begin a close investigation, we should uncover connections between them.

Let us begin with a named author about whom we can discover something. Gilbert Roulston, author of *The Ranters Bible* and a professed ex-Ranter, had been in the 1640s a hack royalist writer … bemoaning the rabble's incursion into politics. *The Ranters Bible* was printed by J.C., as was Samuel Tilbury's *Bloody News from the North*. … A printer of the same initials also printed J.M.'s *The Ranters Last Sermon*. There could be a further link here, through J.M., with *The Ranters Creed* printed by James Moxon. … J.C. also printed M. Stubbs's *The Ranters Declaration*, the woodcuts from which were re-used in G.H.'s *The Declaration of John Robins*. This G.H. may well have been the George Horton who published *The Ranters Monster* in 1652 and *The Black and Terrible Warning Piece* in 1653. There may then be links in terms of printing, publishing and material between at least six of the Ranter sensational pieces and with two others on the Robins phenomenon [John Robins claimed to be God and that his wife would give birth to a new Christ]. …

We can trace other possible links through printers if we begin with *The Routing of the Ranters* printed by B.A. *The Ranters Ranting*, published two weeks later and claiming dissatisfaction with *The Routing*, was printed by B. Alsop. B.A. also published *The Arraignment and Trial with a Declaration of the Ranters* a fortnight later. All three were adorned with crude woodcuts in a similar style. So was *Strange News from Newgate*, printed by B. Alsop in January 1651.

These two possible connections would account between them for ten out of the fifteen sensational Ranter works and two on the Robins phenomenon. The strong impression conveyed is of a small group of printers, publishers and writers eager to ride the Ranter sensation for all it was worth while it lasted. … [We also] need to bear in mind the range of interests involved in the promotion of the myth. It incorporates Grub Street [the sensational press], but also royalist journalists for whom the Ranters could … [personify] the … moral collapse that they had prophesied.

Source 92

The use of atheism and prodigies in contemporary portrayals of the Ranters. [A prodigy is anything that is a cause of wonder or amazement, especially something monstrous or abnormal.] From J.C. Davis, *Fear, Myth and History*, pp. 113–5, 118 and 123.

Powerful myths of deviance are, however revolutionary the situation, never entirely novel. They are made of materials ready to hand. … Part of their power is their … familiarity. … There is no doubt that the atheist is the key image in the make up of the Ranter … What had to be shown was how belief, given free rein and run to excess in enthusiasm, could lead to the same moral and social disorder as unbelief. … The atheist was, in fact, a kind of invented deviant. …

Most of the atheism literature of the early modern period was intended to confirm the godly in their beliefs and practices: 'the personification of ungodliness in an extreme form [was] a means of frightening the pious and encouraging them to show more clearly their allegiance to the opposite pole'. … In many ways the character of the atheist prefigured that of the Ranter. There was the same levity towards religious matters, the abuse of Scripture, scoffing at heaven and hell, and the same general moral laxity. …

The literature of prodigy and monstrosity, to which, in many ways, the sensational Ranter literature bears physical resemblance [was still available and popular in the seventeenth century]. Prodigy books were … a form of inversion … , teaching the natural by exposing the unnatural. The literature of religious inversion or excess readily fused with that of prodigy. Atheists were monsters and so were Ranters:

What age is this that we live in,
What monsters hath it bred;
Who, by their Acts, make Virtue, Sin;
And still the Foot the Head.

So bemoaned *Mercurius Elencticus*, a royalist newspaper to be linked with Samuel Shepherd, author of an anti-Ranter satire.

Source 93

The collapse of censorship. From C. Hill, The World Turned Upside Down (Penguin, 1975) p. 17.

During the brief years of extensive liberty of the press in England it may have been easier for eccentrics to get into print than ever before or since. Before 1641, and after 1660, there was strict censorship. In the intervening years of freedom, a printing press was a relatively cheap and portable piece of equipment. … [There was a] natural harmony … between Leveller writers, printers and hawkers of pamphlets, at a time when printing was a small man's occupation. Printers like George Calvert were prepared to run considerable risks to get radical works published. It may also have been that in a market flooded with printed matter there were sales advantages in calculated eccentricity.

Source 94

The explosion of ideas. From D. Underdown, *Pride's Purge* (OUP, 1971) p. 260.

Out of the multiplicity of sects, out of the excited chorus of political debate, voices were heard calling for absolute freedom. The Diggers repudiated the tyranny of private property, the Ranters the restraints of conventional morality. Zionism, vegetarianism, a dozen other modern 'isms' were in the air. The mad hatter of Chesham, Roger

Crab, reached the irreducible dietary minimum of dock leaves and grass at about the time he gave away all his worldly goods to the poor. During a sermon by Peter Sterry in the austere surroundings of Whitehall Chapel in 1652, a woman in the congregation stripped naked, with joyful cries of 'Welcome the resurrection!' All things were possible, the world was to be made new, the reign of King Jesus was just round the corner.

Yet the humanitarianism was peripheral, most of the militant language mere rhetoric, the exciting experiments confined to the furthest fringe of revolution.

Source 95

Ale-house society. From C. Hill, *Milton and the English Revolution* (Faber & Faber, 1977) pp. 97–8.

Taverns and ale-houses [were] centres of political information and organisation during the English Revolution. ... In 1641 religion was 'the common discourse and table-talk in every tavern and ale-house'. News-sheets were read aloud in taverns so that the illiterate could know what was going on: taverns were distribution centres for pamphlets and news-books. In the early forties information was disseminated to supporters of Parliament in London through 'daily tavern-clubs in each ward'. ... Baptists, Levellers, Ranters, Muggletonians, Quakers and the precursors of the Royal Society [scientists] all met in taverns. Men competed to make themselves famous in the society of taverns and ale-houses.

Source 96

Ranters in the local context: Wiltshire. From D. Underdown, *Revel, Riot and Rebellion* (OUP, 1985) pp. 249–50.

Evidence about Ranters in Wiltshire is more plentiful. ... Tobias Crisp, vicar of Brinkworth from 1627 to 1642, whose unorthodox views seem to have found ready listeners among the husbandmen and weavers of his and the adjoining parishes ... may have left a legacy on which others were later able to draw, for a few miles away at Langley Burrell another radical vicar, Thomas Webbe, established a small Ranter community in the 1650s. Webbe was popular, an enemy charged, with 'divers of the most ignorant parishioners' because of his refusal to collect tithes. He powdered and frizzled his hair, and combined elements of the old festive culture – music and mixed dancing – with an admiration for radicals like Lilburne and the Ranters Joseph Salmon and Abiezer Coppe. But few of the villagers were tempted to follow Webbe into the life of sexual freedom in which he engaged with his wife and companions. Only two or three families in Langley Burrell actually became Ranters, and most of the group were from outside the parish. ... The godly, and even many of the ungodly of the neighbourhood were outraged: Webbe accused the JPs of

prosecuting him for adultery only 'to gain applause amongst the multitude'. He was acquitted, but deprived of his living, after which the community broke up. There may have been other small Ranter groups at Bradford-on-Avon and Salisbury, and perhaps one in the clothing village of Laycock. ...

Heresies traceable to Ranter origins thus continued to surface occasionally, but the Ranters were never more than an isolated handful, and by 1653 they had been broken by persecution.

Source 97

Ranters in a radical context. From C. Hill, *The World Turned Upside Down*, pp. 179 and 203–4.

The view that there is no God but all things come by nature, which attracted George Fox in the early 1640s and was familiar to Muggleton and his circle in the early 1650s, was made specific by Laurence Clarkson, Jacob Bauthumley and other Ranters. In Winstanley and Joseph Salmon it took a more pantheistic form. 'The body of Christ,' Winstanley wrote, 'is where the Father is, in the earth, purifying the earth; and his spirit is entered into the whole creation, which is the heavenly glory where the Father dwells.' ... Joseph Salmon thought that 'God is that pure and perfect being in whom we all are, move and live; that secret blood, breath and life that silently courseth through the hidden veins and close arteries of the whole creation'. The content of the doctrine of either Winstanley or Salmon was equally destructive of any personal God. ...

It is very difficult to define what 'the Ranters' believed, as opposed to individuals who are called Ranters. The same is true to a lesser extent of Levellers or early Quakers; but the Levellers did issue programmatic statements, and the pamphlets of Fox and Nayler can be accepted as authoritative for the Quakers. There is no recognised leader or theoretician of the Ranters, and it is extremely doubtful whether there ever was a Ranter organisation. As so often in the history of radical movements, the name came into existence as a term of abuse.

There are very wide discrepancies between the theology of men like Salmon and Bauthumley, on the one hand, and the licentious practices of which rank and file Ranters were accused, though the ideas of Laurence Clarkson perhaps help to bridge the gap. The same is also true of the early Quakers, whom contemporaries long tended to lump together with the Ranters. There are two possible explanations for this last fact, and it is difficult to know which should weigh more heavily with us. On the one hand there is the unreasoning hostility of conservative critics, who believed that Ranter and Quaker ideas must lead to licentiousness and therefore assumed that they did; on the other hand there is the likelihood that many early rank and file Quakers had, in fact, not entirely shaken themselves free from Ranter ideas and practices. [Hill and some other historians have claimed that many Quaker converts in 1652–4 had previously been Ranters –

a debatable point which will be addressed more fully in Unit 3.4. His general point is valid, although he may over-estimate numbers.]

Source 98

The context of mainstream politics and religion. From D. Underdown, *Pride's Purge*, p. 275.

Most Rumpers obviously put the enforcement of a Puritan code of morality ahead of liberty. Several repressive acts were passed during the summer of 1650, including the strict Sabbath-observance law, the famous measure imposing the death penalty for adultery, and an act against unlawful swearing. More important, as it might be used to undermine religious toleration, was the act against blasphemy. Although milder than the Presbyterian measure of 1648, it was effective enough to deal with the Ranters' disturbing excesses, which were shocking to Presbyterians and Independents alike. The radicals succeeded in carrying minor amendments to the blasphemy and adultery bills. But these were small successes and scarcely affected the general trend towards repression in the summer of 1650. And the change of direction after [Cromwell's victory at] Dunbar was short lived. During the remainder of its life, the Rump made only one more gesture towards toleration; in June 1652 it voted that even recusants could be forced to attend Protestant worship against their consciences.

Source 99

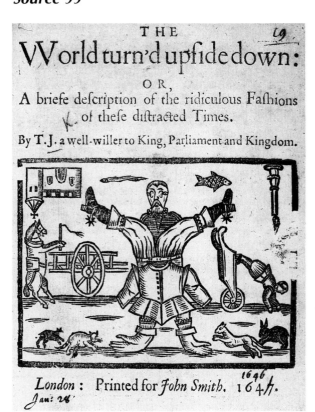

Contemporary Fears. The World Turned Upside Down.

Source 100

The Picture of an English Persecutor: *The theme of 'women on top' used as a basis for political satire*

Source 101

The radicals defeated. From C. Hill, *The experience of defeat: Milton and some contemporaries* (Faber & Faber, 1984) pp. 17–18.

The first defeat of the more extreme radicals came in and after 1649. Leveller leaders were arrested and imprisoned, Leveller-led mutinies in the army were suppressed, culminating in the total rout of mutinous regiments at Burford in May 1649. After that the Leveller leaders abandoned hope of winning control in the army and either subsided into the obscurity from which they had briefly emerged, or took to underground conspiracy, sometimes in conjunction with Royalists. The less numerous Diggers were dispersed in April–May 1650; Ranters were made to recant in 1650–51. Both groupings ceased to exist in any organised form.

Fifth Monarchists appeared strong in the army in 1653, when they collaborated in the dismissal of the Rump of the Long Parliament and its replacement by the Barebones Parliament. But they too had no effective organisation, and were divided in their aims. Very few dogs barked at the disappearance of the Rump or Barebones Parliament. Venner's tiny Fifth Monarchist group staged revolts in London in 1657 and 1661. But apart from their readiness to use violence, their programme differed little from those of other radicals.

Source 102

Patriarchy and the social order. From D. Underdown, 'The Taming of the Scold' in A. Fletcher and J. Stevenson (eds.), *Order and*

Disorder in Early Modern England (Cambridge, 1985) p. 116.

Fears of an impending breakdown of the social order have been common in many periods of history. At no time were they more widespread, more intense, than in early modern England: the 'crisis of order' detected by modern historians in the sixty years before the civil war accords with the perceptions of many people in that period. Among the causes and symptoms of the apparently growing instability were those now familiar problems of excessive population growth, inflation, land shortage, poverty and vagrancy, all of which have attracted the attention of recent scholars. There are those who, like Peter Laslett, stress the stability of English society throughout the entire pre-modern period, and dismiss the signs of tension as minor conflicts that exist in even the most smoothly functioning social system. Few contemporaries would have agreed with them. It could no longer be safely assumed that all Englishmen and women were bound together in the interlocking network of households and communities on which, according to the prevailing orthodoxy, stability depended. 'Was there ever seen less obedience in youth of all sorts, both mankind and womankind, towards their superiors, parents, masters and governors?', the Puritan, Philip Stubbs, demanded in the 1580s, echoing a common preoccupation. Even the patriarchal family, the lynch-pin of the whole structure of order, appeared to be threatened.

Historians and the Ranters

The debate over the nature, extent and significance of the Ranter movement has continued since the publication of J.C. Davis's ideas in 1986. On the one hand, Davis argues that the Ranters did not exist, that they were entirely fictional, a scare created by conservative authorities to justify their claims of social and moral breakdown, and to gather support for repression. On the other hand, while few would deny the lack of definition and organisation which characterised the movement, a variety of historians have argued that some kind of movement, however scattered and limited, did exist, and that it represented a significant mode of thought among ordinary people. The views of different historians are summarised briefly in Sources 103–6 and in two hypotheses which you are invited to test and evaluate.

Source 103

From J. Friedman, *Blasphemy, Immorality and Anarchy: The Ranters and the English Revolution* (Ohio University Press, 1987) pp. xi, xii and 311.

There can be no doubt that the Ranters were the most radical and the most peculiar sect of the Cromwellian Interregnum. ...

It is difficult to make too many generalizations about the Ranters, for most were fierce individualists who found no need for common confessions or lists of dogmas. ...

The Ranters tell us about the sentiments of the poor ... and they come closest to representing the common man normally abused by both institutions of power and then by those who overthrow those institutions. ... Most Ranters simply did not differentiate between the claims of Parliament and those of monarchy. Both were considered property-class institutions and primarily existed for their exploitation of the poor.

Source 104

From A.L. Morton, *The World of the Ranters* (Lawrence & Wishart, 1970) pp. 92–3, 103 and 110–11.

It would probably be incorrect to speak of the Ranters as a Church, or even a sect. There is no evidence of formal organisation or [a] generally received body of doctrine ... All reliable evidence suggests that Ranter meetings were quite small, perhaps ten or a dozen or a score [20] of people meeting privately or semi-privately in a member's house. On the other hand, they were probably both more numerous and more influential than has sometimes been supposed.

If, however, we cannot speak of a Ranter sect, it is possible to speak of a Ranter movement, and this movement has a history which can be traced, at least in broad outline. Many uncertainties must remain because of the nature of the evidence – the writings of the Ranters themselves are ... primarily concerned with doctrine, and any historical details they may contain are incidental. On the other hand the literature about the Ranters ... is uniformly hostile and frequently nothing but the lowest type of gutter journalism. ... On August 9th [1650] Parliament passed [the Blasphemy Act]. ... Some Ranters, like Coppe and Salmon, had already been imprisoned. Now began systematic police raids, often made on evidence provided by informers. ... Under ... these blows Ranterism ceased to exist as a coherent social and religious movement, but its decline was slow and prolonged. All over the country small, more or less isolated groups, and, no doubt, many individuals remained. ... The best evidence for its persistence in all parts of the country in this period, and for its character, comes from Fox ... [who] reports Ranters as late as 1668, and in New England, 1672.

Source 105

From J.C. Davis, *Fear, Myth and History*, pp. 110, 121 and 123–4.

There can be little doubt that there was a fictional or mythical image of Ranterism created in the early 1650s. It was used to discredit or discipline religious enthusiasm and to illustrate, for some, the dangers of religious toleration. ... The speed of its creation and dissemination was made possible by the ready availability ... of the images from which it was constructed, the character of the atheist, sectarian promiscuity and the prodigy [monster] literature. ... The most substantial material relating to Ranters after 1651 comes from Quaker sources, but ... [may be seen as] evidence of the sectarian needs of the Friends rather than the survival of a Ranter sect or movement. ... To illuminate the need for sectarian discipline and boundaries, the image of sectarian indiscipline, a group without boundaries, could be used. Against the agonising problem of ordinances [rules] could be set the Ranterish consequences of the repudiation of all ordinances. ... Ranterism was a weapon used in the movement's own domestic disputes ... [just as the conservatives had used it to reassert authority in the political, social and religious disputes of the nation as a whole].

Source 106

From C. Hill, 'The Lost Ranters?', in *History Workshop*, **No. 24, Autumn 1987, pp. 134–6.**

Davis argues that if we are to be convinced of the existence of Ranters, we must find 'a sect with clear leaders, authoritative tests on entry, and controls over numbers'. Of course, he can't find them. In mid-seventeenth-century England there were no buildings labelled 'Society of Friends', 'Baptist Church'; there were groups gathered around a charismatic preacher or leader. ... Looking back, we can see sects in the process of formation. But in the 1650s ... some Quakers were pacifists, others not ..., [some Baptists] favoured total immersion, others sprinkling; some accepted tithes in the Cromwellian state Church, others did not. ...

From this milieu of free discussion, Quakers, Baptists, Muggletonians ultimately emerged, after many disputes. We can see them as sects, retrospectively, because they survived. Ranters were suppressed because they were thought dangerous. So the Levellers and Diggers had been before them.

I prefer the phrase 'Ranter milieu' to 'sect' or 'movement'. Contemporaries certainly accepted the existence of a milieu, with recognized beliefs and attitudes – hostility to organized Churches, materialism, mortalism, rejection of hell and the devil, scepticism about the special sanctity of the Bible. ... Sometimes this scepticism was extended to God; or God was equated with Reason or Nature, or was located within human beings. They rejected original sin and eternal punishment for the mass of mankind; they preached (and some apparently practised) sexual permissiveness; and they used deliberately violent and provocative language. In the new freedom which existed after the Civil War, men – and, even worse, women – pursued all sorts of heretical ideas provocatively. The word 'Ranter' was used to describe those who participated in, and justified, these discussions: it is difficult to be more precise. ...

After the suppression and silencing of the Ranters in 1650–1, Quakers and Muggletonians wanted to differentiate themselves from the Ranter milieu in which they too originated. For this purpose it was convenient to identify libertinism or excessively enthusiastic behaviour with the Ranters. ...

But this ... description of Quaker practice after the Ranters had been suppressed ... cannot be used, as Professor Davis uses it, to argue against the very existence of Ranters in 1649–51, when there were not yet any Quakers. Many from the Ranter milieu were absorbed by both Quakers and Muggletonians, and each group used the Ranters as a stick with which to beat the other. But there would have been no point in name-calling of this sort if there had never been any Ranters.

Question

9.

> ### Hypothesis A
>
> Few in number, lacking organisation and quickly suppressed, the Ranters were nevertheless significant; they took the radical search for freedom and equality to its logical limit.

> ### Hypothesis B
>
> There was no Ranter sect, no Ranter theology, no Ranter movement. The Ranters were a myth created by conservatives to justify the restriction of religious liberty and the suppression of radical ideas.

On the basis of the evidence in this unit, interpreted in the context of the period, how far can each of the conflicting views expressed in Hypotheses A and B provide a valid explanation of the Ranter phenomenon?

UNIT 3.4

THE QUAKER SCARE

Why were the Quakers successful?

Quakerism, according to the historian Barry Reay in his essay on 'Quakerism and Society', began in the North. It was not, he explains, until 1654 and 1655, with the movement of Quaker preachers southwards, that the movement really made its impact. It was now a national problem rather than a regional nuisance. The prediction of Jeremiah 1:14 had finally proved true: *'That out of the North an Evil shall break forth upon All the Inhabitants of the Land.'*

There is little doubt that many contemporaries saw the Quakers in these terms. As the movement spread, complaints multiplied about the activities of the travelling preachers and their more enthusiastic adherents, and in 1659 the fear of a Quaker rising did much to inspire enthusiasm for the return of the Stuarts as a guarantee of social and political stability. Nor were these fears on the part of magistrates, ministers and the conventional majority in any way surprising. The more picturesque activities of the over-enthusiastic, such as the Friends [as the Quakers called themselves] who ran naked as a sign of their innocence or James Nayler's notorious re-enactment of Christ's entry into Jerusalem, were only the most obvious signs that the Quakers were a threat to convention. The real threat lay in the Quaker rejection of external authority, the elevation of the individual spirit above the laws of church, scripture or society. Moreover, these ideas were spread by wandering preachers, who were in themselves a danger, since they chose to travel as 'masterless men' and establish a national network of meetings in a society whose sense of order depended on local settlement and administration. The more successfully they did this, the more threatening they appeared, and hence the more enthusiastically they were persecuted. Source 107 explains the problem that the Quaker movement posed for contemporaries.

Source 107

From B. Reay 'Quakerism and Society', in J.F. McGregor and B. Reay (ed.), *Radical Religion in the English Revolution* (OUP, 1984) pp. 141–2.

In 1652 George Fox and fellow itinerant preachers moved through the rural areas of northern England linking together groups of separatists. This was the beginning of the Quaker movement. These early 'converts' were for the most part ordinary men and women who had spurned the wishes of their betters and who had already rejected much of the ideology and organisation of orthodox Puritanism. Many were engaged in some form of agricultural work (either as yeomen or husbandmen). Several, it seems, had in the 1640s been in conflict with landlords over their opposition to excessive rents and manorial services; others had been refusing to pay tithes. From the start the Quaker movement was a movement of political and social as well as religious protest....

[Their] success was impressive. Within a decade there were certainly from 35,000 to 40,000 Quakers (men, women and children), perhaps as many as 60,000. They were as numerous as Catholics, more numerous than Fifth Monarchists and Baptists....It must at times have seemed as if the whole of England would turn Quaker. Not one county escaped the effects of Quaker proselytising. Nor did Quakers concentrate on towns and cities; in fact, in contrast with all the stereotypes of early nonconformity as an essentially urban affair, the indications are that (although Bristol and London were important Quaker strongholds) Quakerism was predominantly a rural movement. The Quakers, Bernard Capp has reminded us, demonstrated that sectarianism could flourish in the villages. They were the most successful as well as the most radical of the Revolution sects.

The final sentence of Source 107 encapsulates the paradox created by the early history of the Quaker movement. It was successful in a society whose basic assumptions and attitudes it challenged and threatened; because of that very success, it was the most harshly and relentlessly persecuted of all groups, both before and after the Restoration in 1660; and yet the movement survived and grew, alone among the enthusiastic groups, to become a major Christian Church which operates and is organised on a worldwide basis. As historians, we are therefore required to address the question of how and why the Quaker movement proved, against all the odds, to be so successful.

Historical explanation

Explaining Quaker success involves some preliminary consideration of what it is that we are trying to explain. In the first place, the term 'success' requires some further definition, since success consisted of both gathering and maintaining support, often in the face of persecution. Hence the initial question can be subdivided; we are required to explain both why the movement was able to establish itself (gather support) and why it was able to survive (maintain support) in an exceptionally hostile environment. The same factors may have contributed to both developments, but not necessarily to the same extent and in the same way. It is therefore necessary to examine the role played by different conditional and contingent factors, and to consider their interaction in relation to both the establishment and the survival of the Quaker movement.

Secondly, the process of historical explanation requires us to consider the ideas, actions and events which contributed to the eventual outcome, and therefore to formulate sub-questions relating to each which will define their contributions to Quaker success. Formulating such questions is an essential part of planning an explanation, and these questions will shape and determine the explanation which is offered. Before reading the material provided below, therefore, you should first consider what questions you would like to ask about Quaker ideas and beliefs, about Quaker actions, and about the events and situations which formed the context in which they worked, in order to define how each of these contributed to Quaker success.

Having established these preliminary questions, you will be in a position to interrogate the sources and the narrative below, in order to discover what part ideas, actions and events or situations played in making the Quaker movement so successful. Moreover, as you seek to define the part that each one played, you will also need to consider the relative importance of these different factors in your explanation. Thus the process of formulating sub-questions and seeking to answer them from evidence taken and inferred from sources (primary and secondary) will enable you to produce a planned, coherent and considered explanation of Quaker success.

This unit seeks to enable you to complete this task. The material below contains a number of sources which provide evidence about ideas, actions and events relating to the origins, establishment and survival of the Quaker movement. They are arranged within the framework of a narrative history, which outlines the changing conditions to which the Quakers had to respond and enables their success to be considered in terms of both gaining and maintaining support. The material therefore falls into four main sections; the first deals with

Quaker beliefs and how they were formed, the second concentrates on the activities of the early leaders in developing and spreading their message and on the response and reactions that they met, the third considers the causes and context of their survival after the Restoration in 1660, while the final section looks at the role of ideas, events and actions as conditional and contingent factors in Quaker success and survival. The unit also suggests a number of sub-questions that you might use to interrogate the evidence – although you may well prefer to apply your own.

The Quaker movement

Origins and beliefs

The origins of the Quaker movement lay in the spiritual crisis and meditations of its founder and organiser, George Fox, in the years between 1643 when he left his home in Fenny Drayton, Leicestershire, and the beginning of his active ministry in 1647. The dominance of Fox within the movement has been the subject of some debate. Christopher Hill has argued that, until his entry into Bristol and ensuing punishment destroyed both the credibility and the health of James Nayler, he was regarded as at least the equal of Fox in influence and importance. Others have suggested that the early deaths of other 'Publishers of Truth' such as Richard Hubberthorne (died 1662) and Edward Burrough (died 1663) coupled with Fox's major role in establishing Quaker organisation in the vital years of 1668–9, have given him a position of leadership in the eyes of later generations which would not have been shared by contemporaries in the 1650s. It is certainly true that Fox's religious experiences and the conclusions that he drew from them were far from unique in seventeenth-century England, and that many of his early 'converts' seem to have been already travelling a similar road in a similar direction before meeting with him. Nevertheless, the fact that by 1647 he had developed a coherent set of beliefs which laid out the essentials of the Quaker message, and that from 1647 to 1652 he personally visited and helped to establish most of the Quaker groups in the Midlands and North of England, suggests that the history of the Quaker movement does indeed begin with George Fox.

Source 108

From M. Mullett, 'George Fox and the Origins of Quakerism' in *History Today*, Vol. 41, May 1991, pp. 26–8.

The Quaker founder, George Fox, was born in Fenny Drayton in Leicestershire in 1626. His religious background was that of the highly developed 'godly' English Protestantism which came to maturity under Queen Elizabeth. In his autobiographical *Journal*...Fox paid tribute to his deeply pious parents [and Puritan upbringing]....'When I came to eleven years of age, I knew pureness and righteousness. For while I was a child I was taught how to walk [behave] to be kept pure'.

Nevertheless, in adolescence Fox underwent a profound and protracted spiritual crisis, in common with other great religious figures such as Martin Luther and John Bunyan....[His] adolescent spiritual agony is vividly and poignantly conveyed in the earlier pages of his *Journal*:

'Great trouble and temptation came many times upon me; so that when it was day, I wished for night, and when it was night, I wished for day...my exercises and troubles were very great...I was in great perplexity and trouble for many days...'.

[Eventually, this emotional and spiritual stress led Fox to leave his home and wander in search of solutions. His *Journal* in these years barely mentions the Civil War which raged around him.].

What was at the heart of George Fox's turmoil, making him virtually shut out of his consciousness the epic struggle for freedom and religion in the decade of his youth? In writing of the period from about 1643 he refers to 'a strong temptation to despair...'. What was at the root of this acute despair? He had been brought up, as we saw, in the Puritan or 'godly' tradition of early Stuart English Protestantism, a world view shot through with the reformer John Calvin's doctrine of predestination, which had been elaborated to a high degree in English Calvinism. Predestination traced a clear demarcation between those set apart and preordained by God for salvation and those similarly predetermined to damnation. Chronic anxieties over predestination haunted pious and earnest people such as John Bunyan: indeed we might even go so far as to say that the reiterated inculcation of the so-called 'eternal decree' of predestination, especially by means of countless sermons, caused something like pandemic neurosis amongst a whole strata of religiously serious English people.

However, there is little or no suggestion that Fox's primary problem arose over predestination. Rather, it seems to have emerged out of an acute sense of evil and sin, a further legacy of the Anglo-Calvinist tradition. Fox was strongly aware of sin – and especially of hypocrisy – in others. When he was about nineteen, two of the self-professed 'godly', one a cousin, tried to lure him into a drinking bout at a fair, and he was profoundly shocked by the disparity between their profession and their conduct. Fox retreated into himself, feeling himself commanded by God to 'be as a stranger unto all'...to avoid moral pollution....[His] sense of sin also arose from self-awareness – from guilt, for example, at abandoning his family... – and also from fear of temptations to sin. He tried therapy with a number of adept and well-known spiritual counsellors, 'priests' and 'professors' [people who claimed a measure of religious experience] who handled his problems with farcical insensitivity, advising him, for instance, to 'take tobacco and sing psalms'....

The clumsiness of the professionals gave Fox useful insights into the true nature, as he saw it, of Christian ministry: 'that being bred at Oxford and Cambridge was not enough to fit and qualify men to be ministers of Christ...'. But, even more importantly, the evident futility of merely human aids led Fox inexorably towards Christ: 'There is one, even Christ Jesus, that can speak to thy condition...'. This discovery of Christ and of His redeeming and consoling power at last alleviated Fox's preoccupation with sin; Christ was the remedy for sin and except for Him, 'all are concluded under sin and shut up in unbelief, as I had been...he gave me hope, which is himself revealed in me, and gave me his spirit and grace, which I found sufficient in the deeps and in weakness.'

This breakthrough meant that Fox could at least re-join, as it were, the human race, and in particular, join in the extraordinary, impassioned, infinitely talkative, endlessly experimental religious and social revolution going on in England in the 1640s. Though Fox underwent further temptations...these increasingly had the effect of consolidating the insights he had won, and he was now able to go on, to aid others in their difficulties, through his 'sense of all conditions'. His growing reputation as a therapist, and indeed as a miracle-worker, had to do with the strength and serenity of his converted self, bringing peace to others, like the 'distracted' (deranged) woman in Mansfield Woodhouse to whom he 'brought peace' in 1649.

Fox was also developing a strong line in social justice – he would advise magistrates and tax assessors to 'take heed of oppressing the poor' and condemn capital punishment for crimes against property. He also took a firm stand on social equality, rejecting the various symbols, then current in speech and gesture, of social subservience and deference. Not surprisingly, he came under suspicion from the authorities, and was imprisoned.

Question

1. Consider Sources 109–18 in the light of your own knowledge and of Sources 107 and 108 above, and explain

   (a) the main elements of Quaker belief and attitudes;

   (b) the particular appeal these beliefs and attitudes might hold for seventeenth-century men and women.

   It might be helpful to compile a list of beliefs and attitudes, and then to consider how these might appeal, as a whole or in part, to people in different social, professional and geographical environments.

Source 109

From George Fox's *Journal*. The passages printed here have been selected to illustrate the central message of Quakerism – that God lived within every person and that those who could recognise this Light within themselves and follow its ways, were able to escape from sin. The *Journal* reveals how Fox came to this belief, and the joy and certainty that it offered to those who could follow it faithfully.

When all my hopes in them and in all men was gone, so that I had nothing outwardly to help me, nor could tell what to do, then, O then, I heard a voice which said 'There is one, even Christ Jesus, that can speak to thy condition,' and, when I heard it, my heart did leap for joy....And then the Lord did gently lead me along, and did let me see His love, which was endless and eternal, and surpasseth all the knowledge that men have in the natural state or can get by history or books:...In this I saw the infinite love of God. I saw also that there was an ocean of darkness and death; but an infinite ocean of light and love which flowed over the ocean of darkness....[and] that every man was enlightened by the Divine Light of Christ and I saw it shine through all, and that they that believed in it came out of condemnation and came to the Light of Life and became the children of it; but they that hated it and did not believe in it were condemned by it, though they made a profession of Christ. This I saw in the pure openings of the light, without the help of any man, neither did I then know where to find it in the scriptures, though afterwards, searching the scriptures, I found it.

Source 110

From George Fox, *The Great Mystery of the Great Whore Unfolded*, 1659. In this extract Fox describes how the discovery of the Light led to the creation of the Quaker movement, or Society of Friends.

We found this light to be a sufficient teacher, to lead us to Christ, from whence this light came, and thereby it gave us to receive Christ, and to witness him to dwell in us, and through it the new covenant we came to enter into, to be made heirs of life and salvation; and in all things we found the light which we were enlightened withal...(which is Christ) to be alone and only sufficient to bring to life and eternal salvation; and that all who did own the light in them which Christ hath enlightened every man withal, they needed no man to teach them, but the Lord was their teacher, by his light in their own consciences, and they received the holy anointing.

And so we ceased from the teachings of all men and their words, and their worships, and their temples, and all their baptisms, and churches, and we ceased from our own words, and professions, and practices in religion, in times before zealously performed by us, through divers forms, and we became fools for Christ's sake that we might become truly wise, and by this light of Christ in us we were led out of all false ways and false preachings, and false ministers, and we met together often and waited upon the Lord in pure silence, from our own words and all men's words, and hearkened to the voice of the Lord. [Many Quaker meetings were, and still are, conducted in silence.]

Source 111

From George Fox's *Journal*. This extract reveals a code of morality and behaviour, which became an essential and recognisable hallmark of the Quakers.

When the Lord sent me forth into the world [to preach the Quaker message] He forbade me to put off my hat to any, high or low, and I was required to Thee and Thou all men and women, without any respect to rich or poor, great or small. And as I travelled up and down, I was not to bid people 'Good morrow' or 'Good evening', neither might I bow or scrape with my leg to anyone, and this made the sects and professions to rage....About this time I was sorely exercised in going to their courts to cry for justice, and in speaking and writing to judges and justices to do justly, and in warning such as kept public-houses for entertainment that they should not let people have more drink than would do them good, and in testifying against their wakes and feasts, their May-games, sports, plays and shows, which trained up people to vanity and looseness, and led them from the fear of God – and the days they had set forth for holy-days were usually the times wherein they most dishonoured God by these things. In fairs also and in markets I was made to declare against their deceitful merchandise, and cheating and cozening, warning all to deal justly and to speak the truth, and to let their yea be yea and their nay be nay, and to do unto others as they would have others do unto them, and forewarning them of the great and terrible Day of the Lord, which would come upon them all.

Source 112

From James Nayler, *A Caution to all who shall be found Persecutors*, 1653.

Take heed you that tread the poor and helpless under your feet. Repent, repent, your day is coming on apace wherein the Lord will avenge the poor on him that is too strong for him. And how canst thou stand at that day when thou shalt become as weak as another man and no false pretences will be accepted? Thou must be judged according to thy works, good or evil.

Source 113

From Richard Hubberthorne, *Collected Works*, 1663. Hubberthorne was one of those 'First Publishers of Truth' [the name given to the early Quaker leaders who joined Fox in his missionary work] who spread and upheld the Quaker movement in its first stage of development.

Let everyone that will preach the gospel live of the gospel, and not upon any settled or State maintenance...for the cry of the honest and godly people of this nation is to have a free ministry and free maintenance, and are willing freely to maintain those that minister unto them the word and doctrine.

AN EARLY CONVERT: JOHN WHITEHEAD, 'PUBLISHER OF TRUTH'

John Whitehead provides an interesting example of the men whose dedicated work did so much to encourage and uphold the Quaker movement in its early days. He was converted in the second phase of the movement while serving in the army at Scarborough in 1652. Whitehead's conversion followed a classic pattern among these early adherents, and his account of the process provides some insight into the qualities that enabled the Quakers to attract so much support, as well as the kind of people who were drawn to Quakerism.

Like Fox, Whitehead had been brought up in a Puritan family, 'instructed by my parents in the use of means, as hearing sermons, reading the Scriptures and the like...and so had an outward knowledge of God and Christ.' He had joined the Army at the age of 18, where he 'zealously followed men whom the world called godly ministers' but was still assailed from time to time by a sense of his own sinfulness. By the following year, he had come to believe that 'the kingdom of God is not in outward observations, but that it is within and is righteousness, peace and joy'. Thus, like many early Quakers, he had begun to move towards an inward faith by his own meditations, before any contact with the movement. However, at this point Whitehead concluded that those whom God 'loved once, he loved unto the end' and that therefore he had 'liberty to take pleasure and delight in the world...that though I did commit sin, yet God did not impute it to me; for he sees no sin in Jacob, nor transgression in Israel'. This suggests that he was moving towards an antinomian view, or even a form of Ranterism, although there is no evidence to suggest that he went as far as to act out sin in the manner of Coppe, Clarkson and others. Clearly, however, Whitehead felt that he had lost his way. 'In this state I lay nearly two years and the Lord...sometimes disquieted my earthly spirit, and brought me in some measure into a sense of my condition', but he was unable to see his way forward until 'the Lord in his love sent his faithful messenger, William Dewsbury [a Quaker preacher] into the place where I resided'. At this point, Whitehead received and understood the Quaker message, 'and I saw that I was in a prodigal state...and the judgement of God took hold of me...and in His love He received me and put his fear in my heart which caused me again to depart from all manner of evil'. He attended meetings, waited, prayed and developed his faith before 'the Word of the Lord came unto me and said, if I would be his disciple I must deny myself and take up his cross daily and follow him...and I was separated from my former companions...to wait upon God'.

In September 1654 Whitehead began his active ministry, at first in Yorkshire and later in the Midlands and the south. He established Quaker meetings in Whitby and Cleveland before settling in the Holderness area near Hull. Thereafter his life was that of a travelling preacher, interspersed with imprisonment. In 1654 he was imprisoned in Leicester, and in 1655 he and others from Holderness were imprisoned in Northampton as vagrants. Throughout the period, however, he maintained a regular correspondence with Friends in Hull and Holderness who sought to provide advice and support in difficult times. His letters reveal much about the beliefs and practices of ordinary Quakers in their local meetings. They also demonstrate the network of personal contacts by which the early leadership upheld the movement and enabled it to survive.

Source 114

From *The Written Gospel Labours of that Ancient and Faithful Servant of Jesus Christ, John Whitehead, Collected and Published*, 1704. The extract lays out the main points of Faith to which Quakers should bear witness.

I witness that Christ Jesus is the Light of the world, and enlightens everyone that cometh into the world....And all you who turn to the Lord, and love the Light with which Christ has enlightened you...and walk in it – it will lead you out of darkness and your evil deeds up to God, the Father of lights; and, walking in the Light as God is in the Light, you will have fellowship one with another, and you will witness the blood of Jesus Christ cleansing you from all sin....And I witness that the free grace of God, which bringeth salvation, hath appeared to all men; and it teacheth us to deny all ungodliness and worldly lusts, and to live soberly, righteously and godly in this present evil world. So by the free grace of God we are saved....And God is just, who delights not in the death of a sinner, but rather that he may turn and come to life....And I witness that the Spirit of Truth which convinceth the world of sin, is sufficient to lead and guide into all Truth....And I witness that the gift of God is free, and is eternal life; which life is Jesus Christ, who tasted death for every man.

And I witness that a minister of Christ is not made such by the will of man, nor fitted for his ministry by human learning, or by the sharpness of his wit, or by any natural gift; but by the gift of the Spirit of Jesus Christ; which gift cannot be bought or sold for money, nor limited to times or persons, but is free; and it constrains him who hath received it, freely to minister it to others....And I witness against all those who profess to be ministers of Christ, and receive tithes...and against such as sue people at law for tithes and wages, to whom they neither minister spiritual or temporal things....But all true ministers of Christ I own: by their fruits they are known....And I also own and witness the ordinances of Christ, as self-denial and the daily cross – love one to another – to do to all men as we would be done unto – not to swear at all – if any smite on one cheek to turn the other – to feed the hungry and clothe the naked and the like....And I own magistracy, which is the ordinance of God, ordained for the punishment of evil-doers, and for the praise of them that do well: and those magistrates who are guided by the light of Christ, which is equal and just and who do justice according to the law of God without respect of persons, I own and honour in my soul...But against him who is in the place of a magistrate, and turns from the light of Christ, casts the law of God behind his back, respects the persons of men, perverts all equity, causes justice to stand afar off, lets the evil-doer go free...against him do I witness without respecting his person. Yet no power do I resist, but dwell in that which suffers all things, hopeth all things; and am subject to the will of God, in whom I have that peace which the world cannot give, nor take from me.

Source 115

From John Whitehead, *Gospel Labours*, 1704. The following extracts are taken from letters written in 1662, in which Whitehead is responding to some of the criticisms and accusations that were levelled against Quakers. He seeks to use the weapon of the accusers against them, by justifying Quaker practices from the Scriptures which, it was claimed, the Quakers disregarded. Many of the subjects have been dealt with above, but two in particular may be of significance in understanding Quaker attitudes and the acceptance of their beliefs.

Concerning the Scriptures...
Concerning the Scriptures, I say, we do not slight them, nor cast them off as a dead letter, paper and ink; but own them which Moses and the Prophets, the Evangelists and Apostles wrote or spoke, as they were moved by the Spirit of God,...to be the very words and true sayings of God and therefore not to be slighted but read, believed and practised by every true Christian. But they...whose hearts are not established by the grace of God pervert or wrest the Scriptures out of their right place....Therefore we

direct all to that Word of God which was in the beginning...that is Life and is the Light of men....that so by this Interpreter...people may have the Scriptures opened and feel the power of God....[which] doth [not] make void the Scriptures, but establishes them in their right place as a true declaration....

Concerning Women's Speaking
That daughters did prophesy in the congregation of God's ancient people is evident; for to Israel God spoke by Miriam, in the days of Moses; and again he spoke by Deborah to Israel and judged them by the words of her mouth....And divers women were helpers of the apostles in the work of the ministry...[and] Paul also gave rules how they should prophesy....It is evident that although he did not permit a woman to speak in the church, nor usurp authority over the man, yet he did permit the Spirit of God to speak in women, as we do; for we dare not forbid it, lest in so doing we should quench the Spirit, which they have the promise of as well as men.

Source 116

A seventeenth-century Quaker woman. Women were prominent in the early Quaker movement. Fox's first convert was the Nottingham widow, Elizabeth Hooton.

Sources 117 and 118 further emphasise the important role of women in the Quaker movement, and the respect with which they were treated.

Source 117

A picture of an early Quaker meeting

Source 118

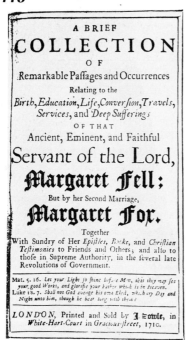

Title page from the works of Margaret Fell. Her devoted service to the movement included the collection of funds as well as the use of her home at Swarthmoor Hall as a place of rest and refuge. It is also of some significance that the Quakers arranged the publication of her autobiography and works after her death in 1702.

The First Publishers of Truth, 1647–60.

The First Publishers of Truth is the name given to the 60 or 70 men and women who, having been converted to Quaker ideas at an early stage, dedicated themselves to spreading its message, at first in northern England and later throughout the country (and beyond). In some cases, for example James Nayler and Francis Howgill, they had embarked on some kind of ministry before meeting Fox, and many had developed beliefs which were similar to the Quaker message before undergoing any process of 'conversion'. Nevertheless, it was as Quakers that they set out to bring a coherent message of hope and salvation to the world. Many devoted their lives to the work, and several, worn out by travelling, beatings and frequent imprisonments, died at a relatively young age. Their story encompasses the early history of the movement and their actions did much to shape its development. As itinerant preachers they set out, not to establish a church, but to convert a world. At the same time, however, they sought to revisit and uphold existing meetings, offering help and advice about organisation, care for the poor, support for the persecuted and maintaining standards of behaviour, which laid the basis of a Church organisation. Gradually, as Quaker numbers grew, this work of consolidation became more important. The increasing frequency of persecution and accusations of Ranterism, blasphemy and immorality led inevitably to a growing concern with defending the Quaker name. The disastrous behaviour of James Nayler in allowing himself to be presented as a new Christ at Bristol in 1656 concentrated the effort to control the more ecstatic and eccentric members. Without ever losing the sense that their message was one of universal redemption, the Quaker leadership did pay increasing attention to the defence of what they had achieved, a tendency which was to be vastly increased after 1660, when the onslaught of a new and barely imagined persecution transformed the task of converting the world into a struggle for survival.

Questions

2. On the basis of the narrative and Sources 119–30 below, explain how the actions of the First Publishers of Truth contributed to the success of the Quaker movement.

3. To what extent did pre-existing conditions or situations help or hinder their work?

From 1647 to 1651, Fox seems to have been engaged in a ministry in his native Midlands area. It is, in fact, difficult to date its beginning with any precision, since he seems to have moved gradually from concern with his own spiritual state into offering the results of his prayers and meditations to others. This stage of his career is described by the historian of the Quakers, W.C. Braithwaite in his monumental work, *The Beginnings of Quakerism*.

Source 119

From W.C. Braithwaite, *The Beginnings of Quakerism* (CUP, 1955) pp. 42–3.

The beginning of propagandist work may be dated back to 1647, but not earlier. To this year, apparently, belong the visits to Dukinfield and Manchester, where Fox first speaks of himself as 'declaring truth'....A little later he attended a great meeting of Baptists on the border of Leicester and Nottinghamshire which was held 'with some that had separated from them, and people of other notions went thither'. Here his mouth was opened, truth was declared, and the power of the Lord was over them all....After the Broughton meeting he began to attract attention....Next year in Nottinghamshire great meetings began, and there was a mighty work of God amongst the people. At Mansfield on one occasion, he was moved to pray in the church, and the lord's power was so great that the house seemed to be shaken. In Leicestershire several 'tender' people were convinced, and many in the Vale of Belvoir, where he stayed some weeks, preaching repentance as he went. We now come to his association with the 'shattered' Baptists in Nottinghamshire, on which much new light is thrown by papers recently unearthed at Devonshire House. A Baptist community had existed in Nottingham and the neighbourhood, which, before Fox came, had lost its spiritual life and become scattered and broken. One portion continued to meet together on the Sunday 'to play at shovel-board and to be merry' the rest became, like so many other groups of dissatisfied persons, a company of Separatists, unaffiliated to any sect. As early as the beginning of 1647 Fox had been attracted to these Separatists...especially one of their number, Elizabeth Hooton of Skegby, near Mansfield. The Baptists...allowed women to preach and...it is probable that she had been a Baptist preacher before she became the earliest woman preacher among Friends....The community as a whole seems to have accepted the message of Fox, and to have formed a new association together under the appropriate name of 'Children of the Light'....These facts respecting the Nottinghamshire Children of the Light are of cardinal importance. It becomes clear that Fox, at the outset of his mission, found material ready to his hand in this broken Baptist community, and, in the most formative and plastic period of his life, impressed his influence on its members and was, in turn, no doubt himself impressed by the Baptist point of view in matters of church life. We have discovered the channel along which many of the Baptist influences which affected Quakerism probably came.

By 1650 this congregation seems to have come to the attention of the authorities, not least because of Fox's insistence on carrying his message to the unconverted by challenging their ministers in and outside of their pulpits. It is easy to forget, especially in the light of Quaker sufferings in the ensuing years, that the early preachers were both enthusiastic and aggressive, and that they regarded it as their duty to challenge the outward religion of the 'hireling priests' of the established Church. In 1650 this led to Fox being imprisoned in Derby, and to the apparent break-up of his congregation, although some, such as Elizabeth Hooton, remained faithful. This pattern of behaviour would also continue throughout the period of the Commonwealth and Protectorate, and was in some measure responsible for persecution of the movement. Cromwell, to whom Fox would later appeal for help, was not unsympathetic to Quaker ideas, and was prepared to try and soften the effects of persecution, as he did with Nayler in 1656, but he would not tolerate the Quaker assumption of a right to interfere with the religious worship of others, whatever their motive. In this area the actions of the early leaders and their dedication to their self-appointed task carried costs as well as benefits.

Upon his release from prison in 1651, Fox decided to leave his native area, partly because of the grief that his behaviour had brought to his family. He accepted an invitation to visit a meeting of separatists who had gathered in South Yorkshire around the village of Balby. The results of this visit would be momentous, for it was here that the spread of the movement into the northern counties began. According to Braithwaite, 'there is some evidence that when in Derby [Fox] had been in correspondence with the group of Seekers near Doncaster, at Balby, Warmsworth and Tickhill, who now gave a welcome to the new movement. I have called them Seekers, but the name is hardly emphatic enough, for they had already found the light'. Fox's arrival, however, seems to have given the group a new coherence, and a new sense of purpose. While he continued his work in other parts of Yorkshire, the Balby group produced several new Publishers of Truth who took up the mission locally, and then elsewhere. Fox met with considerable success in the county, apparently for two main reasons. In the first place, as at Balby, he found groups of existing separatists who were already dissatisfied with their present arrangements, or who had, like the so-called Ranters in Cleveland lost their initial vision and fallen into lax ways. Secondly, he seems to have gained the sympathy of some of those in authority such as Justice Luke Robinson of Pickering and Justice Hotham of

Hutton Cranswick in the East Riding. The latter area in particular produced converts of some standing and substance such as the Storrs of Owstwick, but equally important were those who, without ever joining the movement, respected Fox's purpose and praised his influence. In this sense, the insistence of the early leaders on strict morality in daily life gave the new movement an important advantage. In the words of Justice Hotham, it was 'raised up as a bulwark against Ranterism'.

The sources and brief biographies below summarise the progress made by the Quakers in northern England from this initial base in Yorkshire. By 1654 meetings were established and consolidated throughout the region, the foundations of some kind of organisation had been laid, and a core of itinerant preachers had been gathered, able to provide support and leadership over a wide area. The movement was ready for its next stage of development, the spreading of its universal message to the south of England and beyond.

Source 120

From W. C. Braithwaite, *The Beginnings of Quakerism*, p. 70–1 and 132.

The work in Yorkshire at once resulted in the formation of groups of the Children of the Light in many of the places visited. The Balby group was the first and most important. At Wakefield the members were in part drawn from the Independents; at Selby, York, Borrowby, Stokesley, Staithes, Liverton, Malton, Ulrome, Patrington and probably in some other places, Fox left behind him groups of convinced persons who, in accordance with his advice at Stokesley, began at once holding meetings of a very simple character....Above all, the inward life laid hold so strongly on many that, leaving their outward callings, they formed themselves into what they regarded as a camp of the Lord, and devoted their lives to the publishing of the truth. Fox, in a well-known passage, says that by the spring of 1654 'a matter of seventy ministers did the Lord raise up and send abroad out of the North countries.'....Fox passed on in May 1652 to further strenuous and fruitful service, but under the leadership of Richard Farnsworth and William Dewsbury, the work in Yorkshire continued to make wonderful progress....

RICHARD FARNSWORTH: YEOMAN Born in Tickhill, South Yorkshire, of Puritan upbringing, he joined a group of Independents, but was unsatisfied and eventually ceased attending any formal Church. At this point he seems to have begun meeting regularly with Thomas Aldam, his brother-in-law Thomas Killam and their wives, to 'seek' the Lord. It is likely that they had developed ideas very close to Quakerism before Fox visited them at Balby. All three men took on the task of 'publishing truth', and Farnsworth is described as 'next to Fox, the chief leader of the new movement in the North'.	**JAMES NAYLER: FARMER AND SOLDIER** James Nayler was a yeoman of West Ardsley, near Wakefield. Like many of the early Quakers, he had Puritan and army experience, having fought at Dunbar and Worcester. He had also been a member of an Independent Church in Wakefield, before experiencing a religious crisis that caused him to give up his farm and take up a wandering ministry before ever meeting George Fox. A man of great gifts, he quickly became a leader of the movement and led a very successful mission to London before succumbing to the hysteria of his followers at Bristol in 1656, where he re-enacted Christ's entry into Jerusalem by riding into the city on a donkey. Punished savagely by parliament and disowned by Fox, he was eventually rehabilitated shortly before his death in 1660.
WILLIAM DEWSBURY: SHEPHERD A native of Allerthorpe in the East Riding of Yorkshire, Dewsbury shared the Puritan background that seems to have been characteristic of the early Quaker converts. He was employed as a shepherd in his youth, but was then apprenticed to a clothmaker in Holbeck, Leeds, where his religious doubts seem to have come to a crisis which led to his joining the army to fight for God's cause. He had already tried and rejected the Puritan sects in favour of an inner spirit when he met and was convinced by Fox.	**RICHARD HUBBERTHORNE: SOLDIER** Richard Hubberthorne was the son of a farmer of Yealand who had joined the army in 1648 and served as a captain of cavalry. Returning to his home, he had been attracted to the ideas of the Seekers before meeting George Fox at Preston Patrick in 1652. He suffered a period of intense depression but was finally convinced by Fox in 1653. Thereafter he became a very successful preacher in the south-eastern mission, before dying in 1662 from his many imprisonments.

Source 121

From M. Mullett, 'George Fox and the origins of Quakerism', in *History Today*, May 1991, pp. 28–29.

In 1651 [Fox] moved into the north, to Yorkshire. After a wide circuit of that vast county and of the north-east, in 1652 Fox approached east Lancashire where he had a mountain top vision of 'a great people to be gathered'. In fact his 'great people' lay not so much in Lancashire, where Catholicism was quite well entrenched, as in the dales of North Yorkshire and Westmorland. There Fox encountered a pre-existing form of radical Christianity, the Seekers, a loosely organised grouping of hill-farming and artisan families with a religious attitude of humble waiting for the future unfolding of truth. In Fox and his message it may be said, the Seekers found what they had sought. As the *foci* for their religious gatherings, they met at the chapels-of-ease, such as Firbank Fell Chapel in Westmorland [outside which Fox apparently preached to well over 1000 people in June 1652] which had been provided to supplement the inadequate provisions of the established Church in these scattered and thinly populated northern communities. Already famous preachers, such as Francis Howgill (1618–1669) and John Audland (1630–1664), both soon to become leading Quakers, welcomed Fox and acclaimed him to their auditories: 'This man speaks with authority, and not as the scribes' – that is, the professional priests.

From the area of the Howgill Fells, where he met the Seekers, Fox moved on to Kendal and then along the Furness Peninsula of South Lakeland, eventually coming to the godly, Puritan household of Justice Thomas Fell of Swarthmoor, a place with which [he] was to be associated for the rest of his life. Fox made a mass conversion in the household – except for the head of the family himself, Thomas Fell, who remained a sympathetic but uncommitted supporter. Some years after Fell's death, George Fox married the justice's widow, Margaret, whom he converted in 1652, and who had already distinguished herself by years of devoted service to the movement.

Source 122

From W.C. Braithwaite, *The Beginnings of Quakerism*, pp. 130–6 and 140–5.

Group-life of the simplest kind began inevitably and naturally from the first; indeed it was characteristic of Fox that he won men to an acceptance of his message, not merely as individuals but most often in groups. The Mansfield 'Children of Light', the Balby circle, the great Preston Patrick community, the Swarthmoor household, the groups scattered up and down Cumberland and Cheshire, are illustrations of this, and it seems probable that Quakerism has always consisted of compact bodies of Friends in a limited number of localities. These groups, as we have seen, consisted most often of pre-existing church-fellowships, spiritually prepared for the message of Fox. They were composed mainly of persons who had already dissociated themselves from established Churches, but had found living union with one another because of common convictions and a common search....Fellowship, then of a most intense kind, naturally resulted both from the origin of Quakerism...in already existing groups, and from the centripetal force inherent in the doctrine of the Inward Light. But this does not mean that Fox and his fellow-workers deliberately set about founding a new sect. [Their message] was a message of universal significance, and was proclaimed as a gospel for all men....Such a word as 'sect' is quite inadequate.

[Nevertheless the leadership did try to support and uphold meetings through a rudimentary organisation]. Fox, Farnsworth and Dewsbury exercised real leadership....As early as 1652 [they] gave advice about meetings. By the end of 1652 Dewsbury had settled a General Meeting once in three weeks in the East Riding of Yorkshire and the Westmorland Seekers, before they received the message of Fox, held a General Meeting at Preston Patrick once a month. An early letter of Farnsworth's gives detailed instructions for General Meetings once a month throughout the West Riding, specifying in a most interesting way the constituent meetings [for worship] that are to form each General Meeting, and naming responsible Friends who are to see that the General Meeting is duly arranged....In this way two kinds of periodical meetings, for spiritual fellowship and church-affairs...seem to have grown up quite naturally out of the occasions of the time....In this incipient stage of Quakerism the stress was laid on securing times of religious fellowship and on securing efficient spiritual leadership. The spiritual leadership came in the first place from men like Fox, Farnsworth, Dewsbury and Nayler, who were the apostles of the movement, but men [and women] of spiritual power, who became, many of them, itinerating Publishers of Truth, also exercised leadership according to their gifts. Margaret Fell also took almost at once a place of unique service....She kept open house for travelling Friends and made it her business to create and maintain close relations of personal friendship between herself and most of the leaders of the new movement. The extent of her correspondence is amazing...[and from 1654 she used this network] to establish, develop and administrate a fund, collected at Kendal, to support the Publishers of Truth and the mission to the South.

Source 123

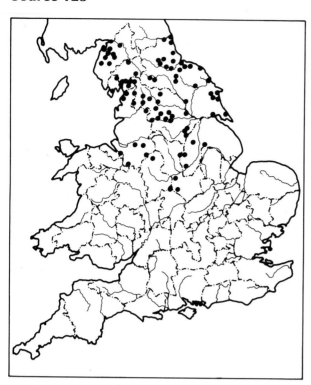

The number and extent of Quaker meetings existing in the North of England in 1654, at the time of the mission to the south.

In 1654 the great 'mission to the south' began. It was a conscious attempt to spread the Quaker message, approached in a highly organised way. The Publishers of Truth were divided into small teams, usually two, rarely more than three, to travel to designated areas spreading the word as they went. Success was immediate. In July 1654, Anthony Pearson, [a JP who had been converted by James Nayler when he sat on the Bench which tried Nayler for blasphemy in Durham in January 1653] wrote to Fox that 'Great is the harvest like to be: hundreds are convinced and thousands wait to see the issue, who have persuasions that it is the truth'. The extent of success varied – the eastern counties, a strongly Puritan area, proved surprisingly resistant – but it was undeniably widespread. In some areas, as in London and Bristol, existing congregations of 'seekers' and 'waiters' were converted, as in the North. By 1656, Fox had reached the far western counties of Devon and Cornwall. He was, in fact, imprisoned in Launceston Castle in Cornwall when the disastrous Nayler affair occurred in Bristol.

With success came persecution. Friends had long faced such difficulties in the north, as a cursory reading of Fox's *Journal* swiftly reveals, but the southward expansion created suffering on a new scale. The strange behaviour of the Quakers, their ecstatic shaking and 'Quaking', inevitably aroused

hostility, and Friends were often attacked by mobs or driven out of towns and villages by enraged inhabitants. Sometimes this was encouraged by local ministers or justices, but the reaction was often spontaneous. The Quaker habit of challenging ministers and entering churches to disrupt services led to further problems, and while Fox makes much of the enmity and injustice perpetrated by those in authority, there is no doubt that the Quakers brought some of their sufferings on themselves. In addition, however, there were frequent and clear instances of malice, injustice and a disregard for the law on the part of the persecutors. One example is provided by the arrest of John Whitehead as a vagrant in Northampton in 1655. (At this time the laws against vagrancy were used more frequently than specifically religious statutes to deal with the itinerant preachers). Whitehead vigorously protested that he had a settled abode where he supported his wife and children, in the East Riding of Yorkshire, as did his companion, a yeoman farmer named Joseph Storr. To prove this, they sent letters to Storr's brother Marmaduke, a grazier who was on business in Stafford, who hastened to the justices to support their claims. Instead of securing their release, this action led only to Marmaduke's imprisonment with them, on no charge whatsoever. The incident had serious results. The three men were kept in prison for several months, without any charge ever being proven, as a result of which Marmaduke Storr lost his home and business, because he was unable to renew his lease. His wife and children were able to survive only because other Quakers supported them.

The Quakers did not accept persecution in any passive spirit. While they steadfastly refused to deny their views, or to give promises of good behaviour which would restrict their religious purpose, they used all the legal processes available to them and argued their case publicly and often effectively. The numerous recorded cases show that some justices, at least before 1660, were concerned to be fair, and Fox himself describes examples of good as well as bad treatment. Moreover, the public occasions afforded by a trial in open court were often put to good use in gaining more converts, and even where the outcome went against them, the Quakers were often able to gain adherents impressed by their courage and steadfast endurance for their beliefs. There is no doubt, however, of the extent of suffering endured, and aside from individual cases where preachers were harried to their deaths, the effect of regular imprisonments on the health of many is revealed by their untimely deaths at a relatively young age. This was greatly reinforced by the persecution which followed the

Restoration in 1660 – John Audland died in 1664, Edward Burrough in 1663, and Richard Hubberthorne in 1662 – but the effect was often a cumulative one, arising from sufferings endured over a period of years.

Whatever the price, there is no doubt about the rapid progress made by the movement up to 1656, when a severe setback occurred in the shape of James Nayler's blasphemous entry into Bristol. Nayler had been in London, where he was immensely successful in establishing and upholding the movement and quite simply seems to have been overcome by his success. A group of hysterical supporters led by Martha Simmonds, who encouraged him to challenge the pre-eminence of Fox, had already created tensions within the movement. At this point, Nayler seems to have been suffering from mental exhaustion, and allowed himself to be persuaded into what was, to him, a symbolic gesture celebrating the advent of a new Christ in the hearts of his people, the Quakers. As a gesture, it was extremely ill-judged, and did great damage to the movement as well as to Nayler himself. Fox immediately repudiated both the action and the man, to the fury of Nayler's supporters. They began a campaign of disrupting meetings, which was eventually stopped by the intervention of Nayler, now in prison. His efforts allowed the movement to re-unite, although Fox refused to be reconciled with Nayler personally until 1660. Nayler's health never recovered from his ordeal, and he died shortly after his release from prison in 1660. The significance of the Nayler affair, its effects, and consequences for the movement are examined more fully in Sources 125–30 below.

Source 124

James Nayler's entry into Bristol, 24 October 1656

Source 125

From C. Hill, *The World Turned Upside Down* (Penguin, 1975) pp. 249–52.

The events following Nayler's symbolic entry into Bristol in 1656, riding on a donkey and with women…strewing palms before him, are well known. Why was so much fuss made? There had been earlier Messiahs – William Franklin, Arise Evans, who told the Deputy Recorder of London that he was the Lord his God, Theaureaujohn, King of the Jews: Mary Gadbury was the spouse of Christ, Joan Robins and Mary Adams believed they were about to give birth to Jesus Christ. They were comparatively leniently dealt with by local magistrates: a short prison sentence, perhaps a whipping for the women. But MPs spent six weeks denouncing Nayler with hysterical frenzy; many demanded sentence of death, and Nayler was ultimately flogged and branded with a brutality from which he never recovered. The explanation is that none of the others seemed so dangerous. Most were holy imbeciles, William Franklin a fraud. But Nayler was a leader of an organised movement which, from its base in the North, had swept with frightening rapidity over the southern counties. It was a movement whose aims were obscure, but which…was recruiting former Levellers and Ranters. Bristol was the second city of the kingdom, where the Quakers had many followers. Above all, MPs were anxious to finish once and for all with the policy of religious toleration which, in their view, had been the bane of England for a decade.…So conservatives in Parliament seized the occasion to put the whole Quaker movement in the dock, and the government's religious policy too.…

It was the parting of the ways for the Quaker movement as well as for the English Revolution as a whole.…The Nayler case was a tragedy for the Quaker movement, already suffering divisions caused by the 'Proud Quakers' [a breakaway group originating in the Nottinghamshire Children of the Light, who rejected Fox's insistence on strict conventional morality] and the surviving strength of Ranter tendencies in the North Midlands. Nayler's case strengthened the arguments for more discipline, more law and order in the Quaker movement.…but [it also] closed the door on much that had been courageous and life-giving in the early Quaker movement. The enormous problem of disciplining this amorphous [force] fell principally to George Fox.…It cost [him] much heart-searching and enmity before he convinced the movement.

Source 126

From a letter written to Nayler by George Fox, dissociating the movement from him and his behaviour, 1656.

Thou must bear thine own burden, and thy company with thee, whose iniquity doth increase, and by thee not cried against. Thou hast satisfied the world, yea, their desires [to find complaints against Quakers] which they look for;

and thou and thy disciples and the world are joined against truth. It is manifest through thy wilfulness and stubbornness. And this is the word of the Lord to thee.

Source 127

James Nayler

Source 128

From W.G. Bittle, *James Nayler (1618–60)* (Ebor Press, York, 1986) pp. 169–174.

Throughout 1657 the turmoil in the movement created by Nayler's split with Fox and subsequent actions in Bristol continued. The affair had resulted in a flurry of petitions against Quakers, and for some time after the trial it seemed as if a general campaign against Quakerism was about to begin. Parliament reacted to the public outcry with a stiffened vagrancy law which went into operation in July 1657. News of the Bristol episode spread to the continent and hampered Quaker missionary work at home and abroad....

Nayler's followers continued to disrupt Quaker meetings....[but] Nayler became deeply troubled by the turmoil within the Quaker ranks and came to understand that more harm was coming to the movement because of his split with Fox than could possibly be caused by what he had felt was Fox's unfair leadership. He realised that if the movement was to survive, unity was essential, and the schism between himself and Fox would have to be healed. He realised also that his acceptance of, and participation in, the Bristol entry had been ill-advised and had proven his own unsuitability for leadership. Nayler knew that the episode hurt the movement, and must have appreciated that Fox's own, more conservative character might have prevented him from taking part in such a demonstration. It may also have been that Nayler, faced

now with the realisation that his most devoted followers were at the least misguided, genuinely forgave Fox for his earlier, hasty condemnation because of them, and now sincerely regretted the break.

[Fox was somewhat slower to forgive, and not until 1660 was William Dewsbury able to bring about a reconciliation between them. However, Nayler's acceptance of his fault enabled the movement to come together and to address the problems of discipline that his error had brought to the surface.] Nayler's indirect, or at least unintentional contributions to the Quaker movement were an outgrowth of the events at Bristol. The immediate impact of these events hampered the spread of Quakerism at home and abroad, as the Quakers were equated with the Ranters and other fanatics. The long range effect was, however, considerably more beneficial. The problems brought about by the episode, as well as Nayler's harsh treatment at the hands of Parliament, cooled the ardour of the more demonstrative of the Friends and, to a large extent, checked any more displays of such unrestrained enthusiasm. Carrol notes, with regard to 'going naked as a sign' and other 'signs and wonders', that there was a notable lack thereof throughout 1656, 1657 and 1658. [The same years saw the beginnings of a national system of meetings.] What is certainly true is that the meeting system established and enforced a doctrinal orthodoxy designed to prevent another James Nayler....[and] ultimately, this restraint contributed to the consolidation and moderation which allowed the Quakers to survive.

Source 129

The Grand Impoſtor
EXAMINED:
OR,
The Life, Tryal, and Examination
OF
ƑAMES NAYLER,
The Seduced and Seducing
QUAKER
WITH
The Manner of his Riding into
BRISTOL.

JOH. 19.7.
We have a law, and by our law he ought to die; becauſe he made himſelf the Son of God.
JOH. 20.31.
But theſe are written, that ye might believe that Jeſus is the Chriſt, the Son of God; and that believing, ye might have life through his Name.

LONDON,
Printed for *Henry Browne*, at the Hand in S. *Paul's* Church-yard. 1656.

Title page of a pamphlet reporting Nayler's entry into Bristol

From 1656 onwards, therefore, the Quaker leaders began to lay increasing emphasis on developing organisation and discipline within the movement. Upon his release from Launceston Castle in 1656 Fox began to arrange a series of General Meetings in the West Country, while Dewsbury and Farnsworth called representatives of the northern Quakers to a similar gathering at Balby. Eventually these led to an annual meeting of the whole movement, which seems to have been first held at Skipton in Yorkshire in 1657, and was repeated in 1658, 1659 and 1660. Thereafter, the onslaught of persecution made such gatherings impossible. From these meetings emerged various documents outlining the arrangements to be made for regular meetings for worship, care for the poor, marriages, the support of widows and apprenticeship of orphan children, and for dealing with 'disorderly walking' on the part of members. This was to be dealt with by the members as a whole, by talking and advising with those who caused concern, not by any sanctions imposed upon them. Nor did the leadership attempt to impose these arrangements upon the movement. The documents were the result of discussion at representative meetings, and were carefully presented as advice rather than instruction. One issued from the Balby meeting ends with the postscript, 'Dearly beloved friends, these things we do not lay upon you as a rule or form to walk by, but that all with the measure of light which is pure and holy may be guided, and so in the light walking and abiding, these may be fulfilled in the Spirit – not from the letter, for the letter killeth, but the Spirit giveth life'. In 1660, on the eve of the Restoration, the Quakers remained a radical movement, committed to spreading a message of universal salvation through the Light of Jesus operating in the individual heart and mind. They had begun to consolidate their earlier gains, and to develop an organisation to support the faith of the individual member, but the core of the movement remained the voluntary gathering of members who shared a common experience and faith, linked and upheld by the itinerant preachers who maintained the fellowship through letters, visits and their network of personal relationships. In Source 130, Braithwaite describes Quaker organisation at this time.

Source 130

From W.C. Braithwaite, *The Beginnings of Quakerism*, p. 314.

The church organisation is still of the simplest, consisting of congregational life under the leadership of local elders, and in the last resort, of the 'fathers' of the Church....There is as yet no appeal to any authority except that of the Light: the central experience of the indwelling life of Christ, which had gathered Friends out of the world into fellowship, was still so generally the living possession of Friends that its vital control held the body together as one organism. But, at the same time, sporadic cases of backsliding and of disorderly life had to be dealt with, and marriages required to be regulated and the poor to be provided for. To suggest wise lines of action in respect to these matters, and to exhort Friends in their various relations of life to walk worthily of their calling, was all that seemed of urgent necessity....And, though Friends were at this time incurring the hostility of the State, there is no sign as yet of that indifference to public life which persecution and nonconformity with the practices of the world gradually fostered: on the contrary, the duty of serving the Commonwealth so far as possible is inculcated.

Questions

Use the narrative provided below to answer Questions 4 and 5.

4. What factors enabled the Quaker movement to survive in the period after 1660?

5. How important were the actions of Quaker leaders in ensuring this survival?

The survival of Quakerism, 1660–89

At the time of the Restoration, the Society of Friends remained an aggressive, expansionist force, its members very much a part of the world that they yet hoped to conquer for the Light. However, such hopes could not survive the onslaught of persecution that came in the years after 1660. The Quakers had not regarded the Restoration as a particular threat, and had even hoped that the king's sympathy for religious toleration might bring them some benefits. However, they were to discover that it was not the king's sympathies that mattered. To both MPs and local Justices, the Quakers were a strange and dangerous phenomenon; their silent meetings, outpourings of faith, and ecstatic quaking identified them as enthusiasts, and their itinerant ministers with their network of meetings and contacts were understandably interpreted as political agents. They were also the most vulnerable of the radical groups. The refusal to pay tithes and church dues provided ample opportunity for prosecutions even before the Quaker Act of 1662, and most important, their refusal to take Oaths, including the Oath of Allegiance, laid them open to prosecution for treason and a whole range of legal abuses. For example, George Harley of Ulrome in Yorkshire was arrested in 1660 after attending a Quaker meeting, and taken to York Castle. At the next Quarter Sessions he was released, but was then re-arrested on a writ of excommunication (for not attending church) and asked to take the Oath of Allegiance, which he refused. Despite offering to make a statement of Allegiance, he was imprisoned, and by these means was kept in prison until 1669, when he died. At that point his widow was seized on a similar writ, leaving ten children effectively orphaned.

The real onslaught began in early 1661 in the aftermath of a hopelessly ill-conceived rising by Thomas Venner's Fifth Monarchists, and continued through the passing of the Quaker Act, the supposed Yorkshire Plot, and the establishment of the Clarendon Code. Examples are far too numerous to cite, but some idea of the scale of the attack can be gained from the numbers released from prison by the king's Coronation amnesty of April 1661. There were over 500 Quakers imprisoned in Yorkshire at that time, and over 4000 in England as a whole. Similar numbers were released in May 1662, in honour of the king's marriage, and again in December of that year by his first attempted Declaration of Indulgence. What infuriated Quakers particularly, was that many of their members had committed no crime, even by the persecuting laws that had been designed to destroy them. Friends were seized and carried before Magistrates without warrant or charge, and tendered an Oath which it was known that they could not take, on no basis other than their known Quaker views. By these means, John Whitehead was kept in prison in Lincoln for over a year, from January 1662 to April 1663. An even worse case appears in the records of Owstwick Monthly Meeting in Yorkshire, where four Friends were arrested in 1665 after Henry Lashley, vicar of Hollym, wrote a letter to the Archbishop of York accusing them of involvement in the Yorkshire Plot of 1663. Although Lashley never offered any evidence to support his claims, and consistently refused to attend Court Sessions to have his accusation examined, the four were kept in the dungeons of York Castle for five months until Friends persuaded JPs in Beverley to enquire as to their whereabouts. Without this intervention, the likelihood is that they would have died there.

More serious from the point of view of the movement as a whole, its leaders and mainstay, the travelling preachers, were particularly vulnerable to persecution, and by 1663 the vital contact that they had maintained between local meetings and the wider movement was destroyed. In 1661 John

Whitehead and Isaac Penington spent several months in Aylesbury Gaol, with 60 or 70 others, and Whitehead was then imprisoned in Lincoln Castle until 1663. George Whitehead and three other preachers were imprisoned for months in Norwich Castle, in a wall recess known as 'the Vice'. Edward Burrough was imprisoned in Newgate in June 1662, and died there in 1663. In the aftermath of the Yorkshire Plot, Francis Howgill and Margaret Fell were imprisoned at Appleby. Despite the efforts of Friends to secure their release, Margaret Fell remained there until 1668, and Howgill died in prison in the following year. William Dewsbury, imprisoned in York in 1661, is described by Braithwaite as 'passing his life in prison, with brief intervals of freedom'. George Fox was taken to Lancaster gaol in 1663, and later transferred to Scarborough Castle, where he was kept in appalling conditions until 1666. In 1665 Howgill listed John Camm, John Audland, Edward Burrough, Richard Hubberthorne, and Caton and Ames, the Westmorland leaders, as having died in, or as a result of, imprisonment. The government's persecution had effectively wiped out the Quaker leadership, through whom, according to Braithwaite, 'far more than through organisation, the Quaker groups had become one living fellowship'.

The effects of this were both obvious and catastrophic. The incipient organisation of 1660 collapsed. No General Meetings were held after 1661, no collection of funds after 1662, and attempts to keep up the county meetings failed, as the lack of records for the period 1663–9 demonstrates. Quakerism was kept alive in the local meetings for worship, at tremendous cost to the lives and property of their members, but inevitably these became more isolated and inward-looking. 'Cut off from wider fellowship and larger vision, [the movement] began to take on a domestic character and to lose something of its universal outlook'(Braithwaite). The Quakers would never again confidently expect to convert the world. They began to see themselves as a Church, and to concentrate some of their efforts on the maintenance of that Church, on the defence of Truth through the defence of their own institutions, standards and reputation. It was in this area that George Fox made a second massive contribution to the success of Quakerism. Recognising the dangers of a localised movement, he used his release from prison in 1666 to embark on a series of journeys covering the entire country, in which he persuaded Friends to accept a new, highly organised and structured system of meetings for worship and administration. Between 1667 and 1669 the meetings for worship were incorporated into a network of Monthly Meetings at local level and Quarterly Meetings at county level, which dealt with administration, record-keeping, collection of funds, and where necessary, discipline among members. Between 1670 and 1675 these were linked up and supported by a system of central, Yearly Meetings of ministers and representatives from the counties, culminating in 1675 in the establishment of the Meeting For Sufferings, which became the central, guiding influence within the movement.

This organisation represented an enormous achievement, and was very much the work of Fox. The effects of persecution, the loss of other leaders, and the need to fight back had convinced him that the movement must become more organised, more disciplined and more directed, even at the cost of sacrificing something of the radical spirit that had suffused the early movement. An unnecessary controversy over the wearing of hats during prayer had been caused in 1666 by John Perrot, a Quaker who had travelled on a mission to Asia in 1657, and attempted on his return journey to convert Rome. He had escaped from this with his life because his eccentricity led the Catholic Church to consider him insane, and place him in an asylum. What Fox recognised was that Quakers like Perrot and the intense individualism that they represented was a luxury that the movement could no longer afford. The new organisation that he created was not designed to dictate to the movement. At every level it represented the membership in a highly democratic way, and sought only to channel and focus their energies. Nevertheless its purpose was to create more discipline, and in this it succeeded. Eccentric gestures, radical outbursts and even 'disorderly walking' became rare among the membership, and by the early 1680s the Quakers had established a reputation for honesty, integrity and good order in their lives that earned the begrudging respect of a previously hostile society.

The benefits of this were clearly demonstrated when a new wave of persecution broke out in the aftermath of the Exclusion Crisis of 1679–82. While persecution had never completely disappeared, its intensity had reduced after 1670, and the laws were never so rigidly enforced after their temporary suspension by the king's Declaration of Indulgence in 1672. The Exclusion Crisis had reopened old controversies, however, and it was followed by an onslaught on dissent of all kinds. Although the Quakers avoided official political commitments, the Whig sympathies of many were well known and resented by their Tory opponents, who seized the opportunity for revenge on those who had acted or voted against them. This time, the Quakers were

equipped to meet the challenge. The effort was co-ordinated by the Meeting for Sufferings which collected funds to support the sufferers and organised a legal challenge to any abuse of the laws by the persecutors. Petitions were presented to the king, and to Parliament, arguing the case for Toleration as well as drawing attention to Quaker sufferings. These were undoubtedly extensive. By mid-1682 there were over 700 Quaker prisoners in England, and many more were impoverished or bankrupted by incessant fines. Nevertheless, there were two significant changes from the situation of the 1660s. The first was that the movement remained strong and its organisation healthy. There was no danger that it would collapse or disintegrate under the pressure of persecution. The second was that there were increasing signs among the population as a whole of a distaste for persecution, and a growing respect for the persecuted. There had been signs of support for some toleration of Protestant Dissenters since the early 1670s. The House of Commons had passed a limited Toleration Act in 1673, which was stopped by the king's influence in the House of Lords. At local levels, many Justices had shown an increasing reluctance to execute the laws against dissent, and it was not unknown for local inhabitants to protect dissenters' meetings and obstruct the work of informers and agents. The growing restraint and discipline exhibited by the Quakers had led to a new respect for their code of life, and Quaker tradesmen were notably successful because of their reputation for honest dealing. All this brought benefits in times of difficulty, and harsh though the persecution of the 1680s was, there was reason for hope in the clear signs of a public reaction against it. Few cases were quite as clear as that in Bridlington, Yorkshire. There, over a period of months in 1682, the local constables refused to arrest members of the Quaker meeting, until they themselves were imprisoned. Thereafter they paid over seventy pounds in fines on the Quakers' behalf, and when they were eventually forced to seize Quaker goods, persuaded the local inhabitants to buy them cheaply and return them to their rightful owners.

In 1685 the accession of James II and his friendship with the Quaker William Penn brought some relief to the movement, and this was followed by James' Declaration of Indulgence in 1687, which effectively brought persecution to an end. In 1689 the Toleration Act finally established the right of Protestant dissenters to worship in freedom, and Quaker survival was assured. What had survived, however, was not the radical, universalist movement of the 1650s. The Society of Friends, the official name by which the movement was now known, was a quietist, disciplined sectarian Church. To some extent the change was inevitable, as a second generation grew up as Quakers by education rather than by conversion, but the process of change had been quickened and intensified by the fires of persecution and suffering. The early Quaker movement had challenged society in fundamental ways, and society had sought to crush it. The Quaker spirit withstood the challenge, but its leaders were forced to reshape the movement in order to do so. The courage and dignity with which Quakers endured the brunt of persecution transformed their image, and made a major contribution to the advent of religious toleration in England – but the movement survived only because it had proved able to preserve its essential vision by adapting its practices in the light of harsh reality.

The role of different factors

The material above reveals a number of factors relating to Quaker ideas, actions taken by Quakers and their leaders, public reactions and the context of events which help to explain why the Quaker movement spread so rapidly and survived so successfully. In order to link these into a coherent explanation, it is necessary to consider more precisely what part each factor played, and how it interacted with others. It is clear that some factors played a conditional role. For example, the speed with which Fox was able to gather groups of converts suggests that there was a pre-existing desire for a faith such as Quakerism – in other words, that the conditions of the time were ripe for a movement of this kind. It could therefore be argued that Fox's ministry, and the ideas that he had developed, were contingent factors, influencing the nature of the movement and the timing of its emergence. This also raises the issue of the relative importance of these factors, which to some extent depends on the questions that are being asked. If we are asked to explain the emergence of a strong radical movement of the enthusiastic type, then the conditional factors may well appear to have been most important. If, however, we are explaining why a movement with the precise beliefs and moral code developed by the Quakers emerged, or why this movement proved capable of adapting in order to survive, then we may attribute greater importance to contingent factors associated with the beliefs held, methods employed and style of leadership adopted by Fox and others.

The sources below adopt an analytical approach to their subject, and seek to consider some of these issues. Sources 131–3, by Reay and Braithwaite, examine the conditions in which the Quakers developed and spread, as well as some of the ideas and attitudes which drew converts to them. Source 134, by Mullett, concentrates on the role of the leadership, particularly George Fox.

Question

6. Using the sources below and your own knowledge, explain

   (a) which factors played a conditional role in the success of Quakerism;

   (b) which factors played a contingent role in the success of Quakerism;

   Do you consider the conditional or the contingent factors to have been more important in Quaker success? Explain and justify your answer.

Source 131

From B. Reay, 'Quakerism and Society', in J.F. McGregor and B. Reay (ed.), *Radical Religion in the English Revolution* (OUP, 1986) pp. 142–5.

What sort of people became Quakers? What do we know about their religious and political backgrounds, about the sect's socio-economic composition?

As far as the better-known Quakers are concerned (the 'ministers' and pamphlet writers) the influence of Puritanism is indisputable. Many, like Isaac Penington, had become 'exceedingly entangled' about Calvin's theory of predestination, 'having drunk in that doctrine, according as it was then held forth by the strictest of those that were termed Puritans'. They were thoroughly imbued with the Puritan sense of sin; they despaired of their salvation. George Fox spent his pre-Quaker days sitting in hollow trees, and tobacco, psalm-singing and blood-letting were suggested to him as potential cures for his despair. Before he became a Quaker, George Rofe was 'smote by the hand of the Lord into many fears as to what should become of me hereafter, and have often wept exceedingly in secret and in my bed, so that I have wetted much clothes with tears'. We could go on. Quakerism was to some extent a reaction to this psychological *malaise*.

Many Quakers began as Presbyterians and then, influenced by radical Puritan doctrine, Familist ideas, and the translated works of continental mystics, progressed to sectarianism. Some were what were called Seekers (those who taught that people should 'sit still, in submission and silence, waiting for the Lord to come and reveal himself to them'). When Quakers entered an area they sometimes carried lists of advanced separatists residing in that area, those who were most likely to be receptive to the Quaker message. Again and again they converted sectaries, sometimes whole meetings: many Baptists, Seekers, some Ranters and Fifth Monarchists. There is also some evidence that in Cambridgeshire (and perhaps in Essex) 'spiritual seeking and unrest was extremely widespread...and that the Quaker position was reached, or nearly reached, *before* the arrival of the Quakers.'

We now know quite a bit about the social origins of the early Quakers. Although there was regional variation in the movement's social composition, it seems that it mainly drew its membership from what were known as the middle sort of people: wholesale and retail traders, artisans, yeomen, husbandmen....Several northern Quakers had been involved in anti-tithe activity in their pre-Quaker days. The same was true of other parts of the country: for example Somerset, Kent, Essex, Suffolk. Many Quakers had a history of active resistance to tithes. Unlike the Levellers, the Quakers responded to agrarian grievances; indeed, during the Revolution, they were among the most unrelenting opposers of tithes.

Then there were radical political connections. A number of Quakers had been county committee men and sequestrators [local administrators for parliament during the Civil Wars]. The New Model Army was an important source of Quaker recruitment. A few had been in the Navy. John Ward, the vicar of Stratford-upon-Avon, (and others) thought that 'Several Levellers settled into Quakers'. Francis Harris and other contemporaries claimed that many Quakers had been Diggers as well as Levellers. Leveller and Digger ideas do crop up in Quaker literature...and we know that the Digger leader, Gerrard Winstanley and the Leveller leader John Lilburne became Quakers. But there is no evidence of any real influx.

Finally, a sizeable number of women joined the Quaker movement. The sect did not offer them equality, but certainly more independence than that offered by society. Quaker women preached, proselytised, wrote and printed tracts, participated in church government (though in separate meetings and mainly in the area of welfare) and assumed a militant role in the sect's various campaigns. Of well over 300 Quakers in trouble for disrupting during the period 1654 to 1659, 34% were women; of the 59 Quaker ministers who arrived in America during the period 1656 to 1663, 45% were women. Gone was the old precept: 'Let your women learn in silence with all subjection.'

Source 132

From W.C. Braithwaite, *The Beginnings of Quakerism*, pp. 18 and 22–7.

The overthrow of authority and the intense religious earnestness of the times combined during the years of toleration [1647–50] to produce a number of quick-growing but usually short-lived sects....The Fifth Monarchy Men were the political zealots of Puritanism, but their extravagance appears sobriety compared with the obscurantist convictions of the Muggletonians, who nourished their faith out of the Apocalypse....The Ranters represented the revolt against authority in its extremist form. [It] was to all intents and purposes a revival of the doctrines of the 'Free Spirit'; there was in England in the

Commonwealth era a real contagion of the idea of God as indwelling...[but] the fact is that the Ranter position afforded no test by which the individual could distinguish between the voice of the Spirit and the voice of his own will. The Quakers on the other hand were 'Children of the Light', and...their message became an antidote to Ranterism....Much more akin to the Quakers, were the Familists...equated by William Penn with the Seekers....After speaking of the rise and degeneracy of the Puritan movement, he says: 'that many left them and all visible churches and societies, and wandered up and down as sheep without a shepherd, and as doves without their mates, seeking their beloved, but could not find Him...whom their souls loved above their chiefest joy. These people were called Seekers by some, and the Family of Love by others...' The Family of Love had originated in Holland about 1530, reaching England about the middle of the century. Their ideas and practices had a close affinity to the Quakers, but they were not strong in numbers....We hear of them as Etheringtonians in London, as Grindletonians in Yorkshire, and as a small sect of threescore persons in the Isle of Ely....The Seekers were, however, the product of the religious travail of the age rather than of any one religious sect, and were recruited also from Independents and Anabaptists, and from Presbyterian and Anglican churches....[Feeling] the insufficiency of the current doctrinal and external religion, and not yet brought into a deeper soul-satisfying experience, [they] afforded the most receptive soil in England for the message of Fox. Some of them won their way for themselves into the consciousness of the indwelling Light of Christ, and on meeting with Fox or some other Quaker Publisher of Truth, at once proclaimed spiritual relationship. More often the Quaker message proved like a spark falling in prepared tinder.

Under the new conditions of religious freedom on the one hand, and active religious controversy on the other, which prevailed in England from the assembling of the Long Parliament, there had been a sudden growth of sects, which took their shape from the light, airy imaginations or the deep spiritual yearnings of their [members]. There were thousands of honest-hearted persons who used their freedom to make a quest after truth, and many of these found no rest, either in forms or in doctrines, and whether they called themselves Seekers or not, were weary with their travelling through the sects and athirst for the gospel of a living Christ. The religious climate was thus singularly favourable to the growth of Quakerism.

Source 133

From B. Reay, 'Quakerism and Society', in J.F. McGregor and B. Reay (ed.), *Radical Religion in the English Revolution*, pp. 149–53.

The success of Quakerism, Christopher Hill has reminded us, witnessed to the continued existence of the radicalism of the 1640s. Perhaps Winstanley had this in mind in 1654, when he told the Quaker Edward Burrough that the Quakers were carrying on the work of the Diggers.

Certainly the Quakers inherited the anticlericalism of the Revolution radicals. The clergy were more concerned with their bellies than with their parishioners souls....Through the system of tithes, priests were maintained in 'idleness' by the 'labours of poor people'....Quakers called for the disestablishment of the state Church and the abolition of tithes. Men and women should hire their own ministers or else ministers should labour to support themselves. The Quakers wanted a movement away from the university-bred, privileged clergy towards a ministry of simple men and women 'who spoke plain words and reached to the consciences of men of the meanest capacity'....But Quaker social comment was not limited to criticism of the Church and ministry. Some Quakers spoke out against the nobility and gentry...'the clergy and the gentry hath the land between them' wrote Elizabeth Hooton....The law, (the 'badge of the Conqueror' according to Edward Billing) also kept 'the poor people in bondage'. Instead of 'covering the naked and feeding the hungry, you set out laws to punish them' Benjamin Nicholson complained in a pamphlet aimed at the magistrates of England. Quakers advocated the removal of lawyers, trial by jury, Anglicisation and codification of the law, [all recognisable demands formulated by earlier radicals]....The society that the Quakers envisaged would have involved some redistribution of wealth....Their political allegiances were relatively uncomplicated....they were against 'the tyrannical Kings and Bloody Bishops'....But they had no coherent political philosophy...[and] could co-operate with any regime that looked like furthering radicalism.

The Quakers of the 1650s were not consistent pacifists. Some do seem to have reached the pacifist position before 1660,...[but] it is not until 1661 that we get, in Hill's words, the first 'official declaration of absolute pacifism in all circumstances'. Before that time it is impossible to talk...of the Quakers as a predominantly pacifist group. Self-preservation after the restoration of the monarchy in 1660, disillusionment with the effectiveness of political action, encouraged them to project their pacifism backwards. 'Pacifism was not a characteristic of the early Quakers: it was forced upon them by the hostility of the outside world'.

Source 134

From M. Mullett, 'George Fox and the Origins of Quakerism', in *History Today*, May 1991, pp. 29–31.

The year, 1652, of Fox's link-up with the Westmorland Seekers and of his first encounter with Swarthmoor and the Fells is widely regarded as that of the inception of organised Quakerism. Fox increasingly turned his attention to the practical organisation of the growing movement. He managed to combine – perhaps surprisingly but by no means unusually in religious history – the persona of a sublime visionary with that of a practical administrator. As a visionary, Fox was liable to

trances and inexplicable intuitions. As an administrator he built up a highly practical pyramidical structure for his movement. At its base was the individual local meeting, above that the administrative hub of Quakerism, the Monthly Meeting, then the county Quarterly Meetings, and at the apex the national Yearly Meeting.

This structure helped Quakerism to survive the storms of persecution following the restoration of the Anglican monarchy in 1660. But Fox's administrative work placed an increasing emphasis on his, or perhaps on his and Margaret Fell's control, an emphasis that precluded alternative styles or *foci* of leadership. [This] highlighted a major collision in 1656...with James Nayler. Fox was already at odds with Nayler before the Bristol episode, and after the incident, when Fox visited Nayler in Exeter gaol, 'the Lord God', Fox recalled 'moved me to slight him'. There were other challenges to Fox's leadership after 1656....[but] in the decades of persecution after the Restoration, his leadership became increasingly pronounced. Other prominent early Friends, such as Audland (d.1664), Burrough (d.1663), Howgill (d.1669) and Hubberthorne (d.1662) were passing away...often quite young, as a result of imprisonment. Fox too could claim full credit for maintaining early Quakerism's heroic record of suffering for faith. He was imprisoned eight times up to the mid-1670s and was frequently beaten up by hostile mobs. However, with his large frame and abstemious habits, he was astonishingly tough and durable, and his very survival, along with his strong will, allowed him more and more to etch his impress on the young movement. He wrote prolifically – books, letters and pamphlets on subjects as diverse as the use of 'thee' and 'thou', the names of the days of the weeks, spelling, Scriptural interpretation, business ethics and 'counsel and comfort'. He was also an incessant travelling missionary in the English tradition of 'itinerant' evangelism, preaching and organising throughout England and Wales, Scotland (1657), Ireland (1669), America and the West Indies (1671–72), and the Continent in the 1670s and '80s.

George Fox's practical shrewdness is evident in his careful management of financial affairs....He was also responsible for a number of social standpoints and concerns that have characterised the Friends for most, if not all, of their history. His pacifism became a fixed characteristic of Quakers...[and] Friends, especially in America, began to evolve a standing testimony against slavery. Fox's key doctrine of an inner light that could enlighten every man and woman implied human equality, and Fox penned an explicit critique of slavery in 1671. Also, and in common with thousands of other early Friends, Fox knew the insides of the English prisons of the seventeenth century, and his awareness of appalling conditions such as those of Scarborough gaol, made him an early prison reformer, initiating a long-standing Quaker commitment to this cause....[Finally] his awareness of illumination potentially available to all men and women developed in him a vibrant sense of female equality....

By the time of his death, Fox had emerged as the revered

leader and principal founder of a movement that has made a unique contribution to the religious experience of mankind. Vigorous and unpolished, he seems to have possessed a natural courtesy, 'civil beyond all forms of breeding' as his admirer, William Penn put it. He could be autocratic and his 'sense of all conditions' did not extend to an appreciation or sense of humour. He was, though, a master of spirituality, a social reformer, [a practical organiser] and a member of that extraordinary group of English religious leaders from Wyclif to Newman.

Evaluating your explanation: Quakers, Ranters and Seekers

One way of considering the success of the Quaker movement is to draw comparisons with other, similar but less successful groups such as the Ranters and the Seekers. All three groups shared an emphasis on the inward spirit as the core of religious experience; all three rejected outward or external forms and authorities, and all three were prepared to elevate the power of the individual spirit above all else. While the Quaker movement survived and lasted, however, the other groups disappeared. It has been argued that Quakerism was, in itself, responsible for this disappearance, that it subsumed the Ranter and Seeker groups in a more coherent, organised and fulfilling faith. It is difficult to judge how far this is the case, since contemporaries, including the Quakers themselves, seem to have attached the label of Seeker or Ranter to any group who manifested some of their tendencies even in the most general way. Even if this is the case, however, we can still validly ask what qualities and characteristics within the Quaker message, organisation or leadership enabled the Quaker movement to take over and maintain support in a way that manifestly eluded the other enthusiastic movements of the time. Source 135, below, is taken from an essay by the historian Geoffrey Nuttall in which he considers Quakers and Ranters as 'enthusiastic' groups and draws a number of comparisons between them.

Source 135

From G.F. Nuttall, *Studies in Christian Enthusiasm* (Pendle Hill, 1948) pp. 81–8.

The relationship between the Quakers and the Ranters is an issue of considerable complication, which needs considerable care in the unravelling. Confusion has been introduced first by a too easy association, and even identification, of the two movements by their contemporaries, and later by the natural desire of Quaker historians to repudiate any association whatsoever....There was a constant contemporary association of the two movements. Thomas Story, writing of Ranters he met in America as late as 1699, says 'they go under the name of Quakers, as the world calls us', but some did distinguish between the two, like the Yorkshire justice who told Fox that 'if God had not raised up this principle of light and life of yours, the nation [would] have been overspread with Rantism'. [It may well be significant in understanding Quaker success, that those who did distinguish seem to have been unusually sympathetic to Quakerism.]

Hostility to the Ranters and disapproval of their principles were regularly expressed by the Quakers...yet they could be surprisingly gentle in admonishing Ranters directly....'I know many of you were once tender and simple hearted' wrote Richard Farnsworth, while William Penn described Ranters as Seekers who had 'ran out in their own imaginations, and mixing them with those divine openings, brought forth a monstrous birth, to the scandal of those that feared God...'. The Seekers represented a transitional stage. The Ranters, that is to say, had a common spiritual ancestry with the Quakers...but certain influences had led to a point of divergence.

Various things assisted the infant Society [of Friends to avoid the pitfalls of Ranterism] and establish itself as, in the main, sane and sensible. Of first importance was its unwearied insistence on the ethical aspect of Christianity....The strongest and clearest differentiation between the Quaker and the Ranter movements was in the sphere of morals. Furthermore, there can be no doubt that Nayler's fall made Friends draw themselves up sharply...and 'walk more carefully, heedful of the special temptations which beset the path of spiritual enthusiasm'. Fox especially walked more carefully, since some were ready to treat him in the way that Nayler's followers had behaved. Certainly Fox's own influence against all extravagances and abnormalities can hardly be over-estimated; and this is the more noteworthy just because his own temperament had what we now call the psychic element unusually well developed. His sturdy strength of character, his practical common sense, his organising abilities were all thrown on the side of decency and order....In this he was supported by a keen pastoral concern on the part of many 'Publishers of Truth'.

Nuttall's analysis is by no means exhaustive; there are numerous other aspects of faith and organisation which can be considered and comparisons drawn between Quaker, Seeker and Ranter characteristics. His survey does, however, demonstrate the kind of comparisons that can be made and some of the conclusions that can be drawn. In evaluating an explanation, of course, these conclusions must then be applied to the issue which is being explained – in this case, the reasons for Quaker success and survival as opposed to the limited influence and rapid disappearance of the other enthusiastic groups.

Question

7. Using the sources in this unit and your own knowledge of radical groups like the Seekers and Ranters, explain

   (a) what similarities you can see between the Quaker, Seeker and Ranter movements;

   (b) what differences you can see between the Quaker, Seeker and Ranter movements;

   (c) how these similarities and differences help to evaluate your explanation of why the Quaker movement was so successful.

UNIT 3.5

═══ THE RADICAL TRADITION: A REVOLUTION ═══ IN IDEAS

Introduction: The historical significance of radicalism

Thus far, radicalism has been examined mainly within the context of the seventeenth century, and debate has focused on its significance for the radicals themselves and for their contemporaries. Some historians, notably Christopher Hill and H.N. Brailsford, have attributed much wider importance to the radical movements, according them a place of historical significance in the development of modern political ideas and popular movements. In his monumental work *The Levellers and the English Revolution*, Brailsford points out that Leveller plans for an elected and decentralised local government 'anticipated what is the normal usage of the United States' and that their insistence on frequent elections to Parliament as a means of rendering MPs truly accountable was 'the Levellers' legacy for many generations to the English Left'. In his introductory chapter 'Seen in Perspective', he argues that the Levellers could have succeeded, and attacks the 'liberal idea of progress' which suggests that the age and the society were not right for radical change of this kind. In Brailsford's eyes, the Levellers represented an opportunity for radical change which would not reappear for two centuries. 'The tragedy was not so much' he continues, 'that Cromwell managed to suppress the Levellers; it was rather that they had no successors, until the radicals of the London Corresponding Society came together during the French Revolution. The brief moment when English institutions under the flame of revolution were malleable passed with the consolidation of Oliver's dictatorship. Thereafter, unable to fight either with sword or pen, the kind of Englishman who had begun under the sea-green flag to work for a true Commonwealth sought salvation, as did Lilburne himself, in some form of subjective religion – in his century the Society of Friends, in the next in Methodism.'

For Brailsford, the historical significance of radicalism is centred on the political legacy of the Levellers, and other forms of radicalism are seen rather as a distraction, absorbing feelings and energies which could have been dedicated to the cause of political change. Hill's views have a different, much wider focus. In his study of *The World Turned Upside Down*, he argues that the radicals of the Civil War years were part of a much longer tradition, reaching back into medieval England and continuing to the present day. This was a tradition of populist belief, critical of privilege and hierarchy in all their forms, which was normally contained by government and society in the name of law and order; periodically, however, it emerged in the form of popular disturbances, riots, rebellions, or in heretical religious movements. The Civil War and Interregnum provided a period of unheard-of freedom and inspiration, in which radical forces were able to develop new forms and arguments. Although crushed at the time, these ideas and attitudes survived, to influence later generations and to re-emerge in more favourable conditions as a new challenge to orthodoxy, hierarchy and privilege in all their forms. His views are summarised in Source 136.

Source 136

From C. Hill, *The World Turned Upside Down* (Penguin, 1975) pp. 19, 25–8, 35, 40–7, 85–6 and 378–86.

There was a greater background of class hostility in England before 1640 than historians have normally recognised. A Scottish observer indeed commented in 1614 on the 'bitter and distrustful' attitude of English common people towards the gentry and nobility. ... In addition to, or expressing, these class tensions there was a tradition of plebeian anti-clericalism and irreligion. To go no further back, the Lollards carried a popular version of John Wyclif's heresies into the sixteenth century. Professor A.G. Dickens has shown how Lollard influence survived in a popular materialist scepticism which makes one 'feel appreciably nearer to the age of Voltaire than is normal in the sixteenth century'. A carpenter in 1491 rejected transubstantiation, baptism, confession, and said men would not be damned for sin. ... The clergy, an earlier Lollard had declared, were worse than Judas, who sold Christ for thirty pence, while priests sold prayers for a halfpenny. The commons, said another, 'would never be well until they had stricken off all the priest's heads'. ... Mr K.V. Thomas has collected a number of similar examples under Elizabeth and the first two Stuarts ... denial of the resurrection, of the existence of God or the Devil; [the claim that] all things come by nature. Such men tended to be called Anabaptists or Familists by their enemies. ... Familism, developing the lower-class scepticism of the Lollards, was an anti-clerical, layman's creed. In this it fitted the temper of Elizabethan society when members of many congregations, increasing in wealth and self-confidence, were more and more critical of traditional clerical claims. ...

[Moreover, English society was much less controlled than is often thought.] First, there were rogues, vagabonds and beggars roaming the countryside, sometimes in search of employment, too often mere unemployable rejects of a society in economic transformation, whose population was expanding rapidly. ... Secondly there was London, whose population may have increased eight-fold between 1500 and 1650. London was for the sixteenth-century vagabond what the greenwood had been for the medieval outlaw – an anonymous refuge. ... [Then there] are the rural equivalents of the London poor – cottagers and squatters on commons, wastes and in forests. ... Unlike the relatively stable and docile populations of open arable areas, these men, cliff-hanging in semi-legal insecurity, often had no lords to whom they owed dependence or from whom they could hope for protection. ... Shading off from these was the itinerant trading population, from pedlars and carters to merchant middlemen. The number of craftsmen in villages in those days of restricted markets was vastly greater than it is today; in bad times they would look for customers over a wider area. Professor Everitt has suggested that these wayfarers, linking heath and forest areas, may have helped to spread radical religious views – as earlier Familists had been weavers, basket-makers, musicians, bottle-makers, joiners, who lived by travelling from place to place. ... An itinerant cobbler was the principal dispenser of the Marprelate Tracts. ... The heath and woodland areas were often outside the parochial system, or their large parishes were left with only a distant chapelry, so there was freedom from parson as well as from squire. ... Dr. Thirsk and Professor Everitt go on to suggest that squatters in forest or pastoral regions, often far from any church, were wide open to radical religious sects. ... The Weald [of Kent] was 'that dark country which is the receptacle of all schism and rebellion'. The densely populated forests of Northamptonshire were centres of rural puritanism, strange sects and witchcraft. The 'cheese' district of Wiltshire, the scene of violence resulting from disafforestation in the early seventeenth century, was also an area of poorly paid, part-time clothing workers and of religious heresy. Ely, [Thomas] Edwards's 'island of errors and sectaries', had long been a centre of plebeian irreverence and resistance, down to the time when Oliver Cromwell, 'the Lord of the Fens', encouraged the commoners. Ely became a Seeker centre in the 1640s. ... In the Isle of Axholme the inhabitants were said to have been virtual heathens till the draining of the Fens; in 1650–1

they supported the Levellers enthusiastically enough. In Cumberland in the mid-fifties, the Quakers met 'in multitudes and upon moors'. ...

There was, then, a long tradition of popular materialist scepticism and anti-clericalism; there was the Familist tradition that Christ was within every believer; there was the sectarian tradition of opposition to a state Church, to the tithes which paid for its ministers and to the patronage system which ensured that its clergy were appointed by the ruling class. There were also the millenarian hopes built up by the puritan preachers. It is hardly surprising that the breakdown of censorship and the establishment of effective religious toleration let loose a flood of speculation that hitherto had only been muttered in secret. ... I have [also] stressed the social background – the isolation and freedom which permitted radical ideas to develop among some communities in woodland and pasture areas; the mobile society of early capitalism, serviced by itinerant merchants, craftsmen, pedlars; the crowds of masterless men, vagabonds and urban poor, who no longer fitted into the categories of a hierarchical agrarian society. The great shake-up of the Civil War suddenly and remarkably increased social and physical mobility. The New Model Army itself can be regarded as a body of masterless men on the move. ... It linked up the hitherto obscure radical groups scattered up and down the kingdom and gave them new confidence, especially in the lonely North and West. ...

The New Model was the match which fired the gunpowder. But once the conflagration started, there was plenty of combustible material lying around. To appreciate this we must look at the development of radical and heretical ideas in England, some religious, others secular; some inherited from the Lollards, some imported from the continent, all modified in the rapidly changing society of sixteenth and early seventeenth-century England. ... In the hectic and exhilarating freedom of the 1640s and 50s all these elements were cast into a melting pot from which unprecedented new compounds were to emerge. ...

[By 1660] the great period of freedom of movement and freedom of thought was over. ... After the Restoration, officers of the New Model returned to their crafts. Preaching tinkers returned to their villages, or like Bunyan, went to gaol. Levellers, Diggers, Ranters and Fifth Monarchists disappeared, leaving hardly a trace. ... Yet nothing ever wholly dies. Great Britain no doubt fared the worse in some respects for rejecting the truths of the radicals in the seventeenth century, but they were not utterly lost. Just as a surviving Lollard tradition contributed to the English Reformation over a century after the defeat of Lollardy, just as a surviving radical protestant tradition contributed to the English Revolution ... so the radicals of the English Revolution perhaps gave more to posterity than is immediately obvious. ... It is unlikely that the ideas of the seventeenth-century radicals had no influence on the Wilkesite movement, the American Revolution, Thomas Paine or the plebeian radicalism which revived in England in the 1790s. Unlikely: but such influence is difficult to prove. [There are, however, some traces.] There were poets – Oliver Goldsmith knew about the Levellers and Blake owed much to the radicals of the seventeenth century. ... Burns perhaps records something of the tradition. ...[He] repeats many of the themes of the seventeenth-century radicals – fierce anti-clericalism, respect for honest poverty ... hatred of the smug hypocrisy of Holy Willie and his like, scepticism about the existence of Hell (except as a social deterrent) ... ribaldry about the Bible, a love of freedom, a belief that 'man is good by nature', and that international brotherhood is coming; his sexual practice disregarded the conventional ties of marriage. More work could probably discover more connections or possible connections. The Brontes' Haworth was in the Grindletonian area, where down to the early nineteenth century 'Oliver's days' were remembered as a golden age. The 'faith in the potentialities of activism ... displayed by the radical groups of the Interregnum' Mr K.V. Thomas tells us, was 'dashed by the Restoration; but the notion that political remedies could be found for social and economic discontent was less easily checked'. ... 'If you destroy these vessels', Edward Burrough told the all-powerful Restoration government, 'yet our principles you can never extinguish, but they will live forever, and enter into other bodies to live and speak and act'.

Questions

1. What do you consider to have been the main characteristics of the 'radical tradition' as described by Christopher Hill?

2. How does Hill explain the survival and dissemination of radical ideas against the wishes of authority?

3. How convincing do you find his arguments?

Professor Hill's view of an enduring radical tradition, and of the significance of the Civil War and Interregnum in encouraging and developing it, requires testing against evidence of popular unrest over a long period of time. In order to do this, we need to define what we mean by radicalism, to establish the characteristics that we expect to see in popular disturbances that indicate the presence of this tradition as an influence on popular behaviour. Taking the points made above, alongside the information about radicalism derived from Units 3.1–3.4, there appear to be four main elements which, in some combination, characterised radicalism in the seventeenth century.

1. Anticlericalism
Dislike of the clergy as a group. It involved more than an attack on individual clergymen, or even complaints of clerical laxity in carrying out their duties. Anticlerical feeling also included criticism of the position and privileges given to the professional clergy, and often extended to attacks on the entire church system that they represented. It could also include claims that orthodox religion was a device for maintaining social control, by the promise of reward or threat of punishment (heaven and hell) in an afterlife.

2. Social justice
Usually involving attacks on wealth and privilege within society, on the unequal distribution of wealth and the unequal operation of the law. Demands for social justice often included reference to the law of God, declaring that God had not made men unequal and that exploitation of the poor and oppressed was offensive to him. Examples of this characteristic would be Coppe's *Fiery Flying Roll*, with its threats of God's judgement against the wealthy oppressors (God as the Great Leveller – see Unit 3.3) and, in a more comprehensive form, the beliefs of Gerrard Winstanley and the Diggers. The idea of imminent divine judgement also encompassed millenarian views of various kinds.

3. Natural rights
The claim that certain rights and freedoms belonged to all men (and sometimes women) because they were rational human beings. In some ways, this overlaps with ideas about social justice, but the key difference lies in the basis on which the claims were made, and in the assertion that the rights extended to all as *natural* human rights. Seventeenth-century radicals concentrated particularly on freedom of religion, but also argued for freedom of expression, free association, equality under and access to the law, and in the case of the Levellers and Diggers, a considerable measure of political and social equality.

4. Political reform
Demanding changes in the political structure to express the principles of popular sovereignty, and eventually to achieve the direct representation of *all* the people. In one sense this is an extension of the ideas underlying section 3 – the demand for natural rights – and it was also often a means of addressing problems of social and economic injustice. These ideas were not always the exclusive property of radicals. Doctrines of popular sovereignty and natural rights were used by the defenders of parliament in the Civil War, and by John Locke and the Whigs thereafter, without accepting the logical implication that political power, as well as rights, belonged to all. In this area particularly, the views of 'radical' and 'respectable' reformers could overlap.

The purpose of this unit, therefore, is to examine incidents of popular unrest from the Peasants' Revolt of 1381 to the emergence of twentieth-century democracy, in order to assess the historical significance of the radical movements of the Civil War and Interregnum. By tracing the development of the four strands outlined above, we should be able to form judgements as to how far these radical movements represented something new, what, if anything, they added to radical thinking, and what, if any, lasting effects they had.

Popular unrest: 1381–1918

The sources which follow offer a selection of evidence regarding popular unrest, and are intended to highlight particular aspects rather than provide an exhaustive coverage of the subject. They should be used in conjunction with the material that you have considered in Development Module 3.1, as well as your knowledge of radicalism in the period of the Civil War and Interregnum. They begin with a consideration of the Peasants' Revolt of 1381. Although the revolt was crushed, the grievances and aspirations expressed within it found further outlet in the Lollard movement of the early fifteenth century, and in the anticlerical echoes that continued thereafter. In the period following the Reformation of the 1530s, popular unrest tended to be directed against rather than for change, but still reflected demands for social justice and a concern for the rights of ordinary people. Moreover, anticlericalism and attacks on the power of the established Church can be seen in the arguments of early separatists during the reigns of Elizabeth, James and Charles I, and while some separatists were orthodox in everything other than their desire to separate, others adopted principles which were in themselves a threat to the existing social and political order.

The period of Civil War and Interregnum saw these ideas flourish and develop on an unprecedented scale, and radical plans for a new heaven and a new earth as well reflected a conviction that England had been chosen by God to lead the struggle to establish His kingdom on earth. With the return of Charles II in 1660, the defeat of radicalism was complete and comprehensive, but the ideas which the radicals had espoused did not entirely disappear. The refusal of religious dissenters to give up their meetings and their willingness to suffer for their faith gradually won the sympathy of moderate men for a measure of religious toleration, at least for Protestants. The political arguments of John Locke and the Whigs asserted a form of popular sovereignty not unlike that put forward by John Milton in his *Tenure of Kings and Magistrates* in 1649. The Revolution of 1688, limited and restricted though it was, expressed doctrines which the radicals had supported, and fatally undermined theories of Divine Right monarchy. There could be no doubt that power emanated from the people, even if its exercise was limited to an élite. Moreover, the claim to derive power from the people as a whole was always likely to encourage the idea of accountability, and therefore of the rights of the governed to be consulted. Thus the accretion of political influence after 1714 to a small number of aristocratic cliques led to demands for political reform from 'country' MPs and their associates and also from those with more radical ideas such as the supporters of John Wilkes. By the end of the eighteenth century, demands for parliamentary reform had gathered pace, and groups of working-men such as those who joined the London Corresponding Society represented the emergence of a genuinely radical movement, inspired by native British traditions as well as by the contemporary influence of the French Revolution.

Demands for natural rights and political reform at this time owed little to the religious inspiration that had been so significant among the radicals of the Civil War. It has been argued that the Methodist movement and evangelical revival of the eighteenth and nineteenth centuries acted as a restraint on popular radicalism, diverting energies into a subjective religious experience that encouraged passive or quietist behaviour rather than political activism. Nevertheless, religious groups maintained a demand for social justice and spiritual equality which had radical implications, and while the Wesleyan Methodists maintained the political and social conservatism of their founder, John Wesley, the Primitive Methodists and other dissenting sects provided an important channel for working-class activity. Strong in some of the new industrial cities and mining areas, the dissenting chapels upheld radical doctrines and provided a training ground for political agitation. Many of the early Labour and Trade Union leaders received an education in their Sunday Schools, an apprenticeship in public speaking as lay preachers, and a belief in social and political justice which inspired and motivated their radical activities. The origins of the modern Labour movement can be found in radical religion as well as in the doctrines of socialism, a fact which distinguishes it from many of its European counterparts.

A major influence in the emergence of nineteenth-century radicalism must, however, be attributed to the economic and social changes which are collectivised under the name of the Industrial

Revolution. By breaking down the village society of Parson and Squire, by gathering an exploited working-class in large urban centres, and by creating social and environmental problems on a hitherto unknown scale, the development of modern industrial society provided the conditions, incentives and motivation for popular political activity. For nineteenth-century radicals, political reform, political rights and political power were not only valid objectives in themselves, but a means by which the power of the State could be harnessed to the cause of equality and social justice. The reformers at Peterloo, the Chartists, the early Trade Unionists and the emergent Labour movement drew on radical traditions and arguments, on existing principles and beliefs to address the problems and issues of their own age. It could be argued that the historical significance of radicalism in the seventeenth century lay in providing arguments and ideas upon which they could draw, and thus in influencing and shaping the radical movements and political developments of a later age.

The radical tradition before the Civil War

Questions

Use Sources 137–50 below, together with evidence from Unit 3.1 of the Development Study and your own knowledge of radicalism and popular unrest, to answer the following questions.

4. In what forms did radical movements and ideas exist before the Civil War?

5. To what extent do these examples represent:

    (a) a series of separate and unconnected incidents?

    (b) a continuing or developing tradition?

Source 137

From R.A. Griffiths, 'The Later Middle Ages', in K.O. Morgan (ed.), *The Oxford Illustrated History of Britain* (OUP, 1984) p. 190.

The cumulative effect of economic, social, political and military strains in fourteenth-century England is seen most graphically in the Peasants' Revolt of 1381. It was exceptional in its intensity, length and broad appeal, but not in its fundamental character, which was revealed in other conspiracies and insurrections in the years that followed. Widespread violence was sparked off in 1381 by yet another poll tax, this one at 1s.[5p] a head, three times the rate of 1377 and 1379. People responded with

evasion, violence towards the collectors and the justices who investigated, and ultimately, in June 1381, with rebellion. Agricultural workers from eastern and south-eastern England were joined by townsmen and Londoners; the grain and wool-growing countryside of East Anglia had felt the full impact of the contraction and dislocation of the economy and the social contradictions of an increasingly outmoded feudal society. Moreover, the rebels were disillusioned by the political mismanagement of the 1370s and the recent dismal record in France, and they feared enemy raids on the coast. Although heretics played no major role in the rebellion, radical criticisms of the doctrines and organisation of the English Church predisposed many to denounce an establishment that seemed to be failing in its duty.

Pressure on the government and an appeal to the new king ... held out the best hope for remedy of grievances, and the populace offered a pool of potential sympathisers. The rebels accordingly converged on London from Essex and Kent (where Wat Tyler and a clerical demagogue, John Ball, emerged as leaders). They threw prisons open, sacked the homes of the king's ministers, ransacked the Tower, and tried to frighten Richard II into making far-reaching concessions which, if implemented, would have broken the remaining bonds of serfdom and revolutionised landholding in Church and State. But the rebellion was poorly planned and organised and more in the nature of a spontaneous outburst of frustration. By 15 June the rebels had dispersed to their homes.

Source 138

From John Thomson, *The Transformation of Medieval England 1370–1529* (Longman, 1983) pp. 28–9. The extract refers to the Peasants' Revolt.

The demand for personal freedom, a recurrent feature in late medieval peasant society, does not reflect only a wish for improved social status, but also a hope for potential economic advantages. As long as a man was unfree, he had no access to the royal courts, but could plead only in his lord's court. A free man, on the other hand, could appeal in the public courts against any increase in the burdens imposed on him. ... Furthermore, he could leave the manor if he so wished, and could therefore negotiate for better terms from the lord by threatening to go if the latter refused concessions. ...

There was little ideology in the revolt, although Christian teachings of social obligation played some part. These were voiced most clearly by the radical priest, John Ball. ... The famous couplet of Ball's sermon at Blackheath:

When Adam delved and Eve span,
Who was then the gentleman?

was adapted from traditional preaching on the emptiness of human boasting. However, although it was not unusual for preachers to criticize social abuses and injustice, this was not necessarily given a revolutionary tone, and the significant point about Ball was that he adapted a traditional idea to revolutionary ends.

Source 139

From R.B. Dobson (ed.), *The Peasants' Revolt of 1381* (Macmillan, 1986) pp. 372–4 and 379–80. The significance of John Ball.

Few features of the early stream of commentary on the great revolt of 1381 are more impressive than the unanimity with which the chroniclers stress the importance of the role played by the 'foolish priest' of Kent. Froissart, Walsingham and Knighton, writers of very different temperaments and interests, all agreed in seeing John Ball as the *eminence grise* of the Peasants' Revolt. Although their search for a scapegoat no doubt led contemporaries to exaggerate Ball's significance and influence, it probably is the case that he was the only rebel leader to have won more than local notoriety for himself before May 1381. ... For modern students of the revolt, Ball's importance lies in the representative rather than exceptional nature of his career and teachings. The crude egalitarianism of Ball's message is now recognised to have been something of a commonplace in fourteenth-century sermons; and it can be argued that Ball is most appropriately seen as an example of those numerous unbeneficed clerks of late medieval England who formed the most radical and 'lunatic fringe' element of both the rising and the contemporary social order. For the English chroniclers, Ball's pernicious influence was more specific still. ... John Ball's activities furthered the cause of Lollardy ... and from that point it was a short, natural and almost inevitable step to the view that Ball was himself a disciple of [Wyclif]. ... Ball's 'confession' [to this effect, however] is an obvious fabrication; and Wyclif ... made clear his personal hostility towards the great revolt within a few months of Smithfield. ... [It is likely that Ball represented a general viewpoint rather than attitudes derived specifically from Wyclif. The only surviving written evidence from Ball himself, six letters preserved by Walsingham and Knighton and attributed to Ball, shed little light on the issue, but do reveal two essential characteristics of the author and his audience – a strong sense of personal identification with the ideal of social brotherhood, and a deeply personal devotion to the most simple and literal truths of the Christian religion. ... More explicitly provocative than the letters ... are several political poems written during the subsequent period. ... [which] declare their love of 'truth', their hatred of 'traitors' and [call on poor men to stand together]. Such letters and verses are fragile evidence from which to prove the existence of a powerful radical tradition in late medieval England; but at least they remind us that the king's low-born subjects were not always and inevitably inarticulate.

Source 140

From R. Hilton, *Bondmen Made Free* (Methuen, 1973) pp. 220–1, 227 and 229–30.

We have seen that some of the continental peasant movements were informed by a negative class consciousness, that is, bitter hatred of the land-owning nobility, sometimes even of all the rich and well-to-do. ... There is a tendency in the recent historiography of late medieval popular movements in England to minimise the element of social conflict and to stress rather that these movements were violent reactions of traditional provincial societies against the pressures of central government and of its agents. ... Whether reactionary or progressive, they were all-class movements of peasants, yeomen, artisans and merchants under their natural leaders, the local gentry. There is quite a strong case for interpreting in this sense the rising of 1450, usually associated with the name of Jack Cade, as well as the various provincial risings in the first half of the sixteenth century ... [but the Peasants' Revolt of 1381 appears to differ]. In so far as we can use medieval social categories, [the Peasants' Revolt] was a broadly based popular uprising of the third estate [commons] against the other two components of the tripartite society [Church, nobility and commons] of the Middle Ages, not a movement of all social groups against a narrow governing clique. There is not the slightest sign of even the beginnings of an alliance between the rebels and any group which had a part to play in the accepted political game: in other words, no friends, no apologists even, either in Parliament or in the Convocations of clergy. Two years later, in fact, the Chancellor, Michael de la Pole, speaking in Parliament, referred to the obedience which the gentry manifested towards the crown during the rising. ... There could hardly be a clearer indication that the leaders of the rebellion, if not the mass following, were far from thinking in terms of the balanced, tripartite society, than the proposals that were put concerning the organisation of the Church. ... These included the abolition of the ecclesiastical hierarchy, except for one archbishop; the abolition of all monks, except for two houses of religion; the distribution of clerical property among the laity; tithes to be paid only by those richer than the parson, and only to parsons leading better lives than their parishioners.

It cannot be said that the rebel leaders of 1381 had a sophisticated, or elaborate, or well worked-out or (above all) realisable vision of what could be put in the place of the social order they were attacking. Nor can it be said that the mass of their followers shared more than some of their long-term ends, though this is true of rebellious and revolutionary movements at all times. Nevertheless, a not incoherent picture emerges, simple though it is. They seem to have envisaged a people's monarchy ... in which there would be no intermediary between the king and his people, that is, no class of landowning nobles and gentry controlling law and administration. Similarly, there would be a people's Church, whose basic unit would be the parish, again with no immediate hierarchy between Christians and the single bishop, or archbishop, who ... was the ecclesiastical equivalent of the people's king. Somehow the people would make the law and administer justice. In spite of Froissart's version of John Ball's sermon, it is unlikely that it was believed that all things should be held in common. A regime of family ownership of peasant holdings and artisan workshops, with the large-scale landed property of the Church and the aristocracy divided among the peasants was probably envisaged. ... Within [this] simple framework ... there were certain elements in the rebels' programme concerned with immediate issues, short-term demands [such as] the execution of the traitors, the king's evil advisers who were responsible for the poll tax and the maladministration of justice. Certain clauses of the Mile End and Smithfield petitions probably refer to the Statute of Labourers and its enforcement – a major cause of social friction. ... But there were other demands, also of a practical-seeming nature [such as the demand for an end to serfdom] which were, in fact, genuinely revolutionary in the sense that, at that time, they could only be realised as an accompaniment to a radical reshaping of the social order.

Source 141

John Ball preaching to the rebel host led by Wat Tyler (left foreground); banners proclaim the rebels' loyalty to King Richard II

Source 142

From M.H. Keen, *English Society in the Later Middle Ages 1348–1500* (Penguin, 1990) pp. 269 and 290.

Some of the best English writing of the late middle ages ... is strongly critical, not just of the friars, but of the clergy in general. Naturally this makes a powerful impression, but before we label the age as anticlerical ... three points need to be remembered. The first is that, if anticlericalism is understood in the modern sense that implies hostility not just to the clergy but to the doctrine and the social morality that their teaching seeks to uphold, then there was none. The second is that criticism of the clergy is always and inevitably rife in a priest-ridden world; it is the price that its clergy pays for their social prominence. The third is that a great deal of the criticism of the clergy in late medieval England came from within the ranks of the clerical order itself, from men who, far from being hostile to clericalism, wished for an improvement in the standards of clerical education and exemplary living, and for a stronger spiritual lead from the clergy.

[Similarly, the emergence of the Lollard heresy reflects the strengths as well as the weaknesses of the medieval church.] The 'devotional literacy' of a wide sector among the laity was the foundation on which Lollardy, the first popular heretical movement of the English middle ages, was built. On its own, popular religious speculation could not have strayed into such a defined set of unorthodox attitudes and tenets as those which gave their colour to Wyclifite Lollardy. Religious literacy was nevertheless a precondition of this development. There was now a spiritually alerted public of persons able to read, who through their reading could reach out to a wider circle of listeners and thinkers. Whether they were literate in the strict sense or not, such listeners could latch on to a teaching that offered a radical challenge to conventional ways in religion just as easily as they could absorb more orthodox spiritual nourishment.

Source 143

From R.B. Dobson (ed.), *The Peasants' Revolt of 1381*, pp. 336–7.

Outbreaks of lawlessness and rebellion were genuinely characteristic of English public life for many decades after 1381. And even the more obviously 'political' rebellions of the Lancastrian period usually reflect some of the grievances expressed by Tyler and his fellows. Thus the rebels headed by Archbishop Scrope of York in 1405 attacked – admittedly in the interests of the northern magnates – governmental corruption and 'excessive and intolerable taxes and subsidies'; and in 1430 Jack Sharpe echoed the views of John Ball as well as Wyclif when he proposed 'that all the temporalities of churches thus appropriated against Christ's law be turned to God, and to the prosperity of the realm'. But for an extensive national rising at least superficially similar to that of Wat Tyler, the historian is inevitably compelled to turn his attention to Jack Cade's revolt of 1450. In its very different way, Cade's rebellion remains as enigmatic and mysterious as that of 1381. At first the resemblances between the two movements seem significantly close. Both revolts began in the late spring and followed a period of English military humiliation at the hands of the French monarchy: both were centred in south-eastern England and both can be interpreted in terms of a disgruntled popular reaction to excessive war taxation. As their 'complaint' shows, the rebels of 1450, like those of 1381, were careful to distinguish their loyalty towards the person of the king and their hatred of the real 'traitors' to his kingdom – the government's central and local officials. It is no coincidence that in both risings, the Treasurer of England lost his head. Above all, the two

rebellions reveal the curious fragility of the late medieval English state and its extreme vulnerability in the face of a sudden popular movement.

But perhaps the differences between the two risings of 1381 and 1450 are more interesting than their similarities. … The identity of the one or two Jack Cades, like that of the several Walter or Wat Tylers, is among the most baffling problems of English medieval history; but it is at least clear that Cade was a politically conscious and devious rebel leader in a way that Tyler failed to be. Their 'complaint' similarly suggests that the rebels of 1450 were capable, as those of 1381 apparently were not, of expressing their aims in a coherent written programme. No doubt this difference was partly the result of the more purely 'political' ambitions of the men who led or joined Cade's revolt. Nevertheless, several of the peasant grievances only incidentally revealed by the chroniclers of 1381 certainly recur sixty-nine years later: the corruption of royal ministers, extortionate taxation, the forest laws and even the statutes of labourers were still among the burning issues of the day. Cade's rebels, like Tyler's, were spokesmen for social as well as political discontent.

Source 144

From A.G. Dickens, *The English Reformation* (Fontana, 1967) pp. 46–7.

That John Wycliffe and his followers anticipated many of the key-doctrines of Protestantism has never been in dispute. The man himself remains in some respects a mystery; we know so much of his thought, so little of his thoughts, so little of the inner sources of his radicalism. An obstinate North-Country mind endowed with the subtleties of the Oxford schools; a combination of disappointed careerist, temperamental rebel, sincere reformer of immense moral courage; all these and yet further complexities seem to dwell side by side. During his last six years (1378–84) Wycliffe was no longer a mere academic radical or a mere revivalist. By all the standards of his time he had become a manifest revolutionary and heresiarch [leader of an unorthodox or heretical religious group]. He accepted the Bible as the one sure basis of belief and demanded that it should be placed freely in lay hands. … He restricted the true Church to those whom God had predestined to salvation. He rejected the doctrine of transubstantiation [that the communion bread and wine were miraculously turned into the actual body and blood of Christ] as a historical novelty and as philosophically unsound, urging that the body and blood of Christ were present in the eucharist [communion service] not corporally but spiritually and symbolically. … Upon the Papal Supremacy, Wycliffe had long cast doubts; he had likewise advocated clerical marriage, denounced monasticism and placed fanatical emphasis upon the need to disendow a rich and mundane clergy. Anticipating the Lutheran glorification of the godly prince, he elevated temporal rulers above human laws and invested them, and other lay magnates with the sacred duty of reforming the Church. Perhaps the only major doctrine of the sixteenth-century Reformers which Wycliffe cannot be said to have anticipated was that of Justification by Faith Alone.

Upon the Reformation abroad he exerted appreciable, if indirect, influence. ... In England [his] teaching underwent strange modifications. Despite its complex and scholastic exposition in his Latin works, it soon found vulgarisers and translators who wrote The Wycket and other English pamphlets falsely ascribed to Wycliffe's own pen. Within a very few years of his death these doctrines developed a widespread appeal among townsmen, merchants, gentry and even among some of the lower clergy. There were limits to their appeal. The economic restiveness of the peasantry did not in general disturb their doctrinal conservatism, while the revolutionary character of the Wycliffite manifestos, together with the attack on transubstantiation, alienated the great majority of the ruling and propertied classes. John of Gaunt, who had formerly utilised Wycliffe in a political campaign against the bishops, seems to have protected him while he wrote his last works in his rectory at Lutterworth, yet neither John nor the other magnates were now prepared to back the heresiarch as in earlier years they had backed the anticlerical reformer. Thus, despite the enthusiasm of a group of knights at court, the Lollards lost any real chance of laying their hands upon the levers of the State. Not, in fact, until the death of Henry VIII was any Protestant group destined to gain full control of this mechanism.

Source 145

From M.H. Keen, *English Society in the Later Middle Ages 1348–1500* (Penguin, 1990) pp. 291–6.

Dr. Anne Hudson has called the Lollard movement ... 'the premature reformation' and the name is just, for like the sixteenth-century reform Lollardy had a political side to its religious programme. Wyclif and his disciples argued explicitly that the secular authority should step in if the ecclesiastical authorities would not stir towards the measures and doctrines that they advocated. In 1410 a disendowment bill, based on an earlier Lollard tract, seems to have got as far as presentation in Parliament: it calculated that the confiscation of ecclesiastical temporalities [property] would support financially 6,200 squires, 100 almshouses, 15 new universities and 15,000 additional pastoral clergy. By this time the clerical establishment was arguing – and in the light of this bill justifiably – that Lollard views constituted a threat to the whole property-owning establishment and to the secular as well as the ecclesiastical social hierarchy. ... [That was the thinking behind the persecution of unorthodox views which began in 1401.] When, in January 1414, the Lollards did attempt a coup against Henry V, led by the heretic peer Sir John Oldcastle, Lord Cobham ... the point was proved. It was also proved how premature Lollard dreams of reformation were. The abortive rising of 1414 discredited Lollardy in the eyes of the secular

establishment, and discredited it finally: after this, there was no chance of it becoming a significant force at a political level.

In its earlier days, Lollardy had attracted some quite significant support in some religiously conscious quarters within the secular establishment. Particularly prominent in this context were a group of knights, mostly associated with the court of Richard II, whose patronage visibly helped to found and foster Lollard communities in localities where they had influence. Both Sir Thomas Latimer at Braybrooke (Northants.) and Sir William Beauchamp at Kemerton (Glos.) presented Oxford-educated Lollards to livings in their gift. The Cheyney family of Buckinghamshire were early patrons of the long-lived Lollard community in the Chilterns and of their pastors. In the late fourteenth century we can see a kind of network of Lollard groups growing up both in towns such as London, Bristol and Northampton, and in specific localities in the countryside, with gentlemen and burgesses (like the Lollard mayor of Northampton, John Fox) supplying patronage and protection for them and their teachers, and university-trained scholars and priests supplying the translated texts that made Wyclif's teaching accessible to lay folk. ... After 1414 ... the establishment patronage disappears: we hear no more of Lollard knights or Lollard mayors, or of Wyclifite scholars in the universities. Influential patronage had nevertheless by then endured just long enough: it had brought together the groups, instilled in them a consciousness of commitment to religious teaching with a particular slant, and above all, had put into circulation the texts that made sure that those teachings would not be forgotten.

So Lollardy survived, surreptitiously and among humbler folk, in the heterodox communities that the years between 1382 and 1414 had established. Its survival bears witness to the appeal, to some at least among the laity of a religious attitude ... opposed to conventional ways. Lollardy was determinedly anti-sacerdotal [against formality in the Church] in its condemnation of prelacy ... and in its questioning of the obligation to pay tithes, and socialistic in its ideas on property and charity. The sense of identity of a tight, puritanical little body of God's elect no doubt helped to give it strength to endure. ... Above all the Lollard movement was nourished and sustained by the reading of Scripture. It was as 'Biblemen' essentially, who maintained that 'no governance is to be held the law of God save that which is founded in Holy Scripture', that they were known in the mid-fifteenth century to Bishop Pecock, who made valiant efforts to put orthodox doctrine into the vernacular to counter their teaching (only to find himself accused of heresy as a consequence). ...

It is impossible to estimate how many Lollards and Lollard sympathisers there were in England at the end of the fifteenth and in the early sixteenth centuries. After 1414 more effective heresy laws cut them off from patronage and from the scholarly impetus that could have given their movement dynamism, and they were driven underground. In some rural localities where they were already well established, such as the Chilterns, and in some towns – London, Bristol and Coventry for instance – there remained enough of them to attract occasional hostile attention, but there is little sign of any significant increase in their numbers.

Source 146

From A.G. Dickens, *The English Reformation*, pp. 47–8 and 49–54.

Persecution forced Lollardy to become a surreptitious congregational sect, lacking effective national leaders and hence precise formularies. Moreover, like most religions which inclined to Biblical fundamentalism and encouraged judgement upon the Scriptures by unqualified persons, it inevitably developed a fringe of cranks. Here, however, we reach a difficult subject, for in some court cases the articles of accusation were doubtless based upon the testimony of foolish or malevolent witnesses. Both ecclesiastical and lay courts often showed gross unfairness toward defendants of any sort. ... Altogether, the weak features of the movement become apparent enough, though a certain strength shines alongside its weakness. It zealously sought to recover from the Scriptures an authentic sense of the person and spirit of Jesus. It argued with force that the materialism, the pride, the elaborate ritual and coercive jurisdiction of the Church found no justification in the lives of Christ and his disciples as recorded in the New Testament. It made a special appeal to the underdogs of feudal and ecclesiastical society by permitting them a far more active role in the management of their religious lives. In short, it had many of the lively features which characterised the English sects of the Stuart period.

This proletarian character of Lollardy developed rapidly during the earlier decades of the fifteenth century, when the movement was stripped of its political aspirations. ... Lollardy became a pertinacious [stubborn] rather than a heroic faith, occupying quiet groups of tradesmen and artisans, but here and there attracting a few priests, merchants and professional men. From the mid-fifteenth century the record of prosecutions becomes less frequent ... [but] if a real decline occurred there must certainly have followed a marked revival in the last decade of the century. From about the year 1490 we hear with ever-increasing frequency of Lollard heretics and of official attempts to obliterate the sect. ... In the early decades of the sixteenth century the most striking group of Lollard communities was to be found in the Chiltern area of Buckinghamshire, then near the southern extremity of the great diocese of Lincoln. Amersham, a prominent centre in 1414, 1425 and 1461 had again developed into a considerable focus of Lollardy by 1495. ... Further important heretical cells existed in the diocese of London, both in the city itself and in the county of Essex. ... A leading figure in this area was John Hacker, known as 'old father Hacker', a water-bearer of Coleman Street. Associated with him, and prominent in later years were John Stacey, also of Coleman Street, and Lawrence Maxwell of Aldermanbury parish close by. These two

were prominent members of the Tilers' and Bricklayers' Company and had wide contacts both inside and outside London. ... In Kent, especially around Tenterden, Cranbrook and Benenden several Lollard communities were denounced to Archbishop Warham, who in 1511–12 received nearly fifty recantations and delivered five offenders to the secular authorities for burning. ... In 1499 eight cases were recorded around Reading, six in and around Faringdon, five in Wantage and one at Hungerford. In the West Midlands around Coventry ... in 1511, about seventy-four heretics (a third of them women) appeared before the diocesan court.

Without question the influence of Lollardy extended beyond those areas where organised Lollard congregations existed, but in the enormous diocese of York ... only three cases of Lollard heresy have been discovered between 1500 and 1528. This may be due in part to the loss of records, but [it does appear that] the Lollard 'revival' so apparent in many parts of England may not have spread to the North in the first two decades of the century. Whatever [may] be the case, from 1528 the recorded situation alters. ... The northern heretics during the later years of Henry VIII afford a spectacle of surprising complexity. Old Wycliffite tenets are beginning to merge with the new continental beliefs; meanwhile the crude radicalism [which had always appeared from time to time] repeatedly asserts itself, but almost always as an obvious derivative from well-known Lollard teachings. One man, objecting to saints' days, made ill-mannered aspersions on the moral character of St. Mary Magdalen, but was so unwise as to broadcast them under the parson's window by the Church of All Saints, North Street, York. Another case is that of William Bull, a young clothworker from Dewsbury, who went off to ply his craft in Suffolk and returned in 1543 with violent, if now old-fashioned views on holy water, extreme unction and the confessional. 'The font', he remarked 'is but a stinking tarn, and he had rather be christened in the running river than in that said tarn, standing stinking by half a year, for when God made the world he hallowed both water and land.' And why, he continued in substance, should I confess to the priest when I have 'japed' a fair woman? If he got the chance, the knavish priest would always be ready to use her in the same way. But if I recite the Creed, and confess directly to God with a sorry heart for my offence, God will forgive me. This is not only the authentic proletarian accent; if a trifle coarsely illustrated, it is also a true expression of Lollardy.

Source 147

From R.J. Acheson, *Radical Puritans in England, 1550–1660* (Longman, 1990) pp. 1–2.

It is traditional in any study of the development of religious tension in early modern England to analyse the contribution of later Lollardy to the English Reformation, particularly within the context of the influence of continental radicalism in the shape of Lutheranism in the 1520s or Anabaptism in the 1530s and 1540s. Such an approach has its adherents: in a relatively recent essay, Christopher Hill has gone so far as to suggest that there may have been a continuous tradition of dissent linking the Lollards of the fifteenth century with the Levellers of the late 1640s. Yet it can equally be argued that the Lollards have no direct relevance to a study of separatism. Whilst it cannot be denied that their assault on 'priestly' authority was a telling blow at one of the fundamental pillars of the pre-Reformation Church, and that their rejection of the efficacy of sacraments was instrumental in laying the foundations for later popular scepticism, there is no hint of a desire to set up an alternative ecclesiastical system in Lollard activities or demands. ...Moreover, although Irving Horst has argued powerfully for Anabaptism as an important influence in England during the 1530s and 1540s, and has rescued its followers from the shadows, he has been able to produce little evidence to suggest that these individuals drew themselves apart into consciously separatist Churches, in stark contrast to their continental precursors. Indeed, although there is plenty of evidence for the existence of Anabaptist ideas in England at this time, there is very little for that of separatist congregations before 1553. A direct relationship between fifteenth-century Lollardy and sixteenth-century Anabaptism on the one hand, and seventeenth-century separatism on the other therefore remains unproven. But there is little doubt that the seeds of the separatism and sectarianism which were to shatter the fabric of the national Church from the 1620s onwards were indeed sown in the latter half of the sixteenth century. ... It was inevitable that under [the Marian] persecution individual Protestants, meeting in secret or merely asserting doctrinal independence, should develop what Patrick Collinson has termed an 'ethic of exclusivism' and an 'alienated mentality and behaviour almost indistinguishable from advanced sectarianism'. ... Out of the ashes of the Marian burnings came a Protestantism which was more multi-faceted than it had been under Edward VI, containing individuals and groups who had experienced the freedom of congregational self-government or the exhilaration of scriptural debate, or who had merely developed critical independence of mind as a result of isolation and persecution.

Source 148

From Alan Smith, The Emergence of a Nation State (Longman, 1984) p. 193. The Pilgrimage of Grace, Kett's Rebellion and the Western Rebellion are dealt with in greater detail in Unit 3.1 of the Development Study, where the main demands of the rebels are enumerated in Sources 33, 35 and 36.

[Sixteenth century] riots and risings...were limited protests by small numbers of men and women against what they regarded as intolerable injustices. As such they were part of a long tradition of riots and revolts which went back to the Middle Ages and was to continue into the eighteenth century. There were also, of course, a number of much more serious rebellions between 1529

and 1660, and Dr. Williams has argued plausibly that these were, broadly speaking, of two types, those in which the leaders attempted to seize political power, and those which were rather protests in force which did not seek to overturn established authority, merely to remedy grievances. ...These large-scale protests were the Pilgrimage of Grace of 1536, Kett's Rebellion of 1549, and the south-western rebellion of the same year. The Pilgrimage was the result of a combination of economic, political and religious discontents ... [but] 'fundamentally the Pilgrims were protesting against an unprecedented intrusion by the crown into their local communities and traditional ways'. The Pilgrimage was, in fact, 'the archetypal protest movement of the century', combining noblemen, gentlemen and commoners in a gigantic effort to secure redress of their grievances from a crown to which they loudly and probably genuinely professed loyalty. Kett's rebellion of 1549 and the south-western rising of the same year had none of the upper-class support which had marked the Pilgrimage. These were movements of the common people, the former essentially economic – a protest against a variety of agrarian grievances in East Anglia, including enclosures, high rents and the overstocking of the common lands by the large sheep-flocks of the gentry – the latter primarily religious – a rejection of the new English Prayer Book imposed on the country in 1549.

Source 149

From R.J. Acheson, *Radical Puritans in England 1550–1660*, pp. 14–17 and 27.

One radical group to be examined ... is the Family of Love, or Familists. Whilst English Familism doubtless owed much to the visionary writings of its Dutch originator, Henry Niclaes (b.1502), it also absorbed radical influences already present in the country. A comparison with English Anabaptism may not be as fanciful as at first appears, since the Guildford Familists who were discovered in 1561 seem to have held several ideas in common with Anabaptists also present in Surrey at the same time. ... It is difficult to identify and quantify Familists [since their beliefs allowed them to maintain an outward show of attending church and abiding by the law]. It may be that English Familism developed during the course of Mary's reign. The main exponent of Familism in England, a joiner by the name of Christopher Vittels, was certainly active in Colchester in 1555. ... In the celebrated description of Familist views published in 1578 by John Rogers and entitled *The Displaying of an horrible sect of gross and wicked heretics*, an interesting picture emerges. The sect appears to have met secretly at night in isolated houses. Scriptural expositions ensued, members speaking in turn according to their seniority within the sect. Goods were held in common ... and new members were welcomed with a kiss. Adultery appears to have been sanctioned, and the value of prayer was denied, as was any belief in the Trinity. The sectarians were convinced of their own perfectibility, and thus implicitly rejected the concept of sin, and subscribed to the view that 'all things come by nature'. We meet this again within the ranks of the Ranter movement of the 1650s.

A royal proclamation of October 1580 signalled the beginning of a campaign to silence the English Familists. ... resulting in a series of prosecutions which were centred on London and East Anglia, the most notable group, numbering sixty persons, being uncovered in the diocese of Ely. After 1580 the Family of Love in England probably ceased to expand. The evidence concerning the Ely Familists shows how tightly knit a group they were, sustained by ties of kinship, a belief that there were many like-minded believers abroad, and a conviction that their names had been entered in a Book of Life, allegedly in Niclaes' possession. ... [The sect] briefly re-emerged in 1606 ... but never achieved the impact that it had on the continent. ... The reasons for its lack of influence remain obscure. The moderate nature of the Elizabethan settlement may be part of the answer; initially, at any rate, hopes for reform of the Church into an acceptable model seemed attainable ... [and] in view of this, Familism would only have appealed to a very small element on the wilder wing of radical religious opinion. Contemporaries also associated Familism with Catholicism, and this may help not only to explain the limited appeal of the sect, but also the strength of opposition to it.

Many of the Familist tenets became familiar themes of the radical milieu which flourished between the years 1640 and 1660, but to assume the existence of a lineal progression from Familism to, for instance, Quakerism in the absence of hard evidence runs the risk of oversimplifying a complex development. It is probably wiser to see Familism as being just one ingredient in the radical 'soup' from which the religious extremists of the Civil War period derived their sustenance. ...

That the Elizabethan period was a time of religious tension and controversy is undeniable. That there were separatists in Elizabethan England is equally so. But to talk of 'Tudor separatism' is in a sense misleading, and to see such activities as 'gadding to sermons' or attending conventicles as evidence of separatism is misplaced. A great deal of 'radical' religious activity stemmed from nothing more than the predilection of a minority of the population to listen to edifying sermons either from nearby ministers or from itinerant preachers. ... [Moreover, this continued to be the case during the reign of James I]. Although Archbishop Bancroft was a disciplinarian in the mould of Whitgift, Puritans soon discovered that it was possible for them to remain within the Established Church without imposing too great a strain upon their consciences [especially under Bancroft's moderate successors]. Of course, there *were* separatists but, like the Catholics, they were nothing more than an irritation at parochial level, and were never in a position to launch a serious challenge to the existing Church. ... Within fifteen years of James I's death, however, England appeared to be swarming with sectaries, separatists and dissenters of all shades of opinion. One is thus driven to the conclusion that the 'triumph of the Saints' was a direct result of the ecclesiastical policy of Charles I and his archbishop, William Laud.

Source 150

From H. Shaw, *The Levellers* (Longman, 1973) p. 104.

What, if anything, did the Levellers contribute to posterity? In a sense, very little. Though they said much that sounds modern and democratic, they were a product of the Age of Faith rather than the Age of Reason; their rationalism was a product of God-given conscience rather than new scientific attitudes, their belief in equality was based on a Christian view of the brotherhood of man, not the utilitarian ethics of later centuries. Standing firmly in the tradition of Wycliffe and John Ball, 'they had', in the words of Dr. Schenk, 'much more in common with William Langland [a medieval poet] than with Thomas Paine or Karl Marx'.

Question

6. In the light of Sources 136–50 and your own knowledge of radicalism and popular unrest, which of the following hypotheses do you find more convincing?

> **Hypothesis A**
>
> Civil War radicalism represented the re-emergence, under particularly favourable conditions, of an enduring tradition of popular protest which sought to secure a more equitable system in Church and State.

> **Hypothesis B**
>
> Protest movements before 1640 reveal deep-seated economic and social grievances, and represented a continuing demand for social justice in Church and State; at no time did they put forward an alternative system of beliefs or challenge the essential legitimacy of the existing structures.

The radical legacy, 1660–1900

The following sources and questions seek to examine the effects of radical ideas and developments during the Civil War and Interregnum on the centuries that followed. The sources provide information and interpretations about radical movements after 1660, in the context of wider political change and development. Source 151 summarises the main characteristics of the Civil

War radicals, while sources 152–7 consider the changes that occurred in the ensuing decades and the ways in which radicals and others contributed to this process. Sources 158–63 focus on the role of religion and the Churches in English life during the eighteenth century and after, and raise questions as to how far and in what forms 'radicalism' can be said to have survived. Finally, sources 164–73 examine the radical groups and the movements for political, social and economic change that developed in industrial Britain in the nineteenth century, and consider the various sources and influences from which they drew ideas and motivation. Questions 7–13 allow the sources to be used to examine various issues, in order to build up judgements about the legacy of seventeenth-century radicalism and its importance in later political, religious and social developments.

Questions

7. What lasting changes took place in English politics and society in the years following the Civil War and Interregnum?

8. How far is it possible to define the contribution to these changes made by radical groups, as opposed to other groups, individuals and influences?

9. In what ways can the period 1640–60 be regarded as a turning point in the place of religion and the Church in British politics and society?

10. What evidence suggests that radical movements in the eighteenth and nineteenth centuries drew on seventeenth-century ideas and experience?

11. What significance would you attach to a radical tradition as compared to the immediate causes and circumstances in which these movements developed?

12. Did the radical attitudes, beliefs and traditions developed in the mid-seventeenth century shape or influence the nature of radical politics in the long term?

13. What, if anything, did they contribute to politics and society in modern Britain?

Source 151

From F.D. Dow, *Radicalism in the English Revolution, 1640–1660* (Blackwell, 1989) pp. 56 and 73.

The historical significance of the Levellers must be recognised. It is true that far from envisaging a completely democratic or egalitarian paradise, they were anxious to retain property, patriarchy and hierarchy. Their creed was that of liberalism and individualism, not socialism or equality. …

Nevertheless, they made significant ideological advances. Unlike other parliamentarians and republicans who were also wrestling with questions of sovereignty and trust, the Levellers developed their doctrines of popular sovereignty and trusteeship into a claim for the broad extension of active political rights. They went far beyond the doctrine of parliamentary sovereignty to place real and continuing power in the hands of the 'people', if not the 'poor'. … To support their programme, the Levellers advanced a radical theory of natural rights which looked forward to the later eighteenth century. Their political ideology was also notable for its rationalist and secularist aspects. Their appeal to reason was innovative, for although they combined this with a vision of the past as the locus of lost rights, they did not have the same view of history-as-precedent or of the sanctity of tradition as their more conservative contemporaries. Finally, although they made heavy use of religious arguments and sanctions for their views, their anticlericalism, their desire to separate Church and state and to treat saints and sinners alike as equal citizens gave political theory 'a push … in the direction of avowed secularism.' …

The positive significance of the religious radicals lies in the realm of ideas, not that of political events. In their religious and social thinking the radicals made major advances, but their political influence was in many ways the reverse of what they intended: instead of bolstering the 'Good Old Cause', in the short term they in fact aided the conservative reaction. In the longer term, however, the balance is different. The existence of dissent, and with it the *de facto* case for toleration, was to be an ineradicable legacy of the Interregnum.

Source 152

From J. Morrill, 'The Stuarts, 1603–88' in *The Oxford Illustrated History of Britain*, pp. 344–51.

The Civil War and Interregnum years saw the disintegration not only of Anglicanism, but of English Puritanism. The structure of the Church of England was abolished or proscribed … but those who dreamed of replacing Anglicanism by a Calvinist Church like those of Massachusetts, Scotland or Geneva were disappointed. The Presbyterian system conceived by Parliament was stillborn. The chaos of the Civil War created a bewildering variety of sects and gathered Churches. …

There was no recovering the old triumphalism after 1660. The Church might be outwardly restored to its ancient forms at the Restoration, but it had neither the self-assurance nor the power to reimpose a general uniformity. Anglican apologetic was defensive and edgy. With the disappearance of High Commission and the rust of disuse settled in its diocesan courts, it lacked the weapons to punish defaulters. The ignominy of its abolition left it institutionally enfeebled. In 1660 the celebration of Easter and the ubiquitous return of maypoles may have been spontaneous and have shown signs of its deep roots in popular culture. But those who chose to defy it were not going to be forced back into its assemblies. The decision in 1662 not to broaden its appeal by adapting its liturgy and by softening episcopal pretensions drove two thousand clergy out of the Church. Despite the attempts to prevent unlawful conventicles, the Baptists, Quakers and other radicals were not to be uprooted. Even more important, the tens of thousands of 'Dissenters' of 1662 who were within the moderate Puritan tradition re-examined whether their desire to be part of a national Church (though not the one on offer) outweighed their desire for a pure worship of God. In the 1580s and the 1600s they had preferred to 'tarry for the magistrate', to stay in the Church and to wait for better times. In Restoration England, they came more and more to opt for separation. In the early seventeenth century they found 'much piety in Babylon'; now they abandoned such temporising and went into schism. The Toleration Act of 1689 was the formal recognition of the fact of religious pluralism.

Source 153

From B. Coward, *Social Change and Continuity in Early Modern England 1550–1750* (Longman, 1988) pp. 95–6.

By 1660 ... it was impossible to restore a comprehensive Church of the type that had existed before 1625. ... Bishops returned, as did the Book of Common Prayer and the traditional Christian festivals. However, one change that the events of the 1640s and 1650s brought about was to identify Dissenters with radicalism and regicide, and 'Dissent is sedition' became a powerful political slogan at the Restoration. [Under the Clarendon Code] the 1660s and 1670s witnessed the greatest period of religious persecution in English history. Nor was that the end of Anglican opposition to Dissenters, which flared up again in the 1690s and early 1700s.

Yet Protestant Dissent survived 'the period of great persecution'. Paradoxically, some Dissenting sects thrived rather than dwindled in conditions of persecution, largely because persecution encouraged spiritual enrichment. ... It is equally clear that the Clarendon Code was not always put into practice with as much vigour as it might have been. Not all Anglican magistrates were willing to penalise Dissenters who they knew were not the seditious radicals they were often said to be. At times too, especially during the reign of James II, the dangers of Catholicism forced Protestants to close ranks, as they did in 1688–9. One outcome of these events was the Toleration Act of 1689, which allowed limited freedom of worship to some (if not all) Protestant Dissenters. So Dissent survived and by the early eighteenth century English Protestantism was irrevocably divided between Anglicans and Nonconformists. One consequence was to create a new (and permanent) divide

in English society as well: between the Church and the Chapel.

It is ironic that ... in reality the threat posed to the Church by Dissent, which had prevented the establishment of a comprehensive Protestant Church, was not as great as it seemed to be. Dissenters were still only a tiny fraction of the population: about six per cent in the second decade of the eighteenth century is the most recent estimate. Moreover, Dissent seems gradually to have lost its spiritual vigour. This coincided with the beginnings of a long association between Dissenters and manufacturing and commercial enterprise exemplified by Quaker families like the Barclays, Lloyds, Whitbreads and Darbys, brought about by their exclusion from politics and polite society. It is no coincidence that groups like the Quakers and Baptists lost much of their early evangelical zeal at exactly this time. Yet Anglicanism was not immune either from a general drift away from 'enthusiasm' in religion in the later seventeenth and early eighteenth centuries. This is most clearly exemplified by the growth of Latitudinarianism in the English Church. Latitudinarian divines, who slowly captured key offices in the Church hierarchy, stressed rational arguments rather than revelation and faith as the basis of their Christian beliefs. They defended religion rationally and coolly. Reasonableness in religion grew, and with it religion lost its central position in some people's lives. ... English society by the early eighteenth century had become secularised.

Source 154

From C.E. Whiting, *Studies in English Puritanism 1660–88* (Cass, 1968) pp. 476–8.

At first the talk was all of comprehension; but how could so many and varying sects be comprehended in one Church? [Bishop] Tenison, writing about reunion in 1683, said the Church might be able to unite with the Presbyterians, and possibly some of the Independents, but as for 'Arians, Socinians, Anabaptists, Fifth Monarchy Men, sensual Millenarians, Behmenists, Familists, Seekers, Antinomians, Sabbatarians, Quakers, Muggletonians – they may associate in a caravan, but cannot join in the communion of a Church.' Some of the Presbyterians continued to desire comprehension, but the numbers of such decreased, and the only alternative was toleration and the movement in that direction swelled greatly as time went on. The Quaker preached it and Charles and James were in favour of it. ...

Various factors were combining to produce a new spirit. As the memory of the Commonwealth faded, and a new generation arose which knew not Oliver, feeling became less harsh; and it could not be forgotten, at any rate by the Dissenters, that the sects had enjoyed religious freedom in his time. Moreover, what was done during the year of Charles II's Indulgence was never quite undone. As the fear of Rome revived between 1678 and 1688, many churchmen began to look to Dissenters as allies and friends in the cause of Protestantism. The Independents and Baptists urged that religious liberty for all Protestants was a guarantee for civil liberty. The Quakers, with their doctrine of the 'Inner Light' looked upon religion as a purely personal matter between the soul and God, and therefore out of the jurisdiction of the State or any secular authority. ... There had always been a number of Anglican divines who were opposed to violent methods, and the growth of the Latitudinarian school, concerned with moral life rather than doctrinal distinctions and influenced by the Cartesian doctrines of the authority of reason and the necessity of a rational basis for religion, helped to spread the milder tendency. ... Theories of natural religion and the Law of Nature caused men like Milton to consider whether religious freedom might not be one of the natural rights of mankind. Milton thought that the only solution of the religious problem lay in the complete separation of the functions of Church and State. The growth of the scientific spirit, exhibited in the foundation of the Royal Society, tended in the direction of tolerance, if not actual indifference to religious questions. Shaftesbury, Buckingham, Halifax and Temple, deistic and indifferent in religion, showed the new spirit in high places, among politicians. ... Following Hobbes, they held that religion, any religion, is only recognised by the State so far as it tends to peace, order and obedience. ...

A new conception of Government arose: that Government exists for the security of liberty and property, for the extension of trade, for the material well-being of the people, and has nothing to do with religion. ... In Holland, where there was a large measure of toleration, trade was prosperous. The inference appeared obvious. The foreign Protestants fleeing from intolerance found a welcome and favour in England because they brought new industries with them, and were also a standing lesson on the evils of intolerance. Persecution crippled business, undermined the rights of property and especially injured the middle-class trader. [In addition] the attempt to restrain by force turned out a failure: in the hottest times of persecution Dissent was in part driven underground, but in times of reaction it appeared as strong as ever. It became commonly argued that compulsory uniformity only covered a hidden discontent, and led to hypocrisy and often to war. ... But how could toleration be given to [Dissenters] and not to [Catholics]? No formula or principle could be found except that Papists were dangerous and Dissenters were not. Hence the one-sided and partial nature of the toleration provided by the Revolution of 1689. The State washed its hands of religious affairs, unless any particular form of religion should be thought dangerous to the government. The Dissenters ... did not at once obtain the same status as the Churchmen, for the Corporation Act and the Test Act remained unaltered. ... [They] were still barred from the universities and their ministers were hampered by lack of education, and came to be looked upon as socially inferior. Their congregations were largely confined to the lower middle class. Arianism and Unitarianism spread rapidly among them, and on the whole, their numbers and influence declined for a long time to come. Nevertheless, the Revolution [of 1688–9] was in essence a Nonconformist triumph.

Source 155

From P. Langford, 'The Eighteenth Century', in *The Oxford Illustrated History of Britain*, pp. 358–9.

It has been customary to play down the full significance of the Toleration Act. An extremely qualified liberty ... [alongside] the substance of the Restoration Settlement ... seemed a poor reward for men who had resisted the temptations offered by the Declarations of Indulgence and had welcomed William of Orange. ... Paradoxically, the resulting exclusiveness of the Church had much to do with England's eighteenth-century reputation as a civilised society in a barbarous world. A comprehensive national Church embracing all but a small number of sectaries and papists would have been a very different matter from a restricted religious establishment, co-existing with large numbers of nonconformists. The difference was perhaps [the creation of] a tolerant, pluralist society. The legal recognition of liberty of worship went far beyond what had been achieved in most of Europe, and Voltaire was to hold it up as the crucial element in the development of a free society.

Source 156

From J. Morrill, 'The Stuarts 1603–88', in *The Oxford Illustrated History of Britain*, pp. 346–8.

In the early and mid-seventeenth century, most intellectuals and most governors believed that there was a divine imperative to bring godliness, good discipline and order to the English nation. God was guiding His people towards a Promised Land of peace and justice in which men would love and worship him as it was their duty to do. The vision of a better world that could be built by man's response to the divine challenge was shared by James and Charles I, by Wentworth and Laud, by Pym and Cromwell. All political writings were suffused by the immanence of God and his Creation, by a deep sense of God's activity in human history and in His providences, His signs of Himself. Shakespeare's plays, Donne's poems, the thought of Henry Parker and the young John Milton all proclaim the same point: the plays of Marlowe are the exceptions that prove the rule.

No such hopes survived the Interregnum. The trauma of regicide left few royalists with faith in the providences of God; the much deeper sense of betrayal experienced by the radicals in 1660 largely explains their political quiescence thereafter. Psychologically, the pain of betrayal after such visible testimonies of divine favour was too great. Instead, most of the Puritans and their heirs internalised the kingdom of God. They accepted the world as the domain of sin and of imperfectability. Within this vale of tears, each person must seek personal peace by building a temple of grace within himself or herself. This acceptance of the limits of what Church and State could achieve dominated the ideology of the late seventeenth century. It is apparent in the way Charles II's jaundiced view of the world was combined with his deep personal mysticism, in the Latitudinarianism of the Bishops and of the clerical establishment; in the Dissenters' abandonment of the quest for a national Church. A few men continued to seek the millennium – Sir Isaac Newton combined his successful search for physical laws with an unsuccessful search for the dating of the Second Coming from the runes in the Book of Revelation – but most settled for making the most of things as they were. John Milton heroically confronted a God who appeared to have guided his people in the 1640s and 1650s only to betray them in 1660. … Perhaps republicans had been tempted into the wrong paths. Samson Agonistes … studied a man given great gifts by God who failed to use them in His service. … But the more typical Puritan work of the Restoration is Bunyan's Pilgrim's Progress which concerns the individual's personal search for peace and salvation.

Christianity was being depoliticised and demystified. The characteristic Anglican tracts of the late seventeenth century had titles like The Reasonableness of Christianity and Christianity not Mysterious. Where God had been in the very warp and woof of nature and life, he now became the creator who set things going, the spirit who worked within the individual and kept him obedient to moral rules. Sermons stressed the merits of neighbourliness and charity. Ministers were encouraged to preach that religious duties meant being kind to old people and animals rather than preaching about the transformation of the world. From the Dissenting side, John Locke, pleading for religious toleration, defined a Church as a voluntary society of men, meeting together to worship God in such fashion as they deemed appropriate. Religion had become an unthreatening matter, almost a hobby. The authorities need not concern themselves with what consenting adults did in private meetings. The Puritans of previous generations could not have conceived anything so anaemic.

This dilution of religious energies, this breakdown of a world-view dominated by religious imperatives can be seen in literature, in science … and in the visual arts. … Political thought was being secularised too [by Hobbes as well as Locke.] The English Revolution does, then, stand as a turning-point. It may have achieved little that any of the parties sought after or fought for. It may have done even less to transform political and social institutions. But it deeply affected the intellectual values, at least of the political élite. An age which derived its momentum from Christian humanism, from chivalry, from reverential antiquarianism [respect for past tradition] gave way to an age of pragmatism and individualism. When John Locke wrote in his second Treatise of Government (1690) that 'all men are naturally in a state of perfect freedom to order their actions and dispose of their possessions as they think fit without asking the leave or depending upon the will of any man' he was proclaiming a message only made possible by the disillusionment with old ideals, but a message which was to make much possible in the decades to come.

Source 157

From R.N. Berki, *The History of Political Thought* (Dent, 1984) pp. 116–8, 128–30 and 142.

What does begin to emerge in the sixteenth century is … something novel and excitingly different from all that we have so far surveyed in the developing Western tradition. … Though intellectual continuity with ancient and medieval thought is evident and easily demonstrable, from this time onwards new colours appear in the composite picture. … [What we might term] the Civic Vision was born and had its greatest intellectual flourishing in the early modern age, roughly between the Reformation and the French Revolution. … The civic vision resembles classical political thought in that it is secular in orientation, humanistic, regards politics as a [distinctive] activity, and approaches the state from human reason … ; [it] has as one of its fundamental principles the notion of legal and political equality … [and] is distinguished from its two predecessors by its 'individualism'. [While the civic vision is greatly influenced by the Protestant Reformation in general, it is ironic that one of the most powerful formative factors was the thought of John Calvin]. In matters of faith Calvinism was harshly intolerant and its tendency was to subject the state to religious domination, as witnessed in Calvin's Geneva and in the New England colonies. Yet in political terms it became the harbinger of modern republicanism and democracy. Calvin, a firm believer in the value of individual conscience, also declared his preference for 'mixed government' over monarchy, [but the position of Calvinists in France and England led them] to assert the right of resistance, even armed resistance by the people under their 'magistrates', to monarchs. … Thus it came about, giving a curious and interesting twist to the development of our tradition, that the twin causes of religious toleration and limited, constitutional government were most effectively promoted by the activities of groups of religious extremists whose beliefs, for the most part, were anything but tolerant. The crucial fact was, however, that they were not in possession of political power. …

The extreme 'left' wing of Calvinism finally led, most notably in the English Civil War … to a plethora of views favouring democracy and republicanism far in excess of what had been intended and preached by the reformers in the sixteenth century. Partly it was the logic of the situation, a protracted state of war, heightened insecurity and the intransigence of the foe, which led even moderate leaders, like Oliver Cromwell himself, towards the acceptance of extreme radical views. The English Rump Parliament's resolution in 1649 'that the people are, under God, the original of all just power', gave symbolic expression to a historic junction of political forces. … The Calvinist emphasis on conscience and individual righteousness [had revolutionary implications in these political circumstances]. … The same intellectual and religious atmosphere saw the birth of several republican and democratic theories of state, government and political obligation, most notably James Harrington's *Commonwealth of Oceana* (1656) which drew its inspiration from classical sources and came to exercise later considerable influence on modern radical thinkers. Another famous republican, the poet John Milton, foreshadows the liberalism of the nineteenth century with his eloquent plea for the freedom of knowledge and opinion. In his *Areopagitica* (1644) … there is as concise a formulation of the civic vision as we are likely to find anywhere … moreover, in the work of the English philosopher John Locke [a generation later], this vision was taken into the mainstream of English politics and exercised a deep influence on thinkers of the eighteenth century.

Source 158

Dissent as a continuing object of suspicion: an engraving from 1709

Source 159

From P. Langford, 'The Eighteenth Century (1688–1789)' in *The Oxford Illustrated History of Britain*, pp. 385–6.

There was a paradox about the Church's position in the eighteenth century. The influence of 'natural' religion in the early part of the century had produced a growing emphasis on works rather than faith. Christians were those who behaved like Christians, and charity was the most obvious expression of religious devotion. But rational religion, however benevolent, did not offer much spiritual consolation to those who lacked the education or the intellect to be rational. The spiritual energy of all the main Churches manifestly wilted under the impact of Latitudinarian tendencies. Mainstream Dissent … visibly declined as a force in popular life and retreated for the moment at least to its traditional support among the urban middle class. … It was left to that rebellious daughter of the Church, the Methodist movement, to offer the poor recompense in the next world for their sufferings in this. The many facets and connections of Wesleyan Methodism make it difficult to generalise about its importance. John Wesley himself was an Oxford don of high-church views and unenlightened politics. Yet to many his influence seemed to express something of the Puritan spirit of seventeenth-century religion. His own spiritual journey was tempestuous and marked by the highest degree of what could easily be seen as recklessness and self-will. But the organisation and discipline which he bestowed on his followers verged on despotism. In theological terms, Wesley was an Arminian; but Calvinism exercised a far-reaching effect on the Methodist movement. Indeed Wesley was preceded in the field by Calvinists such as Griffith Jones and Howell Harris in Wales, and George Whitfield in England. To their enemies all such men seemed dangerous, even seditious characters. Field-preaching could be seen as an open attack on the parish clergy's monopoly of the pulpit; from the vantage point of lay authority, Wesley's readiness to preach his saving message to all ranks and degrees made squires and shires shake. Yet his political views were positively authoritarian, and he offered no challenge to social order. Through his attitudes and those of his followers ran only one concern: the total availability of the evangelist's salvation to all, above all to the poor, to the outcast communities of mining and manufacturing England, neglected by the more fashionable divines.

Source 160

From J.H. Plumb, *England in the Eighteenth Century (1714–1815)* **(Penguin, 1965) pp. 93–5.**

By 1760 Methodism was easily the most highly co-ordinated body of opinion in the country, the most fervent, the most dynamic. Had it been bent on revolution in Church or State nothing could have stopped it. But then, Methodism was not a religion *of* the poor, but *for* the poor. ... In politics [Wesley] was absolutely and completely conservative. He wrote: 'The greater the share the people have in government, the less liberty, civil or religious, does a nation enjoy.' He welcomed Parliament's attitude to Wilkes and regarded the French Revolution as the direct work of Satan. ... For him the proper way to reform the evils of society was to transform the will of the individual.

As a way of life there can be no doubt of Methodism's appeal; it contained so much that was capable of satisfying the deepest needs of human nature. In the exercise of religion there was no emotional restraint. Sobbing, weeping, laughter, hysteria were commonplaces of Methodist fervour – a lack of restraint which seems to us almost pathological. But there was an edge to life in the eighteenth century which is hard for us to recapture. In every class there is the same taut, neurotic quality – the fantastic gambling and drinking, the riots, brutality and violence, and everywhere and always a constant sense of death. At no point did the Anglican or Dissenting Churches of the day touch this inner tragedy of man,

which was the emotional core of Methodism. But Methodism gave far more than emotional release; it brought a sense of purpose and a field for the exercise of both will and power. To men and women who were just climbing out of utter poverty by the dint of their own thrifty endeavour this concentration of will and purpose was particularly appealing. The oligarchical and rigid nature of local institutions meant that there was little scope for ambitious men and women with a social conscience. All doors were closed to them including, of course, those of the established Church, but Wesley provided an organisation in which they could fulfil their need for power and their sense of duty.

Source 161

From J.H. Plumb, *England in the Eighteenth Century (1714–1815)*, **pp. 133–8.**

All was not well. Each year brought fresh disaster and increased the national debt. From the early sixties [1760s] there had been a steadily mounting criticism of every aspect of English life. [The range of complaint was considerable] but the most effective body of men, at least in public propaganda, were the Rational Dissenters, who ... limited their horizons and engaged in practical activity. They dominated the first movement for radical reform.

The Dissenting academies were the major forcing ground for their brand of political radicalism. These academies arose naturally from the fact that dissenters were not admitted to the universities. Because dissenters were excluded from all branches of civil government, it was natural that they should be more critical of it, and that their interest in the rights and liberties of individual men should be strengthened. They were also freer from the traditional pattern of culture; freer to teach new subjects; and freer to receive new ideas. They were also favoured by chance. In Philip Doddridge, Richard Price, and Joseph Priestley they found teachers and leaders of outstanding intellectual ability and complete integrity of purpose. Their aim was primarily theological – the knowledge of God as manifested in the world – but their approach was strictly intellectual. Understanding could be achieved only through a study of history, philosophy, and the science of politics. The dissenting academies were the first schools in which economics, history and natural science were systematically taught, and this gave them an attractive modernity which drew to them pupils from circles far wider than those of dissent. The historical and philosophic approach also gave weight, depth, and a sense of universality to their attitude to politics. Freedom, Liberty, Right, Reason, Necessity, these were the great girders of abstraction upon which they built their treatises of philosophic liberalism. On the other hand, benevolence in its widest sense was absolutely absent from their attitude to life. Liberty and freedom did not mean liberty to be idle and poor. ... The morals of the poor were to be more effectively controlled ... and as in Methodism, [there was a great deal of emphasis on self-help]. Amongst the middle classes the popularity of these views was undeniable, [but] instinctively the poor detested Priestley and, like Guy Fawkes, he was burnt regularly, and, in the end, the Birmingham mob tore down his house.

Universal as their political philosophy was, the Rational Dissenters were forced to adopt particular political attitudes to specific issues – to Wilkes, to America, to the question of parliamentary reform. Both Price and Priestley were completely pro-American: the success of the colonies was the triumph of virtue over sin; it bore the hallmark of Providence. ... They were sympathisers of Wilkes, although they hated his morals. They were leaders in the agitation for parliamentary reform, which they based partly on historical and partly on moral grounds. Their historical arguments were more important, because they helped to foster the strange national mythology of the Victorians. They believed, as the Puritans had believed before them, that Saxon England was the golden age of political democracy. This was destroyed by the Normans and a monarchical tyranny imposed. A long struggle ensued. The first triumph was the Magna Carta and, since 1215, the democratic and libertarian forces, despite setbacks, had gone from victory to victory, but final success was jeopardised by the corruption of George III's government and by the unrepresentative nature of Parliament. [This interpretation of English history was] misleading, yet simple, and it gave to agitation the comforting sense of siding with manifest destiny. This was heightened too by the course of events. The stupidity of the government in its battles with Wilkes, and the handling of the American dispute, made a readjustment in the balance of political power seem more than ever urgently necessary.

But how was this to be achieved? James Burgh, a pupil of Price, had, in 1772–3, demanded in his *Political Disquisitions*, which enjoyed enormous popularity, universal male suffrage, a principle which Wilkes introduced into his measure for parliamentary reform rejected by the Commons in 1776. The same attitude was adopted by another reformer, Cartwright, in his pamphlet *Take Your Choice* (1776), along with the ballot and annual Parliaments; and for the next fifty years Cartwright was the advocate of that extreme political radicalism which was to find its fullest English expression in Chartism. [Extreme or not, the prospect of some parliamentary reform appeared strong at this time; the development of Burgh's Association movement, the work of Sir Christopher Wyvill and the Yorkshire Association and the sympathy of powerful politicians like Pitt seemed to augur success. Unfortunately the cause was set back, first by the Gordon Riots and then by the excesses of, and reaction against, the French Revolution.]

Source 162

From G.M. Trevelyan, *Illustrated English Social History, Vol. 4* (Pelican ,1964) pp. 60–3.

In the lower ranks of society, horror of French Republican atheism helped the Wesleyan movement to spread more widely than ever after the death of its great founder in

1791. Not only did the new Methodist churches increase their membership to hundreds of thousands, but the Methodist spirit was infused into older Nonconformist sects like the Baptists. On the eve of the French Revolution, the Latitudinarian and radical spirit of Priestley and the Unitarians had to some extent penetrated other dissenting sects that were nominally orthodox. But that liberalising influence was destroyed by the reaction with which the century closed, and its place was taken by a strong, narrow evangelicalism. The various Nonconformist sects, thus reinspired to a fresh proselytising activity, undertook the mission of Christianity in the industrial districts, a task for which the Established Church at that time had neither the organisation nor the zeal. While the war [against revolutionary France] lasted, the influence of the new type of Nonconformity was anti-French and on the whole conservative; the governing classes therefore regarded its increasing influence and numbers with less alarm than might otherwise have been felt. ... But as soon as the war was over and anti-Jacobin fears had receded, the unreformed and highly privileged Church Establishment was left face to face with a number of powerful Nonconformist sects, all inspired by a new evangelical vigour, and no longer grateful for a bare toleration. ...

The bridge between Establishment and Dissent ... was found in the small but influential Evangelical party which now effected a lodgement inside the Church. The majority were laymen – Wilberforce, the Buxtons and the Clapham 'sect' – [and] humanitarian activity was the characteristic form in which their religious piety expressed itself. In the cause of the slaves they were ready to co-operate not only with their fellow Evangelicals, the Wesleyans and other Dissenters, but with free-thinkers and Utilitarians. ... The same combination of forces – Church Evangelical, Dissenter and free-thinking Radical – worked for the education of the poor ... and in the following generation for Shaftesbury's factory legislation.

Source 163

From C. Harvie, 'Revolution and the Rule of Law (1789–1851)' in *The Oxford Illustrated History of Britain*, pp. 432–3.

Somewhat different [from the rational religion of eighteenth-century Dissent] was the Evangelical revival. Populist and traditional high church in origin, this drew inspiration from the religious heritage of the seventeenth century – exemplified by Bunyan and broadcast by John Wesley. ...It was respectable without being exclusive, ecumenical and diffusely 'enthusiastic' ... a faith of crisis, valid against atheistic revolution, unfeeling industrial relationships, and brutal personal behaviour. ...The Evangelical revival was politically conservative, yet it soon flowed into peculiar channels. In 1795 the 'Society of Methodists' founded by Wesley left the Church of England because they could no longer accept conventional ordination. Tories they remained, but further Methodist groups such as the Primitives (who seceded in 1811) became more autonomous and more radical. Methodism was northern – 'the real religion of Yorkshire' – elsewhere the Baptists and Congregationalists expanded in industrial towns whose élites were frequently Unitarian or Quaker. … 'Vital religion' accomplished a religious revolution in Wales. In 1800 over 80 per cent of the population still adhered to the established Church whose mid-eighteenth-century missionary efforts, the 'circulating schools', had increased literacy (in Welsh) and enthusiasm beyond the point where it could sustain it. Into the vacuum flowed Calvinistic Methodism and the other nonconformist bodies; by 1851 Wales was 80 per cent chapel-going.

Source 164

From E. Royle, *Chartism* (Longman, 1986) pp. 6–8.

Chartism was a product of the industrial revolution and therefore cannot be understood apart from the economic and social problems of Britain in the 1830s and 1840s, but it was also a political movement with a specific programme for radical reform. So although economic and social circumstances must play an essential part in the historian's understanding of the incidence of Chartist activity … he must also ask why the protest movement should have turned to politics. … The origins of the radical political programme adopted by the Chartists can be traced back to the third quarter of the eighteenth century, though in a more general way the nineteenth-century radicals also saw themselves as part of the Leveller tradition of the seventeenth. In 1774–5 James Burgh, a disciple of the radical Dissenter, Richard Price, published his *Political Disquisitions*, in which he renewed the call for manhood suffrage, and in 1776 John Wilkes echoed the cry in a speech in Parliament. From this time onwards the extension of the franchise was firmly established alongside shorter parliaments, as an essential plank in the reformers' platform.

This same year, 1776, saw the outbreak of the American rebellion and the publication of Major John Cartwright's pamphlet *Take Your Choice*, which set out the essence of what was to become the Chartist programme, with universal suffrage, annual parliaments and vote by [secret] ballot. … Great though Cartwright's contribution was, however, by far the most important of all the eighteenth-century reformers was Thomas Paine [by birth and education a Quaker]. He had cut his teeth in the American revolution with his pamphlet *Common Sense* and his *Crisis* papers. Back in England in the early 1790s, he went on to celebrate the French Revolution with a vigorous defence of its principles, and an equally vigorous attack on the British System in his two-part *Rights of Man* (1791–2). These products of Paine's fluent pen were to become the foundation documents of nineteenth-century British radicalism. As journeymen and apprentices in London, Sheffield, Norwich, Manchester and other towns and villages up and down the country read or heard read aloud extracts from the *Rights of Man* and similar political pamphlets which rapidly became popular, the theme of the necessity for radical political reform began to strike home. The government clamped down on such seditious works, and Paine left for France. … He was both a political pamphleteer and an able political theorist, advocating political, economic and social reforms which only the twentieth century has taken seriously enough to embody in legislative programmes. Even his warmest disciples do not seem to have fully absorbed his teachings on social welfare (including old-age pensions), currency reform, and the foundation of political rights in abstract reasoning. Historical appeals to lost Saxon liberties, denunciations of the Norman Conquest (and sometimes the dissolution of the monasteries as well) long continued to be heard, and for many the Bible continued (in the Puritan tradition) to be regarded as the republican's handbook, even though Paine thought the very reverse. Paine was popular and influential, but his ideas were absorbed rather than fully understood.

The late eighteenth century also bequeathed to the nineteenth the beginnings of radical organisation, as provincial constitutional societies and the London Corresponding Society (founded 1792) met to discuss, educate their members, and prepare for the day when England and Scotland would throw off their monarchical and aristocratic chains and walk in the full freedom of democracy. How far this brand of radicalism had petered out by the end of the 1790s, or how far it had been suppressed but survived as an underground tradition, is a matter hotly disputed among historians. Certainly, formal political organisations largely disappeared but in some parts of the country a minority of extremists does seem to have maintained a revolutionary tradition of subversive activity; and, more respectably, Major Cartwright continued his patient propagandism while Francis Place, master tailor and former member of the London Corresponding Society, began his equally patient career as wire-puller extraordinary in the no-man's land between the popular and respectable worlds of London radicalism.

The events of the 1790s, when the lower-class wing of the British reform movement took heart from the French Revolution, proved to be a turning-point in the development of radicalism. Although the reformers were a small minority of the population, the skilled and literate artisans had now, if not before, taken the step into political consciousness and had accepted the programme of radical political reform. Thereafter, the campaign for reform was to rouse considerable feeling in the ranks below those of the traditional political classes, as this awareness spread to those inhabitants of the new society who were about to be called 'the working classes'.

Source 165

From E.P. Thompson, *The Making of the English Working Class* (Penguin, 1980) pp. 23–4.

At one end, then, the London Corresponding Society reached out to the coffee-houses, taverns and dissenting churches of Piccadilly, Fleet Street and the Strand, where the self-educated journeyman might rub shoulders with the printer, the shopkeeper, the engraver or the young attorney. At the other end, to the east, and south of the river it touched those older working-class communities – the waterside workers of Wapping, the silkweavers of Spitalfields, the old dissenting stronghold of Southwark. ... The L.C.S. was a junction point of this sort. And we must remember that its first organiser lived in Piccadilly, not in Wapping or in Southwark. But there are features, in even the brief descriptions of its first meetings, which indicate that a new kind of organisation had come into being – features which help us to define (in the context of 1790–1850) the nature of a working-class organisation. There is the working man [Thomas Hardy] as Secretary. There is the low weekly subscription. There is the inter-mingling of economic and political themes – 'the hardness of the times' and Parliamentary Reform. There is the function of the meeting both as a social occasion and as a centre for political activity. There is the realistic attention to procedural formalities. Above all, there is the determination to propagate opinions and to organise the converted, embodied in the leading rule: 'That the number of our members be unlimited'.

Such a rule ... signified the end of any notion of exclusiveness, of politics as the preserve of any hereditary élite or property group. ... To throw open the doors of propaganda and agitation in this unlimited way implied a new notion of democracy, which cast aside ancient inhibitions and trusted to self-activating and self-organising processes among the common people. Such a revolutionary challenge was bound to lead on to a charge of high treason. ...

The challenge had, of course, been voiced before – by the seventeenth-century Levellers. And the matter had been argued out between Cromwell's officers and the Army Agitators in terms which look forward to the conflicts of the 1790s.

Source 166

From E. Royle, *Chartism*, pp. 9–10.

The 1790s had seen an explosion in the output of printed material of all kinds, and the man who, above all, continued this process in the early nineteenth century was William Cobbett (1763–1835) a Tory yeoman who belonged to old England by birth and conviction, but who in 1804 read Paine's *Decline and Fall of the English System of Finance* and was converted by it to currency reform and radicalism. In 1816 he decided to address his *Weekly Political Register* to a wider audience, dropped the price from 1s. $\frac{1}{2}$d.[5p] to 2d.[1p], and had a quite remarkable success as his paper found its way into homes throughout the country. In rural Yorkshire, at Malton, radical James Watson's mother was in the habit of reading it and, as Samuel Bamford, a handloom weaver from Middleton near Manchester, recalled: Cobbett's works 'were read on nearly every cottage hearth in the manufacturing districts of South Lancashire, in those of Leicester, Derby and Nottingham; also in many of the Scottish manufacturing towns'. The message was loud and clear, and readily understood. 'He directed his readers to the true cause of

their sufferings – misgovernment; and to its proper corrective – parliamentary reform.

In this sort of way, during the years of distress which followed the French wars, parliamentary reform became the cry. Local Hampden Clubs were founded following the example set by Major Cartwright; groups of Political Protestants gathered to discuss events of the day at the time of the 1818 general election; and Henry 'Orator' Hunt raised crowds to heights of enthusiasm. Other radical publishers followed Cobbett in issuing cheap papers for the people, one of the most influential being Jonathan Wooler, whose *Black Dwarf* brought a young unemployed tinsmith named Richard Carlile into the ranks of the radicals. Carlile then turned publisher himself and made his life's work the reissuing of the works of Thomas Paine.

By organisation, by publication and by oratory, the emergent radical leadership drove home the message to their working-class audiences that the rights of man belonged to them as well as to the rich, and that their sufferings would be permanently relieved only when they achieved full political rights. But if the writings and recollections of contemporaries are to be believed, the advancement of political consciousness was also promoted by certain key events in working-class experience. The American and French revolutions had helped to shape the older generation; the new generation of the early nineteenth century was to be baptised at St. Peter's Fields, Manchester, on 16 August 1819 – the occasion of the 'Peterloo' massacre – when eleven people were killed and hundreds injured as the local yeomanry cavalry charged the unarmed crowd of reformers who had come to Manchester from all the industrial villages and towns in the area, carrying banners and dressed in festive clothing to hear 'Orator' Hunt. They were dispersed in panic, carrying back to their communities their witness of the brutal assault. The event sank deep into the folk memory of Lancashire villages, and further afield. Richard Carlile, who was present on the platform with Hunt, took back to London the story of the 'Manchester Massacre', and working folk everywhere were given the opportunity to read about and to identify themselves with those who had actually been there. If this was the baptism, then a dozen years later came the confirmation, with the agitation for the Reform Bill. ... [In this case] the working-class crowds [were drawn into agitation by] a strange assortment of groups from country gentlemen disgruntled by Catholic Emancipation to pushing industrialists who hoped to enter the world of political power and shape it for themselves. ... [In the event, the working-classes gained nothing in the way of power, but] those still excluded gained something valuable from the events of 1830–32 – that is, experience. The sense of betrayal fortified the popular radical leaders and strengthened their position, for the 'respectable' reformers had proved good teachers. For over two years they had been urging the overwhelming importance of political reform, and they had shown how, by the external pressure of noise and threats, it could be achieved. [Five years later, in the first drafting of the points of the Charter (1837) the new movement began to apply the lessons.]

Source 167

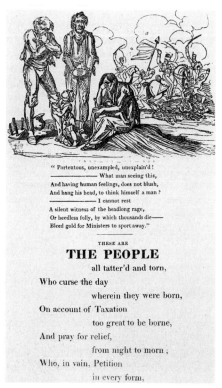

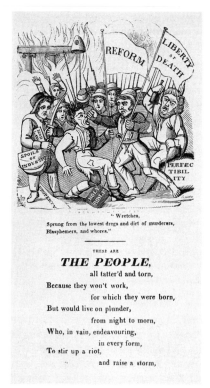

The Propaganda Battle. On the left is an extract from William Hone's The Political House that Jack Built *published in December 1819. With satirical engravings from George Cruikshank, the book attacked the existing system and called for parliamentary reform. In this case, Peterloo is used as the background for a wider complaint. The work sold over 100,000 copies and the use of the nursery rhyme encouraged it to be repeated and recited to those who could not read it for themselves. Its success drew a response epitomised on the right – an attempt to beat Cruikshank and Hone at their own game. Notice the inclusion of a claim of 'Perfectibility' attached to the supposed reformers – a reference to earlier 'dangerous' radicals such as the seventeenth-century Ranters and Quakers.*

Source 168

A detail from the famous satirical sketch, Manchester Heroes, *by George Cruikshank, published in September 1819*

Source 169

From F.C. Mather, *Chartism*, (Historical Association, 1965) pp. 11–14.

To the question, 'What was the cause of Chartism?' Edouard Dolleans returned in 1913 a single, alluringly comprehensive answer. Chartism was 'a reaction of the working class against the Industrial Revolution', a process which had worsened the conditions of life of the common people. Dolleans' conclusion was based primarily upon a study of Chartist attitudes as revealed in the columns of the *Northern Star*, and since he wrote, the researches of economic historians into more objective phenomena have made us acutely aware that the industrial changes of the late eighteenth and early nineteenth centuries varied in character and produced different effects upon the welfare of the workpeople in the many industries, crafts and regions that were affected by them. [The incidence and nature of Chartism varied greatly from area to area, and careful study reveals a complex pattern, from which, however, certain general conclusions can be drawn]. …

On balance, workers in the old, unrevolutionised handicrafts supported Chartism more faithfully than those engaged in modern, large-scale industry. Certain of these crafts – handloom weaving, framework knitting, wool-combing, nail-making – had already entered upon a long and painful process of decline, with wages sinking nearly to starvation level. The men who worked in them were especially militant in Chartism and disposed to persevere in it when others had left it. ... Such evidence is not wholly consistent with the view that Chartism was a reaction against the industrial revolution. It is true that the distress of the declining handicraftsmen was partly the result of competition from power driven machinery, but not entirely so. It was due also to hardships endemic in the unrevolutionised crafts themselves and exacerbated by the great population 'explosion' of the late eighteenth and early nineteenth centuries – overstocking of the labour market, heavy rents paid by stockingers for the hire of their frames and other forms of exploitation by middlemen.

Moreover, when one considers the more highly paid sections of the labour force, one finds again that it was the long established crafts more than the newer ones engendered by the industrial revolution that supported Chartism. The insignificance of the role of the engineering trades in the political movement has perhaps been overstressed, but [the activities of those in Manchester in the Chartist strikes of August 1842] were not typical of their fellow craftsmen, whose outlook remained too narrowly sectional to permit them to become involved in a movement of the whole working class. By contrast, the traditional skills, those of the printers, shoe-makers, cabinet-makers, tailors and coach-builders, played a considerable part in Chartism in its early stages and contributed to a more limited extent afterwards. They formed the backbone of the London Working Men's Association, which originated the People's Charter in 1838, and were still active in the years 1840–42, when the conversion of local trade-union branches to Chartism was reported in the press. ... The practitioners of these established skills constituted, together with the newly risen mechanics and engineers, an aristocracy of labour. They enjoyed a much higher standard of living than most working men. Some of them were self-employed persons rather than wage-earners, and, as a group, they were linked socially with small shop-keepers and small-scale master manufacturers, who also engaged with them to some extent in Chartist activity. For the traditional handicraftsmen Chartism was not a reaction against the industrial revolution. ... [Although economic difficulties] may have intensified their political radicalism in the thirties and forties of the nineteenth century ... their Chartism owed less to transient economic pressure than to steady political conviction. It was one manifestation of a continuing intellectual tradition which stretched back at least to the London Corresponding Society of 1792, and found other expression in a zeal for Owenite and Hodgkinite socialism and in the publication of unstamped newspapers. These labour aristocrats had assets which enabled them to develop a mature political awareness well in advance of the mass of the working force. They had time to read and to study. Through their trade unions they had long acquired the habit of association, and their position on the social ladder facilitated a traffic in ideas between themselves and the radical lower middle class of tradesmen, attorneys, dissenting ministers and small masters. Just as the renegade parson Horne Tooke and the Jacobin attorney John Frost helped the artisan Thomas Hardy to found the London Corresponding Society in the 1790s, so the master tailor Francis Place lent a friendly encouragement to the London Working Men's Association in the 1830s.

Source 170

From C. Harvie, 'Revolution and the Rule of Law', in *The Oxford Illustrated History of Britain*, pp. 443–5.

'I cares nothing about politics neither; but I'm a Chartist' a London scavenger [street-cleaner] told Henry Mayhew, the pioneer social investigator, in 1848. The People's Charter, with its celebrated six points – manhood suffrage, the ballot, equal electoral districts, abolition of property qualifications for MPs, payment of MPs and annual Parliaments – achieved the same impact as the French Revolution and Daniel O'Connell's campaigns in Ireland. But this only gave a superficial and episodic unity to an immensely complex, highly localised movement. Formally it was ultra-democratic (although only as far as men were concerned – a proposal for female suffrage was an early casualty). In its most dramatic nationwide phase it was also short-lived, lasting from 1838 to 1842. But organisation, and heterodoxy, bubbled away in the regions, influenced by the local economic predicaments, political traditions, and the character of the leaders. ... In Scotland and the English Midlands, leadership came from small tradesmen with a sprinkling of business and professional men. In Yorkshire it was militant, following heavy unemployment and the impact of the New Poor Law, but participated with the Tories in their campaign for factory reform. The 'frontier' towns of industrial Wales had already seen plenty of 'collective bargaining by riot', so it was possibly not surprising that a huge protest demonstration at Newport, on 4 November 1839, ended as a bloody confrontation with the military. Fourteen were killed, but subsequent trials led to transportation to Tasmania, not the gallows.

Peel [the Prime Minister] was more humane and tactful than Melbourne in 1831 or Liverpool in 1819, and his policy succeeded. The economic boom of 1843 and 1844 sapped Chartism; its last revival in 1848 reflected the agony of Ireland [during the potato famine of 1845–9] rather than the ambitions of the English artisans or any desire to emulate events in Europe. Late Chartism was more experimental and variegated, as well as more Irish. Feargus O'Connor projected land settlement schemes, Owenite and socialist ideas came back, along with ideas culled from European revolutionaries, many of whom ended up as exiles in Britain. But however fascinating intellectually the friendship of Julian Harney and Ernest Jones with Marx and Engels, the mass movement was dead. Old Chartists remained active in single-issue movements such as temperance, co-operation (the Rochdale Pioneer store of 1844 had Chartist origins) or trade unionism. Others emigrated. Many former Chartists ended up quite respectably integrated into mid-Victorian local government.

Source 171

From F.C. Mather, *Chartism*, pp. 6–8.

An important change in the character of Chartism took place in 1850, when the left wing of the movement, headed first by Harney and later by Ernest Jones, captured the executive of the National Charter Association, and remodelled Chartism as an avowedly Socialist party, intensely class-conscious and linked by ties of friendship with Continental revolutionaries exiled in England. In that year the executive adopted an explicit 'declaration of social rights' calling, among other things, for the nationalisation of the land, the mines and the fisheries, the extension of state credit to all and humane provision for the destitute. [Attempts to link with trade unions and co-operative societies foreshadowed the development of the Labour Party.] ... It would be dangerous, however, to stress the importance of the trend in the total assessment of the Chartist Movement. Before 1850 Chartism certainly could not be identified with Socialism, for it included both Socialists and non-Socialists, and the latter were almost certainly in a majority. Ernest Jones, later to become one of the most ardent Chartist-Socialists, stated in 1847 that the principles of the Charter 'involve socialism no more than despotism', and Feargus O'Connor, by far the most influential figure in Chartist circles, held views on Socialism which were scarcely less adverse than those of an early-nineteenth-century millowner or shopkeeper. It is true, of course, that most people who entered Chartism did so with a view to rectifying some social injustice, but that did not mean that they were Socialists. ...

It was not, in fact, until Chartism became moribund that [Socialists] gained control of the official organisation of the movement and refashioned its programme in accordance with their own ideals. By the time that it became avowedly Socialist the agitation had lost most of its former working-class support. The Chartist 'left-wing' enjoyed freedom to remould the character of the movement because the men who would otherwise have resisted them had turned to other things. Working-class energies in the 1850s were flowing away from Chartism into trade-unionism and the co-operative movement and towards collaboration in politics with middle-class reformers. The later developments in Chartism are, indeed, significant in that they show that what happened in the labour world in the closing decade of the nineteenth century was far less of a complete break with the past than is commonly supposed. This point, however, should not be too strongly made. Because the transformed Chartism was not widely supported, the more successful attempt that was made in Britain after 1890 to create an independent working-class party can have owed comparatively little to it. The later enterprise was in substance the product of new social and political forces.

Source 172

From H. Pelling, *Popular Politics and Society in Late Victorian Britain* (Macmillan, 1968) pp. 19–21, 28 and 31.

The religious historian ought really to bear in mind that the ordinary working-class population was too preoccupied with the needs of day-to-day living to spend much time on the niceties of religious doctrine. People's denominational sympathies, therefore, were likely to be determined by such practical matters as the location of churches and chapels in relation to their homes, the extent of religious charities, the availability of schools for the children, and the degree of influence exerted by landlords, farmers, and employers. ... Working-class religious commitment in the nineteenth century seems to have been most complete in isolated single-occupation districts, where a new sect could secure a degree of identity with the entire community, and some of the community's natural leaders could serve as its evangelists. This seems to have been the case with the Primitive Methodists among the miners of Durham and fishermen of East Yorkshire and perhaps with the Bible Christians among similar communities of the West Country. By mid-century, the Primitive Methodists, or 'the ranters' as the clergy called them, had also made substantial inroads in rural districts, where they satisfied the desire of many an active village craftsman or agricultural labourer to show his qualities of leadership and earnestness. The quarrel with the Church was not doctrinal but organisational: in the 'radical' sects, a man could play an active, perhaps even a key, role without having to be ordained or formally to qualify as a minister. ... One of the greatest weaknesses of the Church of England at this time was its failure to provide any means whereby men of humble origin could play an active part in its religious life or for that matter in its social work. ... But as the nineteenth century went on, the 'activists' among the working class seem to have found other outlets for their energy. As communications improved, so did opportunities for social expression – trade unionism, politics, organised sport and entertainment. There were no noteworthy religious revivals in England after the 1860s, ...

[By the end of the century] the general indifference to worship is fully attested by the investigations made by Booth in the 1890s and by the *Daily News* censors of attendance in 1902–3. Booth's conclusion was that 'the bulk of the regular wage-earning class' was 'untouched' by religion, with one important qualification, namely that 'their children attend Sunday School'.

Source 173

From C. Behagg, *Labour and Reform: Working-Class Movements 1815–1914* (Hodder and Stoughton, 1991) pp. 117–18.

The ILP [Independent Labour Party] was a national organisation with a socialist programme. ... But this was a version of Socialism that was identifiably British in its nature. It drew on three important traditional roots, of liberalism, trade unionism, and Nonconformity, and this made it very different to its more revolutionary socialist counterparts on the Continent. [Keir] Hardie, for example, led the Conference in its rejection of the 'class war' strategies of the SDF [Social Democratic Federation – an early socialist organisation founded in 1884]. Many of the ILP's leading lights in its early years were recent converts from the Liberal Party. James Ramsay MacDonald, a warehouse clerk turned journalist, spent four years as a private secretary to a radical Liberal MP. ... Hardie himself was a Nonconformist [a lay preacher], and a Liberal until 1887. ... Inevitably this influenced the nature of the new party. The programme and approach of the ILP bore the hallmarks of its progenitors' earlier commitment to liberalism. There was, for example, a total acceptance that the parliamentary, rather than the revolutionary, path was the correct one to take. Progress would be made by persuasion, and change would come gradually by a process of reforming existing institutions rather than by overthrowing them. Along with [this] many of the ILP's supporters came to the new party through the experience of trade unionism and this could be seen in the pragmatism of its programme. ...

The third major tradition from which the ILP drew its version of Socialism was Nonconformist religion. In leaders such as Hardie and Philip Snowden, a young clerk from the West Riding, the importance of Nonconformity was clearly evident. These were men who were more familiar with the Bible than with Marx. As Hardie was fond of explaining, 'the final goal of Socialism, is a form of Social Economy very closely akin to the principles set forth in the Sermon on the Mount'. Like Hardie, Snowden's Socialism was never doctrinaire, but his emotional platform style, known to his supporters as 'Phillip's come to Jesus', was a reminder of earlier days when the North had resounded to the oratory of the Chartist leader Revd. J.R. Stephens. This was a version of Socialism that drew heavily on emotive imagery and religious justification. One historian, examining those areas of the North and Scotland where the ILP expanded rapidly over the next few years, has referred to this phenomenon as the 'religion of Socialism'. The enthusiasm generated in some areas certainly seems to have taken on aspects of a religious revival in terms of its energy and its zest.

Question

14. What historical significance would you attribute to the radicals of 1640–60 in the development of popular rights and democratic government in Britain?

Module 4: Comparisons in space and time

UNIT 4.1

A VIEW FROM THE COUNTRY

Module 4 consists of four units, three of which view the 'English Revolution' from different temporal and spatial perspectives, with the fourth addressing the central question of whether, in the light of these different perspectives and the criteria that they establish, there was indeed an 'English Revolution'. Unit 4.1 considers the events of 1640–60 from a local perspective, examining how the study of particular events in different localities reveals the rich variety of reactions and responses to developments in central government, and how this might affect judgements as to the revolutionary nature and significance of what took place. Unit 4.2 compares events in England with others in Europe, considering how far the coincidence of revolution, or rebellion, in a number of European states at this time signifies a general European crisis, and what this may imply concerning the nature and significance of events in England. Unit 4.3 widens both the temporal and spatial perspectives to compare the English Revolution with a number of other revolutionary occurrences, in order to establish whether there is a pattern or model of revolution, or at least whether there are any common and essential characteristics. Conclusions drawn from these comparisons can then be used to consider how far the name 'English Revolution' can justly be applied to the events of 1640–60. Finally, Unit 4.4 attempts to draw together the judgements arising from all four modules in the Depth Study, in order to determine the extent to which the mid-seventeenth century witnessed a revolution in England.

Introduction

In recent decades, historians have become increasingly aware of the significance and extent of variation in the response of local communities to the momentous events that took place in England between 1640 and 1660. A growing number of local case studies have revealed the rich complexity of local reactions to national events, and have, in the process, established the existence of a local or regional perspective which influenced the attitudes of those to whom both king and parliament looked

for support. The importance of these perspectives is explained below in Sources 1 and 2.

Source 1

From John Morrill, *Seventeenth-Century Britain, 1603–1714* (Folkestone, 1980) p. 125.

The new tradition has been built upon the following arguments: (a) That the social, institutional and political arrangements in most counties by 1600 were so distinctive, inward-looking and semi-autonomous that they require to be treated separately. England at this period is more like a federated state than a unitary national state; (b) Effective control over the social, political and (to a lesser extent) religious institutions of each county lay with a fairly self-evident and largely self-sustaining group of gentry families, distinguished from the rest of the community by their wealth, by their interconnections of blood and marriage, and by a distinctive educational background. The crown at any moment chose the actual governors from among the very restricted number of families making up these county communities; (c) The crown could only govern (in particular, could only raise money, enforce its social and economic policies, and maintain law and order) through establishing an identity of interest with these county governors. This meant operating an elaborate system of quid-pro-quos, itself a combination of sticks and carrots. It has been argued by local historians that the early Stuarts failed to operate this system as skilfully as Elizabeth I had done. Most have preferred to see this as a lack of skill on the crown's part rather than the collapse of the system itself from wider forces; (d) National issues did not impinge as directly on provincial squires and others as historians have assumed. Rather, national issues took on different resonances in each local context and became intricately bound up with purely local issues and groupings. Local studies have thus tended to emphasize the uniqueness of each county's response to the crises of the mid-seventeenth century and have also found that much parliamentarianism grew out of an experience of centralist encroachment, and was deeply conservative in nature.

Source 2

From A. Everitt, *The Local Community and the Great Rebellion* (Historical Association, 1969) pp. 5–6 and 8.

The allegiance of the provincial gentry to the community of their native shire is one of the basic facts of English history in the seventeenth and eighteenth centuries. Though the sense of national identity had been increasing since the early Tudors, so too had the sense of county identity; and the latter was normally, I believe, the more powerful sentiment in 1640–60. There were many factors in the development of regional loyalty: the growth of county administration, the development of county institutions, the expanding wealth of the local gentry, their increasing tendency to intermarriage, their growing interest in local history and legal custom, the rise of the county towns as social, cultural and administrative centres. These and many other elements entered into the rise of what Napier once called the 'county commonwealths' of England.

In some respects the Civil War period, by greatly adding to the complexity and volume of local government, increased this sense of county awareness. Certainly the inevitable collision between local and national loyalties implicit in the social development of the sixteenth and seventeenth centuries was precipitated by the political events of 1640–60. Quite apart from the politics of the Civil War, however, there was much in the development of English society that fostered the sense of county cohesion. Despite the well-known fact that many gentry attended the universities and some of the wealthier families spent part of the year in London, the vast majority of country gentry passed most of their lives within a few miles of their native manor-house, in a circle often as limited as that of their tenants and labourers. The brief years at the University and the Inns of Court were no more than an interlude, principally designed to fit them out for their functions as justices, squires and landlords in their own county. After the time spent at Oxford or in London, most of them quickly settled back into the old routine of country life. Henry Oxinden of Maydeacon in East Kent, for example, apparently visited London only once in his life: and when he was there he told his wife that, if he could only get clear of it, he desired never to come thither again. The mother of Edward Hyde, the great minister of Charles I and Charles II, is said to have spent the whole of her life in the county of Wiltshire, and never once to have stepped over its borders into the neighbouring shires. Not surprisingly when people like Mary Hyde and Henry Oxinden spoke of their 'country', they did not mean England, but Wiltshire or Kent, Leicestershire or Northamptonshire, Cumberland or Durham. ...

In 1640, however, local attachments were, if anything, becoming deeper rather than more superficial. For this reason the Civil War was not simply a struggle between gallant Cavaliers and psalm-singing Roundheads. If one studies the history of any particular county community in this period, particularly if one is fortunate enough to find an extensive corpus [body] of family correspondence, one finds that only a small minority of provincial gentry can be exactly classified in either of these conventional categories. This does not mean that most English people were indifferent to the political problems of the time, but that their loyalties were polarised around different ideals.

For them, bounded as they so often were by local horizons, a more urgent problem was the conflict between loyalty to the nation and loyalty to the county community. This division cut across the conventional divisions like a geological fault. The unwillingness of most people to forgo the independence of their shire and to admit that allegiance to the kingdom as a whole must override it was certainly one of the reasons why the Civil War was so long drawn out. In some respects the England of 1640 resembled a union of partially independent county-states, rather as Canada today is a union of self-governing provinces, or America of federated states: and that union, as we all know, is not always a very simple or easy relationship.

Sources 1 and 2 therefore emphasise the importance of the local perspective on two levels. In the first place, it was a part of the outlook of those who participated in the Civil War and its aftermath, and thus an essential element in the decisions that they took and the way in which they reacted to the decisions of others. It was a part of their perception of what was happening, and it is therefore necessary for those who study what was occurring to take it into account. Local needs, local issues and local loyalties contributed to the outlook and actions of contemporaries, and must therefore be understood by those seeking to comprehend the outlook and explain the actions. Secondly, the local perspective reveals the range and variety of reactions occurring across the country in this period. Any explanation of the causes, nature and significance of the Civil Wars must necessarily generalise on a national scale in order to offer a coherent account of events, but the process of generalisation will inevitably simplify the picture and distort the reality of what occurred. The value of local studies has been to restore the local perspective and reveal the complexity of the process by which individuals were drawn into the struggle. The area is not without pitfalls. The historian John Morrill, in a recent survey of local studies, admitted that local complexities and local interests could obscure the genuine and widespread concern with political and religious issues, but continued 'I would still like to make the following claims for the importance of local studies of the origins of the Civil War. First, that localism was an important factor in alienating many people from the government of Charles I by 1640; that it limited the support that both the king and his opponents were able to call on in 1642; and that an understanding of the ways local loyalties lie helps to an understanding of the patterning of allegiance in any part of England. ... If we revert to thinking that we can understand allegiance in the English Civil War as being determined by simple rational choices between two party manifestoes we will not only fail to understand how it came about, but why it had the *shape* that it had, and why it had the outcome that it had.' He goes on to consider a further issue that has arisen in recent local studies – the possibility, once little regarded, of making realistic assessments of how and how far ordinary people, below the rank of local or county government, were voluntarily engaged in the struggle.

The unit which follows therefore attempts to address three issues. First, it seeks to examine the process by which individuals and communities took sides in the Civil War, both at the point of its outbreak in 1642 and at moments later in the struggle when war or its aftermath impinged on their lives. Secondly, it addresses the issue of reactions among 'those who did not rule' and to whom they gave their support, willingly or otherwise. Thirdly, it considers what is therefore implied about the nature of events in this period, and in particular, how far they can be considered revolutionary. The unit falls into two sections, the first of which raises a number of themes and issues in which the local perspective can enhance our understanding of what was happening in the period of civil war and interregnum, while the second is a local case study seeking to demonstrate what may be learned about a particular aspect of the period by studying one area in some depth. The example chosen, the events in Hull in 1642–3, has a specific national significance, but this is not a necessary qualification in deciding upon the value of a local study. The study of Hull could be replaced by any local study, based on any event or issue related to the period, and there is much to be said for students concentrating upon examples which allow them to examine their own local area in some way and to draw upon their own local knowledge. The Hull study raises issues about the process of taking sides, the role of individuals, and the participation of ordinary people in the process. An alternative case study might raise slightly different issues, but in the wider context established in the first section, the value and significance of the local perspective can be assessed in many different ways, each of which can enable us to consider its impact upon our understanding of the period and the extent to which it can be considered revolutionary.

The local perspective: issues and themes

The following sources address a number of issues. Sources 3–11 deal with the process by which individuals and groups took sides, illustrating the

complexities involved; Sources 12–15 remind us of some motives, including national issues such as religion; Sources 16–22 consider the force of neutralism and concern for the peace and protection of particular localities, while Source 23 looks at localism in the context of the Parliamentary committees and also considers the impact of the Civil War on local government. Finally, sources 24–30 raise the issue of the involvement of the common people, or 'those who do not rule', and the extent to which they were motivated, or were free to be motivated, by issues beyond their own immediate necessities.

Questions

1. What motives and concerns influenced those who took sides in the Civil War of 1642–6?

2. How widespread was the desire to remain neutral?

3. How far, and for what reasons, were the common people engaged in the events of this period?

4. In what ways are local studies useful to historians who try to explain the nature and impact of the civil wars in England?

Source 3

Taking Sides. From A. Fletcher, *The Outbreak of the English Civil War* (Arnold, 1981) pp. 379–80 and 400–1.

Many gentry, it seems clear, asked themselves two separate sets of questions as the Civil War broke out, and the answers they gave themselves did not necessarily produce a consistent line of action. The first set of questions was about their allegiance and political sympathies, the second was about the best interests of themselves, their families and their locality. Sir George Booth ... sent his tenants to the Parliamentarian stronghold of Manchester [while simultaneously trying to prevent forces of any kind being raised for action in Cheshire]. ... Lord Montagu showed great vehemence in recruiting for the king in Northamptonshire: for instance he threatened a Lowick yeoman with the gaol if he did not send his two sons to Nottingham. But in a conciliatory letter to the deputy lieutenants on 15 August he and the Earl of Westmorland spoke of their hope 'that with joint consent we may cherish the peace and quiet of the country [county]'. Localism, in other words, was a crucial ingredient in men's thinking and actions.

What was localism? It can be defined as attachment to the interests of and identification with units smaller than the state, such as regions, counties, towns and neighbourhoods. Localism and neutralism were not the same things. Indeed, localism could appear in many guises and be exploited in many ways, some of which are not at all obvious at first sight. But recent work has shown how, in one way or another, the tension between local and national interests was at the heart of many parliamentary elections in the early seventeenth century, the parliamentary debates of the 1620s, the political problems raised by the making of war from 1643 to 1648, and the difficulties encountered by the Cromwellian regime in the 1650s. Because the gentry communities believed that the Long Parliament had reform in hand and understood their concerns, this tension, normally so prominent, was latent in 1641. ... The petitions of early 1642 indicate a quite remarkable degree of unanimity about the nation's problems. Localism, briefly, was largely superfluous, showing its head only in traditional grumbles about the weight of taxation and in the campaigns to remedy a few particular grievances like the billeting money due to Yorkshire, Durham and Northumberland. But in the summer of 1642, everything changed. When the king and parliament sought active support against each other, localism suddenly became a crucial determinant of the responses of both counties and towns to the national conflict.

This discussion of how towns and gentry communities reacted to the Civil War emphasises some of the difficulties in the way of discovering men's real allegiance in 1642. It is hard to believe ... that many well-informed men were pure neutrals at heart. The leading men in the shires, and to some extent the same goes for mayors and aldermen, had been too much involved in the political debate to avoid adopting their own standpoints. Few surely saw a precisely equal amount of right on both sides. Passion and argument had been aroused by petitioning and by numerous informal discussions. Yet at the same time, everyone who was politically aware faced the dilemma that by being true to their deepest feelings they might increase polarisation and destroy local peace. Thus commitment and activism were not the same things: on the one hand activism did not necessarily follow from commitment; on the other hand, there was ... a form of localist activism which did not imply confident or wholehearted commitment to one side or the other. Arguments from men's actions are thus full of pitfalls; intentions need to be interpreted with the utmost care. The terminology of allegiance is still confused, though recent work has made it clear that it is essential to distinguish between moderates and those who became more fiercely committed and between various kinds of collaboration, once the war was under way, with the dominant party in a man's neighbourhood.

Source 4

England divided, 1642. From Clarendon, *The History of the Rebellion and Civil Wars in England*.

Training as volunteers for parliament began ... only in those corporations and by those inferior people who were notorious for faction and schism in religion. ... The people generally (except in great towns and corporations where, beside the natural malignity, the factious lecturers and emissaries from parliament had poisoned the affections) and especially those of quality were loyally inclined. ...

[In the West] most of the gentry were engaged [against the parliament] as they were in truth throughout the kingdom; yet the common people, especially in the clothing parts of Somerset, were generally too much inclined to them. ... [Their leaders were] for the most part clothiers, men who, though they were rich, had not been before of power and reputation there. ... Though the gentlemen of ancient families and estates in that country were for the most part well-affected to the king ... yet there were people of an inferior degree who ... had gotten very great fortunes; and by degrees getting themselves into the gentlemen's estates, were angry that they found not themselves in the same esteem and reputation with those whose estates they had. ... Those from the beginning were fast friends to the parliament. ...

[In Gloucestershire] the yeomanry [have] been most forward and seditious, being very wealthy. ... [In Lancashire] men of no name ... [and] the town of Manchester opposed the king. ... [In Yorkshire] besides the Lord Fairfax ... few of good reputation and fortune ran that way. ... Leeds, Halifax and Bradford (three very populous and rich towns which, depending wholly upon clothiers, naturally maligned the gentry) were wholly at their disposition.

Source 5

England divided, 1642. From Richard Baxter, *Reliquiae Baxterianae*.

A great part of the Lords forsook the parliament and so did many of the House of Commons, and came to the king; but that was after Edgehill fight, when the king was at Oxford. A very great part of the knights and gentlemen ... adhered to the king; except in Middlesex, Essex, Suffolk, Norfolk, Cambridgeshire etc., where the king with his army never came. And could he have got footing there, it is like that it would have been there as it was in other places. And most of the tenants of these gentlemen, and also most of the poorest of the people, whom the other called 'the rabble', did follow the gentry and were for the king. On the parliament's side were (besides themselves) some of the gentry in most of the counties, and the greatest part of the tradesmen and freeholders, and the middle sort of men, especially in those corporations and countries which depend on clothing and such manufactures.

Source 6

The process of division, 1642. From Lucy Hutchinson, *Memoirs of the Life of Colonel Hutchinson*.

Before the flame of war broke out in the top of the chimneys, the smoke ascended in every country [county]. The king had sent forth commissions of array, and the parliament had given out commissions for their militia, and sent off their members into all counties to put them in execution. Between these, in many places, there were fierce contests and disputes (almost to blood) ... [and] every county had the civil war (more or less) within itself. Some counties were in the beginning so wholly for the parliament that the king's interest appeared not within them; some were so wholly for the king that the godly (for those generally were the parliament's friends) were forced to forsake their habitations and seek other shelters. Of this sort was Nottinghamshire.

Source 7

The process of division, 1642. From Thomas May, History of the Parliament.

The eastern counties – Suffolk, Norfolk and Cambridgeshire – were happily kept from the beginning without any great combustion; though it were certain that many of the chief gentry in those counties bended in their affections to the king ... but they were not strong enough to engage their counties in a war, for the freeholders and yeomen in general adhered to the parliament.

[In] Suffolk, Norfolk, Cambridgeshire, Essex, Herts. and Hunts there was much unanimity of opinion ... especially among the common people ... [but] a great number of the gentry ... were disaffected [ill-disposed] to the parliament, and were not sparing in their utmost endeavours to promote the king's cause and assist his force. ... Which might have thrown those counties into as much distraction and sad calamity as any other part of the land had felt, (if not wholly carried them over to the other side) ... if those gentlemen had not been curbed and suppressed by that timely care which the parliament took, and more particularly by the successful services of one gentleman, Mr. Oliver Cromwell of Huntingdon.

[In] the south-western counties the Marquis of Hertford and Sir Ralph Hopton [Royalists] were both opposed in their beginnings ... by private gentlemen of those counties ... besides plain freeholders ... who seemed to understand their own liberties and interest which they had in the commonwealth.

The County of Derby, full of nobility and gentry, was much swayed against the parliament ... but Sir John Gell ... by the help of those freeholders and yeomen that inclined that way, made a party to resist those great ones, at such a time as must needs renown his courage and constancy.

Source 8

Divisions in Kent, 1642. From A. Everitt, *The Community of Kent and the Great Rebellion* (Leicester University Press, 1966) pp. 116–22.

What, then, were the lines upon which the Kentish gentry, in the last resort, had divided? Not on precise lines of class, wealth, antiquity, family rivalry, religion or abstract political principle.... The essential clue to the understanding of party division in Kent, and of the subsequent tangle of relationships between these parties, consists in the fact that there were not two parties in the county, but three groups. ... Much the largest of the three groups ... was the moderates, who shaded off into mild 'parliamentarians' supporting the County Committee, on the one hand, and mild 'royalists' temporarily joining the king in 1642 or waiting hopefully at home, on the other. On either wing of this group were two small groups, hardly more than cliques, of genuine Cavaliers and Parliamentarians.

The genuine Parliamentarians in Kent were mainly men of strong and indeed violent personality. Several of them came of families with a long tradition of opposition to the crown, like the Sandyses of Northbourne Abbey. Some had suffered at the hands of James I or Charles I ... ; some ... seem to have been in economic difficulties. ... Few of these parliamentarians seem to have had strong religious convictions. The Cavaliers of the county came from a rather different milieu. Many of them belonged to families with a long tradition of service to the crown. There were great peers among them like the Duke of Richmond, knights like the St.Legers of Boughton Monchelsea, and small gentry like the Bowleses of Chislehurst and Brasted. Most of them still held some official position ... , several were recusants ... [and] on the whole they were younger men than the Parliamentarians. The one characteristic which the Cavaliers held in common with the Parliamentarians, and which distinguished them from the moderates, was that they were often relative newcomers to the shire and derived part of their income from some other source than the land. In other words, neither Parliamentarians nor Cavaliers represented the deepest interests of the county.

Source 9

Divisions in Yorkshire. From L. Stone, *The Causes of the English Revolution 1529–1642* (Routledge & Kegan Paul, 1972) pp. 142–3.

Despite the prodigious amount of research devoted to the subject in recent years, the motives for the alignments of the gentry when the war began are still not wholly clear. Everything points to the fact that right up to the last minute a great majority of the gentry were anxious to avoid armed conflict, and that very substantial numbers contrived to stay neutral throughout its course. In Yorkshire, 240 out of the total of 680 gentry in the county never committed themselves to either side. Neither a study of the MPs themselves, nor local studies of the county gentry, have succeeded in showing any clear association of wealth with political sympathies in 1642, although such a correlation does appear after 1645. The theory that the Parliamentarians were 'mere gentry' as opposed to the court-connected Royalists is not supported by the available facts. Nor has the theory that the Parliamentarians were men of declining fortunes embittered by economic decay fared any better. In Yorkshire, of those gentry families who appear to have been in financial decay and who took sides, three quarters threw in their lot with the king, and only one quarter with Parliament. ...

Far more decisive than any socio-economic correlations is that with religion. In Yorkshire over one third of the Royalist gentry were Catholics, and over a half of the Parliamentarians were Puritans. ... All the Parliamentary leaders in Yorkshire had a previous record of strong Puritan sympathies. There is reason to think that those who had opposed the crown on purely constitutional and political grounds in the 1620s and 1630s tended to swing back to the king with Sir Edward Hyde in 1642, while those who had also opposed the crown on religious grounds were far more likely to stick to Pym and fight for the Parliamentary cause.

Source 10

Taking sides: the city of York. Extracts from the *Victoria County History of the City of York*, pp. 181–201.

The economy of seventeenth-century York was largely determined by the city's function as a regional capital. Its role in ecclesiastical and secular administration and in county politics brought much business into the city, although the abolition of the Council in the North, which had attracted many visitors, probably caused some 'decay of trade'. The city was something of a metropolis, the focus of a regional trade in which the raw products of the countryside were exchanged for imported or locally manufactured goods and services. It was becoming, moreover, a social capital of some significance, a centre of consumption based not only on the prosperity of its more substantial citizens but also on that of the growing numbers of gentry who resided, temporarily or permanently, in the city. ... The position of York merchants in overseas trade was being weakened by rivalry with better placed ports, and was further weakened during the century by the interruption of continental markets, lack of adequate shipping, piracy and the rivalry of London and local merchants. ... Complaints were voiced against merchants of the Leeds district, who were nearer the cloth manufacturing areas, and against those of Hull, who enjoyed superior port facilities. It was alleged that the trading regulations of the Eastland Company and the Merchant Adventurers of England favoured London at the expense of the outports. ... [Nevertheless merchants remained predominant in the government of the town].

[York was governed by a corporation which consisted of Mayor and Aldermen, a common council of burgesses and an upper or 'privy' council of 24 who assisted the aldermen on behalf of the burgesses.] Throughout the century, the dominance of the aldermen over the 24 was maintained. Moreover, an analysis of the attendance at meetings shows that from time to time small groups of men became preponderant within the bench and thus made the civic oligarchy the more exclusive. ... The office of Lord Mayor was filled according to certain conventions. Immediate re-election was not allowed by the charters, [but] a second term of office was lawful, and was indeed usual until 1662. From 1603 to 1701 the mayoralty was held on 60 occasions by merchants. ... This strikingly emphasises the economic and social dominance of the merchants in York and prompts three further observations. First, the aldermanic bench was recruited from only a very narrow section of the city's trading and industrial community; secondly, the provision of 78 out of 101 mayors between 1603 and 1701 by merchants, grocers and drapers mirrors the importance of the distributive trades in York's economy; thirdly, gentry and professional men such as attorneys played an insignificant part in the government of the city. ... Although it is impossible ... to obtain an exact picture of the wealth of the city's ruling group, there are some pointers to the social and economic status which some at least of the aldermen attained. First, ten aldermen were knighted between 1603 and 1702. Secondly ... many of the principal citizens owned not only city property, but also rural estates, and some resided in the country for long periods. ... For example, Sir William Allanson, the son of an Ampleforth yeoman, had land at Crayke (North Riding) and Ousefleet (West Riding) as well as in the city. A few important families eventually left the city, to reappear in county society, for example the Thompsons of Escrick – [while others intermarried with gentry or within the city oligarchy]. For long periods the governing body of the city included men related by blood and marriage as well as successive generations of the same families. ... Members of Parliament for York between 1640 and 1660 were men closely associated with the city, five of the seven being aldermen, and one other, Sir Thomas Widdrington, serving as Recorder. All were sympathetic to the Parliamentarian cause, and some were closely associated with the revolutionary governments. Sir William Allanson and Alderman Hoyle who were elected in 1640 remained to serve in the Rump and before his death in 1650 Hoyle was a remembrancer in the Exchequer. ... Sir Thomas Widdrington served as Speaker of the House of Commons [and played a significant role in offering the crown to Cromwell in 1657]. ...

The outstanding characteristic of church life in York under the early Stuarts was the expanding influence of Puritanism. This was no doubt assisted by the tolerance and sympathy of Archbishops Hutton and Matthew, who did little to disturb Puritan-minded clergy and laity. ... The corporation encouraged preaching and 'exercises' in the city by using its authority to enforce attendance at church services and by appointing Puritans to the office of city preacher founded in 1581. [Three ministers appointed

– Richard Harwood, Henry Hooke and Henry Ayscough – were all moderate Puritans in outlook.] During the 1630s, Puritan clergy were entrenched in important central parishes in the city and were attracting investigation by the officials of the two successive Laudian archbishops, Samuel Harsnett and Richard Neile, especially the latter. During this period, incumbents in some twelve different York parishes were cited at different times for Puritan irregularities such as non-use of the Prayer Book. …Perhaps the most notoriously Puritan parish at this time was St Martin's, Micklegate, where John Birchall became Rector in 1633. He followed two earlier Puritan incumbents, and it seems likely that Archbishop Neile decided to make an example of this parish and its rector. The churchwardens were cited for conniving at clerical nonconformity and at lay irreverence in church – in which three aldermen were implicated – and they were obliged to submit and to 'beautify' the church after the Laudian manner. Birchall was charged with a variety of Puritan offences, including non-adherence to the prayer book, failure to catechize or baptize, administration of communion to non-parishioners, and conducting conventicles in York and elsewhere, and this attempt to discipline a recalcitrant Puritan dragged on for six years before Birchall submitted. It seems that Puritan clergy enjoyed lay support for there is no evidence of popular opposition during this period. … [In addition] several prominent members of the corporation were closely associated with Puritanism. Aldermen Hoyle, Breary and Topham had links with Birchall…; Aldermen Micklethwaite, Dickinson and Allanson had connections with other Puritan clergymen; Archbishop Neile regarded Alderman Vaux as the leader of the Puritans in the city. … Even as late as 1643, when the three principal Puritan aldermen surviving – Hoyle, Allanson and Vaux – had left the city, the corporation refused to accept a royal nominee as city preacher and clearly wanted the Presbyterian John Shaw [then living in Hull] in that place.

[At first sight, then, York has all the makings of a Parliamentarian town, and indeed the city might have opted for parliament or neutrality had a free choice been possible. This, however, was never a real option, because York was the king's northern capital, with strong court connections, and perhaps most important, the base that Charles chose to work from after he fled London in January 1642.]

In 1640 during his negotiations with the Scots, Charles had been in York for some weeks. In March 1642 he moved his court to York which, during the succeeding six months, served as the royal capital. Foreign ambassadors and many of the nobility, gentry and officers of State resorted to the city. This forgathering of royal supporters aroused so much suspicion in the House of Commons that a parliamentary committee was sent to take up residence in the city, ostensibly to provide communication between Court and parliament, but also to keep watch on the king's proceedings. … During the spring and summer the king considered petitions from his subjects and the terms for negotiation offered by parliament. Gradually Charles gathered volunteer troops around him and summoned two great county meetings to York, one in the castle on 12 May, the other at Heworth Moor on 3 June, at which he successfully appealed for help in further recruitment, despite some opposition. Offers of aid flowed in thereafter in answer to the royal commissions of array. From York the king made two unsuccessful expeditions – one to Hull on 23 April, the other to Beverley at the end of July; soon after the latter, he announced his intention of raising his standard, but left the city before doing so.

The place of York in national affairs early in 1642 could not fail to be reflected in the work of the mayor and corporation. The obvious steps were taken to protect the city against attack. …The corporation, though it cautiously issued a declaration praying for a peaceful settlement, promised to protect the king. In the same spirit, the lord mayor decided to consult the recorder for legal advice before committing the city to putting the militia – 600 strong – at the king's disposal. At the end of July Charles was petitioned that the militia should not be called away from the city. The civic authorities persisted a little longer in their non-committal attitude; on 2 September they refused an offer of advice on the safety of the city from a group of royalist gentry on the grounds that it was in no danger. Even as late as November the aldermen considered the possibility of securing a treaty of neutrality with the parliamentarian leaders. By that time, at the request of the royal commander in Yorkshire, the citizens had been organised into a strict armed watch, 20 strong by day and 80 by night; the posterns and the ferry at St Leonards were locked up at night, and the corporation devoted an increasing amount of time to military matters. York had considerable national as well as local strategic importance since it lay near to the main north-to-south route; as a fortified stronghold, valuable also in terms of prestige, it was well fitted to be the centre of royalist activity in the North. After the king's departure, the city was held by a succession of royal governors, [including the ex-governor of Hull, Sir Thomas Glemham] under the supreme command, after December 1642, of the Marquis of Newcastle. During the ensuing months York was the royalist base for operations against Hull, in the West Riding, and in the Midlands, but the city itself experienced no fighting at this time. Although Charles did not again visit his important garrison, the queen was in York in March 1643, bringing arms from abroad, distributing food and money to Parliamentarian prisoners, and heartening the royalist soldiers by her presence. …

[The royalist hold on York, however, was probably not as strong as they would have wished, and this accounts for a series of interferences with the city government which aroused considerable local resentment]. When the king came to York in 1642, the Mayor, Edmund Cowper, was clearly affected by the presence of his sovereign, and when his loyalty was rewarded with a knighthood, he became a devoted royalist. In 1643, Newcastle, no doubt wishing to keep a firm and experienced sympathiser in office, asked for the re-election of Sir Edmund Cowper as lord mayor. The corporation, pleading the charter, refused to comply, whereupon Newcastle, on royal authority, forbade the mayoral election and had troops sent to the Guildhall to prevent it. He renewed his request in January 1644, refusing an interview with the corporation which decided that it would be futile even to assemble at the Guildhall. [Assurances that those standing to replace Cowper were loyal to the crown were apparently unconvincing.] After the fall of York [in 1644 in the aftermath of Marston Moor] Cowper was removed from the mayoralty on the order of parliament [but apparently with the ready compliance of a resentful corporation], Alderman Hoyle MP being elected by the normal procedure to succeed him. Before the regular mayoral election in January 1645, however, six active royalist aldermen were removed from the bench, although they were not disenfranchised and only one was fined for delinquency. The corporation was careful to fill the vacancies in the customary way. ...

Source 11

A Devonshire Parliamentarian. From *The Apology of John Weare*.

I undertook not this service for private interest, revenge or pay. I had an estate left by my ancestors; the office of a justice of peace I long had executed in my country; and I wanted not solicitations [did not lack invitations] to adhere to the king's party. ... But upon assembly of the gentry that were that way affected, hearing some discourse that tended both to the dishonour of God and the overthrow of the common liberty, I ... fully resolved with my utmost to promote the purity of religion and the public peace [by raising a regiment for the parliament].

Source 12

A Yorkshire Royalist. From *The Diary of Sir Henry Slingsby*.

I went with the Bill [for excluding the bishops from the House of Lords, but] I was against the bill for taking away the function and calling of Bishops. ... I am of opinion that the taking of them out of the Church ... may be of dangerous consequence to the peace of the Church. For, admitting that government of bishops be not of divine right, ... but considering that this government hath continued from the apostles, or near the apostles' time, it were not safe to make alteration from so ancient a beginning. ... The common people judges not with things as they are with reason or against, but [from] long usage. So that they would think themselves loose and absolved from all government when they should see that which they venerated so easily subverted.

Source 13

Religious zeal. Nehemiah Wharton, a sergeant in Lord Essex's army, to his master, Mr Willingham in London, 16 August 1642.

Wednesday: Mr Love gave us a famous sermon this day. Also, the soldiers brought the holy rails from Chiswick and burned them in our town. At Chiswick they also intended to pillage the lord of Portland's house, and also Dr Duck's; but by our commanders they were prevented. ...

Thursday: I marched towards Uxbridge. And at Hillingdon, one mile from Uxbridge, the rails being gone, we got the surplice, to make us handkerchiefs; and one of the soldiers wore it to Uxbridge. This day the rails of Uxbridge, formerly removed, was with the service book burned. This even[ing] Mr Harding gave us a worthy sermon.

Source 14

Religious zeal. Dr Thomas Paske to the Earl of Holland; from Canterbury, 30 August 1642.

Colonel Sandys arriving here with his troops, ... the soldiers entering the church ... began a fight with God himself: overthrew the communion table, tore the velvet cloth from before it, defaced the goodly screen or tabernacle work, violated the monuments of the dead, spoiled the organs, broke down the ancient rails and seats ..., forced open the cupboards of the singing men, rent some of their surplices, gowns and Bibles, and carried away others, mangled all our service books, bestrewing the whole pavement with the leaves. A miserable spectacle to every good eye.

Source 15

Conservative reaction. From Thomas May, *History of the Parliament*.

A great party whose livelihood and fortunes depended on [the bishops] and far more whose hopes of preferment looked that way ... began to be daily more disaffected to the parliament. ... Another thing which seemed to trouble some who were not bad men was that extreme licence which the common people ... took to themselves of reforming without authority, order or decency. ... To this were added those daily reports of ridiculous conventicles, and preachings made by tradesmen and illiterate people of the lowest rank, to the scandal and offence of many.

Source 16

Localism and neutralism. From D. Hirst, *Authority and Conflict 1603–58* (Arnold, 1986) pp. 223–4.

Everywhere men sought an escape in neutralism. The ruin of Germany during the Thirty Years War, and the scattered agrarian unrest that had broken out all over the country in 1640–2 as political controls began to fracture, only reinforced the natural human preference for peace. Even those whose loyalties were clear, such as the Parliamentarian Fairfaxes in Yorkshire, could recognise how much they had to lose and strove to neutralise their own areas – Sir John Hotham's fear lest 'the necessitous people ... set up for themselves to the utter ruin of all the nobility and gentry', was widely shared. In county after county gentlemen shunned both the militia ordinance and the [king's] commission of array: the extreme case was Staffordshire, where the gentry tried to raise a third force to resist outsiders. Towns like Leicester shut their gates, and most ordinary countrymen infinitely preferred to follow the plough than the drum.

If neutralism was so prevalent, how was civil war possible? Why did fortress Staffordshire fall and all the other neutrality pacts collapse? The haphazard beginnings of the Civil War illuminate both the strengths and the weaknesses of the endemic localism. For the neutrals found that their counties and towns were by no means autonomous, and that pressures existed both within and without. The conflicting principals acted as magnets to the area around them, a fact which helps to explain the well-known geographical division into a Parliamentarian south-east and a royalist north and west. Parliament easily disarmed neutrals in neighbouring Kent and Hertfordshire; conversely, the movements of the king undermined the efforts of many in the north to stay out of the fray. In other areas, paradoxically, the need to preserve social order did the work of the belligerents. Thus, anti-Catholic disturbances amongst industrial workers suffering from the deepening depression drove frightened gentry to collaborate with the regionally dominant power, whether Parliamentarian in Suffolk or royalist in Staffordshire. Indeed, such considerations of prudence rather than principle – who was most to be feared locally? Who was most likely to win? – probably determined the allegiances of the majority of the population throughout the war.

But zealots could be found everywhere, and the neutralists could not build quarantines against them. The Worcestershire minister Richard Baxter gave a moving account of how royalist violence against otherwise peaceful Puritans drove many to Parliamentarian garrisons for refuge, and thus willy-nilly to align themselves. As Lucy Hutchinson in Nottinghamshire observed, 'every county...had the Civil War within itself'.

Source 17

Neutralism in Cheshire. The treaty of Bunbury, 23 December 1642.

An agreement made the day above at Bunbury in the county of Chester, for a pacification and settling of the peace of that county by us whose names are subscribed, authorised hereunto by the lords and gentlemen nominated commissioners of array [Royalist] and deputy-lieutenants [Parliamentarian] of the said county.

1. It is agreed that there be an absolute cessation of arms from henceforth within this county; and no arms taken up to offend one another but by consent of the king and both houses of parliament, unless it be to resist forces brought into the county. ...
4. That the fortifications of ... any town in Cheshire, lately made, by either party, be presently demolished. ...

7. It is agreed that the commissioners of array shall not any further put the commission of array in execution; nor the gentlemen nominated deputy-lieutenants the ordinance of the militia. ...
8. That all parties join in a petition to his majesty and both houses of parliament, for putting an end to the great distractions and miseries fallen upon this kingdom, by making a speedy peace.

Source 18

Neutralism in Yorkshire. From Clarendon, *History of the Rebellion and Civil Wars in England.*

The gentlemen of the several opinions proposed between themselves that neither [the commission of array nor the militia ordinance] should be meddled with; but that all should be contented to sit still, without engagement to either party. ... [At Rothwell on 29 September] articles were solemnly drawn up, consented to and subscribed by the Lord Fairfax and Harry Bellasis, the heir apparent of the Lord Fauconberg. ... With them, the principal persons of either party subscribed the articles. ... The parliament no sooner was informed of this transaction than they expressed their detestation of it. ... Upon this declaration and vote ... the lord Fairfax himself and all the gentlemen of that party ... prepared themselves to bear a part in the war and made all haste to levy men.

Source 19

Popular reaction. A declaration made by the Earl of Bath from Devon, 1642.

There came [to South Molton] the Earl of Bath, my Lord Chichester, Baronet Pollard, Sir Popham Southcott, Sir Ralph Sydenham ... and divers others. ... The common sort of the town fell in a great rage with the mayor and his company for giving licence that they should enter; and swore that if they did attempt anything there or read their commission of array, they would beat them all down and kill them. ... I do verily believe they were in number at least 1000, some with muskets loaden, some with halberds and black bills, some with clubs. ... The women had filled all the steps of the cross with great stones, and got up and sat on them, swearing if they did come there they would brain them. ... The gentlemen, seeing that, betook themselves every one to house; and after that, not one of them, nor their servants, durst show themselves in the street. ... And when the Earl rode forth of town, they did throw stones after him and his men.

Source 20

The Clubmen. From J. Morrill, *The Revolt of the Provinces* (Longman, 1980) pp. 98–100.

In the course of 1645, Clubmen Associations were formed in Shropshire, Worcestershire and Herefordshire (January-March), Wiltshire, Dorset and Somerset (May-

September) Berkshire, Sussex and Hampshire (September-October) and South Wales and the border (August-November). The seriousness of the threat was partly based on the geographical extent of the movements. But it derived also from the numerical strength of the Clubmen. Although in the event they did not prove an effective military force, their numbers invariably impressed observers and initially inclined both sides to conciliate them. Neither side seriously questioned the Clubmen's claim to be able to raise 20,000 men in Wiltshire and Dorset at forty-eight hours notice. ... The Berkshire Clubmen claimed 16,000 adherents, the Glamorganshire 'Peaceable Army' about 10,000. Again, independent observers accepted these figures. ... Even if such figures were wildly exaggerated, the numbers must have been substantial at a time when only three armies in the kingdom consisted of 12,000 men or more. It is likely that the Clubmen outnumbered local forces in most Clubmen counties.

Each Association began as an essentially popular peasant movement, growing out of a series of confrontations between village communities and soldiers demanding quarter or provisions (or general plunder). In most cases, leadership then passed to the leading gentry who gave the associations greater administrative coherence and wider political programmes. Yet every Association remained distinct and retained characteristics reflecting local problems within a context of unity to the traditional values of provincial society. At the heart of all the movements lay a yearning to halt the war, most Associations looking not just for a local pacification but for a national settlement along the same conventional lines as the bemused neutrals of 1642 had sought. Meanwhile, they sought a local truce. Sometimes they envisaged themselves taking over full responsibility for raising and distributing contributions to remaining garrisons, sometimes they hoped to persuade both sides to withdraw all their forces, leaving the Clubmen as the sole military power. There were persistent demands for the full restoration of traditional methods of local government.

There is overwhelming evidence that most of the Clubmen were neutrals. ... This certainly did not preclude Associations from assisting either king or parliament in particular circumstances, but this need not imply a betrayal of their neutralism. A tactical alliance with Fairfax, for example, helped the Devon and southern Somerset Clubmen to rid themselves of Goring, who represented a threat to provincial liberties far greater than that posed, in the short term, by the New Model. The Clubmen were not seeking to help parliament win the war. They were using parliamentary troops to clear their own counties of the most potent immediate threat. Again, it is vital to point out that at the beginning of 1645, the war appeared evenly balanced; that the creation of the New Model did not immediately alert the country to a major shift in the balance of power; and that it took several months for the importance of the Battle of Naseby to be appreciated. The Clubmen were assuming that a military stalemate still existed. Their primary task was to prevent their own shires from becoming major battlegrounds.

Source 21

Clubmen grievances. From the *Petition of the Sussex Clubmen*, 26 September 1645.

1. The want of Church government whereby our Churches are decayed, God's ordinances neglected, orthodox ministers cast out without cause and never heard, mechanics and unknown persons thrust in ... whereby God and the Parliament are dishonoured and the people grieved.

2. Whereas for three years last past we have through much labour and God's blessing gained the fruit of the earth and had hoped to enjoy the same, but by free quarter and plunder of soldiers our purses have been exhausted, corn eaten up, cattle plundered, persons frightened from our habitations and by reason of the violence of the soldiers our lives not safe, and have no power nor authority to resist the same. ...

3. The insufferable, insolent, arbitrary power that hath been used amongst us, contrary to all our ancient known laws, or ordinances of parliament, upon our persons and estates by imprisoning our persons, imposing of sums of money, light horses, and dragoons, and exacting of loans by some particular persons stepped into authority who have delegated their power to men of sordid condition whose wills have been laws and commands over our persons and estates, by which they have overthrown all our English liberties and have endeavoured thereby to make us desperate. ... [This last complaint is probably a reference to the county committees set up by parliament as a wartime administration. A discussion of their work is provided in Source 22, below.]

Source 22

Clubmen organisation. Articles of Association of the Clubmen of Dorset and Wiltshire, 1645.

Made and agreed on at a meeting at Gorehedge Corner on 25 May 1645, and read at Bradbury in Dorset by Mr Thomas Young, a lawyer; when there were present near 4000 armed with clubs, swords, bills, pitchforks and other several weapons.

1. Every town, tithing, parish and great hamlet, make present choice of three or more of the ablest men for wisdom, valour, and estate, inhabitants of the same, unto whom at all times they may repair for assistance and direction.

2. That the Constable, Tithingman and other officers of the town etc. ... set a constant watch of two at the least, and they watch every night well-armed, and if required, by day also. ...

5. That all such as pretend themselves soldiers, and are taken plundering or doing any other unlawful violence, be presently disarmed and after examination (having confessed into which army he doth belong) to be safely guarded thither (together with sufficient witness to prove the offence).

6. That to avoid false alarms no man shall rise into arms but such as are summoned by the watchmen, unless they see apparent violence, or in case the watchmen be defective or surprised. ...

9. That if quarter be demanded according to Order Martial, the soldier is to be friendly entertained behaving himself fairly in his quarters, but if he plunder or offer any other violence then he is to be restrained and delivered up to the Commander in Chief to be by him corrected.

10. That whatsoever person, though seemingly associated ... shall be found to occasion any outcry or by any means to assemble any in favour or opposition to either party, king or parliament ... he shall be accounted unworthy of our protection.

The impact of war was not only felt through military action, but also through the county committees set up by parliament to administer the areas under its control and to ensure that its armies were kept supplied. The committees were greatly resented, partly because of their need to mobilise resources, but also because it was claimed that their members lacked the social position normally expected of those who ran local government, an accusation also levelled at the administrations of the Interregnum. In considering government from this local perspective, John Morrill reveals its variation and complexity, the impact and upheaval of war, and the extent to which parliamentary divisions and disputes were reflected in the localities.

Source 23

Parliamentary administration. From J. Morrill, *The Revolt of the Provinces*, pp. 114–9.

One of the few easy generalisations to make about this problem is that public confrontation and mutual denunciation characterised the history of most parliamentarian county establishments at some point during the years 1643–7. This is, in itself, a sign of the instability of the parliamentarian ideals. Again and again the charges and counter-charges resulting from these disputes return to a few principal themes. One was the question of overlapping jurisdictions. ... Another was the lack of definition in the relationship of military and civilian authorities. Questions of corruption and favouritism often joined with clashes of personality or even the continuation of ancient feuds and rivalries. ... In most counties, deeper political and religious divisions cut across or coincided with these more immediate problems.

This is perhaps most clearly seen in the religious divisions of the period. Obviously the essentially national conflict over the basic nature of the religious settlement was in itself reflected in each county. But while at Westminster politicians and divines struggled to work out a blueprint for the future ... in the provinces committees were daily required to cope [with immediate practical issues]. ... A host of *ad hoc* decisions had to be made long before a strategy for the future could be worked out. In general, historians have oversimplified religious issues and once again presumed the very real polarities of the artificial world of Westminster to exist in much the same form elsewhere. The terms 'presbyterian' and 'independent', like the terms 'royalist' and 'parliamentarian', 'Puritan' or 'country', must be used with the utmost care. It seems to me that at a local level, in explaining the religious tensions of the 1640s in the counties, the terms are positively misleading. ...

On the one hand, committees were divided about the religious nature of the revolution. Rigid presbyterians and congregationalists might agree that the revolution was a prelude to the creation of a godly nation, fired by enthusiasm and sound doctrine and forced into obedience to their vision of the moral commonwealth by godly magistrates. Men like Oliver Cromwell looked for men representing 'the different forms of godliness in this nation', who shared this essential faith in an imminent Zion. In Cheshire, strict presbyterians and visionary congregationalists made common political cause against the 'worldly' party. Only at the end of the 1640s and early 1650s does this union disintegrate. Other men, including 'presbyterians', congregationalists and episcopalians, sought only to purge remnants of popery from the existing Church, discharge unfit men from the ministry, cleanse and restore the Church to an exalted but not dominant role in a flawed and fallen world. ... While at Westminster, the establishment of a national liturgy and doctrine, and the theological problem of toleration created different polarities ... in the localities the realities of coping with ecclesiastical anarchy on a day-to-day basis did create alliances unthinkable at a higher level.

Men who wanted to purge the nation of its evil ways and inaugurate a new age were likely to adopt punitive attitudes towards those responsible for the Civil War. On the other hand, moderates were acutely aware of the accidental ways by which many of their opponents had found themselves unhappily active for the royalists. Many common civilities and contacts continued despite the war, and many county committees found themselves expected to sequester and harass old friends, relatives and neighbours. Quite apart from such bonds, many moderates temperamentally favoured conciliation of the defeated as a better way to restore security and peace than repression. To the Godly, however, condign punishment of all who had opposed a just cause was necessary and proper. The position of neutrals was one which excited particularly fierce controversy within county committees. Certainly the campaign by radical groups to enforce rigorously the terms of the sequestration ordinances became a major source of conflict. In many counties, moderates retained control of sequestrations and reacted sympathetically and generously to individual tales of misfortune and mischance. Elsewhere the 'Godly' maintained a rigorous and austere husbandry over the estates and persons of the delinquents. ...

[These divisions and variations were complicated by

changes in the personnel of local government.] Before 1642 local officials could be fairly easily divided into three groups whose responsibilities matched their social status. ... The Civil War introduced a much less rigid hierarchy of duties [and a greatly increased workload]. ... As the need for senior officials grew at a time when the divisions and casualties of war reduced the pool, social mobility within the structure also increased. ... In many areas, county committees came to recruit senior men from backgrounds which would have barred them from membership of the pre-war élites. In some counties ... the new men (minor gentry with a sprinkling of townsmen) proved to be political and religious radicals who further alienated and sometimes displaced those members of the old traditional élite who had earlier constituted the parliamentarian leadership. ...

[It is important not to overstate the case.] In a majority of English counties that group of traditional governors who adhered to parliament in 1642–3 remained in control until 1649. This included most of East Anglia ... the south ... and the Midlands. In counties where the royalists had held overall control for any length of time, parliament found it difficult to find former governors who had not compromised themselves, and necessarily looked to less prominent men who had avoided committing themselves or who could more readily disguise past indiscretions. This was the pattern in much of northern England and Wales: also in counties like Worcestershire. Nonetheless, the social background of many of the new committee-men did form an important element in the struggle for power in a number of counties, of which Kent, Sussex, Somerset, Staffordshire, Cheshire and Nottinghamshire are prominent examples. In all these cases the 'new men' tended to be more radical in religion, more determined in the harassment of delinquents, [and] tougher in their preparedness to sacrifice the independence of the county to win local or regional military control. ... The factors interacted differently in each county [but the cumulative effect was to increase the impact of the war, to bring about more radical change in some areas, and to add to the complexity of the picture overall].

Source 24

The role of the common people. From D. Underdown, *Revel, Riot and Rebellion* (Oxford, 1986) pp. 120–1 and 124–5.

There is, in fact, plentiful evidence that in the early seventeenth century ordinary Englishmen had opinions on national issues that reflected their underlying concern for law, custom and 'good rule'. They tended, naturally enough, to view these issues primarily in terms of their impact on their local communities. ... The early years of Charles I's reign were ... the crucial period of politicization. By 1627 the circulation of subversive writings had become ominously common ... [and] some, like those sung by three home counties fiddlers, were openly aimed against the king's chief counsellor, the Duke of Buckingham. Disaffection was spreading even

among the military: when Londoners, conscripted as punishment for resisting the 1626 Forced Loan, arrived at Portsmouth, troops from the garrison demonstrated in their favour. By January 1628 the scholarly Sir Robert Cotton was worrying over the strength of feeling 'amongst the better sort of the multitude'. ... As with Ship Money and other aspects of Charles I's policy of centralisation, these measures were *new*, and thus an affront to popular as well as élite notions of law and good rule. ... The common people had their own version of that 'ancient constitution' to which their superiors in parliament were so constantly appealing.

Source 25

Popular reactions: Parliamentarian volunteers in Somerset, 1642. From John Ashe, *A Perfect Relation*.

Upon Friday morning they all marched together unto the place appointed for that day's meeting, in the town of Chewton. And thither came unto us all the trained bands ... doubled twice over by means of volunteers, who came best armed and were most ready in the use of their arms. ... And our company was increased to the number of 40,000 ... all the gentry and yeomanry and lastly youths that inhabited in the north-east part of the county. ... There came also out of those parts of Wiltshire near Sir Edward Hungerford's quarter about two or three hundred horsemen. ... There came likewise 300 lusty stout men ... of the city of Bristol. ... There came from Gloucestershire a company of foot, well armed, consisting of 250 or 300 men, all volunteers.

Source 26

Popular reactions. From the Minute Books of the Sessions of the Peace for Exeter, 1642.

29 July: Richard Bennett of this city, goldsmith, accused ... for speaking some scandalous words of the parliament ... and of Mr Pym: as that Mr Pym was a traitor, as the king had so called him. ...

9 August: Simon Seagar alias Tanner, of Minehead, accused ... for speaking very seditious and traitorous words of the king's most excellent majesty in the house of Richard Martin, inn-holder, viz. that the king's majesty had given his broad seal to the rebels in Ireland against the Protestants, and that the king [did] maintain papists about him against the Protestants.

12 August: [John Gollop of Netherbury in Dorset, musician, was committed to prison for] the singing of one other scandalous song this week at the Bear, touching the Lord Kimbolton and the five members of the house of Commons [at the request of Edward Seymour, esquire.]

24 August: [William Morrell of Exeter, worsted-comber, was committed for saying that] the prince was come to Sherborne Castle ... [and] if he might be butler there but

that one night, he would put poison in all the drink and poison them all.

16 November: [Thomas Warner, worsted-comber, was imprisoned for saying] that he did think that all those that had made those works in Exeter for the defence of the city, to keep out the king and his company, would be hanged for their labour, and he did hope so … [and] that he had been to drink a health to the king and the Cavaliers, and to the confusion or condemnation of the Roundheads and the volunteers.

[Philip Job, apprentice, was imprisoned for saying] that the parliament's laws were not worth a turd.

Source 27

Popular support for parliament. From B. Manning, *The English People and the English Revolution* (Heinemann, 1976) p. 235.

In the West Riding of Yorkshire, south-east Lancashire, the Birmingham area and elsewhere the smallholding handicraftsmen were the firmest and most radical supporters of parliament. They were part-farmers and part-manufacturers, not wholly dependent on the gentry, nor wholly dependent on the merchants or larger manufacturers; men not rich nor yet impoverished, independent in their economic life and in their opinions. The clothiers of Halifax and Bradford, the weavers of the Manchester area, the metal-workers of the Birmingham district, exhibited a close resemblance in their attitudes and actions during the Civil War. Their motives were many: fear of attacks by papists, royalists and plundering soldiers; distress at the disruption of their livelihoods by economic depression and war; hope that parliament would redress their grievances and give them a more secure future. They were yet sustained by ideals of religious reformation and political democracy as cures for all their problems and ills, and they were fearful and suspicious of the intentions of all superiors, whether Royalists or Parliamentarians or what.

Source 28

Popular support for the king. From Clarendon, *History of the Rebellion and Civil Wars in England*.

There was in this county [Cornwall] … a wonderful and superstitious reverence towards the name of a parliament, and a prejudice to the power of the Court; yet a full submission and love of the established government of Church and State, especially to that part of the Church as concerned the liturgy, or Book of Common Prayer, which was a most general object of veneration with the people. And the jealousy and apprehension that the other party intended to alter it was a principal advancement of the king's service.

Source 29

Popular reactions in the fens. From K. Lindley, *Fenland Riots and the English Revolution* (Heinemann, 1982) pp. 257–8.

The vast majority of fenland commoners remained virtually oblivious to the great issues debated at Westminster in the months leading up to the outbreak of the Civil War. The chief significance of the political crisis for most of them was the ideal opportunity it afforded to level enclosures and regain their commons, and if they demonstrated any political allegiance it was secondary to and often in pursuit of the regaining of those lands. There is no real evidence that the generality of fenmen had been politically educated by their experiences in the 1630s [in a campaign against the fen drainage schemes] and the political and constitutional points made by their most articulate spokesmen, like Sir John Maynard, were addressed to fellow members of the political élite and made little, if any, impact upon the consciousness of the fenmen themselves. Like their forest counterparts, the fenmen's main preoccupation, as the English Revolution ran its course, remained much the same as it had been in the 1630s, the defence of an open fen, and the official favour extended by successive political regimes towards fenland drainage ensured that it would remain so.

Source 30

An individual reaction. From 'The Life of Adam Martindale', *Chetham Society Vol. IV* (1845) pp. 31–2.

It was in the Christmas time that I was dismissed, in that fatal year 1642. Going home to my father, he received me kindly; but things were now woefully altered for the worse from what I had formerly known them. My sister was married to a noted Royalist, and, going to live about two miles from Lathom, which the parliament's forces accounted their enemies' headquarters, they were sadly plundered by those forces passing the road wherein they dwelt. The great trade that my father and two of my brethren had long driven was quite dead; for who would either build or repair an house when he could not sleep a night in it with quiet and safety? My brother Henry, who was then about twenty-four years of age, knew not where to hide his head, for my Lord of Derby's officers had taken up a custom of summoning such as he and many older persons, upon pain of death, to appear at general musters, and thence to force them away with such weapons as they had, if they were but pitchforks, to [the siege of] Bolton; the rear being brought up with troopers, that had commission to shoot such as lagged behind, so as the poor countrymen seemed to be in a dilemma of death, either by the troopers if they went not on, or by the great and small shot of the town if they did.

This hard usage of the country to no purpose (for what could poor cudgellers do against a fortified place?) much weakened the interest of the Royalists … and many yeomen's sons, whereof my brother Henry was one, went to shelter themselves in Bolton and took up arms there.

A Case Study: Hull and the Civil War

Source 31

Beverley Gate, Hull, in 1776, from which Sir John Hotham denied Charles I entry to the town in April 1642

The town of Kingston upon Hull played a vital part in the Civil War and its final outcome, not because, as has been claimed, the war began there, but because it was secured for parliament in 1642, and remained in parliamentary hands throughout the period. The famous incident in April 1642 when the governor Sir John Hotham denied entry to the king, who was demanding access to the magazine stored in the town, did not spark off military activity, although it did lead to a propaganda war between king and parliament which revealed and widened the breach between them. The real significance of Hull was its position as the main supply port for the north of England, and its strategic value as a secure base in Yorkshire. In 1642 there was a considerable store of arms in the town which had been collected by the king for the Scottish wars, but after the incident of April 1642, the arms were quickly shipped to London where they were used to supply the parliamentary army when war began in August. This was no doubt useful to the parliamentary side, but what was far more important was that while they held Hull, they could send supplies to their northern armies and effectively prevent the royalists from doing the same. In August 1642 Queen Henrietta Maria was already in the Netherlands where, with help from Charles' brother-in-law, William of Orange, she had collected a considerable quantity of arms. In 1643 she did succeed in landing a shipload of these at Bridlington, but this was little compared to the possible supplies of money, arms and even men that Charles might have been able to call upon from his fellow sovereigns if he had controlled an accessible port such as Hull. Moreover, from Hull the Humber estuary gave access to a network of rivers which covered much of northern England and the eastern Midlands. The Ouse ran to York, the Aire and Calder to the West Riding, the Don to Doncaster and Sheffield, while the Trent made its way through Lincoln to Nottingham and as far south as Leicester. Control of such a port was a permanent strategic advantage, and would prove to be of crucial significance in the eventual outcome of the war – for Hull supported the cause of parliament throughout the period.

The sources below provide evidence concerning the town, its significant characteristics, its inhabitants and the events in which they were caught up, particularly in the crucial year of 1642–3 when the town withstood two royalist sieges. Sources 32 and 33 provide an outline of the main events, while Sources 34–44 focus on the characteristics of the town and those within it who influenced the outcome. By considering these sources in the light of Questions 5–11 you should be able to establish an explanation for the fact that Hull supported parliament in the Civil War, rather than the king.

Questions

5. Read Sources 32 and 33, and write a brief summary of events in and concerning Hull from 1639 to 1644.

6. Why was Hull easy to defend and difficult to capture?

7. What factors in Hull's economy, social and political structure, or religious outlook might make its citizens sympathetic to the cause of parliament?

8. What part did Sir John Hotham play in securing Hull for parliament? What were his main motives and intentions?

9. Why did Hotham later try to betray Hull to the Royalists? Why did he not succeed?

10. What part did the Hull Corporation and MPs play in these events?

11. How far is it possible to determine the attitudes of the ordinary citizens in Hull at this time? To what extent were they able to influence the outcome of events?

Source 32

From B.N. Reckitt, *Charles the First and Hull,1639–45* (Mr Pye Books, Howden, 1988) pp. 1, 6–7, 13–14 and 17–18.

When Charles I was at York in April 1639, on his way North to meet the invading Scots, he sent a message to the Mayor of Kingston upon Hull to say that he would visit the town in three days time. ... An inspection in the morning of the second day was the real object of the king's visit. In Hull were stored large quantities of arms and ammunition for the Scottish war, partly brought from Holland and partly collected from other parts of the country. In three years time the possession of this magazine was to become of vital importance, for it was by then larger than any other in the country and could provide the equipment for perhaps 16,000 men. The king regarded the store almost as his private property, for he had himself supervised its collection. ... So Charles personally looked over the store and viewed the defences of the town containing it. He had sent Captain Legge to supervise the storage, so passing over the existing Governor of the town, Sir John Hotham. This he had done in spite of representations from Sir Thomas Wentworth, who had strongly advised him to rely on Hotham. Hotham was fully capable of the task and, moreover, was certain to resent such an affront. But Charles had been adamant [possibly because Hotham was known to have opposed Ship Money] and was to suffer severely for his stubbornness. The name of Sir John Hotham is noticeably absent from the list of those receiving the king and he probably deliberately kept away. ...

After the royal forces had been defeated at Newburn-on-Tyne in August 1640, the army [was] dispersed and its equipment returned to store in Hull. To ensure its safety the king appointed as Governor a staunch Royalist, Sir Thomas Glemham, whereupon the Mayor, Robert Morton, stood upon his dignity and claimed his own right to be Governor under the Charter granted by Edward VI. ... Why a similar stand had not been taken on the appointment of Sir John Hotham in 1628 is not clear. To this protest the Earl of Strafford sent a reply to the effect that the appointment of Sir Thomas Glemham was to be regarded as evidence of the king's princely zeal for the safety of the town and he asked the Mayor to submit to the king's wish. But the Mayor still stood his ground until the king announced that he proposed to pay another visit to the town and requested that preparations be made for his reception. [Not only was this a veiled threat, but the cost of a second visit within the year would be a significant burden to the town.] This was enough. Sir Thomas was immediately admitted with a garrison of a thousand men and the keys of the town and blockhouse were handed over to him. The threatened royal visit was cancelled.

The affair was the more galling perhaps because submission involved the local billeting of troops. The city of Hull had already recently suffered from this and had found it particularly irksome because, since the soldiers were seldom and irregularly paid, a virtue had to be made of necessity and credit given for necessary provisions. True, a letter of thanks and some money had been sent on the last occasion but it was unlikely, in view of Charles's straitened finances, that repayment would be again forthcoming and certainly not a letter of thanks after this incident. In July 1641 the regiment at Hull was disbanded and Sir Thomas Glemham gave up his post and left for London. ...

On 4th January 1642, the king made his ill-fated attempt to arrest the five members of the House of Commons. ... Civil war became almost inevitable and both sides began jockeying for position. The importance of securing Hull with its magazine was immediately recognised by both parties. The king made his move at much the same time as parliament and sent the Earl of Newcastle, who was to be his commander in the North, with Captain Legge to secure the town. They took no forces with them and entered incognito, but they were soon recognised and brought before the Mayor. To him the Duke showed the royal commission, but it was already known that parliament intended to appoint Sir John Hotham; indeed, according to Legge, his troops had already been refused entrance by the Burgesses. [see below] The Mayor, 'perceiving an estrangement between the king and his parliament', hedged and petitioned the king to decide whether his own direct nominee or his representative designated by parliament was to be admitted. He also wrote to parliament explaining what had happened and asking that, in the unfortunate event of troops having to be quartered in the town, he, as Mayor, should be appointed Governor in accordance with the Charter. Parliament promptly summoned Newcastle to take his seat in the Lords. After consulting the king, who was not yet ready for an open breach, the Earl accordingly left for London with Legge. So the Royalist attempt to gain control of Hull was frustrated and it was now Parliament's turn.

On 11th January the Lords and Commons agreed that Sir John Hotham should be appointed Governor of Hull, that he should take control of its magazine with the help of some of the Yorkshire Train Bands [local militia] and that he should not deliver up the town or the magazine 'without the king's authority signified by the Lords and Commons in parliament'. This was a very important phrase, and was to be reiterated later. Sir John was in the House at the time and, standing up, pronounced the following words, 'Mr Speaker, fall back, fall edge, I will go down and perform your commands', thus showing that he fully appreciated the risk he was running in accepting so precarious an appointment. Perhaps he did not fully appreciate that 'fall edge' was really a serious possibility, but he may well have done so in view of his past relationship with the king. ... Sir John himself does not appear to have gone up to Hull until the early part of March for there are records of his activities in parliament until then, but he sent his son and heir, Captain John Hotham, to secure Hull for him. Captain John, like his father, had already seen service on the continent. He was of reckless, dare-devil bravery and his exploits for the Parliamentary forces were soon to make his name a byword in the North. In the judgement of his fellow MPs at this time he was more wholeheartedly of their party than his father. ...

When he arrived in Yorkshire he raised a force of about 800 of the Train Bands and advanced towards Hull. But the Mayor, Henry Barnard, warned of his coming, had the gates closed and the walls manned, claiming that he was the king's representative in Hull just as his predecessor had done when Sir Thomas Glemham had come as Governor-extraordinary. Captain John had to withdraw and appeal to parliament for further orders. (It was during this time that the Earl of Newcastle and Captain Legge tried to gain control.) On the former occasion the king had secured the entrance of his nominee by threatening a royal visit. Parliament secured their end by sending peremptory orders for the admission of Hotham and his forces. The Mayor and Aldermen yielded rather than 'incur the heavy displeasure of the House and perhaps be obliged in the end to submit'. But even then they were not out of trouble. It appears that when Hotham marched in with his troops the townsfolk refused them billets and they were forced in mid-winter to camp out in the streets. Hotham complained to parliament and the Mayor and Aldermen were sent for to explain their actions. They appeared before the House and boldly claimed that no soldiers could be billeted in the town without the inhabitants' consent, as, indeed, parliament itself had asserted in its own Petition of Right [1628]. The claim had to be admitted. Hotham was ordered to make his peace with the Mayor and Aldermen, and they in turn were asked to provide billets, which they promised to do. By the end of January Captain John was securely ensconced in his father's command.

Source 33

From *The Victoria County History Of Hull*, **pp. 102–7.**

The deepening division between king and parliament in 1641–2 was bound to affect a seaport and stronghold with the strategic importance of Hull. As early as January 1642 both sides endeavoured to take control of the town and the large magazine still stored in the manor-house. On 11 January the king named the Earl of Newcastle as Governor and ordered Captain Legge to assist him, while parliament nominated Sir John Hotham and asked his son, Captain John Hotham, to secure the town at once. Within three days Newcastle and Legge found that the Corporation was unwilling to recognise their commission or to admit any troops under their command, although Legge reported that he had at least been able to persuade the corporation not to admit Captain Hotham either. This may have been so, for Hotham was refused entrance at first, and the corporation allowed him to enter later with some of the county trained bands only at the express command of parliament. Even then the corporation made difficulties about billets which were provided only after the Mayor and Alderman James Watkinson had been summoned before the Commons; the town's obstruction, however, was largely due, not to politics, but to a desire to uphold its chartered rights against interference.

The troops in Hull were provided with arms and ammunition from the magazine and were reinforced after the arrival of Sir John Hotham, who made other defensive preparations at the walls and gates. Before the end of March the king and the court had moved to York, which during the next few months counterbalanced Hull by acting as a focus of royal strength. Meanwhile there were discussions in parliament about the transfer of the magazine to London and the next royal attempt to win Hull was made partly to prevent such a step. On 22 April the Duke of York, the Elector Palatine, and their entourage arrived in Hull informally, were entertained by the mayor and the governor, and stayed overnight. Sir John Hotham, however, had already suspected a trap, and his alarm was increased when he was told that the king was on his way to rejoin his son in Hull with a troop of horse. With his resolution stiffened by the advice of Peregrine Pelham MP, Hotham ordered the gates to be closed and came out on the walls near Beverley Gate to refuse entry to the king. Despite a heated argument with his sovereign, who alternately threatened and bargained, and in defiance of the Mayor's wish to admit the king, Hotham stoutly maintained his refusal. Charles withdrew to Beverley, followed shortly after by the Duke of York and his party who seem to have been kept in ignorance of the incident. Hotham was proclaimed a traitor, and next day refused the offer of a royal pardon if he would conform to the royal wishes. His act of defiance in the interests of parliament marked an important stage in the onset of the Civil War and formed the subject of sharp exchanges between king and parliament in which royal complaints against the governor of Hull were flatly rejected.

Soon afterwards a large part of the magazine was removed to London, but measures for the safety of Hull continued: a parliamentary committee was sent to support Hotham and to raise the trained bands for defence. The capture of Hull remained a prime objective for Charles who, with his headquarters at York, needed a defensible seaport to provide access for possible aid from abroad. Early in June some Royalist troopers under a local gentleman made an ineffectual demonstration outside the walls, and there were two futile attempts to win the town by treachery. Towards the end of the month, however, Lord Digby, who had been captured at sea, was landed at Hull where, by concealing his identity, he was able to talk to Hotham. What happened is uncertain for the evidence is conflicting, but the governor may have given Digby some grounds for hoping that Hull would return to its allegiance. This possibility may have prompted Charles to send a force of soldiers to Hull early in July. For about three weeks the town was loosely besieged: attempts were made to prevent the passage of supplies, some windmills were burnt and a bombardment was mounted. But there was no sign of any treachery within Hull and its resistance was stronger and more effective than expected: bastions were erected outside the gates, walls were strengthened, parliamentary supply ships reached the haven, and the surrounding country was flooded when the dykes and river banks were cut. The defenders made two successful sallies in the second of which the Royalists were driven from their quarters at Anlaby and were obliged to raise the siege.

During the following weeks the walls and the castle were repaired, and regular watch and ward was maintained, partly for security, partly to prevent disorders among the garrison. There was little military activity in the neighbourhood of Hull, but parties of soldiers from the town harried Royalists in the East Riding, and Captain Hotham broke Yorkshire's treaty of neutrality by taking troops to capture Cawood Castle. Shortly afterwards

another treacherous attempt to deliver the town was frustrated.

It is difficult to ascertain the political temper of Hull during 1642. After defying the king the Hothams may have been reluctant to see the conflict widened, and before the end of the year Sir John had quarrelled with Pelham, who supported the 'war party' in parliament, while Captain Hotham was in touch with Newcastle, the Royalist commander in Yorkshire; both had already shown jealousy towards the Fairfaxes. Moreover, on his arrival in Hull Hotham declared that the town was 'five parts of seven' for the king, and there is evidence that some of the townsmen wished Charles to be admitted in April. Such sympathies found little support, however, among the corporation. Although aldermanic attendances at meetings fell during the autumn, James Watkinson was the only Alderman to withdraw from Hull to join the king. [There is some doubt about this point. Other sources say that William Dobson was the only member of the Aldermanic Bench to join the king. Watkinson certainly joined the king in York where he became Keeper of the Magazine, but he was not officially removed from the Bench until 1644. In 1646 he was sequestered for his royalism. William Dobson, an Alderman and Sheriff of Hull during the kings visit in 1639, appears at Aldermanic meetings until 1642, and was a member of the defence committee established in January 1642. It was Edward Dobson, also a member of the committee and possibly a brother of William, who was sequestered and fined for royalism in 1646. In 1648 William Dobson was Mayor of Hull, which seems unlikely if he had been an active Royalist. Whatever the facts, it is clear that very few of the Aldermen displayed any strong royalist feelings.] The Mayor, Barnard, did not support Hotham's stand in April, and bad relations between the two men seem to have persisted, but Barnard remained in the town and assiduously attended corporation meetings. Indeed, throughout 1642 the major share of municipal work was born by a small group which included Barnard, his successor Thomas Raikes, and Aldermen Jefferson and Smith. These men and their brethren felt sufficiently involved with the parliamentary side to ask their MPs to ensure that if peace were made they would be included in any act of oblivion.

During the winter of 1642–3 the main fighting took place in other parts of Yorkshire, but some parliamentarian troops were supplied from Hull, where the garrison remained on the alert. The walls, castle, and blockhouses were surveyed, and further steps were taken to strengthen them, while the townsmen were required to help with the work as well as to maintain a regular watch when the spring heralded a renewal of the campaign against Hull. The governor was already in dire straits for money to pay his troops and feared that he might have to ask the inhabitants for free quarter.

By this time, however, the Hothams had lost any enthusiasm for the parliamentary conduct of the war and were communicating with Royalist leaders. But their intention to surrender Hull was suspected by parliament and their failure to act quickly enabled the parliamentary leaders to warn Sir Matthew Boynton and others of the danger. On 28 June these men met the Mayor, some of the Aldermen, and Captain Lawrence Moyer of the parliamentary ship *Hercules* to concert a plan to prevent the betrayal of the town. Early next day the crew of the *Hercules* landed and, with the help of soldiers and citizens, quickly secured the castle, blockhouses, walls, and gates. Captain Hotham was arrested but Sir John escaped through Beverley Gate with some of his bodyguard in the nick of time; he was captured in Beverley and then imprisoned on board the *Hercules*. Both men were closely guarded until they could be taken to London to await trial and punishment.

There was no show of popular support for the Hothams: Sir John's relations with the citizens had been difficult, he had not favoured the activities of the 'preciser clergy', and feeling against him had been stirred up by Alderman Pelham. The corporation acted to prevent his treachery with commendable efficiency and constituted a small committee of defence. The committee included Thomas Raikes, the Mayor, Aldermen Denman, Popple. Roper, and Henry and John Barnard, William Styles, the vicar of Holy Trinity, and Boynton. It assumed control of the town with the Mayor acting as governor. It is probably a sign of the corporation's confidence in its mastery of the situation that details of the events of 29 June and the precautions taken were at once entered in the Bench Book. Moreover, the frustration of Royalist hopes of Hull's defection came at a crucial point in the struggle for it coincided with the climax of Royalist successes in Yorkshire at Adwalton Moor which left the king's side in almost undisputed control of the whole county except Hull. Early in July, therefore, the Fairfaxes were able to retreat to the safety of the town where their forces were succoured by the committee of defence. The committee pleaded successfully for Lord Fairfax to be made governor, although it later expressed some dissatisfaction that its own share of the command was not more clearly stipulated.

In July and August the preoccupation of Newcastle's Royalist forces in Lincolnshire gave the governor and corporation the chance to reorganise the defences against the expected attack. This began on 2 September when Newcastle approached the town with a large army. At first the siege was not a close one and the attackers' siege-works were far enough from the walls to enable the governor to destroy much of the Charterhouse hospital and to use the ruins as a gun emplacement. From their batteries further north the besiegers poured red-hot shot into the town in the vain hope of starting fires, and most of the fighting during the earlier half of the siege consisted of artillery duels and skirmishes along the north side of the town. When Fairfax cut the banks to flood the country on 14 September, however, the Royalists switched their attack to the west. More siege-works were prepared by both sides and the bombardment continued sporadically. Sallies by the defenders achieved little, the royalists were hampered by wet weather, and both sides suffered accidents: in one, due to carelessness, the north blockhouse was partly blown up, and in the other much of Newcastle's magazine was destroyed in an explosion.

Although the besiegers had cut the town's fresh-water supply at the start, brackish water was available from wells within the defences. Parliamentary ships were able to carry in supplies, Col. Oliver Cromwell brought reinforcements on 26 September, and after the arrival of Sir John Meldrum with more troops Fairfax determined to break the siege. On 11 October a strong force made a sortie and after bitter fighting overran the Royalist positions. The siege was raised the next day, and for some years 11 October was observed as a day of public thanksgiving. [In the following year the battle of Marston Moor and the seizure of York for parliament removed any remaining threat of further attack.]

Casualties do not seem to have been heavy, but the inhabitants suffered some privations and mortality was high. Members of the corporation stayed in their posts, but because of the gravity of the situation they asked Raikes to serve as Mayor for another year; the governor joined his pleas to theirs, and Raikes reluctantly agreed. The successful resistance of Hull immobilised the royal army in the north at a vital time and prevented the king from gaining the full advantage of victories earlier in the year. It also retained for parliament a strategically important stronghold and base, which the Fairfaxes used in military operations in the county during the rest of 1643, while the corporation, whose general administration had been curtailed, worked to bring local life back to normal. ... The corporation made great efforts to retain its military independence once the emergency of 1643 was over, but despite its wishes the town was attached to the Northern Association in 1645.

Source 34

From P. McNicol, *Horrible News from Hull* (Hull, 1987) p. 5.

Hull was strongly fortified. By nature it was bounded on the east by the river Hull and on the south by the Humber. East again of the River Hull was a line of fortifications built by Henry VIII, with two blockhouses north and south and a castle in the middle. Protecting the city on the landward sides, the town walls ran westwards from the Hull, turning southwards to reach the Humber. These were built of brick between 1321 and 1400, four feet six inches thick and fourteen feet high. They had twelve towers and four gatehouses – the North Gate, Beverley Gate, Myton Gate and Hessle Gate. To strengthen further what was already a strongly fortified town, the inhabitants of Hull had the ability to flood the low-lying meadowlands under the west walls by pulling up sluices that kept out the water at flood tide. This inundated the country around Hull for about two miles and left only a few roads above water. So Hull was virtually impregnable. Charles himself seems to have realised the difficulties of taking the city by force and is recorded to have asked Sir Thomas Glemham, a former governor of Hull, 'Cannot I starve Hull? I am told I can take their fresh water from them.' He was told by Glemham that Hull was so marshy that 'every man can dig water at his door'.

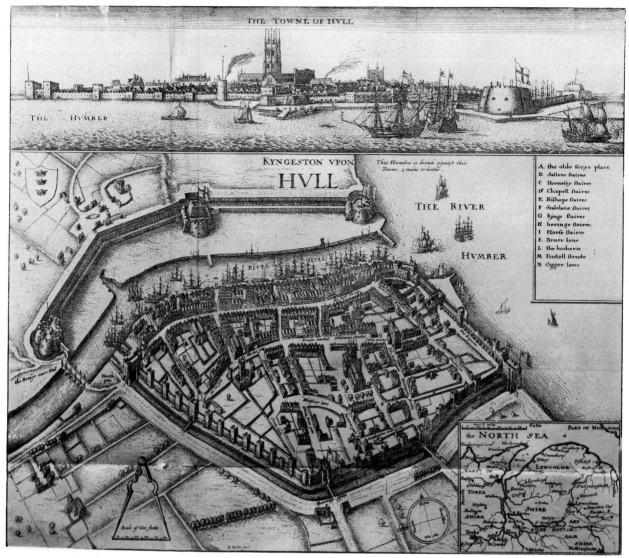

Plan of Hull, 1640, engraved by Wencelaus Hollar

The extracts from *The Victoria County History* (Source 35), summarise the character and characteristics of the town, covering its economic, social and political structures, as well as its religious arrangements. While these are treated separately, it is important to consider how the different factors interacted with one another. It is also important to be aware of the European context in which Hull traded in the mid-seventeenth century. Her main contacts were with northern Europe, where at this time the Protestant powers were under attack from the Catholic armies of Spain and the Austrian Emperor, in the Thirty Years' War. The war was brutal and bitter, both sides being guilty of atrocities, but it was the Protestant version of events that would be conveyed to the merchants and seamen of Hull.

Source 35

From *The Victoria County History of Hull*, pp. 96–8, 100–02, 120–5 and 133–8.

Economy

[Hull was first and foremost a seaport, relying mainly on overseas trade. In the early sixteenth century her medieval trade in woollens and wine had begun to decline. However] maritime activity at Hull began to increase again about the middle of the sixteenth century. … Furthermore, an increase in the size and number of vessels owned at the port suggests longer voyages and expanding trade. … The commercial basis of Hull's maritime growth was the expanding manufacture of cheap kerseys [cloth] in the West Riding. Exports of this northern cloth rose rapidly for about twenty years after 1565, as the town began to take advantage of the products of its promising hinterland, and a further sharp increase took place in the 1590s. The activity of Hull's merchants and mariners in the Baltic trades began to increase at the same time. ...

Hull's commerce in the Baltic was adversely affected during the later 1620s by Swedish military campaigns which occasionally stopped the traffic and which caused generally depressed trading conditions. ... The Dutch were playing an increasing part in the Baltic trade, with important effects on Hull. The second and third decades of the seventeenth century saw the growth of the indirect supply of Baltic goods through Amsterdam and Rotterdam: in 1633 one fifth of the flax entering Hull came from Holland, while of the newer imports, more than two thirds of the pitch, tar and iron was carried in by the Dutch, as well as a large proportion of the timber. Thus the expanding traffic in these goods added little to the business of Hull's Baltic shippers. Hull joined in the general outcry against the Dutch carrying trade, but such protests were of little avail when the Hollanders were able to bring Baltic and Norwegian products to Hull more cheaply than English traders shipping direct to the port. Hull's staple exports were still hides and the cheap West Riding cloths. Although the traffic soon fell from the peak reached during the 1590s ... this branch of the town's commerce usually flourished during the first quarter of the seventeenth century. ... During the first forty years of the seventeenth century, therefore, the growth and the changes in Hull's overseas trade were associated with the development of Amsterdam as an entrepot [exchange depot] for Baltic goods, brought from there to Hull in increasing quantities. This exchange with the Netherlands thus replaced the earlier direct traffic with the Baltic, which had flourished vigorously during the preceding half-century. Hull's trade ... continued during these years to grow steadily, if not dramatically ... [but] it ranked only fourth or fifth among the outports in tonnage of ships owned at this time, and its shipping was undoubtedly threatened by Dutch competition. ... Piratical attacks were another menace ... [with] growing difficulties throughout the early seventeenth century.

As a maritime town, Hull was [always] liable to contribute to the cost of ships for the navy. In 1558 it unsuccessfully sought help from York ... [and in the emergency of 1588] the Privy Council ordered York to contribute. [In the 1590s this was extended to the cloth towns of the West Riding, but Hull always had great difficulty in actually collecting any money.] The whole question was reopened by the issue of ship money writs in 1626 [when] Hull and York appealed jointly against the size and apportionment of the assessment. ... [After] a lengthy and heated debate ... Hull was relieved of two-thirds of the levy, and in the following year [1627] it joined in the general resistance to further payments for the provision of ships. The writs of 1634–40 [however] gave little opportunity for obstruction: Hull attempted unsuccessfully to pass part of the charge of the first writ on to other places, but [probably because these towns were now being assessed for contributions anyway, since the king had extended the tax inland] thereafter it regularly [if reluctantly] paid its share of the tax, like the rest of Yorkshire, until 1640, when nothing was collected.

Town government and MPs

[By its charters, Hull was governed by a corporation of Mayor and Aldermen, who also sat as JPs, and sent two MPs to Parliament]. Under the charters the Mayor and Aldermen formed a largely self-perpetuating body with the major influence in the choice of town officers. ... They nominated candidates for Mayor, Aldermen, Sheriff and Chamberlain, the final choice being made by themselves with an unspecified number of burgesses [citizens]; by the 1690s, 100 or even 150 of the latter were voting in these elections, but clearly the choice of candidate was all-important. ... The corporation met frequently, but mainly at irregular intervals, either in Holy Trinity or in one of the Guildhalls. ... The political crisis of the early 1640s resulted in much more frequent meetings, mainly for business connected with defence. ... The mayor was normally present but the attendance of the Aldermen varied considerably ... ; [some] small groups were most assiduous in attendance, and the preponderance of these men made the ruling group seem even more exclusive. ... There was some formality about the conduct of meetings: Aldermen took precedence in speaking and other matters by seniority. ... On at least two occasions men challenging the corporation grumbled about the lack of a representative body for the commons, but there is no sign of any widespread agitation to institute the sort of common council existing elsewhere. ... The corporation consulted selected burgesses on certain matters of general concern. ... Nevertheless, voting on candidates selected by the Mayor and Aldermen and intermittent consultation on a limited range of subjects gave the burgesses, however senior or substantial, no very effective voice in municipal affairs.

Scarcity of biographical material and the absence of inventories make it impossible to draw a clear picture of the wealth of the town's ruling group, but the surviving evidence gives some pointers to the social and economic status of its members. The occupations of rather more than half of the Aldermen can be determined, and of these the overwhelming majority were merchants, whose preponderance on the bench was maintained throughout the period. By comparison few other aldermanic occupations have been identified: ... in the seventeenth century there were ... five shipmasters, four drapers, a grocer and an apothecary. Whether other occupations enjoyed better representation among the sheriffs and chamberlains is not known, but it is clear that, even if this was so, promotion to the bench came most readily to the merchants. ...

Although a few of the Aldermen suffered declining fortunes in later life, the great majority remained men of substance to the last. ... Aldermen usually possessed a certain amount of property in the town, and rent, as well as trading profits, formed part of their income. ... Rural property was no less attractive to most of the Aldermen, although many of them confined their interest to holdings in the hinterland of the town. ... Nevertheless, some leading townsmen had extensive possessions in the country. ... Marriage alliances with the gentry were not uncommon, and these also linked the town with the countryside.

Intermarriage between the families of the town leaders was much more frequent. ... Thus the list of Aldermen usually included several men related by blood or marriage, and two other features also combined to give the bench the character of a closely-knit oligarchy; these were long service and the presence of successive generations of the same family. ... In the seventeenth century Bernard was an Alderman for 30 years, while Nicholas Denman held a place on the bench for 27 years and Sir John Lister for 24: The Mattison, Stockdale, Thurscross, Rogers, Chambers and Maister families, among others, all provided more than one Alderman during the period. Above all, four families played a pre-eminent part in municipal life. The Barnards provided three aldermen and two recorders. Four members of the Dalton family served as Aldermen, two of these were also MPs, and another, Sir William, was Recorder. The elder John Lister was succeeded on the bench by his son, Sir John, and their combined service totalled 46 years. Finally the Ramsdens, in addition to their outstanding parliamentary record, supplied three aldermen in the seventeenth century.

[In the sixteenth century most of Hull's MPs were members of the bench, town officers, or close associates] but in the early seventeenth century Hull was less successful in avoiding interference in its choice. ... Four of the eight members returned in James I's reign were Aldermen but four were outsiders. ... [However, by 1628] the corporation were resolved to elect only burgesses to parliament, and this rule was followed [thereafter, with the exception of Sir Henry Vane, the Lord High Admiral, and his son, who was elected in November 1640.] He was selected primarily because his father had been instrumental in freeing Hull from a lawsuit about the repair of the castle. Between 1604 and 1640 only one of the six local men served more than once, namely John Lister. ... It may be of great significance that when Lister [a staunch Royalist] died in December 1640, Peregrine Pelham, a merchant and ex-sheriff, was elected to succeed him as Vane's parliamentary colleague, and both men gradually moved into opposition.

Religious life
By the time of the Elizabethan Settlement [1558–9] local Protestantism had firm roots, and further evidence of its strength was quickly forthcoming in the lay attack on the Marian vicar, Thomas Fugall, who was ... deprived [of his post]. ... His successor at Holy Trinity was Melchior Smith who, significantly, was persuaded by members of the corporation to come to Hull from Boston (Lincs.) where he had already identified himself as an advanced Protestant. ... Smith professed several characteristically Puritan beliefs: bitter hatred of popery, dislike of ceremonies, and emphasis on the Bible, above all upon preaching, which he considered to be 'the highest and most excellent function of a priest'. He remained vicar until 1591, and from the widespread influence of his teaching during his long incumbency grew much of the reputation of Elizabethan Hull as a centre of militant Protestantism.

The corporation was in harmony with the Puritan desire for sermons and [with the help of the sympathetic Archbishop Grindal, founded a lectureship at Holy Trinity]. ... The first lecturer was Grindal's nominee, Griffith Briskin, who in 1578 and again in 1581 was before the Ecclesiastical Commission for conduct which suggests non-acceptance of parts of the Prayer Book. [By contrast, Catholic] recusancy took very little hold either in Hull or in the surrounding country. ... There were, [however] strong cross-currents of religious opinion in the town during early Stuart times. ... [The vicar] of Hessle and Hull was Richard Perrott, a conforming Anglican later to be associated with High Church views. During his ministry Perrott faced opposition. His attempt to have the organ at Holy Trinity repaired and used won only lukewarm support and failed. He also had a disagreement about preaching in 1625 with the newly-appointed lecturer, Andrew Marvell, the elder. Marvell became a most influential minister and a respected figure in the town: he was a moderate Puritan who renewed earlier complaints about local Separatists. Perrott's teaching could also have been counteracted by John Gouge, the curate chosen by the corporation in 1627 [and] by various Puritan clergy in the neighbouring parishes. ...

By this time the diocesan authorities had launched their counter-attack on Puritan worship in towns like York, Beverley, and Hull. Perrott himself served on commissions to survey churches, and in 1633 orders were issued to 'beautify' both Holy Trinity and St Mary's after the Laudian manner; the churchwardens apparently complied. Moreover, Perrott had already introduced a daily service at Holy Trinity to promote the Prayer Book in the affections of his parishioners. In this he probably had some success, at least among the moderates. The service was suspended during the plague of 1637 but once that danger was passed the Mayor and some of the Aldermen asked for the service to be resumed. Perrott professed himself willing to comply but could not do so because of the opposition of his curate, Gouge, who was already lapsing into nonconformity; Perrott was warned that any attempt to discipline Gouge would cause uproar in the town. Members of the corporation maintained their pressure, however, but when they failed to persuade Gouge to conduct the service Archbishop Neile intervened to order him to do so, and he was hauled before the diocesan courts. The inability of the vicar and his aldermanic supporters to coerce Gouge shows that their views were not representative of popular opinion. Neile's officials were able to achieve their aim of frequent services by acting as arbitrators in the dispute. Their interest in Hull's religious life continued in 1639 when Marvell was disciplined and instructed to read more of the Prayer Book liturgy before his weekly lecture.

Their success was short-lived. When Marvell was drowned in 1641 the corporation, with much popular support, chose another moderate Puritan, William Styles, to succeed him in preference to a Laudian prebendary of York. About the same time Gouge complained to the House of Commons about one of Perrott's sermons; the vicar was impeached but died before the year ended. Styles thereupon succeeded to the vicarage and to the task of upholding the town's religious traditions. [Thereafter the Puritan grip on Hull was firm, with disputes in the ensuing decades arising from a personal animosity between Styles and the new, staunchly Presbyterian, lecturer, John Shaw, and a continuing battle between these two upholders of a national Church and the Separatists. During the war the latter received encouragement from the Independent, Philip Nye, who was associated with Sir Matthew Boynton of Barmston in the East Riding, and John Canne, preacher to the garrison from 1648. In 1644 Hull saw the foundation of one of the earliest Independent Churches in England, in Dagger Lane.]

Source 36

From P. McNicol, *Horrible News from Hull* pp. 2–3.

Seventeenth-century Hull was first and foremost a busy trading port, then the fifth most important in the country. It looked out to sea for its trade and most of this trade was with Holland. Consequently many of its influential inhabitants were descendants of Dutch merchants whose Calvinist leanings ensured the gradual growth of a strong Puritan element in Hull. Happily the Puritan virtues of thrift and industry offered material as well as spiritual profit to the merchant classes. These men resented the autocratic methods of Charles' rule for three reasons. First, they maintained that, as they both contributed to and benefited from the prosperity of the nation, they should therefore have some voice in its administration. Secondly they disliked the methods used by Charles during his eleven years of personal rule to raise money for his government. The tax called Ship Money, originally levied to provide a force to rid coastal waters of pirates, now diverted to wider usage, was detested nation-wide. John Hampden, Sir John Hotham and Sir Hugh Cholmley refused to collect the money and pay it over, even when they learned of the king's displeasure. Thirdly, they felt that they had good reason to complain against Archbishop Laud's harsh persecution of non-conformists, for Laud at this time was very active in his campaign against puritanism. On the other hand there was an age-old tradition of loyalty to the monarchy which usually balanced any anti-royalist feeling. Edward I had founded the port of Kingston-upon-Hull and later it was presented with its royal charter. The people of Hull were very proud of their royal foundation and there was a large Royalist following in the city at this time. Indeed, Sir John Hotham thought it necessary to order all the townsfolk to remain indoors until sunset on that fateful day when he refused his king entry into the city – a precaution, no doubt, against a hostile reaction to his 'treason' from a substantial minority of the citizens.

Source 37

From B.N. Reckitt, *Charles the First and Hull, 1639–45* (Mr Pye Books, Howden, 1988) pp. 18–20.

Sir John Hotham, member of one of the oldest and most influential families in Yorkshire, was knighted by James I at York and saw service abroad fighting for Frederick, Elector Palatine, who was son-in-law to James I. In 1621 he was created Baronet and four years later was elected Member for Beverley in the first parliament of Charles I. He continued to represent that town in all five parliaments of the reign. He was appointed Governor of Hull in 1628 and High Sheriff of Yorkshire in 1635. Politically, he stood for the rights and liberties of the subject within an all-embracing cloak of monarchy, and he had therefore joined himself with the anti-court party of Eliot, Hampden, Pym and Wentworth in the early parliaments of the reign. But he would probably have agreed with Wentworth [Strafford] who later went over to the royal side, that 'the authority of a king is the keystone which closeth up the arch of order and government'. … But Hotham's parliamentary activities were sufficient to bring him into disfavour with the Court and to mark him as on the Parliamentary side when the final split came about. …

Wentworth had hoped to win Hotham to the king's support when, as President of the Council of the North, he appointed him to high positions in the royal service in Yorkshire, and, indeed, for a time he may have done so. But the damage was done when the king insisted on appointing Captain Legge as military commander in Hull. Wentworth then wrote a revealing but ineffectual letter (27 March, 1639): 'I know his [Hotham's] faithfulness to be such as I durst answer for him with my life; nor am I ignorant that in party he is eager, and in truth over-earnest, yet it were very easy to have him as forward on the king's party, and more than in any other private animosity. Believe me, he is as considerable a person as any other gentleman in the North of England, and therefore it were well in my opinion not utterly to cast him off, as by taking the government of that town [Hull] you shall infallibly do'. Thereafter Hotham took umbrage against Wentworth, whom he probably imagined to be to blame for Legge's appointment, and against the royal authority. He refused to collect or pay ship money and Wentworth took action against him, as recounted by Sir Hugh Cholmley of Whitby in his Memoirs: 'My Lord [Strafford] had also put Sir John Hotham out of all commissions for refusing ship money; and him, and my cousin Mr Henry Bellasis, eldest son of the Lord Falconberg, into the Fleet [prison] for some words they had spoke in this Short Parliament (1640). All which I wish from my heart had not happened; for it did not only produce inconvenience and prejudice to my Lord's person, but even to the nation too, I fear, as you may conjecture by the story.' As one consequence Hotham gave damaging evidence against Wentworth, or Strafford as he then was, at his trial.

Hotham was also in the bad books of Charles for his critical attitude in parliament and for joining in a petition in 1640 against the billeting of soldiers in Yorkshire. For this Charles sent for Sir John and Sir Hugh Cholmley, who had also signed the petition, and personally upbraided them, saying that if they ever meddled, or had a hand in any more petitions, he would hang them. Such an insult was an attack on Sir John's personal honour and on his liberty as a subject and his resentment was naturally extreme. There followed the appointment of Sir

Thomas Glemham as Governor of Hull over his head – a bitter pill administered at a time when he was wavering and when his own appointment might well have drawn him back to the Royalist fold. But the key to his future actions lies in the fact that though his quarrel with Charles was deep, it was not a quarrel with the principle of kingship and at the back of his mind he still reverenced the position and powers of the crown, into whatever rash acts the hastiness of his temper might lead him and whatever the resulting appearances to his own ostensible party might be.

Source 38

From Clarendon, *The History of the Rebellion and Civil Wars in England.*

Though Hotham had concurred with them [Parliament] in all their violent ways, yet they well knew that he was not possessed with their principles in any degree, but was very well-affected in his judgement to the government both in church and state, but had first been engaged by his particular malice against the Earl of Strafford, and afterwards terrified by their votes against Sheriffs and deputy lieutenants. … He could better resolve upon deliberation than on a sudden, and many were of the opinion that if he had been prepared dexterously beforehand, and in confidence, he would have conformed to the King's pleasure; for he was master of a noble fortune in land, and rich in money; of a very ancient family, and well allied, his affections to the government very good; and no man less desired to see the nation involved in a civil war than he; and, when he accepted employment from the Parliament, he never imagined it would engage him in rebellion; but believed that the King would find it necessary to comply with the advice of his two houses; and that the preserving that magazine from being possessed by him, would likewise prevent any possible rupture into arms.

Source 39

From Sir Hugh Cholmley, *Memoirs Addressed to his Two Sons.*

That unfortunate but noble gentleman Sir John Hotham, my cousin-german once removed and dear friend … was a man of good understanding and ingenuity, yet of a rash and hasty nature, and so much wedded to his own humour, as his passion often over-balanced his judgement, and yet he was able to give good counsel and advice, where his own interest was not concerned; he was valiant and a very good friend; and if his own particular interest had not been concerned would not have forsaken his friend for any adverse fortune; he was a man that loved liberty, which was an occasion to make him join at first with the Puritan party, to whom after he became nearer linked merely for his own interest and security; for in more than concerned the civil liberty, he did not approve their ways. Some of his most intimate friends who often moved him to quit the Parliament and come to the King, found him very inclinable, making protestation,

that he did but expect a treaty, when if the King should but offer that which was reasonable and the Parliament not accept, he would desert them.

Source 40

Portrait of Sir John Hotham

Portrait of Captain Hotham

140

Source 41

From a letter written by Captain John Hotham to the Earl of Newcastle, 9 January 1643.

My lord, there is no man that hath any reasonable share in the commonwealth can desire that either side should be absolute conquerors … : it is too great a temptation to courses of will and violence. … If the honourable endeavours of such powerful men as yourself do not take place for a happy peace, the necessitous people of the whole kingdom will presently rise in mighty numbers. And whosoever they pretend for at first, within a while they will set up for themselves, to the utter ruin of all the nobility of the kingdom.

Source 42

From P. McNicol, *Horrible News from Hull* pp. 7–9, 11–13 and 16–17.

As Charles saw clearly that it would be difficult to take Hull by force, he resorted to plots and bribery to worm his way in. … The first two plots, organised from the outside, failed when they were discovered by Hotham who quelled them and reported diligently to parliament. The third plot was much more subtle and came very near to success. A certain Lord Digby was captured in a ship off Hull by the parliamentarian vessel *Mayflower*. He had been trying to assist the royalist ship *Providence* which was carrying arms for the king. When the *Mayflower* reached Hull, Digby, pretending that he was a seasick Frenchman, managed to gain an audience with Hotham, to whom he revealed his true identity as an ardent Royalist. No doubt Digby possessed considerable powers of persuasion, for he was soon in Hotham's confidence. Hotham listened to Digby's largely untrue estimations of the powers at Charles' disposal and eventually agreed to his plan to give up Hull to the king. The one problem was his honour, but it was soon agreed that Charles should come to Hull with a force of men, fire one shot, and then the town would be given over to him. Hotham's honour would thus be satisfied and he could accept the pardon and the money that Digby promised in the King's name. …

That was why Charles and the Earl of Lindsey appeared before Hull at the beginning of July 1642 with so few men that the Earl, knowing nothing of Digby's plan, was in despair. The royal army consisted of three thousand foot and one thousand horse, ill equipped and badly armed. Presumably the token shot was fired and immediately it was clear that Digby's plan had failed. Hull stood firm and the siege dragged on throughout July: the third humiliation for Charles with respect to the city. The reason for the failure of Digby's plot is not clear. The most obvious answer is that parliamentarian support in Hull was much stronger than Hotham had reckoned, so that the surrender of the city was impossible. It is also possible that Hotham had second thoughts about the validity of Charles' offer of pardon for one who had humiliated him so deeply in April. …

The prospect of the siege must have caused great apprehension amongst the ordinary citizens of Hull. The decision had been taken for them that they must take up arms against their anointed monarch. Pamphlets such as the royalist *Horrible Newes from Hull*, with its lurid description of the devastation the enemy would work after they had entered Hull, would add greatly to their fears for their lives and their property, at the same time adding to their determination to protect themselves and their city to the best of their ability. … On 10 July a small royalist force was sent to burn down windmills outside the walls, to cut off food supplies and to act as a show of strength. On Hotham's orders they came under fire from the town walls, whereupon they dropped their weapons and fled. Incensed but triumphant, the citizens strengthened their defences, kept ever on the alert by the dark rumours of Charles' intended revenge should he take the city. … Charles relinquished command on 17 July to the Earl of Newport and returned to York. Newport was faced with a hopeless task with underpaid men and little ammunition. Morale was low and the siege was soon raised. With the parliamentarians in command of the sea, Hull would never have surrendered. …

A little more than one year [later] Hull was again besieged … [this time by] an effective fighting unit led by the Earl of Newcastle and with the advantages of excellent weaponry and successful experience of the craft of warfare in Lincolnshire. … Much had changed inside the walls of Hull also. The gradual progression of hostilities had made both Sir John and Captain Hotham less and less enthusiastic towards their original alliance. … In February 1643 Captain Hotham was to be found visiting the Earl of Newcastle in Bridlington and meeting the Queen. … Hotham had previously written seventeen letters to the Earl, a correspondence which had begun with negotiations about prisoners and ended with an admission of loyalty to the king and the expression of a desire to join the royal cause. Subsequent meetings of Captain Hotham with the Queen and Earl produced the promise from Hotham that his father would hand over Hull to the king in return for certain royal favours.

The reasons for the inept manoeuvrings of the Hothams during 1642 and 1643 were both political and personal. Sir John was known to disapprove of the lengths to which the parliamentarians were prepared to go against the king and he disliked the unreasonable terms proposed by parliament in the negotiations at Oxford after the king had raised his standard at Nottingham. It would seem that Sir John genuinely desired a peace settlement which the parliamentarian terms made quite impossible. Religiously Hotham had little in common with the Puritans in Hull, and it would seem that he was generally unpopular in the town, having disputed with the Mayor and Aldermen over many decisions during the first siege. Most of all Hotham resented the appointment of Ferdinando, Lord Fairfax as the commander of the parliamentarian forces in the North and the promotion of his son, Sir Thomas Fairfax, as General of the Horse over the head of Captain Hotham who was made Lieutenant-General. But whatever their motivation, the behaviour of the Hothams appeared equally discreditable to both sides. [To make matters worse, while parliamentary agents were investigating the suspected treachery of Sir John in Hull] the newly-created Lieutenant-General Hotham was arousing deep resentment amongst the parliamentarian forces in Nottingham. He had been sent there as part of a force to repel the royalist advance from Yorkshire led by the Earl of Newcastle. Perhaps elated by the imminence of his change of allegiance, he let his forces run riot and plunder throughout Nottingham, and quickly earned the dislike of his superiors, including Colonel Oliver Cromwell, in a series of violent disputes with them. [After threatening Cromwell with a pistol he was briefly imprisoned by parliament, but escaped to return to Hull.] His escape was brief, since he arrived in the town in time to be arrested alongside his father for their planned betrayal. … By 15 July, both the Hothams were safely in the Tower of London.

The arrest of the Hothams came only just in time for the parliamentarian forces. On 30 June, Lord Ferdinando and Sir Thomas Fairfax had been defeated by the Earl of Newcastle's army at Adwalton Moor, [and] they retreated towards Hull. With Hotham as governor, the city gates would have been firmly closed to them, but as it was they found a parliamentarian town offering them welcome. … [A defence committee of the Mayor, Aldermen and local gentry had taken over the town from Hotham] and Fairfax was appointed Governor on the recommendation of Thomas Raikes, the Mayor, on 22 July. [In September Fairfax was to return the complement, for when Raikes was asked by the Aldermen and Burgesses, in view of the emergency, to act as Mayor for an unprecedented second term, it was apparently the persuasions of Fairfax that finally overcame his reluctance. Thus when the Earl of Newcastle drew back from his march south via Lincolnshire, to deal with a parliamentarian Hull which was serving as a base for raids in royalist Yorkshire he found a united city which had been given time to strengthen its defences.] When the siege began on 2 September, 1643, the defenders of the city stood together behind their leaders who themselves staunchly supported the parliamentarian cause. All decisions resulting from discussions between the new Governor, Lord Fairfax, and the Mayor and Aldermen were unanimous. [The energetic defence of the citizens, aided by the ability of parliament to send supplies and reinforcements by sea] held off an efficient and effective royalist force. … On 14 September Lord Fairfax decided to open the sluice-gates to flood the area round the city. As a result the royalists were encased in mud, their [siege] works blocked and useless. [Finally, on 11 October a sally led by Sir John Meldrum overran the royalist positions; on 12 October came news of a significant Royalist defeat at Winceby, in which both Col. Cromwell and Sir Thomas Fairfax had taken part. The same day] the Royalists were seen to be raising the siege and leaving the area. … Newcastle must have realised that, had he abandoned the futile siege of Hull at an earlier stage, his forces, joined together with those already in Lincolnshire, would have made all the difference to the outcome of the battle. As it was, he marched into Lincolnshire to join the defeated Royalists, too late to help them and with a defeat of his own to report.

Source 43 which follows consists of extracts from the Bench Books and miscellaneous documents which record the proceedings of the Corporation and Committees which administered Hull during and after the Civil War. The Bench Books make no reference to the king's attempts to enter the town, and provide little more than oblique and passing comment on the first siege. For much of the period, the business transacted seems entirely normal – wills, leases, town maintenance and minor transgressions among the citizens, and this serves as a timely reminder that the national upheaval of Civil War had a varying, sometimes indirect, and intermittent impact upon the lives of individuals in the thousands of towns and villages that made up the local communities of England. As official records, the Bench books reveal little of the attitudes, beliefs and motivations behind the decisions made, but the accompanying letters and documents show something of the attitude of the town – a fierce local independence and concern for the town's liberties and privileges, care and concern that those who made decisions in these difficult times should be protected and indemnified for their actions, respect and deference towards those of rank and position in society accompanied, however, by a determined defence of the citizens' rights and a refusal to be collectively overawed by superior rank.

The following extracts have been selected to illustrate events and issues referred to in the sources above, but they also focus on the difficult issue of discerning the attitudes and feelings of ordinary citizens. Inevitably, the records refer mainly to the activities of the small group of leading citizens who served on committees, administered the town and made decisions which affected the rest. Nevertheless, it is possible to infer certain ideas about the attitudes of the wider population. Plans for the defence of the town in Source 43(a) show complete confidence in the Corporation that the inhabitants of the town will participate and support their decisions. The re-election of Thomas Raikes as Mayor, described in Source 43(c), reveals the acquiescence or even the positive support of the burgesses, in contrast to the resistance demonstrated at York in a similar situation. The arrest of Hotham and his co-conspirators in Source 43(b) shows that only the Lister family and Sir Edward Rhodes, whose estates lay in south Yorkshire and who had no specific connection with Hull, were considered to be actively in support of Hotham's plans, and there was certainly no support for Hotham from the citizens. Finally the small numbers of citizens who were sequestered for royalist activities in 1646 [Source 43(d)] as compared with those from the surrounding country also indicates that few were actively opposed to what their leaders chose to do. Such evidence is fragmentary and uncertain, resting on the interpretation of scattered references and the reading of implications from a limited range of actions. Undoubtedly, the issue of survival in a situation created by others can explain much of the apparent enthusiasm of the Hull citizens in resisting the royalist attacks. It can be said, however, that the citizens of Hull followed their local leaders and pursued their policies to a degree that precludes positive royalist sympathies even if it does not express enthusiasm for the parliamentary cause.

Source 43

From Hull Corporation Papers, Hull City Record Office.

(a) Bench Books: Monday, 27 March, 1643.

Whereas it hath been, of late, divers times moved to Mr Mayor in private by sundry burgesses, that in respect of the present dangers and distractions of these times, and especially considering the great army now on foot in York and Yorkshire under command of the Earl of Newcastle, that some course might be settled for the townsmen's watching of the Town, Castle and Blockhouses in the night time during these troublous times. And thereupon Mr Mayor gave order to the Constables of the several wards to summon the Burgesses and Townsmen inhabitant to appear in the Council house of this town this present day, to the end that that business might be seen and there propounded and further considered of. And according to the summons, divers of them appearing: It is ordered by the Mayor and Aldermen, with the consent of Sir John Hotham, Knight and Baronet, Governor of the Town (now also present) and with the consent of the Burgesses assembled that from henceforth strict watch shall be kept every night throughout the Town, Castle and Blockhouses by the Burgesses and Townsmen inhabitant without pay, and that half a ward shall watch every night. And that so many and such of the half ward as shall be by Mr Mayor, or by the Aldermen of every ward shall be thought fit, be set to watch at the Castle and Blockhouses and the rest to watch at the lane ends in the Town as the Mayor and Aldermen shall appoint.

(b) Minutes and Orders of the Town Committee.

29 June, 1643: Whereas upon the apprehension of some fears and jealousies by the Townsmen, that treachery hath been intended against the town to deliver the same up to some forces, enemies to King and Parliament, the townsmen have put themselves into a military posture for safeguarding and keeping of the Town and forts for the use of King and Parliament until the Parliament's pleasure and directions be signified therein and further as shall be directed. And have to that end taken into their custody this morning the Town, the Magazine and Forts, with the ordnance and ammunition in and about the same. Whereupon Sir John Hotham, knight and baronet,

who was formerly appointed governor by the Parliament, is of a sudden this morning departed and hath wholly left the Town. It is therefore thought fit and agreed that a Governor and Committee be forthwith appointed for settling of the present distractions in the Town and regulating the affairs of the Town and of such occurrences as may happen: And hereupon Mr Thomas Raikes, now Mayor, is appointed the present Governor of the town; and Mr Roper, Mr John Barnard, Mr Henry Barnard, and Mr Denman, Mr Popple (Alderman) and Mr William Styles (Vicar) of the Town; Sir Matthew Boynton, Sir William St Quintin, Sir Richard Darley, Sir William Allenson, Mr Robert Johnson and Mr John Penrose are appointed a Committee in the premises.

1 July, 1643: Ordered that Mr Samuel Lister be presently removed from the prison where he now is and confined to the house of Lady Lister, his mother, and he to enter bond of £200 by himself, Mr John Lister, and Mr Hugh Lister, his cousin, with condition to appear before the Parliament at any time, or before the Mayor and Committee or Governor of Kingston upon Hull as shall be thereunto required by them.

3 July, 1643: Ordered that Mr John Hotham shall, for his more security, be removed from the Chamber in Mr Somerfield's house where he now lodgeth, to Mr Ripley's house in Church Lane this night, there to be safeguarded until further order. … And that Mr Hotham's children shall have free liberty to go abroad in the Town and to the School, and a maid to wait on the children, and that Lady Anderson [Hotham's mother-in-law] have liberty to view the trunks in the Mayor's house to see if her trunk be amongst them.

(c) Bench Books: Saturday, September 30, 1643.

This day … there was put in election to the Burgesses in the Guildhall assembled, Mr Peregrine Pelham [MP for Hull] and Mr John Chambers, Alderman, for one of them to be sworn Mayor of this town of Kingston-upon-Hull for the year to come: But the Burgesses assembled, taking into consideration Mr Mayor's vigilance and carefulness of the town's affairs for the year past, and his fidelity to the public cause, and the great danger that the town is now in, being at present strongly beleaguered by the Earl of Newcastle's forces lying nigh and daily shooting into the Town with their great Ordnance, earnestly prayed Mr Mayor either to continue Mayor as he is, or otherwise that he would give way to be elected Mayor again as of now for the year to come. But Mr Mayor being very unwilling thereunto, as the business was in debate, the Right Honourable, the Lord Fairfax, Governor, came into the said assembly in the Guildhall and requested Mr Mayor to take upon him the Mayoralty of the Town for another year, assuring him that his extraordinary charges would be satisfied him by the Public. And divers of the Burgesses also then promising that these charges should be borne; whereupon Mr Mayor (after much entreaty) being persuaded to be added as a third man to go on with Mr Pelham and Mr Chambers in the said election; he, the said Mr Thomas Raikes, now Mayor, was elected and sworn to continue Mayor of the said Town for the year to come.

THE SIEGE RAISED – NOTA!

Memorandum impervetuum to the praise and glory of God, that the 11th October 1643 the Siege was raised which had been continued against this Town by the Earl of Newcastle's great Army for the space of 14 weeks last past.

(d) List of Sequestrations, 1645–6. The list shows those who compounded and were fined for royalist activities during the war. Very few were from Hull itself.

Robert Cartwright of Hull, draper – a captain in Newcastle's army.

Stephen Thompson of Humbleton – owner of Scarborough Castle.

Edward Dobson of Hull, draper – left Hull for royalist York.

Christopher Hildyard of Winestead – in arms against Parliament.

Henry Hildyard of Winestead – ditto.

James Watkinson of Hull, merchant – left Hull for York, became Keeper of the Magazine there.

Matthew Topham of Hull, merchant – left Hull for York.

Christopher Hildyard of Routh – in arms.

Sir Michael Wharton of Beverley – attended King's meeting at Heworth Moor.

Sir Henry Griffiths of Burton Agnes – Colonel in Royal army.

Sir Robert Hildyard of Patrington – served King in his Privy Chamber.

Michael Wharton of Beverley – Captain in Royal army.

Sir Francis Cobbe of Ottringham – Lt.-Col. and Esquire of His Majesty's Bodyguard.

Sir Hugh Cholmley of Whitby.

Source 44

From P. McNicol, *Horrible News from Hull* pp. 18–19.

It is true to say that the Civil War was basically a struggle between two privileged classes. … Major decisions were taken by men of influence on both sides; the common people had little or no say; indeed, in some parts of the country unaffected by actual fighting, life went on much as usual, and the people were hardly aware … that there was a war in progress. But the citizens of a town under siege followed their leaders perforce. It was not the common people of Hull who made the decision to support the Parliament, to deny the King entry or to refuse to give up the town to the Earl of Newcastle. These matters were arranged by the leading figures in the city including the members of Parliament for Hull and the Governors, Hotham and Fairfax, who were appointed by the Parliament. Yet the ordinary citizens were vitally concerned with the outcome of the siege. A town forced to come to terms with the enemy faced humiliation and large financial loss, while a stronghold taken by storm was confronted by a disaster, the scale of which depended on the extent to which discipline could be imposed on the victorious troops by their commanders. It was wise to fear the worst and to unite in fighting to prevent it.

Politically the common people had no reason in the world to support the parliamentarian cause: Parliament was not defending their liberties or championing their rights. Indeed, the natural inclination would have been towards the king as a traditional father-figure. But if ordinary people were not greatly concerned with politics, they were profoundly concerned with religion. Nearly all had an inbred hatred of popery, intensely suspicious of the elaborate ritual which Charles and his Archbishop, Laud, were imposing upon the Church of England. … The free and easy attitude to religious observances of the Cavaliers was also offensive to many Puritans and they accused the court party of licentiousness and frivolity. Parliament was seen to be the champion of the Puritan cause, and in cities the prosperity of which was based on commerce, the majority of the common people, influenced partly by their leaders, but largely by their religious convictions, favoured the parliamentary cause. This was most probably the situation in Hull, though the existence of a large royalist minority is also likely. The decision, once taken, was irrevocable. There would be little point in a citizen telling a gang of looting soldiers that he had not been in favour of the siege in the first place.

Question

12. Why did Hull support parliament throughout the Civil War?

The sources above have provided sufficient information to enable you to answer this question, but a good explanation will require some consideration of the kind of question that is being asked. Hull's support for parliament can be seen as an event, in which case the factors which caused it can be seen as conditional and contingent, and the importance of each weighed up. Alternatively, the question can be seen as involving two events – Hull's initial support for parliament in 1642, and the maintenance of that support despite attempts to betray the town to the king. The explanation of each event will differ slightly, and certainly the causal factors will have a different role and importance in relation to the two events. It is, however, possible to see this question in other terms. If 'Hull' is seen as meaning the citizens of Hull, then their support for parliament can be viewed as an action – or a series of actions – and will require an intentional explanation of why such actions were taken. It will also be necessary to consider who were the citizens. If the explanation focuses on the leading citizens, the corporation and its allies, then it will be necessary to explain what they intended by the decisions they took, and by raising second order questions about the situation before 1642, and/or the attitudes and beliefs that shaped their intentions, to compare the significance of long-term preferences as opposed to immediate necessities in dictating their actions. If, however, the term 'citizens' is extended to include the ordinary residents of Hull, then the question must be raised as to how far their actions were voluntary, and the Corporation, as well as the Governors, must become factors in influencing the decisions made. A range of approaches to the question can be valid – what is essential is to decide upon the nature of *what is to be explained* before attempting to construct the explanation and to decide upon the role and importance of the various elements and factors involved.

Evaluating the explanation

Once you have established your explanation it can be developed further and the importance of certain factors highlighted by a process of evaluation. One way of doing this is by a comparison with another, similar occurrence, another is by considering possible alternative outcomes.

1. Evaluation by a comparative study – York in the Civil War

The cities of Hull and York were similar in many ways. Both were ports in the seventeenth century (since the River Ouse was navigable as far as York) and both had a substantial merchant community. The economy of York was less dependent on overseas trade since it was also the northern capital, seat of regional government, and the social and administrative centre for the north of England. Both towns had a strong Puritan element although the influence of the Church authorities must have been more immediate and direct in York, with its Archbishop and Cathedral Chapter. Both were governed by a Mayor and Corporation, although in York they were assisted by a council of 24 who fulfilled an intermediate role between the Corporation and the burgesses which did not exist in Hull. Finally, both were military strongholds, with a garrison and military governor, who operated alongside (and sometimes in partnership with) the borough authorities. In 1642 Hull declared for parliament, while York became the centre of royalism in Yorkshire.

Therefore, although the two cities were comparable in many ways, the outcome of the political struggle in each differed in 1642. Only the defeat of Newcastle's army at Marston Moor in 1644 allowed the parliamentary forces to gain control of York.

Thus by comparing York and Hull, and discovering the ways in which they differed, it may be possible to highlight the factors which were crucial in explaining why Hull supported parliament throughout the Civil War. Source 10, pp 123–5, provides more detailed information about York in the seventeenth century. Read this source, and compile a list of the ways in which Hull and York were similar, and the ways in which they differed in the Civil War years.

Questions

13. How did the situation in York differ from that in Hull from 1642 to 1645?

14. What does this suggest about the factors that led Hull to support parliament rather than the king?

---

2. Evaluation by considering alternative possibilities

An alternative method of evaluation is to consider whether any other outcome to the situation was historically possible, and by examining why such outcomes did *not* occur, to highlight which factors were of particular importance in bringing about the actual outcome. In relation to Hull's support for parliament, it may be useful to consider whether it was historically possible for Hull to have supported the king. If there is evidence of some royalist feeling in the town, it might have been possible for the Royalists, rather than the supporters of parliament, to have gained control of important posts and positions in 1642. Had that occurred, for example if Newcastle and Legge had taken up the position of Governor or if the royalist MP, Sir John Lister, had not died in 1640 to be replaced by Pelham, we would have to consider whether the underlying support for parliament in the town would have been sufficiently strong or sufficiently organised to have reversed the situation. Certainly the royalist hold would have been more tenuous than that of parliament, but the instincts for survival and protection of home and property which encouraged many citizens to fight with parliament might well have operated in the reverse direction. Perhaps most important, if Charles had been able to enter Hull in April 1642, his presence and ability to appoint officials in vital positions might well have rallied the citizens to him and left behind a framework for royalist control.

If these are valid historical possibilities, then certain factors which prevented them from occurring become crucial in explaining why Hull supported

145

parliament – the role of the Hull MPs, the Corporation's willingness to accept Hotham rather than Newcastle, the action of Hotham in denying the king entry. Similarly, we need to examine whether Hotham's plot to betray Hull could have succeeded, and what actions or events prevented this. Finally, in both cases, we need to consider the extent to which, at both crucial moments, the actions and events which prevented Hull from becoming royalist arose from deep-seated, underlying factors in the situation, or from personal, specific, or even random elements and considerations.

In examining why Hull supported parliament we have also revisited some of the ideas addressed in the first section of this unit, about the process by which men took sides in the struggle, about the beliefs, attitudes and considerations which motivated them, and about the extent to which 'those who did not rule' were able or willing to involve themselves according to their own preference. In the light of all the information contained in this unit, you should now consider the value, and the implications, of the local perspective in drawing conclusions about the Civil War.

Questions

15. Do the sources above, interpreted in the context of seventeenth-century attitudes and beliefs, provide any evidence of a significant Royalist minority in Hull?

16. In the light of this, could Hull have been Royalist?

17. What factors prevented this (a) in 1642, and (b) in 1643?

18. What does this indicate about why Hull supported parliament throughout the Civil War?

Questions

19. What do you consider to be the advantages and disadvantages of studying the Civil Wars and their aftermath from the local perspective?

20. How far do claims that men were motivated by major issues, such as religion or the liberties of parliament and people, survive testing against evidence taken from local studies?

21. To what extent does the local perspective support or undermine the concept of an English Revolution?

UNIT 4.2

THE GENERAL CRISIS IN EUROPE

Introduction

Thus far we have considered the English Revolution in a mainly English and occasionally British context, and attempted to consider its nature as a 'revolution' in terms of its roots in, and impact on, English society. Yet the British monarchy was far from unusual in experiencing upheaval in this period, and the years of civil war and interregnum saw at least five other major rebellions in Europe – in Catalonia, Portugal and Naples (all possessions of the King of Spain), in France, and in the Netherlands. As a whole, the seventeenth century was a period of almost incessant warfare, both within and between European states. The beginning of the century saw France emerging from a series of devastating civil wars occasioned by religious division and the ambitions of her nobility, and a struggle in progress between Catholic Spain, her Protestant provinces in the Netherlands, and their Protestant English ally. England and Spain made peace in 1604, but the independence of the Netherlands was not secured until 1609, and after a 'twelve years truce', the Dutch were again fighting the Spanish from 1621. This was part of the wider struggle between Protestant and Catholic in Germany and between France and the Hapsburgs (rulers of Spain and Austria) for the dominant position in Europe, which flared up in the Thirty Years War of 1618–48 and continued intermittently until 1714. Indeed, given that war is often a cause of political upheavals, it is ironic that the most serious of the internal rebellions should have occurred in Britain, since the British monarchs were almost alone in Europe in being able to avoid participation in foreign war (except the brief struggles with their Dutch commercial rivals and Cromwell's limited expeditions) from 1604 until the Glorious Revolution led to conflict with the overweening power of Louis XIV. This does not, of course, mean that events in Britain were unaffected by this era of conflict – the threat of the Catholic powers and the misery of German Protestants were a potent image in the minds of those who looked suspiciously on the activities and ambitions of Charles I, and later of his sons.

This context of upheaval, and the coincidence of a number of crises and rebellions in the monarchies of Europe, has also prompted historians to raise another question regarding the nature and significance of the English Revolution – to ask whether it was a unique, British occurrence, to be explained by investigating British problems and conditions, or whether it was a part of a wider phenomenon, a European crisis arising from structural problems related to the economic and political development of Europe as a whole, manifested in different ways in different states according to local and cultural conditions. The idea of a general European crisis was raised by historians in the 1930s, but the modern debate was initiated by the work of Eric Hobsbawm and H.R. Trevor-Roper in the 1950s, and brought to a head by the publication in 1965 of a collection of essays, putting forward different viewpoints, under the title of *Crisis in Europe, 1550–1650*, edited by Trevor Aston. Since then other historians have examined aspects of the issue and drawn conclusions based on different areas of research into European history. The views of a number are summarised below.

Questions

1. How does each of Sources 45–50 describe the nature and impact of the six 'revolutions' which occurred in Europe between 1640 and 1660?

2. Do any of the sources seem to share a common viewpoint?

3. What do you consider to be the value, if any, of concepts such as the 'general crisis'?

Source 45

From E.J. Hobsbawm, 'The Crisis of the Seventeenth Century', in T. Aston (ed.), *Crisis in Europe,1550–1650* (Routledge & Kegan Paul, 1965) pp. 4–5.

I wish to suggest that the European economy passed through a 'general crisis' during the seventeenth century, the last phase of the general transition from a feudal to a capitalist economy. ... The seventeenth-century crisis thus differs from its predecessors in that it led to as fundamental a solution of the difficulties which had previously stood in the way of the triumph of capitalism as that system will permit.

Source 46

From H.R. Trevor-Roper, 'The General Crisis of the Seventeenth Century', in T. Aston (ed.), *Crisis in Europe, 1550–1650*, pp. 94–5.

Such, as it seems to me, was the 'general crisis of the seventeenth century'. It was a crisis, not of the constitution nor of the system of production, but of the State, or rather, of the relation of the State to society. Different countries found their way out of that crisis in different ways. In Spain the *ancien regime* survived: but it survived only as a disastrous, immobile burden on an impoverished country. Elsewhere, in Holland, France, and England, the crisis marked the end of an era: the jettison of a top-heavy superstructure [the Renaissance monarchy and court], the return to sensible mercantilist policy. For by the seventeenth century the Renaissance Courts had grown so great [and were so unproductively expensive, absorbing so much wealth and energy] that they could only flourish for a limited time, and in a time, too, of expanding general prosperity. When that prosperity failed, the monstrous parasite was bound to falter. In this sense the depression of the 1620s is perhaps no less important, as a historical turning-point, than the depression of 1929: though a temporary economic failure, it marked a lasting political change.

Source 47

From T.K. Rabb, *The Struggle for Stability in Early Modern Europe* (Oxford, 1976) pp. 3–4.

What I will be trying to demonstrate is that Europe entered a new era very roughly during the middle third of the century and that the best indication of this profound transformation is the very different atmosphere that reigned in the succeeding decades. Between say, the early 1630s and the early 1670s (though it would be foolish to insist on crisp cut-off points in so far-reaching a process) there was a change in direction more dramatic and decisive than any that occurred in a forty-year period between the beginnings of the Reformation and the French Revolution. And it is precisely by recognising how different Europe's situation was in the aftermath of these events than it had been during or immediately preceding the great shift that we can come to appreciate the extent of the alteration that had been wrought.

Source 48

From R.B. Merriman, *Six Contemporaneous Revolutions* (Oxford, 1938) p. 89.

The causes, courses and results of these six revolutions ... afford an admirable example of the infinite variety of history. Though contemporaneous, they were curiously little alike; their differences were far more remarkable than their similarities.

Source 49

From H. Kamen, *The Iron Century* (New York, 1971) p. 330.

There is a real danger in the whole concept of a General Crisis, just as any covering explanation tends to be fallacious [misleading] in detail. It is misleading to think that the long-term problems of European States were the same, for they obviously were not. England and Spain shared little in common in 1640 except for the same date for their revolutions; Moscow and Paris in 1648, Amsterdam and Stockholm in 1650 coincided in time rather than in problem. It is one thing to look at the common difficulties shared by social classes in different countries, quite another to generalise from the very uneven development of European states to the existence of a particularly significant crisis. A turning-point did, of course, exist, and the occasion was supplied by the economic difficulties of the decade 1640–50. In those years of fiscal instability and price inflation, of bad harvests and the beginnings of a trade recession, the accumulated problems of governments and the grievances of their subjects exploded in a continent-wide outburst of revolution.

Source 50

From A.D. Lublinskaya, *French Absolutism* (CUP, 1968) p. 4.

For a long time the seventeenth century lacked, so far as the whole of Europe and the whole of the century were concerned, a special resounding epithet to describe it. The situation has markedly altered. ... Many new works of a wide scope have appeared together with new theories which endeavour to systematise the knowledge that has accumulated, arranging it in some kind of general pattern which will embrace all or most of the countries of Europe and reveal what it was that determined the common features (or at least the similarity) of the processes taking place in these countries. In these theories the seventeenth century figures as something special, as a century of very acute contradiction, a century of economic, social and political crisis, of a *crise de conscience*. It has at last been given its descriptive epithet and become the century of 'general crisis' and of 'general revolution', the 'tragic century'.

Many of these conceptions are dubious and even quite unacceptable ... but they are interesting in that they try to penetrate deeply into the essence of events, to track down some sort of fundamental causes of those processes of outstanding importance which were common to all the countries of Europe.

The purpose of this unit is to examine the question of a European crisis in order to consider what light, if any, it sheds on the nature and significance of the

English Revolution. The task is to consider whether there was a European crisis, and if so, how and why it occurred. This is approached in two ways. The first is to examine the five other 'revolutions' of 1640–60, and consider whether any factors or characteristics are shared with the events in England. If such common factors existed, then not only may they suggest the existence of a European crisis, but also serve to emphasise the significance of those factors in the English Revolution. The second approach is to consider a range of historians' views as to what such a crisis might consist of and why it might occur at this time. The results can then be applied to the English Revolution and their implications considered. Finally, in the light of the views that you have developed through this process, you will be able to review and reassess your own judgements as to the nature and significance of the English Revolution.

Questions

4. Read the following accounts of the five 'revolutions' and compile a list of the similarities that they shared with the English Revolution. It may be useful to pay particular attention to: causes; aims of the revolutionaries; leadership; social/economic groups involved; and results.

5. What do you consider to have been the main differences between these events and those which occurred in England during the 1640s and 1650s?

European revolutions 1640–60

Revolutions in Spanish possessions

Catalonia

The province of Catalonia, situated on the north-eastern coast of Spain, with its ancient capital in Barcelona, had become a part of the Spanish monarchy through its association with the kings of Aragon. With its culture and economy focused on the Mediterranean, and extensive links with neighbouring France, it was always distinct from the dominant Castilian centre of the Spanish kingdom, and intensely proud of its regional laws and customs embodied in the constitutional agreement known as the *fueros*. Throughout the 1630s the demands of war against France were placing a strain on relations with Madrid, largely because King Philip IV's chief adviser, Count Olivares, wasted little tact and persuasion in his demands for troops and taxes with which to fight

Count Olivares

the French. His manner and attitude raised Catalan fears that he intended to infringe or reduce their local rights, and the financial burdens arising from his demands created an additional source of tension. In 1639 Catalonia was invaded by a French force, and the town of Salces captured. Despite pleas for help from Madrid, the Catalans were largely left to fend for themselves, and it was a local force which drove the French out of Salces in December 1639. Far from reducing his high-handed demands, Olivares now placed Castilian troops in the province, requiring free quarter for them, and when two members of the municipal council of Barcelona protested, they were imprisoned. On 12 May 1640 the citizens of Barcelona stormed the prison to rescue their leaders, and by June the whole province was in open revolt. Olivares was furious, and declared his intention of both crushing the revolt and abrogating the *fueros* to destroy Catalan autonomy for the future. An appeal to the king having proved fruitless, the Catalans were left with little choice but to seek French help, which Richelieu, realising that the revolt would weaken his enemy, was more than willing to provide. In January 1641 the French king, Louis XIII was elected as Count of Catalonia and the province now embarked on a war of independence. In 1641 a Castilian attempt to capture Barcelona was repulsed, but the revolt was already beginning to weaken. Many Catalans were suspicious of the French, and when King Philip declared in January 1642 that the *fueros* would be confirmed and respected, rural support began to melt away. In the winter of 1642–3 Olivares fell from power, and the way to reconciliation was open. In the conditions of war it was not finally achieved until the fall of Barcelona in 1652, when further royal promises to respect Catalan autonomy led to the surrender of the city. Philip kept his promises, but in 1659 when French victory against Spain meant the surrender of some territory, it was the Catalan provinces of Cerdagne and Roussillon which were sacrificed. Thus the ultimate result of the revolt was the maintenance of their customary rights at the cost of territorial mutilation.

Portugal

The kingdom of Portugal had been formed during the struggle to free the Iberian peninsula from the Moorish invaders, being granted by the king of Castile to Prince Henry of Burgundy as a reward for his military support in the struggle. Later Spanish monarchs had tried to reclaim the land, with its long and strategically useful coastline, but military force having failed, it was through intermarriage and inheritance that Philip II was finally able to secure control of the territory in 1581. Philip respected the independent identity of his new kingdom, but after his death there was an increasing tendency to replace Portuguese officials with Castilians, and to give the Castilian nobility the lucrative and important posts in the Portuguese administration. The protests of the native nobility and populace were disregarded. It was not, however, until 1636, that war, the needs of the Spanish treasury and the centralising policies of Olivares brought matters to a head. Disregarding the supposed immunity of the Portuguese from Spanish taxation, Olivares imposed a 5 per cent property tax, and easily dealt with a minor uprising in Evora which resulted. Encouraged by his success, he sought to impose an enormous fine on the whole of Portugal, and publicly considered the abrogation of all the rights and customs agreed in 1581–2 and the merging of Portugal with Castile. As with Catalonia, his determination to centralise and refusal to compromise drove the semi-autonomous kingdom into open revolt. Moreover the war and the financial weakness of the Spanish monarchy which had helped to bring matters to a head now also helped to determine the outcome. By 1638 the Portuguese nobility had persuaded John of Braganza to accept the throne, and secured the help of Richelieu in a bid for independence. In 1640, encouraged by the Catalan revolt, they attacked the Spanish garrisons and officials in Lisbon, aided by a French fleet which appeared off the Portuguese coast. Braganza was publicly declared as King John IV on the following day. The rebellion was accomplished with ease, and, preoccupied by war and Catalonia, the Spaniards were slow to respond. Olivares attempted to use a group of sympathisers among the Portuguese nobility to plot the murder of King John, but when this was discovered and foiled, he took no further action. In 1643, after his fall, the Spanish government attempted the reconquest of Portugal, but were held off until the marriage of

Catherine of Braganza to Charles II of England in 1660 provided enough help to tip the balance in Portugal's favour. Peace, and the recognition of Portuguese independence, was finally concluded in 1668.

Naples

The kingdom of Naples had been conquered by the Spanish in 1443, but had continued until 1504 to be governed by a line of client kings and a native feudal nobility. In the early sixteenth century it was brought under the direct control of Spain, and was thenceforth ruled by a Spanish viceroy, in the interests of Spain. Backward, poor and deprived of local rights and customs, it was plundered by the Spanish treasury and in the words of R.B. Merriman, 'Naples suffered at once from all the bad consequences of an antiquated feudal system and of modern absolutism, and got none of the compensating advantages of either.' In the 1640s discontent built up to a new peak. A succession of bad harvests, an eruption of Vesuvius, plagues and the Barbary pirates combined to increase popular misery, and in 1646 an uprising in neighbouring Sicily exposed the weakness of the authorities. The final straw came when the viceroy, the Duke of Arcos, sought to impose a tax on fruit, the principal food of the poor. Led by a Neapolitan fisherman, nicknamed Masaniello, the Neapolitans attacked government officials and forced the viceroy to make concessions. There followed a vicious battle of wits and intrigue between Masaniello and Arcos, which saw betrayal and brutality on both sides. The rebellion was confined to the lower classes; the middle class and nobility were repelled by the violence of Masaniello and his adherents. Not, however, until Arcos sought to use the visiting troops of the Spanish general, Don John of Austria, in order to teach the populace a lesson, did the rebels openly reject Spanish authority, and in desperation, seek French help at the end of 1647. Little was forthcoming, and in February 1648, the Spanish were able to recapture the city. The rebellion had been little more than a popular outburst, lacking effective leadership or coherent aims. Like the other revolts in Spanish territory, however, it had been provoked by financial exactions, the needs of war, and the lack of respect shown by the central government for the peoples who made up the periphery of a vast and far-flung royal estate.

Revolution in France – the Fronde

The rebellions known as the 'Fronde', aptly named after a children's game, occupied the energies of the French government for approximately three years, from 1648 to 1650. There were two main revolts – the Fronde of the Paris Parlement in 1648, and the Fronde of the Princes which came to a head in 1650. The two overlapped, as different groups and factions sought to use each other's grievances and interests in pursuit of their own, and were fought out against a background of provincial rebellions, but at no point was there anything approaching a coherent national rebellion which could merit the term 'revolution'. In the words of a recent French historian, 'The nation did not participate'. According to R.B. Merriman, 'It was from first to last a struggle of classes, of factions, of localities, each with grievances of its own; they could not – perhaps one may safely say they would not – effectively combine against the crown. ... The *idée monarchique* was the only concept of government existent in the France of that day, and there was not the remotest chance of replacing it with any other. ... ' The parliamentary Fronde was about customary rights and privileges, the Fronde of the Princes a struggle for power within the royal court, a defence perhaps of what the great nobility regarded as their customary right to influence royal policy, especially during the minority of a child king. The focus of resentment in both cases was the chief minister, Cardinal Mazarin, an Italian by birth who had succeeded Richelieu in the directing of French government and thus usurped the position of native, and traditional, advisers.

Cardinal Mazarin

In 1642 Cardinal Richelieu, who had masterminded French government throughout the reign of Louis XIII, died, having indicated to the king that his protégé, Mazarin, could succeed to his position. Five months later, Louis himself died, leaving the four-year-old Louis XIV to be guided by a Council of Regency made up of his mother, Anne of Austria, and seven members of the greater nobility. By manipulating the two rival princes of Orléans and Condé, Anne and Mazarin managed to achieve sole regency for the king's mother, and she was willing to be guided in all matters by the Italian cardinal. Thus the nobility were already alienated when, in 1643–4, financial problems were creating increasing difficulties with the populace and with the Parlement of Paris in particular.

That body bore little resemblance to the English parliament, in either its nature or its functions. Essentially it consisted of lawyers and professional administrators who had been able to buy hereditary offices. By the French custom known as the venal system, and nicknamed the Paulette, certain jobs and positions could be bought and handed down within the family of the purchaser, becoming, after three generations, a title of nobility which was distinguished from the feudal nobility (nobility *d'epée* – the military nobility) by the name of 'nobility *de robe*' (a reference to the lawyers' robe). Such titles conferred privileges, exemption from certain taxes, and a position in such bodies as the Paris Parlement. The Parlement claimed the right to authorise royal decrees as law, but had never been able to establish that legality depended on this, nor did it have control of royal finances. Unlike the English monarchy, the French king enjoyed the right to tax and a system of collection which was quite independent of any other body. Moreover, when the Parlement had occasionally refused to authorise royal decrees, a ceremony known as the *lit de justice*, involving a personal visit from the monarch, was enough to force them through.

In the 1640s, the real function of the Paris Parlement was to serve as a channel and focus for the rising popular discontent created by years of war and the resultant heavy financial burdens. By 1644 the French population had paid for nine years of war against Spain and the Hapsburgs, the financial position of the monarchy was growing desperate, and the desire for peace was openly expressed. When Mazarin introduced a new tax on buildings outside the walls of Paris (there being little space for fine new houses inside) the Parlement refused to authorise the decrees. A *lit de justice* forced them through in 1645, but in 1646 there was fresh resistance. At court, the influence of Mazarin and his family was bitterly resented, and the population of Paris also focused their resentment on the foreign cardinal. By 1648 the situation was already difficult when Mazarin provoked the Parlement to fresh resistance by an attack on the Paulette – the system of selling offices. An attempt to buy off the members by protecting their positions at the expense of other office-holders backfired, and led to unified resistance which forced the government to drop the scheme. Encouraged by their ability to protect their traditional rights, the Parlementaires now put forward a scheme for reform which would considerably enhance their own powers and those of similar bodies in other parts of France. The government wrangled for six months, until the great victory of Condé over the Hapsburg forces at Lens, and the ensuing popularity of the government, encouraged it to try and seize the initiative. In August 1648 the leading Parlementaires were arrested, and barricades went up in Paris. Trapped in the Palais Royal in Paris, Anne and Mazarin had to concede defeat, but were later able to leave the city for Rueil. With the help of Condé they were able to negotiate a dignified withdrawal by announcing a programme of reforms on the same day as the signing of the Peace of Westphalia in October 1648. The court returned to Paris amid the apparent popular victory.

In fact the government had no intention of accepting the reforms in practice. Unlike Olivares, Mazarin knew when to bend. The war with Spain continued, but the peace in Germany had freed some troops for use elsewhere, and when the court moved to St Germain on the pretext of keeping the king safe from continuing disturbances in Paris, Condé was persuaded to use them to blockade the city. The magistrates took measures for defence with the help of Condés younger brother and rival, the Prince de Conti. In 1649 the threat of Spanish intervention led to a short-lived agreement at Rueil, but by the end of the year little real progress had been made. The government of Anne and Mazarin depended on Condé, who envied and despised Mazarin and took every opportunity to insult him. Opposed, however, by Paris and Conti, and unable to trust the regent, Anne, he could not openly seize control. In the meantime, unrest in the provinces continued sporadically, and the war against Spain dragged on.

In January 1650 Mazarin attempted to break the stalemate. Concluding an agreement with the Parlement, who hated Condé, he ordered the arrest of Condé, Conti and the Duc de Longueville. The effect was to spark open revolt among the nobility and their dependants. Madame Longueville and the leading French general, Turenne, allied with the Spanish to invade from the Spanish Netherlands while the Princess Condé fled to join rebels in Bordeaux, who were also appealing for help from the English. Mazarin was able to defeat both attacks, but in his absence a coup in Paris led by the Duc d'Orléans and his daughter, Mlle de Montpensier, forced him into exile, and the arrested princes were released. The nobility were in control, and the Regent could do little to resist. Their aims, however, were largely personal and their unity was short-lived. With the hated Mazarin no longer present to serve as a unifying factor their differences soon began to resurface, to be exploited by Anne, who remained in contact with the cardinal. The arrogance of Condé alienated many and in July 1651 he left Paris, concluded an alliance with the Spanish and handed over several forts to them. Rebellions broke out in Provence and Anjou, and in the last three months of 1651 the French suffered a series of humiliating defeats at the hands of Spain. In this desperate situation, the regent again summoned Mazarin to her side, and this time the resistance of the Parlement was overridden by the young king who attained his majority [became old enough to rule in person] in early 1652. With Louis now able to serve as a focus for unity, the government's hand was greatly strengthened, and with Mazarin keeping a low profile, control was gradually restored. The return to allegiance of Turenne improved military organisation and in May 1652 he defeated the Spanish in the north. Condé and Orléans refused to accept the king's majority and tried to overawe Paris, but by July 1652 they had been forced to abandon the city, and in October of that year, as Condé fled into exile, the king and his mother returned to Paris in triumph. Mazarin wisely continued to organise the campaigns against Spain and the rebels, and when he returned to Paris in early 1653, he had given positive proof of his loyalty to France through his military victories. By the end of 1653 the last embers of revolt, the republican rebels of Bordeaux who had allied with England, were finally extinguished, and Mazarin remained as the chief adviser to Louis XIV until his death in 1661.

The Frondes arose from the strains of war, financial problems which caused the government to threaten ancient rights and privileges, and the temporary weakness of the monarchy. They failed because their adherents were fighting first and foremost for their own, often conflicting interests, without a coherent cause or philosophy to unite them. In a time of national danger, their self-interest could be seen as treason. Perhaps their most lasting effect was on the young king himself. It was no coincidence that he removed his residence from Paris to Versailles, freeing the court from the

A 'Frondeur' rousing the citizens of Paris to revolt against Mazarin during the Fronde

physical presence of the city and its people, destroyed the pretensions of the Parlement, reduced the nobility to courtly ornaments kept far from their provincial centres of influence, and established in France an absolute monarchy which became a model for monarchical ambition throughout Europe.

Crisis in the Netherlands

The United Provinces of the Netherlands had been established as an independent state through rebellion against Spain in the late sixteenth century, finally securing recognition of its independence in 1609. The circumstances of its birth, and its widely varying regions had created a constitutional conflict within the state that came to a head in 1619 and again more seriously in 1650. The country consisted of seven provinces, each with its own character and economic base, of which the province of Holland was by far the largest and most influential. In theory, government lay with a Council of State and parliament known as the States-General, which had wide theoretical powers but whose members were forced, in practice, on many important issues to refer back to the provincial estates which they represented. The military struggle for survival had also led to the accumulation of much power in the hands of the Stadtholder, an office held by William the Silent, Prince of Orange at the time of the revolt against Spain and becoming hereditary to the house of Orange in the ensuing decades. By 1609 Maurice of Nassau, William's son, was Stadtholder of Holland, Zealand, Gelderland, Utrecht and

Overyssel, five of the seven provinces, while other members of his family held the position in the other two. Originally a representative of the King of Spain, responsible for the administration of justice and power over a number of appointments, the office of Stadtholder represented central authority, a unifying influence which was much needed in conditions of war.

William of Orange

Thus by 1609 power in the Netherlands was divided between two centres. On the one hand lay the House of Orange, monarchical in outlook, centralising in practice and necessary in time of war. On the other was the Grand Pensionary of the largest province, Holland, representative of the estates of Holland, commercial and republican in outlook and concerned to defend the rights of the individual provinces and those of Holland in particular. The conclusion of the Twelve Years Truce in 1609 represented a victory for the Pensionary, John van Oldenbarneveldt and the commercially-minded merchants of Holland, but the ensuing decade saw a bitter struggle between the Pensionary and Maurice of Nassau, in which issues of power and commerce became inextricably intertwined with religion. A dispute had broken out between the strict Calvinism of the theologian Gomarus and the more tolerant views of Jacob Arminius, in which the Gomarists were supported by Maurice against the attempts of the Hollanders to encourage a tolerant atmosphere favourable to peace and commerce. The struggle came to a head in 1619, when Maurice managed to have Oldenbarneveldt convicted on a dubious charge of treason and executed. The renewal of the war with Spain in 1621 further strengthened the power and monarchical ambitions of the Orangists.

From 1619 to 1648 the Orangists were triumphant. The national struggle against Spain made centralised authority and military leadership essential, and Maurice's half-brother and successor, Frederick Henry, was able to establish hereditary rights to the offices that had been gathered, and consolidate his power. In 1647, when he died and was succeeded by his son William, the creation of an Orangist monarchy seemed imminent, and this was certainly the ambition of William himself. He had already concluded a royal marriage with Mary, daughter of King Charles I of England. Nevertheless, he faced certain difficulties. The Spanish monarchy, preoccupied with the struggle against France, signified a willingness to conclude peace and recognise Dutch independence, and a war and tax-weary nation breathed a sigh of relief. The Estates of Holland, led by a new Pensionary, John de Witt, raised their heads and renewed the struggle for power. Despite William's opposition and the efforts of the French, the Dutch envoy Adrian Pauw negotiated a commercially advantageous peace with Spain which was signed on 30 January 1648. William's opposition delayed ratification until May, but could not prevent it. In order to attack the problem of debt which was threatening the prosperity of the state, Holland now demanded that the benefits of peace be felt in a reduction of the size and cost of the army.

More than any other institution, the army was the source and symbol of the Stadtholder's power. William was able to persuade the other six provinces that it was too early and too dangerous to consider such a reduction, but the Hollanders were determined, and the size, status and financial contribution of their province made it difficult to ignore their argument. Throughout 1649 the argument centred on Holland's right to unilaterally disband a small company of 600 foot-soldiers paid by the provincial Estates. In June 1650 they ordered a disbandment, and the colonels of the regiment refused to take orders from anyone except the Stadtholder and Estates-General. A deputation from the latter tried to appeal, with William, over the heads of the Dutch Estates to the cities of Holland, but received little support. It was clear by now that what was at issue was not the army, but the ultimate source of authority in the United Provinces. In August William tried to break the deadlock by arresting the leaders of Holland and seizing the city of Amsterdam, but the attack was bungled and led to a siege of the city. The city was reluctant to fight, and agreed to dismiss the burgomaster, Cornelius Bicker, who had organised the resistance, but the central issue of power was not resolved. While William had a certain legal right on his side, there was no doubt that his desire to renew the war with Spain and conquer new territory in the Spanish Netherlands lacked support in Holland, and his financial demands were bitterly resented. In order to recoup and consider his position he retired to his estates in Gelderland, from where he renewed his negotiations with the French. It is likely that he was planning a French-supported coup and probably the establishment of a monarchy when, in late October 1650, he fell ill with smallpox. By early November, he was dead. In 1651 the Estates of Holland abolished the office of Stadtholder and invited the other provinces to do the same. Following a constitutional conference in the same year, a new constitution devolved central power to the provinces, and under the guidance of the Grand Pensionary of Holland, John De Witt, the United Provinces entered upon a commercial 'golden age'. Ironically, the fortunes of the House of Orange were to be restored by the son born eight days after William's death, another William, who based his life and career on the fight against his father's French ally in the struggle to defend both the Netherlands and England against the overweening ambitions of Louis XIV. In that sense the revolution in the Netherlands in 1650 was instrumental in bringing about the revolution in England in 1688.

Question

6. How far do the similarities and differences between these five 'revolutions' and the events in England lead you to accept the idea of a 'general crisis'?

Sources 51–5 below provide a range of different views held by historians on this issue of a general crisis. Some of them suggest that such a crisis did exist, others reject the idea, while still finding useful parallels and points of comparison. Using these sources and the information above, consider and review your initial response to Question 6.

Source 51

From R.B. Merriman, *Six Contemporaneous Revolutions* pp. 89–91. Merriman does not accept the existence of a general crisis, but does point out some striking similarities between the situations in different parts of Europe.

These six revolutions … had, at the outset, certain features in common. … In the first place, the immediate, though not always the most fundamental cause of every one of them was financial. In each case it was arbitrary taxation in one form or another, and the complaints that it evoked, that gave the pretext for revolution. The demands of Olivares for money, in defiance of the law of the land, started the movements in Catalonia and Portugal which culminated in declarations of independence. In Naples it was the fruit tax against which the people rose. In England it was the financial straits to which Charles was reduced that forced him to summon the Long Parliament, and one of the first acts of that memorable assembly was to pass bills which deprived the Crown of all the sources of its independent revenue. In France it was again the financial exactions of Mazarin which caused the Parlement de Paris to come forward in defence of the liberties of the realm. In the Netherlands the demands of the province of Holland for successive reductions of the naval and military forces of the union and of the expense which they entailed were the first important steps towards constitutional revolution. The results, indeed, were widely divergent. In Catalonia the revolution was put down, but the government in Madrid promised henceforth to respect the *fueros*. In Portugal a kingdom regained its independence. In Naples the revolt was suppressed, but the fruit tax, which gave rise to it, was withdrawn. In England, the principle of parliamentary control over the royal finances was permanently established, whereas in France, after the Fronde was defeated, the royal exactions continued and increased. In the Netherlands the protests of Holland against the financial demands of the Stadtholders led to a constitutional rearrangement which enabled her to dictate the policy of the United Provinces for a period of twenty-two years. But in every case, the point of departure was the same.

Secondly, it is worth noting that, in five of the six rebellions we are considering, the outbursts in their origin were directed rather against dominant and unpopular ministers than against the monarchs whom they served. In Spain, this was perhaps inevitable. Philip IV, politically speaking, was a nonentity; it was Olivares, and in Naples Arcos, against whom the people rose. In England nothing is more notable than the unwillingness of Parliament, at the outset, to lay the blame where it really belonged, on Charles; Strafford and Laud had to be sacrificed long before men could be brought to admit who the real culprit was. In France it is more striking still. Mazarin was the public enemy; most of the demands of the Frenchmen were made in the name of the child king against the detested minister. The institution of monarchy, in other words, was still, generally speaking, sacred. Only in England was it abolished, and its abolition proved but temporary there. All that the revolutionaries really demanded was that its powers should not be abused. Everywhere we find them invoking, in one form or another, 'the ancient liberties of the realm'. Even in the Netherlands, where there was no king, the advocates of provincial autonomy could justly maintain that their programme was far more closely in accord than was that of the Stadtholder with the principles laid down in the Union of Utrecht of 1579, from which the Dutch derived their independence.

In view of the fact that all six of these revolutions broke out at the end of the period which is generally known in European history as the century of the Wars of Religion, it is interesting to observe how little the majority of them were affected by differences of church government and creed. England, of course, is a marked exception in this respect. There the religious question … was in the final analysis the most fundamental of all; and this doubtless goes far to explain why the English revolution was able to attain results so much more far-reaching than those of any of its contemporaries. But elsewhere the picture is very different. In Portugal and Naples there was no religious issue at all. In Catalonia … the cause of Rome was most unjustifiably utilised as a war cry by both sides. In France the Huguenots were regarded by the government rather as potentially dangerous political rebels than as adherents of a dissenting creed. Mazarin was only too glad to let them enjoy full possession of all the liberties that Richelieu had left them, provided that they did not breed trouble for the state. In the Netherlands the ferocious antagonism between the Gomarists and the Arminians, which reached its climax in 1619, had dwindled into comparative insignificance by 1650. The embers of it continued to smoulder, no doubt, but it did not again burst into flame. It was overlaid by considerations of politics and commerce. The story of all five of the continental revolutions is an interesting evidence of the extent to which Europe had already begun to change its point of view about fighting over differences of faith.

If the English revolution was an exception … in its emphasis on religion, it differed from them still more widely in the lengths to which it showed it was prepared to go. The three revolts against the authority of the King of Spain had dealt blows to his power and prestige, but they had none of them really threatened his authority in Madrid. The Fronde, it is true, began at Paris, but the interests of the people concerned in it were so conflicting that it never seemed really likely that it would achieve any permanent results. But in England the Independents were convinced that their cause was the cause of God. No reverence for tradition or established order restrained them. They cut off their king's head 'with the crown upon it' and established a republic.

Source 52

From G. Parker and L.M. Smith (eds.), *The General Crisis of the Seventeenth Century* (Routledge & Kegan Paul, 1978) Introduction, pp. 8–14. The extract focuses on one possible explanation for a general crisis, arguing that there was an economic crisis in seventeenth-century Europe, which had political consequences, but that rather than a crisis of capitalism, the problems arose from changes which are known to have taken place in the climate.

A fall of one degree C in overall temperatures – and that is the magnitude of the change during the 'Little Ice Age' – restricts the growing season for plants by three or four weeks and reduces the maximum altitude for cultivation by about 500 feet. The expansion of population in the sixteenth century had led to the cultivation of many marginal highlands: a colder summer would reduce, or perhaps remove, the yield of such areas, leaving their populations on the threshold of starvation. Diminished food reserves, producing (effectively) serious overpopulation, presented a favourable terrain for the spread of diseases. ... There was no real escape from this; the inputs and outputs of the agricultural system had reached a balance that could be broken only by heavy capital investment and new technology. This, European agriculture could not provide. Wherever improved yields were achieved, whether through better methods or increased area of cultivation, the surplus produced was soon swallowed up by the growing population: there was little capital accumulation, therefore little land improvement or technical innovation, and therefore little increase in the supply of daily bread. There were only three choices facing a population caught in this trap: migration, death or revolt. ...

'The peasant revolt', wrote Marc Bloch, 'was as common in early modern Europe as strikes are in industrial societies today.' He was right. The number of rural uprisings, at least in certain areas, is indeed astonishing: in Provence, for example, there were 108 popular uprisings between 1596 and 1635, 156 more between 1635 and 1660 (16 of them associated with the Fronde of 1648–53) and 110 more between 1661 and 1715. ... There was, however, an important difference between the usual

target of the popular revolt and the strike. Whereas the latter aimed to influence the employer, landlord or owner for whom the strikers worked, the early modern revolt was directed overwhelmingly against the State, particularly during the period 1625–75. Neither the exactions of the Church and nobles nor their exemption (in many countries) from taxation seems to have been a leading grievance of the rioters, at least in western Europe. Of course, these matters played their part in generating unrest; but increased seigneurial labour services or the activities of the church courts rarely triggered off a widespread revolt at this time. These burdens were regarded in the same light as the weather, or a bad harvest: inescapable but immutable. Rebellions were directed against grievances that could, in theory, be changed – the policies and demands of government – and the victims of the rioters were normally the officials trying to enforce those policies, especially tax-collectors. ...

New taxes, or the increase of old ones, played a part in provoking almost every revolt during our period, from the ship money of Charles I in England to the *media annata* of Olivares in Castile. Many revolts – those of Naples, Palermo, Normandy and Moscow, to name but a few – were directly triggered by the imposition of a new tax at a time of dearth. ... However, if this type of analysis can explain away several of the revolts that marked the 'general crisis' it cannot account for them all. There is no way in which the 'Little Ice Age', the bad harvests of the 1630s, or even ship money can be shown to have caused the English civil wars. The same is true of all the major political crises of western Europe in these years: the Fronde, the revolts of Portugal, Catalonia and the British Isles, the confrontations in Holland and Sweden. In each of them the cause is to be sought, not in the social structure and economic situation of the populations at large, but in the innovative policies of their governments, especially in the fields of finance and religion.

Source 53

From Niels Steensgaard, 'The seventeenth-century crisis' in Parker and Smith (eds.), *The General Crisis of the Seventeenth Century*, pp. 36–44. Steensgaard takes up and develops the point made at the end of Source 52, that the need for resources to be raised by taxation led to new fiscal policies, and that it was the impact of these policies as well as the sums raised, that offended societies at a number of social levels, including, but not confined to the peasantry.

Many historians have indicated in general terms the possibility that wars and taxes were contributory causes of the economic difficulties and social conflicts of the seventeenth century, but only a few have tried to estimate the extent of the taxes in relation to the total production. ... Did the State's share of the national product in the seventeenth century increase? We shall never possess the statistical information that would permit an exact answer to this question, but we may maintain without any hesitation that the seventeenth century, crisis or no crisis, witnessed an enormous growth in public expenditure. In the seventeenth century the largest armies since the time of the Roman Empire were established, and before the end of the century most of the states also had standing armies in peace-time. Military organisation was one of the century's most advanced forms of enterprise: fortresses, navies and royal palaces constituted the century's biggest efforts in planning and organising, and its most precious investments. ... [On one level] state expenditure stimulated the economy as a whole, but ... only if the resources that were used in establishing the armies or in undertaking the year-long campaigns and erecting the fortresses were previously lying idle. If on the other hand the resources were transferred from other sectors, there is no reason for surprise when we find that these other sectors manifested symptoms of crisis.

[Moreover, it was the methods used to find these resources that were often the most crucial issue. H.R. Trevor-Roper found the 'general crisis' to be the result of a clash between court and country in which the Court was seen as a parasitic bureaucracy; however] the revolts were by no means directed against a stagnating parasitism, but against a dynamic absolutism which, with its taxation policy, violated the customary laws and threatened to disrupt the social balance or deprive parts of the population of their livelihood. In Catalonia and Portugal the revolts were precipitated not by dissatisfaction with the established order, but by dissatisfaction with Olivares' attempt to alter the established order when he demanded that the viceroyalties should contribute towards the costs of Spain's foreign policy side by side with Castile. The revolt in Naples followed after a number of years of large contributions to the Spanish war chest, which not only had been economically devastating, but also had created chaos in the traditional distribution of authority and wealth. ... The opposition of the Parlement of Paris in the 1640s had no ideological aim, but was concentrated against the Crown's fiscal legislation; and the Fronde of the Parlement was triggered by a legislation that would have increased the Parlement's own privileges [protection of their offices and titles while threatening others]. In England the trends are less clear, but even in this case there is an apparent conflict between the monarchy's attempt to strengthen its economic independence and the taxpayer's defence of his customary rights. Even in the coup d'état in the Netherlands the fiscal element is present. ...

The common factor in the contemporaneous revolutions is thus something far less subtle than Trevor-Roper's dualism between court and country. We do not need to look for abstract similarities between the social structures of the societies in revolt, for there is the concrete similarity between the policy of the governments concerned, that is in their attempts to increase their income or to secure control over the state revenue regardless of customary rights. This statement, which is supported both by our knowledge of the revolts and by the analysis of the economic crisis presented above, can be further substantiated if we extend the comparative investigation to include those countries that did not suffer internal armed conflict in the middle of the seventeenth century. ... That it came to armed conflict in some states is not a valid criterion; the chosen starting-point should be the conflict, be it armed or unarmed, that is common to all the states. Behind the conflict we find the same thing everywhere: the State's demand for higher revenues. In some cases the tax demands were coupled with financial reforms that were not necessarily unfair, but which undermined customary rights; in other cases the increased burden of taxation came to rest on the population groups already living below the bread line. The different reactions in different countries, regardless of whether or not it came to armed conflict, or whether the protests led to any results, depended on the social and economic situation of the country in question and on the policy chosen by the governments (not least upon the choice of the social groups with which they chose to co-operate and the social groups upon which they chose to lay the burden of the increased taxation). But in every case it was the governments that acted in a revolutionary manner: the tax demands disrupted the social balance. They did not create a revolutionary situation: they were in themselves a revolution. The six contemporaneous revolutions can only be seen as one if we rechristen them 'the six contemporaneous reactions'.

Source 54

From Parker and Smith (eds.), *The General Crisis of the Seventeenth Century*, Introduction, pp. 4–6. This source extends the idea of a general crisis beyond Europe, emphasising the general features which apply to all states in this period, by looking again at the effects of climate and economic change. However, it also emphasises the limits of what such explanations can offer, and suggests that economic and political crises are not necessarily interlinked.

Voltaire drew attention to an important feature of the 'general crisis' which most later writers have forgotten: the 'crisis' was not confined to Europe. ... There were rebellions and upheavals in almost all areas of the Old World, and also in some parts of the New. ... The world-wide extent of these upheavals suggests that, beneath the more obvious local causes, some very basic and deep-seated influences were at work, such as a general deterioration of the global climate leading to relative over-population and food shortages, to mass migrations (perhaps armed) from poorer to richer lands, to swift-spreading pandemics [diseases] and to frequent wars and rebellions. If such a climatic explanation of the General Crisis is to be taken seriously, the evidence of deterioration in the weather must be sought in many parts of the globe, not just in a small region such as Europe: parallel manifestations should be observable over a wide area. And, indeed, in the mid-seventeenth century there were. Similarities of experience were sometimes very close. For example, the peasant revolts in Ming China from 1628 to 1644 had a great deal in common with the simultaneous wave of popular uprisings in the France of Richelieu: a picture of increasing military expenditure and growing court extravagance at a time of economic adversity has been painted in remarkably similar colours for both societies. There were even disastrous plague epidemics in both countries: 1639–44 in China; 1630–2 and 1647–9 in France. One recent study has compared the consequences of the late Ming peasant wars in the 1630s and 1640s to the destruction caused by the Thirty Years War in Germany, with the population decimated and the area of cultivated land almost halved, from 100 million acres to 58 million acres.

But the similarities end here. There is little resemblance between the events of 1644 in Peking, those of 1648 in Paris and those of 1649 in London beyond the elimination of a sovereign of undisputed legitimacy by 'usurpers'. ... The road from a general economic crisis to a major political upheaval was governed by personalities, local conditions and unforeseen accidents to a degree that makes generalisation hazardous. The 'general crisis' is, in fact, two contemporaneous but separate phenomena: one, a series of individual political confrontations, some of which developed into revolutions; the other a truly 'general crisis' in the demographic and economic development of the world.

Source 55

From Parker and Smith (eds.), *The General Crisis of the Seventeenth Century*, Introduction, pp. 15–18. This source reinforces some of the reservation expressed in Source 54, by emphasising the factor of religion which cannot be explained by economic or climatic factors. It also offers a reason for the exceptional scope and success of the revolution in Britain.

At the back of all the major revolts of our period lay a consciousness that governments were trying to change the *status quo*. ... To take the example of England, it was the initiative of the Crown – whether in matters fiscal ... or diplomatic, economic ... or religious – that shook the *status quo* and provoked discontent. [In the period prior to the revolutions, Europe had also experienced a period of 'confessional absolutism' as in state after state, the religion of the individual ruler was enforced]. ... Confessional absolutism produced results, but success had a high price. In all those areas where the court's culture was not shared by the population at large, a new gulf was created which allowed disaffection to develop. ... It was only religion that was capable of producing an ideology which could unite the opponents of a regime. At the same time it created an alienated élite capable of championing those whose religion seemed threatened. 'Confessional absolutism' was therefore the form of government action most likely to lead to revolution. Possession of religious ideology was something that

distinguished the successful revolts of this period (Scotland, England, the Ukraine) from the unsuccessful ones (Catalonia, the Fronde); the exception was Portugal, and there King John IV could draw on strong national feeling. Finally, religion was more likely to mobilise a degree of international support for the rebels. It was no accident that the leaders of the anti-Hapsburg factions in Austria, Bohemia and Moravia were all Calvinists, or that they allied with their co-religionists elsewhere to form a 'Calvinist International' based on Heidelberg, The Hague and Prague to oppose the 'Catholic International' based on Rome, Vienna, Brussels and Madrid. No one can hope to understand the coming of the English Civil War without knowing about the Bishops' Wars in Scotland and the Confederation of Kilkenny in Ireland. The Stuart monarchy was a personal union of three crowns, and the policies of Strafford were tried out in Ireland before they were attempted in England; those of Laud were implemented simultaneously in England and Scotland. ... It has been correctly pointed out that 'the initiative that the Long Parliament took against the royal prerogative in 1640 and 1641 depended heavily on the presence of the Scottish Army in England. Later, during the Civil War, parliament could hardly have carried on without Scottish military help'. And the tie upon which that Scottish assistance depended was the 'Solemn League and Covenant' which undertook to enforce a Presbyterian (i.e. Scottish) religious settlement upon England (and Ireland) 'according to the word of god and the examples of the best reformed Churches'.

The sources above have challenged the original claims of Hobsbawm and Trevor-Roper for the existence of a general crisis, and have suggested alternative explanations for the parallels and similarities which undoubtedly existed between events in different parts of Europe in the mid-seventeenth century. In the place of a general crisis they suggest the existence of certain wide-ranging conditions, which account in different combinations for the upheavals of the period, and do also serve to highlight the particular significance of some of these conditions in causing and influencing the English Revolution. Recently, however, these ideas have been taken further by the work of Jack Goldstone, Professor of Sociology and a specialist in Comparative History in California. Professor Goldstone has attempted a synthesis of many of the arguments put forward above, and by developing the ideas further, is able to offer a new concept of a general crisis. He suggests that the root cause of the crisis is demographic – a rise in population which presses on resources in a number of ways and at a number of levels. He also argues that the easing of this pressure accounts for the greater stability of the eighteenth century, and that a new rise in population creates a renewal of revolutionary activity in the nineteenth century, from which Britain's industrial revolution provided some immunity. His synthesis cannot accommodate all the factors present in seventeenth-century upheavals, but it does offer a link between the economic, climatic and political crises described separately above. In Source 56 these links are explained, in Source 57 the ideas are applied to the English Revolution, and in Source 58 a comparison is drawn between events in England and France.

Source 56

From J.A. Goldstone, *Revolution and Rebellion in the Early Modern World* (University of California Press, 1991) pp. 35–6 and 24–5.

The causes of revolutions and major rebellions … need not be sought solely among sudden events. Such events can be considered as 'triggers' or 'releasers' of pent-up social forces, but they are not the fundamental causes. Indeed, such 'releasing' events are themselves generally the result of cumulating social pressures. A long-term cumulative factor, such as population increase, can therefore readily lead to a sudden event. What matters is whether the existing social and political institutions are flexible enough to move easily in response to such pressures. …

Large states of the early modern period, whether monarchies or empires, faced certain common constraints. They needed to raise sufficient revenues to support their armies and reward their retainers. They needed sufficient allegiance from the élites to secure loyal officials for government service and, perhaps more importantly, to secure loyal local authorities in an era when centrally appointed officialdom rarely penetrated below the county level. And they needed to provide sufficient stability and sustenance for the working and cultivating population so that the latter could pay their taxes and other obligations and yet not be inclined to support rebellion. Thus any train of events that simultaneously led to fiscal deterioration, élite factionalism and disloyalty, and a major decline in popular living standards or undermining of popular traditional rights, threatened the ability of states to maintain their authority.

Put simply, large agrarian states of this period were not equipped to deal with the impact of the steady growth of population that began [in the sixteenth century] throughout northern Eurasia, eventually amounting to population increases in excess of the productivity gains of the land, [especially if these were reduced by climatic changes]. The implications of this ecological shift went far beyond mere issues of poverty and population dislocation. Pressure on resources led to persistent price inflation. Because the tax systems of most early modern states were based on fixed rates of taxation on people or land, tax revenues lagged behind prices. States thus had no choice but to seek to expand taxation. This was all the more true as population increases led to the expansion of armies and hence to rising real costs. Yet attempts to increase state revenues met resistance from the élites and the populace and thus rarely succeeded in offsetting spiralling expenses. As a result, most major states in the seventeenth century were rapidly raising taxes but were still headed for fiscal crisis. Moreover, élites were seeking to secure their own relative position. Population growth increased the number of aspirants for élite positions, and their demands were difficult to satisfy given the fiscal strains on the state. Élites thus were riven by increasing rivalry and factionalism, as pursuit of positions and resistance to state demands led to the formation of rival patronage networks in competition for state rewards. Finally, population growth led not only to rural misery but also to urban migration and falling real wages, owing to the especially rapid expansion of youth cohorts that accompanied the population growth. Thus both urban workers and rural artisans staged food riots and wage protests.

Ideological battles flared as well, for state weakness, élite competition, and popular discontent combined to fuel religious conflicts. In these periods the state's fiscal difficulties undermined their financial support for established Churches, and the attempts to use the Church to buttress their increased demands for taxes and other resources led to entwined religious and political opposition. Dissident élites and dissatisfied artisans were thus widely recruited into heterodox religious movements. As all of these trends intensified, the results in each case were state bankruptcy and consequent loss of control of the military, élite movements of regional and national rebellion, and a combination of élite-mobilised and popular uprisings that manifested the breakdown of central authority.

Naturally, these trends showed numerous national and regional variations. … Moreover, while this framework emphasises material changes as the *cause* of state breakdown, these material changes dictated no particular outcomes. … State reconstruction offered a variety of choices to élites, and whether such reconstruction involved radical change or the strengthening of traditional institutions, depended chiefly on particular cultural frameworks and the development of élite ideologies. Clearly, material and ideological factors influenced both the causes of state breakdown and the outcomes. However, this framework suggests a particular balance of material and cultural forces; it gives a predominant role to material factors in bringing about state breakdown, but a predominant role to culture and ideologies in shaping state reconstruction.

Source 57

From J.A. Goldstone, *Revolution and Rebellion in the Early Modern World*, pp. 141–5.

Neo-Marxists have argued that the social causes of the English Revolution lay in the changes wrought by the growth of agrarian and overseas capitalism. However, these arguments are difficult to sustain. By the mid-seventeenth century, virtually every group among the élite – including the Crown – was involved in commercial exploitation of their land or in collection of profits from trade. Rural conflicts chiefly involved artisans protesting grain shortages, high prices, and the extension of arable land, not cultivators protesting [against] unlawful enclosures. Further, in the early seventeenth century enclosures were more often instances of collaboration than of conflict between Crown and gentry. Finally, as overseas trade stagnated from the 1570s, the largest overseas traders maintained their support of the Crown in return for royal monopolies. England's economy grew more commercial and capitalist after 1500, but the hypothesized causal links between this growth and state breakdown are absent. Whig historians have argued that constitutional and religious struggles underlay the revolution. But they have not been successful in demonstrating that such struggles were rooted in long-term social causes that presaged an eruption into open conflict in the mid-seventeenth century, or in explaining why a state fiscal crisis and popular uprisings were particularly likely to develop in those decades. Recent revisionist historians have therefore argued that the English Revolution had no long-term social causes at all but rather was the result of errors of judgment and administration by Charles I.

Yet all parties have failed to examine closely the links between the inability of English economic, fiscal and social institutions to adjust to the sustained population growth of the years 1500–1640 and the causes of state breakdown. State finances, the stability of the élite hierarchy and popular employment were all adversely affected by population growth and consequent inflation. These relationships are schematically shown in Figure 3.

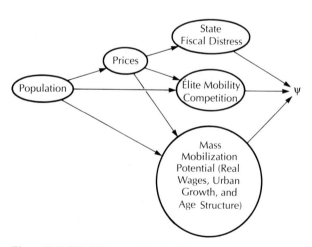

Figure 3: Political demography of early modern England: basic relationships

I have suggested ways to measure changes in all three of these areas by using a rough scale of state fiscal distress, employing university enrolments as an indicator of élite mobility and status competition, and constructing a compound estimator of mass mobilization potential. Each of these three indicators is graphed ... in Figure 4. Clearly, each set of scores is somewhat higher in the early

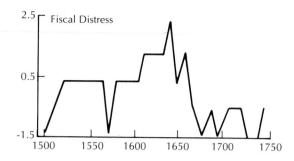

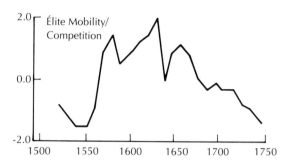

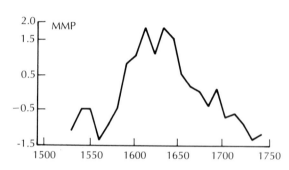

Figure 4: Fiscal Distress, Mobility/Competition and MMP in England: – Z-scores, 1500–1750

seventeenth century than in earlier or later periods; however, the changes are not of remarkable proportions.

In any case, the crucial factor making for state breakdown is not that any one of these factors was high. After all, states survive bouts with bankruptcy, élite divisions and popular disorders when they occur separately. My claim is that the mid-seventeenth century was exceptional in that all of these factors, being driven by the underlying force of population growth in the preceding century and a half, created a synergistic stress [i.e. a stress caused by different factors co-operating together] that caused the breakdown of state power. In terms of a causal model, such a synergistic combination can be represented by an interaction effect. Thus, if our model of the origins of the revolution is correct, we should find that the interaction product

ψ = Fiscal Distress x Mobility/Competition x Mass Mobilization Potential

rises to a distinctive peak in the mid-seventeenth century, unmatched by a similar rise in either the sixteenth or eighteenth centuries. I have named this function by the Greek letter π [psi], serviceable as an acronym for 'political stress indicator', hereafter psi ψ.

The course of the function *psi* from 1520 to 1750 is depicted in Figure 5. This function sharply distinguishes the period of mounting crisis and revolution in the early seventeenth century from other periods in early modern English history.

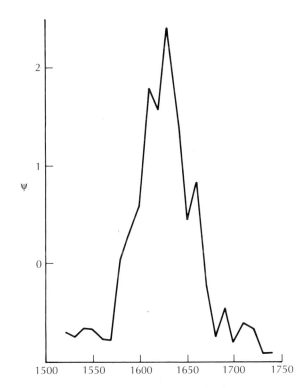

Figure 5: Pressures for crisis (psi) in England, 1520–1749

This data analysis makes clear that the early seventeenth century was a period of unique social character, and that its uniqueness lay precisely in an unusual combination of factors. However foolish Charles may have been, the differences between the early seventeenth century and the centuries that immediately preceded and followed it were not merely in the realm of royal policies. The constitutional struggles and religious conflicts of the time were underpinned by an extraordinary combination of decaying finances, rising élite mobility and competition, and falling real wages, all propelled by rising population. This combination of ills reached a peak in the middle third of the century unmatched at any time throughout early modern English history. The English Revolution was in part a religious, in part a constitutional, and in part an economic conflict. What is undeniable from the preceding analysis is that these conflicts combined to reach fatal acuteness precisely when English society was undergoing a unique level of social and economic stress, a stress that can be precisely defined and measured through the function *psi*. The *psi* function clearly differentiates the mid-1600s from the preceding and succeeding centuries as a period of exceptional predisposition to state breakdown. The burden of proof thus shifts heavily to those who

continue to claim that the breakdown of the English state in 1640 occurred in an 'ordinary' situation unaffected by long-term social and economic changes.

Source 58

From J.A. Goldstone, *Revolution and Rebellion in the Early Modern World*, pp. 158–163. A comparison between the French and English civil wars.

From 1500 to 1650 France's population grew rapidly, though not quite as rapidly as England's. … And many of the same trends as were seen in England during the sixteenth and seventeenth centuries were equally visible in France: a sevenfold rise in grain prices; a convergence of surplus rural population on Paris, which grew over 15 per cent per decade from 1550 to 1650; and a sharp fall in real wages. The social and political consequences of population growth and price inflation were also similar to the English experience. The Crown's tax system … rapidly gave way to the rising costs of war … and the monarchy thus had to resort to the same measures that had alienated the English élite and exhausted Charles I's credit. … Forced loans were exacted … but these measures were still not enough, [and] in the 1630s taxes were increased at unprecedented rates. … Inflation posed problems for the nobility as well [but] provided profit opportunity for some. … Displacement and turnover among the élite is visible in the replacement of the traditional nobility in the royal service by recruits from the Third Estate. The Crown, partly to raise revenue and partly to counter-balance the traditional nobility, created a virtual new class – the *noblesse de robe* – by selling roughly fifty thousand official posts during the late sixteenth century. … By the early seventeenth century, the sale of offices had virtually put the bureaucracy and judiciary beyond royal control. Thus new officials – the intendants – were appointed to supervise the officials, and the *paulette* came under attack. The Crown thus found itself opposed by the robe nobility for attacking their privileges and by the traditional nobility for the special favour shown to the robe. Noble opposition, from both the traditional grandees and the newer nobility of office-holders was made more fearsome by the threat of popular revolts … reflecting the increased revenue demands of state taxation falling on a growing population that found it ever more difficult to feed itself. …

Thus, state breakdown in France can be traced to factors quite similar to those in contemporary England: state fiscal crisis, exceptional élite mobility and competition, and heightened mobilisation potential among the populace. … However, the different contours and outcomes of the conflicts reflect significant differences in the resources of the combatants. The Tudors had reduced the power of the great lords, although they lacked a standing army and a large bureaucracy. Having relied on the support of the country gentry, Parliament and London since the time of Henry VIII, the English Crown had few supporters to fall back on when its fiscal and administrative expedients undermined the confidence of Londoners and brought attacks from Parliament. Radical

Protestantism, moreover, could cloak itself in nationalist appeals against a suspect, papist administration. Hence, aside from marshalling reluctant traditionalists, who felt that defence of an objectionable king was preferable to the radical parliamentarians' courting of popular revolution, Charles I had few options. But in France the great older nobles – the dukes and princes – were still independent powers, and the crown could exploit their resentment of the urban, office-holding élite. Protestantism, though a serious threat to stability, could not pose as a nationalist ideology to lead the nation. Thus, unlike in England, there was no clear basis for a nationalist, cross-class coalition against the crown. Adroit manipulation of alliances and divisions among the princes, the *officiers*, and the populace allowed the French Crown to survive through feint, retreat, and eventual triumph.

Question

7. Using all the information provided in this unit, reconsider your response to Question 6 and explain

   (a) how far the revolutions of 1640–60 represented a general crisis in Europe.

   (b) what such a general crisis, and/or the continental revolutions, suggest about the causes, nature and outcome of the English Revolution.

UNIT 4.3

═══ WHAT DO WE MEAN BY A REVOLUTION? ═══

Introduction

In Unit 4.2 the English Revolution was considered in a wider spatial context in order to assess whether it was part of a general crisis and, by comparing it with other upheavals of the time, to evaluate our explanations of its causes, nature and significance. Unit 4.3 now seeks to take this process further, by widening both the spatial and temporal contexts in which we consider its significance and by extending the comparisons to other major revolutions. The first approach to comparison is to widen the temporal context and to consider the Civil Wars in relation to events that followed – in particular the Glorious Revolution of 1689 and American Revolution. This allows us to consider the different kinds of events that have been labelled 'revolution', and to assess something of the long term significance of the events of 1642–9. The second approach is to consider the English Revolution alongside those in France and Russia, which have been widely acknowledged to have been turning points in European history, and through the ideas that they embodied, to have influenced political developments throughout the world. Initially, comparisons have been made for the specific purpose of evaluating the nature and significance of the English Revolution. By examining the similarities and differences between these events, it is possible to highlight factors which may be considered particularly influential or important in the events in seventeenth-century England. However, historians who have studied a range of 'revolutions' have also sought to consider common and individual factors in order to offer more general explanations of how and why revolutions occur. The final part of this unit addresses some of these questions, and considers whether, by comparing a number of different revolutions, we are able to define what a revolution is, whether there is any pattern of causation, development or outcome, and how far these concepts may be usefully employed in assessing the nature and significance of events in England between 1640 and 1660.

Comparative history

The extension of the temporal context raises issues concerning the basis on which such comparisons can be made, and the nature of the conclusions that can be drawn from them. In Source 59, the historian John Morrill outlines some of the problems.

Source 59

From J. Morrill, *The Nature of the English Revolution* (Longman, 1993) pp. 34–5.

I can now see that the deployment of the term 'England's Wars of Religion' was a revisionist statement. By locating the mid-seventeenth-century crisis in an early modern context away from what I took to be misleading and unhelpful comparisons with modern revolutions from 1789 on, I was seeking to reject a fundamentally anachronistic approach to the seventeenth century, one designed to render the event explicable by assimilating it to a category familiar to modern experience and social theory. It represented and represents what I still believe to be a salutary reaction against various forms of modernisation theory. It was an essential part of the revisionist claim for the particularity of past experience, and for the gulf between our mental world and that of the seventeenth century. Thus I was consciously seeking to assimilate the events in seventeenth-century England to a class of events [wars of religion] which belong distinctively to the period under study and not to the social and secular divisions alleged to underlie most modern revolutions. And yet, paradoxically, one aim was to enhance the claims of the 1640s and 50s to be a great turning-point by suggesting that the overthrow of monarchy, the House of Lords and confessional [religious] state constituted a fundamental transformation which – even without the social transformation sought by the model-builders and even given the reversals of 1660 – changed political consciousness. As I put it recently, the present may not have been determined by these events, but it tastes of them.

Dr Morrill's objection is not necessarily to comparative history, but to the type of comparison that seeks to establish 'models' and risks the

163

distortion of historical events in order to fit them to the model, or to explanations of events in the early modern world that apply structures and assumptions related to later periods. What he is emphasising is the need to assess an event in the context of its own time, even when comparing it with others from different periods. This is particularly the case with occurrences such as revolutions, which by definition have some effect on the events which come after them, and often leave a legacy of ideas which influence and even lead to other revolutionary outbreaks in the future. It is therefore important that the limits of comparative explanation are clearly understood, that the type of comparison made is appropriate to its purpose, and that the conclusions drawn are specific in both their scope and application.

One example of comparative history is provided by a straightforward extension of the temporal context so that events occurring at different times in the same state can be compared and the results can be used to define the relationships between them as well as to assess their relative significance. This type of history was employed by J.G.A. Pocock and his colleagues (Source 60) to consider the comparative significances of the English Revolution of the 1640s, the 'Glorious' Revolution of 1688–9, and the American Revolution against Britain in 1776.

Source 60

From J.G.A. Pocock (ed.) *Three British Revolutions: 1641, 1688 and 1776* **(Princeton, 1980) Introduction, pp. 3–5, 12–14 and 17.**

There now seems to exist a new way of looking at the Puritan Revolution, the Glorious Revolution, and the American Revolution in their chronological order. ... We see the Revolutions of 1641 and 1649 as occasioned by the breakdown of a certain aristocratic order, the Tudor, but as leading toward the reconstitution of another, the Whig; we see the Revolution of 1688 as an important but not the final step in the construction of the Whig order; and we see the Revolution of 1776 as the greatest but not the only insurgence against that order in the reign of George III. What renders the last Revolution 'American' is its role in the creation of a continental republic and nation; in this [context] we are concerned with it in its 'British' character. ...

In line with these perceptions, Lawrence Stone ... presents a 'seismic rift' running, from 1620 to 1720, through the relations between government and society in English history. [Stone's view has already been presented more fully in Unit 2.6, Source 182. The corner-stone of the Tudor system was the crown's relationship with the gentry.] The role in these relations of the territorial aristocracy – who were country gentlemen writ large –

was to act as independently operating transmitters and dispensers of [government] patronage through their personal contacts with the Court at one end of the chain and with the county communities at the other. If the Civil War broke out – [as Harrington believed at the time] – through a breakdown in their ability to act as intermediaries, it is not surprising that the Restoration is preceded by a loud demand for 'the old Lords' in their role as 'a screen and bank' between king and people, and followed by a reconstitution of political aristocracy. ... [In a new situation, with the parliament playing a larger role in government, part of the new task of the Lords is to provide the king's ministers and organise his government. Thus the term 'court' takes on a new, more political definition. In addition, in an age of large electorates and religious/ideological strife, the aristocracy divides on party lines, in which the party favoured by the monarch becomes the 'court' party and the other, the 'country'. The Tories are the court party in the reign of James and of Anne, the Whigs in the reign of William and after 1714. The revolution of 1688 is made possible by a temporary alliance of Whigs and Tories, driven together by the impatience and misjudgements of the king. Hence the revolution] appears a momentous event indeed, having far-reaching consequences (notably for the Church), but not in itself a major alteration in the structure of British politics. The structural change comes a few years later, in what we are now accustomed to calling the Financial Revolution; and though it was a consequence of the events of 1688, it was neither foreseen nor intended by the actors in that memorable year. By 'the Financial Revolution' is meant the successful creation, centring around the foundation of the Bank of England in 1694, of a structure of public credit through which England's trading wealth could be invested in the security and stability of government and give that government the power to engage successfully in long-range war for political and commercial ends. It was public credit [that laid the foundations of the British Empire]. At the same time, it vastly expanded the government's resources in patronage, to which the country gentry were already objecting. To the increasingly Tory 'Country party' of the 1690s and after, it seemed that Whig rule, high taxes and standing armies were being imposed upon the gentry by a 'monied interest' investing in the stability of an increasingly bureaucratic regime.

In the reign of Queen Anne, the Tory gentry staged their last great revolt against Whig rule; but under the heading of a 'growth of oligarchy' a complex counter-revolution can be traced following the reversal of party fortunes in 1714. Whig politicians, restored to office under George I, passed the Septennial Act of 1716, which increased the duration of parliaments and so rendered political contests less common. The 'growth of oligarchy' was in fact a systematic reduction of political competitiveness and so of the participation of the electorate in politics, which could never have happened if Tory as well as Whig gentlemen had not turned against the borough electorates that their forefathers had been steadily enlarging for at least a hundred years. The thesis of an electorate large in the seventeenth but restricted in the eighteenth century means that the Whig aristocratic order attacked by American revolutionaries and British reformers was not an *ancien regime* and had no feudal character, but was a recent outgrowth of mercantile and patronage politics instituted in the search for social stability combined with expanding empire. ... [By its nature, oligarchy does without ideology and was therefore unlikely to split on that basis ... but it does sharply restrict power, and therefore ideology can play a part in attacks upon it. In the reign of George III dissident Whigs, disturbed by the actions of the king], joined forces with surviving Tories, country gentlemen with urban radicals and drew heavily on both Country and Commonwealth sources surviving from the time of Charles II, if not that of Cromwell ... [to attack the oligarchy and demand change. Not surprisingly, the oligarchy was at its weakest on the peripheries, where its powers of patronage were thinly spread.] ... The minds of Americans before, during and after the Revolution were to a remarkable degree dominated by the ideology of opposition to the Whig regime, to the point where it became possible to look upon the Revolution as a Country movement of a sort like, and yet unlike, those to which the English counties and boroughs might give rise. ...

What we have done is to present the American Revolution as a schism in Whig political culture, in such a way that our three revolutions form at last a single sequence. The seismic rift was healed by the establishment of the Whig oligarchy, but the latter sharply limited the distribution of political power. New rifts consequently opened, and the revolt of the North American colonies can be ranked with English parliamentary reform and Irish parliamentary nationalism as one of a series of reactions against the rule of the oligarchy. Even the republicanism with which the Founding Fathers rejected the parliamentary model of government itself was initially 'commonwealth' in character and owed much to speculations put forward in the Cromwellian phase of the first English Revolution.

The source above does not, and does not attempt to, provide a clear and comprehensive analysis of the three revolutions to which reference is made, nor does it enable the full significance of each to be assessed. Indeed, very little reference is made to the results of the revolutions at all. What are considered are the common elements in causing these revolutions, each explained in its own context; and the results suggest that they are part of a longer process of development. When applied back to the original subject of study these conclusions serve to enhance the importance of one factor – the crisis of the 'Tudor' aristocracy – in explaining the outbreak of civil war, and to suggest that the Civil Wars as a whole have considerable revolutionary significance. They are portrayed as representing a major collapse of the English system of government, arising from significant structural weaknesses, and raising problems which were not resolved until the early eighteenth century at best. The Revolution of 1689 is reduced in significance, being part of the gradual resolution of issues arising from the Civil Wars and even the American Revolution is seen in part as arising from the same source, reflecting the failure of the eighteenth-century solutions. This interpretation could be further supported by a similar study of the political ideologies of the period. The justifications of parliament's actions in 1642–9 were taken up by the philosopher John Locke, writing in the aftermath of the Exclusion Crisis of 1679–83 and published in the aftermath of the 'Glorious' Revolution. His arguments concerning the nature and source of government power, the rights of property, individual liberty, and the nature of representation formed the basis of the American case against the British government. Thus comparisons arising from the study of three revolutions in a developmental, temporal context extending from c.1620 to c.1780 result in a new, or adjusted, explanation of the nature and significance of one of them: the English Civil Wars of 1642–9.

Questions

1. To what extent does any developmental relationship that might exist between the events of 1640–60, 1688–9 and 1776 influence your view of how far each constituted a 'revolution'?

2. How might your conclusions about the revolutionary significance of the Civil Wars and Interregnum be affected by extending the temporal context back to 1450, to include the Wars of the Roses and the 'Tudor Revolution in government'?

(Material on the Wars of the Roses and the 'Tudor Revolution' can be found in Unit 1.4 of the Development Study.)

A more obvious form of comparative history is that which is called by Professor Jack Goldstone 'case-based' comparison, of which his own work, *Revolution and Rebellion in the Early Modern World*, affords an excellent example. In such comparisons no developmental relationship between the events is assumed, although such a relationship may exist. Each set of events is studied within its own context, and similarities and differences are noted. These may then be used to shed light on the nature of particular events, such as the English Revolution, or to devise broader explanations encompassing the range of events studied.

Source 61

From J.A. Goldstone, *Revolution and Rebellion in the Early Modern World* (Oxford, 1991) pp. 52–3.

The central goal of comparative history is not merely to find analogies or generalities in historical experience. It is to find causal explanations of historical events. Given that historical variation reveals both continuity and change, comparative history proceeds by asking which elements of the historical record were crucial. Thus to study merely the history of two cities, or of two countries is to practice parallel, but not comparative history. The latter depends on identifying some key difference between the cases and asking which of the many distinct elements in these cases were responsible for the particular difference in question. … Comparative history often starts with apparently similar situations among which there are nonetheless striking differences that call for explanation. Yet the reverse pattern of historical variation also sometimes arises – that is, in historical situations that seem markedly different, similar sequences of events unfold. There are striking similarities between the French Revolution of 1789 and the Russian Revolution of 1917, despite their vast separation in time and enormously different historical settings. Thus the comparative historian may also approach historical variation from the angle of significant similarities: why, in contexts that seem to differ widely, are similar patterns of events observed?

A wider unifying explanation being Professor Goldstone's primary purpose, he has chosen his revolutions from a particular historical period, the early modern, but if the purpose of comparison is the more limited goal of using comparative case studies to further understanding of a particular set of events (the English Revolution), it is possible to draw examples for comparison from a wider temporal and spatial context. Hence the following comparative examples are the French Revolution of 1789 and the Russian Revolution of 1917. In such cases it is important to be aware of how far the differences between revolutions from different periods of time reflect the particular social, political and cultural characteristics of the periods in which the revolutions occurred. For example, the parliamentary opposition of 1640–2 had no blueprint for change, and were reluctant to consider such a possibility. The constitutional reformers of 1789 in France had some vision of change, derived in part from the English experience, and were quick to go beyond this into claims of natural right and a perception of change for the purpose of improvement. This does not make them more revolutionary in relative terms, but reflects the change in attitudes which had taken place in the 150 years that had elapsed since the English Revolution. Similarly, the planned revolution of the Bolsheviks in 1917 reflects the legacy of events in France.

A characteristic of 'case-based' comparison is that there must be reasonable knowledge of each of the cases in comparison. If the primary purpose, as in this study, is to enhance our understanding of the English Revolution, then the other examples are used for comparison and do not require examination in the same depth. However, comparisons which are based on little or no understanding of the other revolutions will tend to be facile, and reveal little of value. It is therefore sensible to limit the cases so that a reasonable knowledge of the comparative examples can be acquired. In addition, it is useful to compare like with like. In each of our case studies we are considering the collapse of a national government, and a national upheaval. We are also, as Source 60 has demonstrated, examining revolutions which were the first of a sequence. In each case the revolution in question has raised issues that were not entirely settled by the outcome of that revolution, but which formed the basis of further crises and upheavals in the years that followed. The French Revolution was defeated in 1815, but its message led to further revolutions in France in 1830 and throughout Europe in 1848. The socialist message of Russia in 1917 has dominated political struggles – revolutionary and otherwise – throughout the twentieth-century world. Like the English Revolution of 1642–9, their echoes were heard long afterwards and in many places.

The following material falls into two sections. In the first, there are some examples of the kind of comparisons that can be made, in the form of sources taken from the work of historians who have studied these revolutions and in the brief biographies of the monarchs who were their victims. In the second, a short account of the French Revolution is set out in order to enable the historians' comparisons to be tested and others made. No account of the Russian Revolution is provided here because it is considered in detail in Module 4 of the Development Study, and reference should be made to the material provided there.

Questions

3. Read Source 62. How useful is Russell's idea of two 'revolutions', drawn from the Russian Revolutions of 1917, in clarifying the nature of the English Revolution?

4. Read Source 63. What light do Goldstone's opinions on the relationship between reform and revolution shed on explanations of the outbreak of the English Civil War?

5. What do the biographies of Louis XVI and Nicholas II, used in conjunction with your knowledge of Charles I (see Unit 2.1, pp. 94–5), tell you about the role played by monarchs in precipitating revolutions against them?

Source 62

From Conrad Russell, *The Origins of the English Civil War* (Macmillan, 1991) pp. 2–3.

Uncertainty about what we are trying to explain is deepened by the fact that the English Civil War, as much as the Russian Revolution, was two revolutions, and the aims of these two revolutions were as profoundly opposed to each other as the aims of Mensheviks and Bolsheviks. ... In 1642 the supporters of both revolutions were in alliance, and the balance of power within this alliance is still uncertain. The first revolution is the one symbolised in the execution of Strafford, the legislation of the Long Parliament, the Militia Ordinance, and the outbreak of Civil War in 1642. The second is the one symbolised in the creation of the New Model Army, Pride's Purge and the execution of Charles I. The first was, in anthropologists' terms, a rebellion rather than a revolution; it was not a social revolution but a split in the governing class: a movement by a large number of peers and gentlemen to force a change of policy and a change of ministers on Charles I. The second revolution was a revolution in the full sense of the term: it was an assault on the existing social structure, and particularly on the position of the gentry. Unlike the first rebellion, the revolution of 1647–9 was supplied by the Levellers and Fifth Monarchists with truly revolutionary ideologies. In the face of this second revolution, the vast majority of the leaders of the original rebellion against King Charles grew so frightened of their own followers that their sympathies returned to the king. ... The second revolution was the revolution of the army as the first was the revolution of parliament, but even after the army, through Colonel Pride, had purged parliament to its liking, parliament was so keen to broaden the basis of its support that it admitted conformists and time-servers in such numbers that ... they [soon] outnumbered the genuine revolutionaries. ... We have then a political rebellion which was to a limited extent successful, and a social revolution which, largely as a result of the gentry's unbroken control of local government, was almost totally unsuccessful.

Source 63

From J.A. Goldstone, *Revolution and Rebellion in the Early Modern World*, pp. 316–7.

There is a long history of debate on the relationship between reform and revolution. [Alexis de] Tocqueville [in The Old Regime and the French Revolution, 1856] noted that Louis XV and Louis XVI had initiated many reforms in France and alleged that their reforms hastened, rather than delayed, the coming revolution. The Russian tsars and the Chinese imperial court also implemented reforms in the last decades before their downfalls. These events suggest that reforms can be blamed for undoing regimes – they contribute to revolution rather than avoid it. But this view overlooks two very successful reform movements in nineteenth-century Europe: the English reforms of 1828–32 and the Prussian reforms of 1807–14. In both cases, the nations emerged stronger and more stable from their reforms. Equally significant, in France in 1830 and 1848 ... resistance to reform turned situations of political crisis into actual revolutions. ...

The critical question about reforms is not how many occurred but rather what kind of reforms and in what circumstances. In France under Louis XVI, in Russia under Nicholas II, and in China under the empress dowager, the reform regimes were already under tremendous strain. ... But the reforms adopted by these regimes were all quite modest, entailing reorganisation of central and local administration designed to give more power to the central government while offering advisory posts to dissident élites. There were no attempts to change the fundamental structures of power, status, or economic organisation. In contrast the reforms adopted by England and Prussia involved substantial changes in access to political power and status. In England obstacles to full political participation by Catholics and Dissenters were removed, and the electorate expanded by more than was accomplished in France through the Revolution of 1830. A full active (not merely advisory) sharing of power with new groups tied them to the old élite and separated them from lower-class protests. ... In addition, England and Prussia made their reforms under pressures that, though real and insistent, were far more modest than those faced by France, Russia and China. Prussia had been soundly defeated by Napoleon at Jena, but the state was still intact; England was facing difficult social and political pressures in 1830, but its fiscal structure was sound and its military firmly reliable. Thus, both cases of successful reforms were made in times of difficulty, but not of extreme duress. The reason that reforms hastened revolution in France, Russia and China is so simple that it hardly bears repeating: the reforms were too little and too late. The successful reforms were more extensive in terms of power-sharing and were undertaken while the regimes were still in positions of considerable strength.

The influence of individuals

Louis XVI

Louis became King of France in 1774 following the death of his grandfather, Louis XV. Brought up in the isolation of Versailles, he had little idea of how the French people lived, and thus his genuine desire to do his duty as their King and father was of little practical use. A devout Catholic, he married the sister of the Austrian Emperor, Marie Antoinette; the union was a happy one, and Louis was a good husband and father, unlike his philandering grandfather. Unfortunately, in political terms this laid him open to the influence of his wife's opinions, which were singularly superficial and ill-informed. The famous story that she recommended that the starving crowds, who were demanding bread, should eat cake instead may, or may not, be correct – the significant point is that it was credible. When beset by an angry mob attacking the Tuileries in 1792, she refused to be rescued by Marshal Lafayette, whom she hated for his support of reform in the early stages of the Revolution. She declared that she would rather die than be saved by him – she later got her wish! Marie Antoinette's worst

influence on the king arose from three factors: her total lack of understanding of the situation with which he was faced; her constant urging him to be strong when genuine concessions might have changed the situation; and her encouragement of his secret contacts with Austria. None of this would have been possible were Louis not already inclined to make the wrong decision at the worst possible time. The problem was that while he understood the need for reform, he was incapable of thinking as a constitutional monarch. Moreover, he was far too easily persuaded to change his mind, as a series of reforming ministers learnt to their cost. Believing that he had the king's support, Jacques Necker attempted to re-organise royal finances after 1783 in the teeth of aristocratic opposition – only to find that Louis refused to support him at the crucial moment. When faced with the demands of the Third Estate in 1789, Louis first refused, and then gave in to pressure, thus losing the opportunity to gain political support while lacking the strength, practical or temperamental, to resist demands for reform. The pattern was repeated throughout the following year, when the royal family were forcibly moved to Paris, in the acceptance of the decrees of the National Assembly, and particularly in accepting the attack on the Church. It was this assault on his genuine and deeply-held religious beliefs that finally drove him to break with the reformers and attempt the flight to Varennes. If any event could sum up the inadequacies of Louis and his wife in this situation, it was the attempt to flee France without either military protection or disguise to aid their escape.

In the end, Louis died and the monarchy perished because his subjects could not trust him. With a combination of political stupidity, temperamental weakness, and a total lack of understanding that his royal role had changed, he failed to be decisive when he could, offered too little too late, and revealed with absolute clarity that he would betray his people and his state in order to protect his throne and his religion. 'When you can keep together a number of oiled ivory balls you may do something with the King.' This verdict of his cousin sums up Louis' weakness and vacillation. In his situation, it proved fatal.

Louis XVI

Nicholas II

Nicholas inherited the throne in 1894, having been brought up in the isolated atmosphere of the court of Alexander III. The architect of his father's policy of repression, Pobedonostsev, was his tutor – thus it was hardly surprising that Nicholas had imbibed all the traditions of Russian autocracy. He married a German princess, Alexandra, and like Louis XVI and Charles I, was a devoted husband and father. His wife was a great, and not always constructive, influence in his life. The historian, Anthony Wood (Source 65), summarised his personality and outlook as those of a benevolent, considerate but weak autocrat.

Source 64

Tsar Nicholas II and Tsarina Alexandra in jewelled robes dating from the time of Peter the Great

Source 65

From A. Wood, *The Russian Revolution* (Longman, 1986) p. 4.

Nicholas II was a man of great personal charm, deeply religious and devoted to his family. He could be resolute, as he had shown when he insisted upon marrying Princess Alix of Hesse-Darmstadt against the initial objections of his father. Unfortunately this quality of determination was marred by a sensitivity that inhibited him from openly opposing views with which he disagreed, and his ministers and officials could never be sure of his genuine acceptance of their advice, nor even of their tenure of office. On one issue at least, Nicholas did not leave them long in doubt. At the beginning of his reign the provincial *zemstvo* [council] of Tver addressed an appeal to him for an extension of representative institutions. 'I am informed', said Nicholas in his reply, 'that recently in some of the *zemstvo* assemblies voices have made themselves heard from people carried away by senseless dreams about participation by representatives of the *zemstvo* in the affairs of internal government; let all know that I, devoting all my strength to the welfare of the people, will uphold the principle of autocracy as firmly and as unflinchingly as my late unforgettable father'. For Nicholas the autocracy was sacrosanct, a responsibility divinely entrusted to him, and the note of finality in his statement created an obstacle for the reformers that was to frustrate them until the last hours of the monarchy.

Nicholas' attitude was reflected in his actions throughout his reign. The tsar and his chief minister, Sergei Witte, the architect of Russian industrial development, faced a serious threat of revolution in 1905. Nicholas' belief that he could control discontent by uniting the nation in war was rudely destroyed by the disastrous defeat against Japan. Faced with peaceful protest in St Petersburg in January 1905, troops were ordered to fire on the demonstrators. The resultant bloodbath sparked off strikes and demonstrations throughout the country, and in October it was Witte who saved the regime by persuading Nicholas to concede a parliament, the Duma. When it proved less pliable than Nicholas expected, it was Witte who paid with his position. He was replaced by the brutal but effective Stolypin, and the government embarked on a savage repression. Thousands were hanged, exiled, shot, or simply disappeared. At the same time, the powers of the Duma were whittled away until they became meaningless, thus going back on the promises that Nicholas had made in the October Manifesto of 1905.

The outbreak of war in 1914 proved the final catalyst leading to the collapse of the monarchy. After an initial outburst of patriotic fervour, the population found themselves fighting without adequate resources, fleeing as refugees, or enduring rocketing prices and shortages in the cities. These problems cannot be laid entirely on the shoulders of Nicholas – he inherited a system beset by structural weaknesses. Nevertheless, he resisted any change in that system for 20 years. Moreover, after 1914 he made a series of catastrophic errors. The first was to allow himself to be advised by a wife who had no understanding of Russia, was hated as a possible German spy, and almost invariably advised him to show strength when concessions were needed. The second was to acquiesce in her relationship with the monk Rasputin. Despite rumours, it is unlikely that their relationship was sexual, but the Tsarina was fatally influenced by the monk's personality and healing powers with her haemophiliac son, and Rasputin was undoubtedly corrupt. His presence at court destroyed respect for the Tsar within the élite upon which the autocracy ultimately relied. The final error came in 1916 when Nicholas chose to take personal control of the war. From that point on, defeats could be laid at the door of no-one else. In the end, the monarchy collapsed in February 1917 because the élite had come to believe that Nicholas was unable to carry out its functions effectively, and forced him to abdicate. When his nominated successor refused the throne, the Duma finally took control.

Like Louis XVI and Charles I, Nicholas was personally principled and honourable. He was also weak and indecisive, or at least unwilling to express his decisions openly, except in a blinkered defence of his autocratic powers, which he regarded as a privilege and duty placed upon him by God. Unable to compromise in any meaningful way, yet reluctant to offend or disappoint, he appeared vacillating and unreliable. Educated in lofty isolation, he had little understanding of his people and the sufferings that they endured. Both in 1905 and 1917 he was shocked by the depth of popular feeling. Yet, ultimately, it was his inability to provide leadership for the élite that led to collapse. The failure in war and the corruption of Rasputin convinced the Generals and leading ministers that the person of Nicholas must be separated from the office of Tsar in order to save the latter. But when Nicholas abdicated it was the signal for a collapse of the regime that ultimately opened the way to revolution.

Revolution in France: 1789–1815

Question

6. Read the following account of the French Revolution and refer to the account of the Russian Revolution in Module 4 of the Development Study.

   What similarities and differences between the English, French and Russian Revolutions can be identified in terms of

   (a) the causes,

   (b) the progress,

   (c) the outcomes of each revolution?

   When identifying the causes and outcomes of each revolution, you should consider both the short and the long term.

The system of government in eighteenth-century France, the *Ancien Regime*, was essentially the work of Richelieu and Louis XIV, who had centralised the administration, destroyed the power of the old nobility, and established an absolute monarchy which became a model of government throughout seventeenth-century Europe. Its weaknesses were threefold: it relied upon an active and energetic monarch; its acceptance by the nobility and the provinces was bought by granting them economic and financial privilege; and as a result, it was extremely difficult to adapt, update or develop to meet changing conditions. By the 1780s the system was so overstretched as to be almost creaking to a halt. So chaotic was the organisation of government that there still existed 360 different feudal codes of law applying to different parts of France. Internal trade was strangled by appalling roads and a system of river tolls – a boat bearing wine from the south of France to Paris paid over 40 tolls and lost a fortnight in the process. In theory government was in the hands of the king and his ministers – chosen and dismissed by the king at will – and the Intendants who supervised the administration of 40,000 townships and departments. The king's word was law, and there were no restrictions on his power. In practice the government was racked by inefficiency, blocked by inertia, and above all, paralysed by financial problems.

The root of the problem was that those who could afford to pay – the nobility and the Church – were exempt from most taxes. Louis XIV had concluded an agreement with the Pope and the French Church which guaranteed him their support in return for the suppression of French Protestants and freedom from state taxation. He had broken the power of the old nobility in the aftermath of the Fronde by summoning them to Court and forcing them to dance attendance upon himself. The price of this surrender of political power was the granting of social status and tax exemptions. These exemptions were also granted to the *noblesse de robe*, the officials and functionaries who made up bodies like the Parlement of Paris. France was divided into three Estates, or classes of people. The First and Second Estates, the Church and Nobility, numbered about 300,000 out of a population of approximately 25 million. They owned almost all of the land. The

Third Estate consisted of all the rest of the people, from relatively wealthy lawyers and merchants to the poorest peasants. It was these people who bore the weight and expense of French government.

The financial burden of the peasant was crushing. Not only did he pay the poll-tax and *vingtième* (one twentieth of income, one of the few taxes also paid by many of the nobility) but in addition he paid a tithe to the Church, another large land tax to the king, and a salt tax based on a compulsory purchase of 7 pounds of salt by everyone over the age of seven; he also owed feudal dues to his lord, and though labour services had often been commuted to a money payment, he was still obliged to take his corn to be ground in the lord's mill, his grapes to be pressed in the lord's press and to pay for the privilege. He paid customs duties if he took his produce through a village, watched his crops ruined by huntsmen and their prey who were protected by game-laws, was liable to be conscripted for military service, and was often forced to work on local roads and bridges, without pay under the forced labour or *corvée* system. Perhaps worst of all, the funds raised by the sufferings of the peasantry were nowhere near adequate for the expenses of government.

By the 1780s it is clear, therefore, that the system of government in France was not only unjust, but massively inefficient, and the more educated members of the Third Estate were well aware of it. While not suffering the economic burdens of the peasantry in the same way, they resented the restrictions on trade, the oppressions of the Church, the inefficiency of the law and, above all, their own total exclusion from power and influence. In the words of one of their leaders, 'What is the Third Estate? Everything! What has it been hitherto in our form of government? Nothing! What does it want? To become something!'

Attention had been drawn to these problems during the eighteenth century by two particular factors. The first was the 'Enlightenment', the eighteenth-century intellectual movement which sought to encourage rational thought, order and efficiency. Writers such as the great sceptic Voltaire were quick to point out the stupidity and injustice of the system, while others, such as the Encyclopaedists led by Diderot, recommended reforms. Montesquieu argued for reforms on the British model, while Jean Jacques Rousseau put forward democratic ideas, based on the idea of a social contract. In many ways Rousseau's ideas were impractical – indeed the closest they came to practical expression was in the Jacobin system of popular dictatorship in 1793 – but the spirit of democracy was influential and his arguments for human equality and natural rights did create a vision of a new and more just society. The second factor which highlighted the weaknesses of the system was the decline of France as a great power, particularly in comparison to her great commercial rival, Britain. Since 1714 a series of wars had seen France try to combine the role of great territorial power in Europe with that of holding an overseas empire, stretching her resources beyond their limit and losing out to Prussia in central Europe and Britain in India and the American colonies. In 1783 she had gained some revenge, being instrumental in Britain's defeat by the Americans and the loss of her colonies, but the effort had overstretched her already weakened finances and brought about financial collapse. In addition, the revolutionary ideas put forward by the Americans were imported into France by her military heroes like Marshal Lafayette and by radical enthusiasts like Tom Paine. In that sense, French success in 1783 was achieved at some considerable cost.

In order to pay for the American War, the minister of finance, Jacques Necker, had been forced to borrow heavily, adding to the crown's already massive debts. By 1781, over half of income was going in interest payments! Necker attempted to reform finances by appointing new tax receivers and by controlling the expenditure of the army and navy. Immediately he was opposed by a faction of the nobility who would lose their lucrative offices, and the military interests, and when the king failed to support him, he was forced to resign. His successors continued to borrow until in 1787, faced with imminent bankruptcy, the new finance minister, Calonne, persuaded the king to call representatives of the nobility in an Assembly of Notables in order to persuade them to accept a greater share of the tax burden. Not only did they dislike the proposed land tax, but the Notables saw, in this appeal for help from the crown, an opportunity to strengthen their own position and spread power more widely among themselves. Refusing to vote taxes, they demanded the summoning of a States-General, so that grievances could be considered and reforms established. Awareness of the need for reform was genuine, and spread through all classes, but since this body, the only representative of France as a whole, consisted of the three Estates meeting and voting separately, it would be assumed that any reformist movement would be led and controlled by the two upper houses. In other words the expectation behind this 'revolt of the Notables' was that power would be shifted from the king to the aristocracy, but no further.

The States-General

Preparatory to calling the States-General, the government asked for *cahiers* of grievances. It got over 60,000. The demands from all over the country were the same: tax reform, the abolition of feudal dues, the rule of law and a parliamentary monarchy. Instead, however, of accepting the demands and placing himself at the head of the movement for reform, Louis XVI showed a marked reluctance to accept change. At first he demanded that the three Estates should sit and vote separately as usual, thus ensuring that even though he had agreed that the Third Estate should have twice as many representatives, they would be unable to outvote the two upper houses. He was thus robbed of any credit for his willingness to reform, and, not for the last time, undermined the ability of his subjects to trust in his goodwill or judgement. As it was, the Third Estate under the leadership of Mirabeau declared itself to be the National Assembly, meeting on a Versailles tennis-court when they found their hall closed. In the famous 'Tennis-court Oath' they swore to remain united until a constitution had been granted. In the face of this defiance Louis backed down, thus indicating that he could be pressurised into granting reforms with which he personally disagreed. By June 1789

the first Estate had joined them, and at the end of the month the king officially amalgamated the three Estates into one National Assembly. In early July it gave itself the title of the Constituent Assembly, in recognition that its main task was now to draw up a constitution. However, events outside the political classes were now beginning to take over. Unrest in Paris had grown steadily with high bread prices and the flow of news, and on 12 July new troops were sent in to guard the royal stronghold of the Bastille. This merely provoked further reaction and on 14 July, encouraged by the speeches of a young journalist, Camille Desmoulins, an angry mob stormed the Bastille, symbol of royal authority and tyranny, in Paris. That night the Parisians established their own local government, an elected committee known as the Commune, and their example was followed all over France. On 17 July the king came to Paris (under protest) to recognise the Commune, and wore a *tricolore*, the emblem of the revolution in his hat; elsewhere peasants attacked chateaux, burned records of their feudal obligations, and townsmen set up their own local committees and communes. When the Constituent Assembly abolished feudal tenures on 4 August 1789, it was in some ways recognising a *fait accompli*.

Source 66

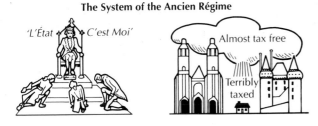

The Work of the Philosophers

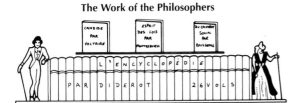

The Example of the USA

The bankruptcy of the Crown

A summary of the principal causes of the French Revolution. From D. Richards, Modern Europe *(Longman, 1945) p. 13.*

The intervention of the common people marked a new stage in the revolution, and over the following years their influence was often decisive. As a preface to the new Constitution, the Assembly issued the Declaration of the Rights of Man, a truly radical political statement of universal rights and liberty. When the king resisted this and the abolition of feudal tenures, the citizens of Paris – led by the women – marched to Versailles and forced both king and Assembly to return to Paris where the Assembly's debates could be attended by the citizens and both intimidated by the threat of mob violence. The king's anger at this cavalier treatment of God's representative on earth was further fuelled in 1790 when the Assembly sought to solve France's financial problems by seizing Church lands. This was followed by the Civil Constitution of the Clergy, which rejected the power of the Pope and turned the French Church into a department of state. His genuine religious convictions led Louis to be appalled by these steps, and when the change was condemned by the Pope in April 1791, Louis listened to the arguments of his wife, Marie Antoinette, that they should flee to her brother (the Emperor of Austria) and raise an army with which to return and destroy the revolution. Unfortunately they neglected to adopt any disguise, or to take troops for protection, and having been recognised at Varennes, they were returned in disgrace to Paris. It was this revelation – that Louis could not be trusted – which really sealed the fate of the monarchy. The following year saw the growth of Republican Clubs, of which the Jacobins were the most important. In addition, a working-class Cordelier Club founded in Paris began to adopt genuinely democratic ideas. When the Assembly finally revealed its Constitution in 1791, the more radical groups were infuriated by the power left to the king and the imposition of a property qualification for voters. The constitution also gave great autonomy to the local communes of France, which further reduced the Assembly's ability to maintain control. When they compounded their naivety by declaring themselves ineligible for election to the new legislative assembly, power passed rapidly into the hands of the more radical groups.

By the end of 1791 the progress of the revolution was being further influenced by the threat of invasion. Members of the nobility who had fled the upheaval were supported by European monarchs who were infuriated by the treatment of the king, and saw in these new ideas a threat to their own power. The Republicans now dominated the Assembly, and one group of deputies from the Gironde area began to see in war the possibility of both exposing the king's treachery and uniting the country behind a republic. In April 1792 France declared war on Austria, but fared badly in the early battles. Suspicions that the king had betrayed French plans to the Austrians grew, and in August the Jacobins, with the help of the Cordeliers Club and its leader Danton, seized control of the Paris Commune. The mob invaded the palace of the Tuileries and Louis fled to the Assembly which had little choice but to imprison him. The Jacobin leader, Robespierre, called for the dissolution of the Assembly and the calling of a Convention to establish a more democratic constitution. When elected, this proved to be extremely republican in character. The Jacobins had triumphed, but at a terrible cost. Over 2,000 had died in the attack on the Tuileries and this had been followed by the massacre of 800 royalist supporters. The trend to violence continued. In September the king was formally deposed, and rebellion broke out in the devoutly Catholic Vendée. The rebels were appalled at the treatment of the king and the Church, but also infuriated by the republican attempt to conscript men for the war. In Paris the citizens suffered from high prices and fear of invasion (Prussia having now joined the coalition against them) and reacted by further massacres of royalists and priests. Over 2,000 were murdered while in prison in September. At this point the hastily gathered army of volunteers drove the Prussians back at Valmy, to give the Republic some breathing space, and the Jacobins declared war on tyranny everywhere. In January 1793 the king was put on trial. The Girondins and Danton appear to have wished to spare his life, but, ominously for any future moderates, dared not say so, and the policy of Robespierre, which was execution, was accepted. The revolution now entered its most bloody and violent phase. From January 1793 republican France was at war with Prussia, Austria, England and Spain (who had been drawn in by threats of French expansion), beset by civil war at home as more moderate provinces sought to break from republican authority, and undermined by inflation and food shortages brought on by the stress of war. In Paris the Jacobins ruled the Convention and the two administrative committees – the Revolutionary Tribunal and the Committee of Public Safety. In the mind of their leader, Robespierre, the people of Paris represented France, and their reactions were the expression of the democratic General Will. Hence their hatreds were tantamount to law, and egged on by their orators – some visionary, some grotesque – they condemned any who argued for moderation, balance or restraint. The last of the Girondin deputies were arrested in June 1793, and for a year Robespierre enforced the control of Paris and of the Republic through a Reign of Terror, designed to destroy the enemies of revolution and purify the nation. Anyone accused of disloyalty was executed, with or without trial. In Paris the guillotine claimed about 3,000 lives, but this and worse atrocities were repeated in cities throughout France. By April 1794 Danton, horrified by the excesses, tried to call a halt, and was himself executed as a traitor. By July 1794, the Republic was supreme throughout France and able to direct its energies against external enemies. At this point, Robespierre himself fell victim to his own machinery of Terror, when an alliance of personal enemies and those tired of the bloodshed united to denounce him and send him to the guillotine. Personally incorruptible, his ruthless devotion to an ideal did not allow for men who were motivated by more political concerns.

What followed from 1794 to 1799 was a more 'moderate' revolutionary government based on a five-man Directory. They were supported by the middle-class financiers and businessmen who had benefited from the Revolution and who were opposed to both mob violence and to a royalist reaction. Increasingly, however, they had to rely on the army (now organised, trained and professional while still representing democratic and revolutionary ideals through its promotion by merit, etc.) to protect them against both foreign invasion and popular unrest at home. The result was the rise to power of the leading general, the brilliant and ambitious Corsican, Napoleon Bonaparte. In 1799 he seized power, and when the elected assembly failed to support him, he sent in troops to drive them from the building.

Between 1800 and 1815 Bonaparte ruled France, first as Consul and then as Emperor. His dictatorship was efficient and effective, and his government provided important and lasting reforms. He restored the Church (under government control), reformed the law and provided economic and political stability. He never gained the support of extreme royalists or of the Jacobins, but the great majority backed the regime. This was partly due to the lack of any viable alternative, but there is no evidence of any effective movements against him.

Source 67

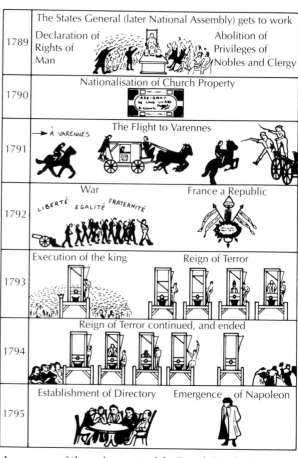

A summary of the main events of the French Revolution. From D. Richards, Modern Europe, *p. 31.*

What eventually undermined Napoleon's regime was the cost of incessant warfare, and what overthrew him was military defeat at the hands of Britain and her continental allies in 1814. Even then he was able to return from his first exile in Elba, rally sufficient support to drive out the newly-restored Louis XVIII, and mount a new campaign which ended only with defeat at Waterloo in 1815. By sending him into a more remote exile on the island of St Helena in the South Atlantic, the allies ensured that a further return was impossible.

It was no surprise that monarchy was restored in France in 1815. Throughout Europe the concept of monarchical rule, justified by hereditary right, was the form of government best known and understood. Even in France there had been no intention to overthrow monarchy until 1792, but rather to reform it. Experiences thereafter had done little to recommend republicanism and popular participation. Monarchy was to most people the natural form of government. Even Napoleon had sought to legitimise his seizure of power by becoming an Emperor and marrying into the Hapsburg royal family. He was not opposed to the institution of monarchy, but sought to make his family a part of it. He made one brother King of Naples and another the King of Holland. As kings themselves, the victors of Waterloo would inevitably see a return to legitimate monarchy as the best basis for stability in France and in Europe as a whole. But legitimate monarchy had been unmade and remade too many times to survive unscathed.

Within 15 years of the king's return, France was again in the throes of revolution. Louis XVIII had proved an astute, if uninspiring, ruler and had made a reasonable success of the weak parliamentary constitution upon which his government had been based. When he died in 1824, he was succeeded by the stubbornly autocratic and devoutly Catholic Charles of Artois, his younger brother, who appeared to have learned little from his period of exile up to 1815. The leader of the ultra-conservatives, his attempts to restore the power of the Church and to reduce the influence of liberals in parliament led to his overthrow and exile in 1830. He was replaced, at the invitation of parliament, by a cousin, Louis Philippe D'Orleans, who governed as a genuinely constitutional monarch. In 1848, however, at a time of economic stress and unrest in Paris, a combination of liberal-democratic reformers and ambitious politicians were able to force Louis Philippe to abdicate and replace him with a short-lived Second Republic which eventually fell prey to a Bonapartist coup and the foundation of a second Napoleonic Empire.

While there were many specific causes and triggers of these later 'revolutions', the repetition of forms and structures made familiar following 1789 suggests that the issues behind and within the French Revolution of that year had not been settled or worked to their conclusion in the events of 1789–1815, but remained to haunt French government throughout the nineteenth century.

Questions

7. In the light of the comparisons with the French and Russian Revolutions, what relative importance would you attach to the different factors that

   (a) caused the English Revolution?

   (b) shaped its outcome?

8. How far do comparisons with the French and Russian Revolutions strengthen or weaken the claims of the mid-seventeenth-century crisis in England to be regarded as a revolution?

Models of revolution

Thus far, comparison has been used for the limited purpose of defining similarities and differences, and evaluating interpretations of the nature and significance of the English Revolution. However, some historians have taken the process of comparison further, to consider the nature of revolution itself. The following sources give some examples of historians' interpretations, based upon a number of models and case studies of revolution. Source 68 outlines some models of the causes, progress and outcomes of revolution, challenging the idea that revolution has played a significant part in the political evolution of Europe. Source 69, which focuses on the Glorious Revolution of 1688–9, reminds us that historians have defined the term 'revolution' in widely differing ways and that definitions of the term have an important bearing on explanations of the event. Sources 70–2 consider some differing definitions and assumptions about 'revolution' and about the categories of events to which the term can or should be applied. In the light of these various interpretations, you are then asked to reconsider what constitutes a revolution, and how the process of definition can, or cannot, aid our understanding of the subject of our enquiries, the English Civil Wars and Interregnum.

Source 68

From J.A. Goldstone, *Revolution and Rebellion in the Early Modern World* pp. 171–4, 434–5 and 478–9.

(a) Causes

There is a remarkable parallel between recent trends in the historiography of the French and English Revolutions. In both cases explanations that have focused on long-term social changes, particularly the rise of capitalism and capitalist groups, have been undermined by decades of critical scholarship [by those labelled revisionists who have emphasised short-term and individual factors]. ... The sociologist Theda Skocpol has offered a broad explanation of revolutions based on international as well as domestic politics ... [arguing] that the French Revolution was the result of France's inability to compete with England in sustaining the expenses of war, owing to a lagging precapitalist economy. ... [This explanation] focuses on aspects of French institutions – for example the weakness of the state in the face of international pressures and the crucial role of peasant villages – that were also found in other instances of social revolution, namely Russia in 1917 and China in the period 1911–49. ... Skocpol's goal is not merely to explain why France had a political crisis but also why it had a *social* revolution. Since France was the only nation in early modern Europe to have a social revolution, as opposed to a mere state breakdown, [her explanation stresses] precisely how France's state and agrarian structures *differed* from those of other states. Her parallels are drawn not between the French Revolution and other early modern state breakdowns but rather between the French Revolution and social revolutions in twentieth-century states struggling with the beginnings of heavy industrialisation. ... The fundamental contribution of Skocpol's work is the demonstration of what made France unique in early modern Europe, and why its revolution had elements in common with the later socialist revolutions in Russia and China.

[However] state breakdown in France in 1789 comprised a combination of elements: a state fiscal crisis, élite rebellion and sharp intra-élite conflicts, and urban and rural unrest. As we have seen, precisely the same combination occurred a century and a half earlier in the English Revolution and in the French Fronde ... [see Unit 4.2 above]. Neither Skocpol's analysis nor the particularistic explanations of the revisionists shed any light on why this specific combination of elements occurred *in all three instances*. In addition, we have noted that the French Revolution was part of a wave of state breakdowns from 1770 to 1850 that stretched all across Europe, into Russia and China. ... I [would] argue that the breakdown of the French state in 1789 was rooted in the same causes that gave rise to the crises of the seventeenth century. That is, following a period of demographic decline from 1660 to 1700, which brought an interval of stability, when population rose in the eighteenth century France was again thrown into crisis by the inability of its economy, its system of taxation, and its mechanisms of élite recruitment to cope with sustained population growth. ...

Two caveats are critical here. First, this argument seeks to explain only the breakdown or 'crisis' of the Old Regime. If one thinks of the 'French Revolution' as being chiefly the events from 1791 to 1815 – that is, the struggles for dominance, the emergence of Jacobin leadership, the Reign of Terror and the rise of Napoleon – then the revolution is not explained here. ... The factors that explain the breakdown of the Old Regime are not, in general, sufficient to explain what happened in the ensuing struggles over power and state reconstruction. Second, to say that the French Revolution was rooted in long-term social changes that affected all of Eurasia in the period 1770–1860 is not to say that such social changes alone caused the revolution, or that those changes had the same effects everywhere. The impact of long-term social changes, as I indicated in discussing the contrasts between the English Revolution and the Fronde [see Unit 4.2 above], always depends on the particular social and political structures exposed to those changes. In the period 1660 to 1730, England and Prussia underwent major transformations in their political institutions and their economies; hence they each responded to the population pressures of the eighteenth and nineteenth centuries in their own specific fashions. France ... modified but did not replace its earlier economic and political structures under Louis XIV; thus his successors encountered fiscal pressures, intra-élite conflicts, and popular unrest similar to the events of the seventeenth century.

(b) Course and Development

Historians have often puzzled over why revolutions characteristically show a progression to the 'left', toward more extreme radicalism. ... Furet traced, in the French Revolution, a process of rhetorical competition and escalation leading to terror and democratic despotism, [which] is common to social revolutions: Napoleon succeeded Robespierre; Cromwell replaced Pym; Stalin succeeded Lenin; Chiang Kai Shek and, later, Mao Zedong replaced Sun Yat Sen. ... In the conditions of social dislocation that precede state breakdown, ideologies are a diverse mix. ... When the crisis reaches the point where the Old Regime is clearly breaking down and has lost the initiative, attempts are made to unite the opposition ... by broad slogans that can bridge both the folk and élite views of the problem and the various particularistic complaints. Examples include the call to defend the 'rights of Englishmen and the true religion' in England in the 1640s; the call for the Estates-General in France in 1787–8; the slogan 'Peace and Land' in Russia in 1916–7; and the simple 'Down with the Shah' and 'Somosa must go' in contemporary Iran and Nicaragua. Such simple unifying slogans are not always present in revolutionary contexts. The Fronde in seventeenth-century France, for instance, was never able to unite its diverse elements. But such slogans, where they do occur, dominate the early stages of revolution, deferring conflicts and focusing enmity on the Old Regime.

The collapse of [the regime], however, creates a new situation, in the sense that competition is now open among formerly subordinate élite groups to dominate the polity and offer solutions to the problems that brought down the Old Regime. In this competition, groups that have prior national organisation and programs are at an advantage. It is not necessarily their radical views that put them at the forefront; for example the Puritan gentry in the 1630s and the Jacobin Clubs in the 1780s were clearly moderate and reformist, not revolutionary. Rather, their organisational advantage allows them to take the lead in disseminating their viewpoint. Nonetheless, their success in dominating the polity, given the lack of accepted institutions and of adequate military force, rests on their ability to win the allegiance of key groups. This means appealing to desires for rectification, redistribution and national authenticity. [These are not always easy to attain, especially in the conditions of upheaval or difficulty that cause and are exacerbated by revolutionary outbreaks. Hence there is a tendency to put forward competing, and often increasingly radical bids for support. Where a popular, social revolution has occurred, this creates a populist or 'leftward' pressure. In certain cases, however, it can cause a move towards stability, or even dictatorship].

(c) Outcomes

The struggle for power that follows state breakdown tends to overwhelm moderate, and later, radical efforts to rebuild the state. Instead, the common outcome of episodes of state breakdown is the thirst for order, and hence, within a decade or two, the rise of a nationalist, populist dictatorship. In England the state breakdown of 1640 was followed in the mid-50s by military rule under Cromwell. Even after the Restoration of 1660 the result was a reactionary monarchy driven by a backlash against Puritan and parliamentary freedoms. In France the state breakdown of 1789 was followed, a little over a decade later, by the Napoleonic Empire. And just two decades after the state breakdown of 1830, France was again ruled by an imperial despotism led by a Bonaparte. In Germany the legacy of 1848 was the Kaiser's bureaucratic and military empire. Even after the second German Revolution, in 1918, it took only a decade and a half for a nationalist dictatorship to emerge under Hitler. In Russia, socialist revolutionary fervour gave way to military nationalism under Stalin. ...

In short, history shows an almost uniform tendency of episodes of state breakdown to culminate in populist, usually military, dictatorship. ... Regardless of the aims or ideology of revolutionaries, the task of rebuilding state authority requires the broad-based mobilisation of popular and élite groups to support a new regime, as well as the defeat of internal and often external opponents. The exigencies of this struggle generally lead to terror, disorder and the growing dominance of military men. The rebuilt armies of the revolution embody its energy and ideals but have little patience with national democracy and individual freedom. ... Revolution is not part of the solution to authoritarianism and tyranny; instead it is part – indeed a recurrent part – of the problem. ...

Democracy developed in the West through the combination of (1) visions of secular improvement and wider political participation articulated by marginal élites; (2) military defeats and occupations that discredited central authorities, forged broad élite coalitions in favour of republican institutions, and created opportunities for liberal ideas to bear fruit; and (3) reform legislation that expanded the franchise and guaranteed individual rights and liberties. That we associate revolutions with democracy is an illusion that arose because revolutions offered marginal élites the greatest opportunities and incentives to invent and propagate democratic ideologies. We then ignore or treat as regrettable 'deviations' the almost universal failure of revolutions to entertain such ideologies for more than a few years before succumbing to despotic rule.

Source 69

From W.A. Speck, *Reluctant Revolutionaries* (Oxford, 1989) pp. 241–2.

Whether or not the events of 1688 deserve to be remembered three hundred years later as a revolution depends on what is meant by the term. Like 'feudalism' and 'class', it is one of those words which historians use all the time. Indeed, despite warning each other that it is constantly being used in an imprecise and even nebulous way, they continue to spawn new usages for it. Thus, it had the adjectives 'agricultural', 'commercial', 'financial', 'industrial', 'moral', 'sexual', and even 'Thatcherite' attached to it. Clearly, this is a debasement of the term, so much so that some scholars have recommended its removal from the historical lexicon altogether. Yet we seem to be stuck with it, not least because it is a useful shorthand.

Several attempts have been made to give it a more precise definition. Thus models have been extrapolated from events which everybody recognizes as revolutionary, such as those in France in 1789 or in Russia in 1917, and used to test the claims of other upheavals to the same status. One problem with this approach, however, is that the analyses have come up with different and even conflicting definitions. After reviewing some of the rival models, Theda Skocpol concluded that 'there are enormous differences among the major types of social-scientific theories not only about how to explain revolutions, but even about how to define them' [T. Skocpol, *States and Social Revolutions*, Cambridge, 1979, pp. 12–3]. ...

Most historians nowadays would distinguish political from social revolutions. A political revolution is seen as one which changes the polity of a society but does not alter its social structure, whereas a social revolution transforms the structure of society and its dominant ideology.

Source 70

From W. Doyle, 'The Legacy of the French Revolution', in *Modern History Review*, February 1992, p. 20.

What makes the French Revolution a living issue? It is the fact that it marks the beginning of a whole range of attitudes, values, ideals, institutions and ways of doing things that have swept the world ever since and are very largely still with us. ... Take for example the very idea of Revolution itself. Our modern conception of it goes back no further than 1789. Before that, revolution simply meant political change. The fall of a minister, a change of monarch, a change of policy, even – all these were indiscriminately called revolutions by eighteenth-century men. But what happened in France in and after 1789 changed all that. It was a revolution, of course, in the old sense, a spectacular political change. But the extent of that change, as it developed over subsequent years, was so great, and so far-reaching, that it soon became clear that this was an upheaval quite unlike any other that had happened before, and that if this was a revolution then the meaning of the word had to be changed. And so it was. Ever since then we have always been careful to distinguish between mere change, and even simple *coups d'état*, and real full-blooded revolution.

Source 71

From Jonathan Clark, *Revolution and Rebellion* (Cambridge, 1986) pp. 3–4 and 37–8.

In contrasting 'revolution' and 'rebellion' in the title of this book I am referring to modern debates: I am not suggesting that those terms carried their present meanings in the seventeenth or eighteenth centuries. Until after 1789 the term 'revolution' indeed often signified a reversion to a previous pattern, as a wheel comes full circle. Clarendon reserved the title 'revolution' for the events of 1660, not 1642; Whigs used the same term of 1688 to signify the repair of the constitution after what they claimed had been James II's innovatory tyranny. ...

Our own meanings are somewhat different. Without wishing to rest much weight on definitions, it might be suggested that we still understand 'rebellion' to mean a fundamental challenge to the title to legitimacy of political institutions, often (in the past) a religious title. But this concept now tends to become subsumed in that of 'revolution', since we often take a revolution to be a successful rebellion; and by 'revolution' we now understand, in addition to the political aspects, a fundamental challenge to the legitimacy of social structures, including patterns of hierarchy or stratification, and titles to economic ownership or control. Too much recent writing, it is suggested, rests on this anachronistic sense of 'revolution': the revisionists' preferred category is 'rebellion'. ...

So to distinguish these two explanatory categories helps us to disengage ourselves from the assumption that revolutions are always 'forward-looking', that they embody the progressive aspirations of 'rising' social classes to speed up developments being impeded by 'the forces of reaction'. Rebellion is a concept more evidently devoid of such implications; it helps our appreciation that many conflicts (like the Civil War or 1688) can better be described as reactions against innovations, a deeply rooted resistance to undesired change. ...

It was not an Englishman but a Frenchman, François Guizot, whose *Histoire de la Révolution d'Angleterre* (Paris, 1826–7) was the first to apply the term 'revolution' to the Civil War in place of the traditional 'rebellion'. Guizot had been struck by an analogy between England in the 1640s and the events of 1789 in France, and developed the comparison at length: 'both are victories in the same war', he believed.

> 'Created by the same causes, the fall of the feudal aristocracy, the church and kingly power, they both laboured to obtain the same result, the dominion of the public in public affairs. They struggled for liberty against absolute power, for equality against privilege, for progressive and general interests against stationary and individual interests. [The revolution of the 1640s] though disappointed in its premature hopes ... caused English society to take a wide step from the monstrous inequality of the feudal system. In a word, the analogy of the two revolutions is such, that the first would never have been understood had not the second taken place.' (F. Guizot, *History of the English Revolution*, Oxford, 1838, vol. I, pp. x and xx–xxi.)

Equally, the term 'Industrial Revolution' was not an English but a French invention, again of about the same time, and again inspired by an analogy with the upheaval of 1789. The idea of a *révolution industrielle* gained currency in France only in the 1820s. In 1837, the economist Jérôme Blanqui claimed in his *Histoire de L'Économie Politique en Europe*: 'While the French Revolution was making its great social experiments over a volcano, England was beginning hers on the solid ground of the industries. ... Hardly was the industrial revolution born from the brains of those two men of genius, Watt and Arkwright, when it took possession of England'. Yet such a concept, even when formulated, was not self-evidently valid in English eyes: not until the 1880s and after was the phrase naturalised in England.

Despite its dubious ancestry, the word 'revolution' by now has a Pavlovian effect on some historians: applied to any event, it leads at once to eager expectations of radical structural change, profound discontinuity, a sweeping away of the old order. We may indeed wonder whether England has ever experienced revolution in the extensive terms of the social scientists' definitions in the 1640s, 1688 or 1714, or even under the later impact of 'Industry'. How much was destroyed in the Civil War? Apart from the large extent to which royalist peers and gentry retained their estates, local studies suggest the widespread and deeply rooted survival of Anglican religious loyalties and practices, even reinvigorated by the experience of persecution.

Source 72

From G. Watson, 'How Radical is Revolution?' in *History Today*, November 1988, pp. 42–3.

Revolution is not what it was. It was once thought that the modern age had been made by it; nowadays a sustained stability looks more interesting, since stable societies are not just more comfortable but at times more radical too. 'I suppose what connotes a revolution is shots', William Gerhardie once remarked gaily, 'they have a way of conveying a sense of importance'. And it is that importance, or self-importance, that has dramatically faded in recent years. ... Why, it is now asked, were revolutions ever supposed by nature to be radical? Why should societies not change faster and more efficiently without them?

The surprising truth is that revolution was not always thought of in radical terms at all: that use is exceptional before the nineteenth century. The word was once conservative. That this should be thought odd looks even odder when one reflects that many revolutions in recent times have been preservative in effect, in intent, or in both. Hard to resist the conclusion that theories of revolution in the past hundred years have been out of touch with political reality, doubly out of touch with such far-from-radical events as the English Revolution of 1689. What has recently been gained is an appreciation of stability and of what it can achieve in the way of social change. What we still have to recover is a sense of preservative revolution.

Modern theorists have commonly assumed revolution to be indissolubly linked to radical ideology, transforming social systems in favour of the poor by deliberate design. In that familiar model, intellectual élites like Jacobins or Bolsheviks demand social change; the demand is violently acted on; and societies change, and for the better, as an effect – a sort of word-made-flesh.

All that now looks hard to swallow. For one thing, societies are surely inclined to change of themselves, and without any ruler – revolutionary or otherwise – intending it. For good or ill, change is natural to human societies, at least in industrial states; so that intellectuals do not need to write or speak, or rulers to act, to make it happen – although they may often have to act to prevent it from happening. It is the stationary state that is exceptional. Again, new rulers who seize power through revolution may hold much the same views about the social order as old ones. And above all, social changes deliberately wrought by governments, and especially by revolutionary governments, are notoriously unreliable in achieving what was meant. Politics is a world of unintended effects, and our own century is littered with instances of counter-effective revolutions, so to speak: seizures of power designed to be popular entrenching the privileges of the ruling caste. The Soviet system is one notorious instance among many. There can be no easy assumption in public affairs that intent equals effect. The sober truth is that modern theories of revolution by now fail to account for many or most of the instances. Our theory of revolution is a fantasy of revolution.

Full circle: Islamic clergy outside the US Embassy, Tehran, June 1980. The Iranian Revolution was a classic return to fundamentalist values.

In this unit you have now considered the following under the name of Revolution: two civil wars in England, one of which (during the 1640s) is labelled a revolution, while the other (the Wars of the Roses) is not; a radical reorganisation of state and society, carried out by the English government in the 1530s; a limited aristocratic coup backed by foreign invasion (in 1688–9); a colonial war of independence (1775–82); a major economic upheaval (the Industrial Revolution) and two great national upheavals which transformed the nature and justification of government, accompanied by a restructuring of social and economic patterns (the French and Russian Revolutions). In answering Questions 8, 9 and 10, and again in Unit 4.4, you should employ the knowledge and understanding you have acquired of these different phenomena to reconsider what you understand by the term 'revolution'. Having ascertained the essential characteristics of revolution, you will then be in a position to finalise and evaluate your conclusions as to whether or not there was a mid-seventeenth-century English Revolution and, if so, what its characteristics were.

Questions

9. How far is it possible to define what is meant by the term 'revolution'?

10. Does defining what we mean by revolution and applying the definition to different case studies help or hinder our understanding of particular 'revolutions'?

11. What do you consider to be the essential characteristics of a revolution?

UNIT 4.4

WAS THERE AN ENGLISH REVOLUTION?

You have now considered the English Revolution from a variety of perspectives, enabling you to assess its complexity, the relative importance of the different factors in its occurrence, development and outcome, and its long-term impact. You have considered the events in England in a wider European context, and in a longer temporal context in order to assess their nature and significance. Finally, you have examined a number of revolutions in order to address the idea of revolution itself and what the use of the term may imply. The purpose of this unit is to enable you to apply what you have learnt from these processes to the central question of whether or not there was an English Revolution, and if so, what it comprised and when it occurred.

In addressing this question you should utilise your knowledge of historical development, and particularly of development in English or British government and politics, as well as your understanding of seventeenth-century England and of the nature of revolutions. The first step is to draw on these understandings to construct a list of criteria by which your judgements can be made. The second is to utilise your knowledge of the period from 1640–60, and your awareness of what took place in the longer term, before and after these years, in order to assess how far the events and outcomes of 1640–60 meet the criteria of 'revolution'. There follows a list of suggested characteristics that a 'revolution' should have. It is by no means exhaustive, nor does it constitute a definition or model. In the light of your previous conclusions, particularly those drawn at the end of Unit 4.3, you may well wish to change it. It serves only as a starting-point for you to draw up your own criteria.

Questions

1. How adequate are the ten statements below as criteria for defining what constitutes a revolution?

2. Explain and justify any alterations or additions to these criteria that you would wish to make.

A revolution requires:

1. Long-term structural problems, of sufficient scope and intensity to make some kind of conflict or upheaval in government and society probable, if not inevitable.

2. Short-term triggers (events, actions or personalities) which cause the problems to come to a head at a particular moment.

3. A weakness in, or breakdown of, existing structures which allows revolutionary ideas or actions to develop.

4. An ideology which gives coherence to at least some grievances, factions and aims.

5. A change in government structure and organisation brought about by violence or the threat of it, rather than by peaceful reform.

6. Some change in the social structure, in terms of the distribution of wealth, status or power.

7. An element of rapidity or shock which brings about a hostile reaction.

8. Contemporary judgements that some extraordinary change is taking place.

9. The introduction of some new elements (in structures, attitudes or ideas) which constitute a break with the past.

10. Lasting effects – which may be intended outcomes, unforeseen results or unexpected by-products of the events in question.

In considering how far the English Revolution meets these criteria, you may find it useful to award marks on a scale of 0–5 for each criterion, with 0 representing a total absence of that criterion and 5 representing its strongest possible presence and influence. You could then apply the same criteria and scale to one or more other 'revolutions' and compare the results. This exercise (particularly if repeated over a number of occurrences some accepted by historians as revolutions, some not) would serve to test the effectiveness of your criteria as well as evaluate your judgements about the nature of events in England. Your conclusions could play an important role in answering Question 3, the answer to which should represent a distillation of the knowledge and understanding you have acquired throughout all four Modules of this Depth Study.

Question

3. Was there an English Revolution in the seventeenth century? If so, did it occur in:

(a) 1640–2?

(b) 1647–9?

(c) 1688–9?

(d) a combination of two or more of the above?

Explain and evaluate your answer.

Index